Management for Professionals

More information about this series at http://www.springer.com/series/10101

Robert Kepczynski • Raghav Jandhyala • Ganesh Sankaran • Alecsandra Dimofte

Integrated Business Planning

How to Integrate Planning Processes, Organizational Structures and Capabilities, and Leverage SAP IBP Technology

Robert Kepczynski
Zurich, Switzerland

Ganesh Sankaran
Walldorf, Germany

Raghav Jandhyala
SAP LABS LLC
Tempe, Arizona, USA

Alecsandra Dimofte
SAP Switzerland
Regensdorf, Switzerland

ISSN 2192-8096   ISSN 2192-810X (electronic)
Management for Professionals
ISBN 978-3-319-75664-6   ISBN 978-3-319-75665-3 (eBook)
https://doi.org/10.1007/978-3-319-75665-3

Library of Congress Control Number: 2018934952

© Springer International Publishing AG, part of Springer Nature 2018

This work is subject to copyright. All rights are reserved by the Publisher, whether the whole or part of the material is concerned, specifically the rights of translation, reprinting, reuse of illustrations, recitation, broadcasting, reproduction on microfilms or in any other physical way, and transmission or information storage and retrieval, electronic adaptation, computer software, or by similar or dissimilar methodology now known or hereafter developed.

The use of general descriptive names, registered names, trademarks, service marks, etc. in this publication does not imply, even in the absence of a specific statement, that such names are exempt from the relevant protective laws and regulations and therefore free for general use.

The publisher, the authors and the editors are safe to assume that the advice and information in this book are believed to be true and accurate at the date of publication. Neither the publisher nor the authors or the editors give a warranty, express or implied, with respect to the material contained herein or for any errors or omissions that may have been made. The publisher remains neutral with regard to jurisdictional claims in published maps and institutional affiliations.

Printed on acid-free paper

This Springer imprint is published by the registered company Springer International Publishing AG part of Springer Nature.
The registered company address is: Gewerbestrasse 11, 6330 Cham, Switzerland

Preface

The idea of this book came to light after one of the Integrated Business Planning workshops. My colleagues **Mariel Ramirez and Emmanuel Bieth** have encouraged me to put planning knowledge and experience on paper, so global and country implementation stakeholders could benefit from it. We shared the same opinion that the book may help many other companies to have a better start in their IBP journey. I gathered some ideas and topics on many post-its and grouped them into logical content, and guess what . . . initial structure of the content has emerged.

I thought the best way to proceed is to gather people whom I worked with and who have "make things happen" approach and that is why I asked **Raghav Jandhyala, Alecsandra Dimofte, and Ganesh Sankaran**, if they want to be coauthors. This was a moment when IBP book was not anymore "MY" project but transformed into "OUR" project. As we have discussed process and technology aspects of IBP at the meetings, we came to conclusion that we need some input from Human Capital to make "People" side exposed appropriately to importance in IBP. We asked **Katherine Stankiewicz and Malgorzata Kalarus** to provide input in talent acquisition, retention, and career development. Those topics came up in all projects as vital element of IBP transformation success.

Once the book was pretty much ready, we asked chemical company **Regional S&OP Manager** and **Solution Architect for Demand and Supply Planning** to provide content review. Content would not be ready without our colleagues, who provided project support and managed figures and references. Therefore, we would like to thank **Federico Sasso, Ivan Kostakev, Vladimir Dorodnitsyn, Giulio Zunino, and Tommaso Nardi** for their contribution.

Last but not the least, we were lucky to have **Alexi Koifman** as true IBP book supporter.

Integrated business planning will be covered in a small series of books. This book is intended to help you to:

- Understand value of IBP
- Connect strategic, tactical S&OP, and operational planning processes
- Design IBP "fit for purpose" organizational structure and capabilities
- Leverage SAP IBP functionalities, explained with selected use cases
- Define measurement of IBP success

- Understand role of maturity "as-is" assessment
- Plan future of your IBP

The next book is intended to talk more about the practical side of integrated design and implementation of IBP enabled on SAP IBP.

Zurich, Switzerland   Robert Kepczynski

Contents

1 **Recent Past Disconnected Planning** 1
   1.1 Summary 7
   Reference 8

2 **Why Move to Integrated Business Planning** 9
   2.1 Value of IBP Process and Organization Transformation 9
      2.1.1 Process Value 9
      2.1.2 Organizational Value 12
   2.2 Value of SAP IBP on HANA in Cloud 12
   2.3 Value of SAP IBP Pre-configured System 19
   2.4 Value of Operating IBP in Holistic Way 28
   2.5 Summary 29
   References 30

3 **What Makes Integrated Business Planning** 31
   3.1 Integrated Design 31
   3.2 Connect Planning Processes: Strategic, Tactical,
       and Operational 38
      3.2.1 Strategic Annual Business Planning and Tactical S&OP
          Integration 38
      3.2.2 Monthly Strategic Product Planning and Tactical S&OP
          Integration 39
      3.2.3 Operational Planning and Tactical S&OP Integration 41
      3.2.4 Summary 42
   3.3 Extend S&OP 44
   3.4 Connect Org. Structures and Capabilities 50
      3.4.1 Connect Functions 51
      3.4.2 Connect Organizationally Planning Processes and
          Levels 52
      3.4.3 Create Overlap of Capabilities 53
   3.5 Connect Data and Systems 57
      3.5.1 Time Series Integration 59
      3.5.2 Order-Based Integration 69
      3.5.3 Other Integration Options 71

		3.6	Summary	71
	References			72
4	**How to Run IBP: Use Cases**			**73**
	4.1	Strategic Planning		73
		4.1.1	Improve E2E Strategic Initiative Simulation	73
		4.1.2	Improve Strategic Product Demand Planning	77
	4.2	Tactical S&OP		78
		4.2.1	Improve Focus with Segmentation	78
		4.2.2	Improve Efficiency and Effectiveness with Differentiated Forecasting	86
		4.2.3	Improve Availability with Safety Stock Planning	95
		4.2.4	Improve Supply Chain Costs with Optimizer	102
		4.2.5	Improve IBP Supply Chain Planning with ARIBA Supplier Collaboration	108
		4.2.6	Improve Financial Outcomes with "What—If" Simulations	111
	4.3	Operational Planning		116
		4.3.1	Improve Responsiveness with Demand Sensing	116
		4.3.2	Improve Responsiveness with Short-Term Demand Prioritization	122
	4.4	Summary		128
	References			128
5	**How to Manage Organization and Capability Change**			**129**
	5.1	Talent Acquisition		129
		5.1.1	Talent Acquisition Is Not Synonymous with Recruitment	129
	5.2	Talent Retention		140
		5.2.1	Why Should Companies Invest in Retaining Employees?	141
	5.3	Career Path Development		143
		5.3.1	What Is a Career Path?	143
		5.3.2	What Are the Career Path Development Stages?	143
		5.3.3	What Are the Key Factors for Successful Implementation of Career Pathing?	144
	5.4	IBP Center of Expertise: Leadership!		145
		5.4.1	Let Us Talk About IBP COE Leadership!	148
	5.5	Summary		151
	References			152
6	**How to Enable Change with SAP IBP Technology**			**155**
	6.1	SAP IBP Applications Overview		155
		6.1.1	Application Modules in SAP IBP	155
		6.1.2	IBP for Sales and Operations Planning	157
		6.1.3	IBP for Response and Supply	159

		6.1.4	IBP for Inventory	163
		6.1.5	IBP for Demand	165
	6.2	Process Modeling		166
		6.2.1	Global and Local Processes	166
		6.2.2	Process Cadence and Orchestration	167
		6.2.3	Hierarchy of Processes	169
		6.2.4	Process Management	170
		6.2.5	Process Template	171
		6.2.6	Process Steps	172
		6.2.7	Process Instance	173
		6.2.8	Process Visualization and Monitoring	174
		6.2.9	Task Management	174
		6.2.10	Process Automation	175
	6.3	Organization Modeling		176
	6.4	Data Modeling		179
		6.4.1	Elements of a Planning Area	183
		6.4.2	Master Data Types	183
		6.4.3	Key Figures	184
	6.5	Versions, Scenarios, and Assumptions		187
		6.5.1	Versions	188
		6.5.2	User-Defined Scenarios	188
		6.5.3	User-Defined Scenario Management	189
		6.5.4	Version and Scenario Comparison	189
		6.5.5	Assumptions	190
	6.6	Collaboration		191
		6.6.1	Collaboration in SAP IBP	192
		6.6.2	JAM Collaboration	192
		6.6.3	Validating Options	195
		6.6.4	Meetings and Decisions	195
		6.6.5	Store and Share Documentation	197
		6.6.6	Case Management	198
	6.7	Summary		198
	References			199
7	**How to Measure Transformation Success**			**201**
	7.1	Why Measure, Relevance in Performance Measures		201
	7.2	What to Measure		203
	7.3	How to Measure		209
		7.3.1	Components of a Process Metric	215
	7.4	Process Measurement		218
	7.5	How to Measure Effectiveness, Efficiency, and Adherence		219
		7.5.1	Correlation of Metrics	223
	7.6	Big Picture: How to Link Measurement to Shareholder Value		225
	7.7	When Things Go Wrong		230
	7.8	Summary		233
	References			233

8	How to Build Transformation Path	235
	8.1 Qualitative Assessment	235
	8.2 Quantitative Assessment	240
	8.3 Improvement Opportunities and Prioritization	242
	8.4 Road Map and Business Case	244
	8.5 Summary	246
	Reference	247
9	"Quo Vadis" Integrated Business Planning	249
	9.1 Observations of Disruptive Technology Trends	249
	9.2 Process Trends	252
	9.3 Planning Applications Observations	261
	9.4 Organizational and Capabilities Trend	262
	References	265

About the Authors and Contributors

Authors

Robert Kepczynski has more than 20 years' experience in supply chain management and technology. Robert does assess, design, and implement people capability models and process design and delivers efficient technology solutions. Robert specializes in supply chain planning processes and technology. Robert took business roles:

- In plant supply/production planning and sequencing, inventory and materials management, warehouse and duty operations, and costing and budgeting
- In market IBP and S&OP and distribution planning
- In regional and global S&OP, sales forecasting, demand planning and demand management, and process ownership

Robert did lead x-functional transformation programs delivering functional optimization and differentiation. Robert contributed to the 2nd in the world SAP IBP implementation, which have started in 2013 and proved that Robert has heart, head, and hand for IBP.

Raghav Jandhyala is a senior director of product management at SAP for SAP IBP responsible for sales and operations planning and unified planning processes and best practices in IBP. Raghav has over 16 years of experience in different fields like supply chain management, retail, and banking along with strong technical background in development and adoption of business applications. Raghav held various roles in his career as business consultant, development architect, solutions manager, and product manager. Raghav is responsible for developing the roadmap for S&OP solution and works with multiple IBP customers for new innovations and as a trusted advisor for their global rollouts.

Ganesh Sankaran is a supply chain management technology practitioner. Ganesh helps clients solve business problems and generate value from their supply chain processes, particularly in the planning domain. Ganesh possesses a skill set that combines deep theoretical insights into SCM and rich implementation experience in SAP solutions further enriched by around 7 years of prior software development experience.

Alecsandra Dimofte is working for SAP where she started as a supply chain management consultant. Alecsandra was involved in several IBP/S&OP implementation projects which allowed her to play different roles, from integration consultant to functional design lead. Alecsandra contributed to the development of the S&OP practice within her delivery unit and to the growth of the IBP online community by active participation in the space dedicated to IBP.

Contributors

Katherine Stankiewicz is a human capital practitioner. Katherine has over 8 years' international experience in HR and post-merger and acquisition integration management along with experience in developing, leading, and maximizing performance. Katherine is a strong leader in creating and driving change through the implementation of processes and initiatives.

Malgorzata Kalarus is human capital practitioner. She has over 5 years' experience in human capital area across various industries (construction, power and utilities, chemical, and gas and oil). Malgorzata effectively drives change initiatives within international organizations.

Reviewers

Regional S&OP Manager in a large chemical company—He has more than 30 years of experience in supply chain management, logistics, and information technology. He is currently a supply chain and logistics manager for a global manufacturer of differentiated chemical products. He has a solid background in IT solutions and led design and implementation of S&OP from site to global level.
Solution Architect is currently a solution architect in supply chain planning at a large consumer products company, where he is helping to shape a multiyear process renovation program centered on SAP IBP. He has 15 years of experience designing software solutions for supply chain planning, having previously worked in the packaging, chemicals, and machinery manufacturing sectors in Switzerland, the United States, Sweden, and South Africa. Prior to that, he worked as a software developer at SAP in Germany. He completed a master's degree in mechanical engineering at the University of Cape Town in 1993.

Project Support

Federico Sasso focuses on logistics processes and particularly in production planning and material management area. He completed his master's thesis on outlier detection and correction for seasonal and intermittent products. In IBP, he focuses on statistical forecasting and data analysis and inventory planning.

Ivan Kostakev has over 3 years of shop-floor experience in the manufacturing industry, both as a logistics manager and project engineer. He specializes in integrated business planning.

Vladimir Dorodnitsyn brings experience in the design, implementation, and integration of SAP EWM and SAP ERP. He works in the domain of supply chain planning with a strong focus on integrated business planning including both business and technology transformation topics.
Giulio Zunino has gained insights into the automation of cross-industry production processes and in the automotive industry as a whole. Here, he particularly focused on ways to address the new challenges that the digitalization of the production processes is causing.

Tommaso Nardi works in supply chain management practice. Over the past few years, Tommaso developed a deep understanding and hands-on knowledge of supply chain planning and operational transformations in the life sciences sector.

Recent Past Disconnected Planning

In the course of our careers, we have observed that broadly understood planning processes happen over short-, mid-, and long-term horizon.

Short-term operational planning processes happen over 4–12-week horizon, tactical planning processes cover up to 3 years, and strategic planning processes shape business even up to 10-year horizon.

If we take a closer look into those three planning horizons, we have come to the conclusion that planning processes executed in respective time horizon were characterized differently by:

- Objective
- Impact
- Stakeholder decision power (position in the company hierarchy)
- Stakeholder degree of connection to operational execution or strategic directives
- Frequency
- Granularity
- Time bucket
- Degree of embedding financials into decision-making process
- Degree of embedding product/technology information into decision-making process
- Degree of embedding of customer/market information into decision-making process
- Industry needs
- Systems and technology support

Since those characteristics were different for each of the planning type, many companies face enormous amount of challenges to integrate planning process under one coherent integrated business planning framework. Companies struggle to unlock value of those planning processes being integrated and managed holistically.

In order to understand how to integrate planning processes, let's attempt to describe them one by one as per strategic, tactical, and operational planning.

Strategic planning—We have realized that companies have one strategic planning process which defines business direction and strategy for long-term horizon and the other one which was focused on strategic assets and products but impacting mid-term horizon. Both processes were highly important and had a high impact on company performance.

We have seen that strategic planning which set company direction was executed on annual basis (sometimes twice a year) and was normally led by business development or business planning team. Let us call this process as **annual business planning**.

We have seen that strategic planning processed focused on strategic assets and products was executed on a monthly basis and was typically led by senior supply chain planning managers. Let us call this process as **monthly strategic product/assets planning**.

Annual business planning addresses a global view on business development and business strategy where strategic initiatives affecting technology investments, market positioning, developments, and channel growth are captured, discussed, reconciled, and monetized.

On the demand side, this process addresses issues associated with introduction of new sales channels, entering new markets, and competitor's trends.

On the supply side, this process addresses internal or external manufacturing footprint assessment, investments in operations, warehousing, long-term capacity challenges to be solved with internal or external manufacturing/tolling/3–4PL and CAPEX discussion. Quite often as part of this process, large technology shifts or extensions are being discussed. Length of strategic horizon is much aligned to R&D of the products or technologies.

On the financial side, this process addresses financial risk and opportunities like exchange rate fluctuations, macroeconomic trends, impact of potential acquisitions, and mergers.

This process is typically executed once per year and does cover inputs from various functions considering up to a 10-year future horizon. Process is being led or managed by a global senior management of the company which has a decision power to make changes in company strategy and approve strategic initiatives but do not have hands-on influence on short-term execution.

Experts who support execution of this process prepare data and analysis on aggregated level like product lines or business lines, regional or global scope, and profit or cost center groups. Normally data is being prepared on annual bucketing and mainly in monetary terms.

Decision-making process fundamentally is based on evaluation of assumptions and pros/cons discussion of the financial impact on future company performance. Decision-making process in essence is about developing "what-if" business risk and opportunity scenarios and aims to visualize the management scenario impacts like CAGR (compound annual growth rate). The output of this process was communicated to various functions in the organizations including local management.

Monthly strategic product/assets planning addresses regional or global, mid- to long-term view on strategic products, raw materials, and assets. Examples of those could be:

– Active ingredients in the chemical industry
– Active pharma ingredients (drug substances) in the pharma and health-care industry
– Steel in kitchen appliances
– Seed varieties in the agriculture industry

Those strategic products are very often linked to high cost contribution in the final products, sometimes even above 70%. This process regularly generates impact and improves transparency on monthly tactical S&OP process executed on country to global level but where products discussed have higher form of customization. Link between strategic product planning and tactical S&OP enables organizations to reach the objective of:

– Raising awareness
– Managing feasibility of tactical S&OP plan realization in a better way
– Analyzing projected performance against budget on a regional/country/product family level

Typically, this process was executed in a mix of so-called top-down (by marketing as demand for strategic form of the product) and bottom-up (by supply chain as demand based on consumption of strategic form of the product), where two streams of inputs are being compared and reviewed.

This process runs on a monthly basis with a monthly time bucketing for horizon of up to 5–7 years.

Key stakeholders who lead and manage the monthly strategic product planning are typically on the level of functional manager on global and regional level, mostly from marketing and supply chain. Typically they are not accountable for business strategy but have influence and provide inputs to annual business planning.

Decision-making process fundamentally is based on evaluation of demand inputs, unconstrained and constrained supply planning linked to supply propagation to countries/markets. Fair share of profitability is often used as criteria to allocate strategic form of the product to demand locations. Allocation in tactical horizon is supported with "what-if" business risk and opportunity scenarios which aim to visualize impact of budget realization and operating profit impact of the company as a whole and its business units (markets, countries).

This process and stakeholders have stronger impact on execution of the country/market operational plans.

Tactical planning/sales and operations planning—This process addresses a country-regional-global view on product, demand, supply, financial, and volumetric reconciliation (pre-S&OP meeting) and sign off by management (S&OP meeting). It does focus on addressing issues associated with top-line revenue and volumetric projections, definition of country or product group or channel price tactics, bottom-line profits exposed from constraints, gaps to budget, financial element projection (like exchange rates), and alignment to strategic initiatives. It is a main process which impacts realization of operating plans like budget.

Process is very cross functional, and since it's executed from local to global level, stakeholders can have different accountability and impact on execution. The main process objective is to deliver a balanced plan in volume and value with documented assumptions. The process is not focused on resolving very short-term issues but rather focused on how to achieve business objectives for the current year and current year plus 1.

Decision-making process consolidates inputs through product-demand-supply-pre-S&OP to S&OP meeting. In each of the steps, "what-if" business scenario planning is used to model risk and opportunities. Very often scenarios go cross-process steps like for tender demand to supply and pre-S&OP reconciliation or for new product launch to demand, supply, and financial impact assessment.

Data which was being used had a monthly granularity on various levels on product and commercial-geographical hierarchy. Process on country/market level was often executed on SKU/product group/sales zone/country level. Process on regional/global level was reviewed on product lines/country/group of country level. Process on site level was executed mainly on key manufacturing assets or key strategic product level. Time bucketing was typically monthly, with specific focus on subtotaling like:

- Year to date, year to go, and full year
- Weeks, months, quarters, and years which help to quickly assess situation

We have observed that time horizon of this process varies from the current year to current year plus 2.

In the last few years, we have observed that tactical S&OP process is more and more tightly integrated with financial planning, but this is not yet very common. There are a lot of companies which run their S&OP process in volume only and disconnected from financials.

Tactical S&OP process in many industries is linked tightly at minimum of once per month with operational planning. Tactical S&OP sets a detailed framework for operational planning in which it is even further optimized and resolved especially in demand-supply balancing but on a more granular level.

S&OP has many forms, variations, and definitions, but let us bring one from the leading practitioner:

Sales and Operations Planning is communication and decision-making process:

- To balance demand and supply
- To set plans for volume that will guide the detail mix
- To integrate financial, product development and operating plans

(Dougherty & Gray, 2006)

Operational planning—This process addresses very often in country/sales zone demand and supply imbalances. This process was very down to earth and operated with resources and assets which were available at a certain point in time for short horizon. We have seen that operational planning was introduced in the companies when monthly S&OP process was not granular enough to solve demand-supply imbalances driven by product type or channel. We observed various frequencies of this process from daily, weekly, to bi-weekly. What we have found very interesting is that this process was switched on and switched off during the year especially in case of:

- Highly seasonal products
- Limited life products and offers
- Short peak seasons
- Large promotional campaigns
- Customer-specific products
- Commodity business

This means that operational planning can be driven by product or industry characteristics.

We have observed that time horizon of this process varies from a few days up to 12–16 weeks.

Operational planning focuses to **extract the biggest value from available materials, manpower, machines, and money. These four dimensions may be called "4 M."**

Data which was typically needed had a very high granularity, order level (sales/production, inventory) on daily/weekly bucketing. Due to the amount of highly granular information, exception management did play an important role in the process.

Participants/contributors of operational planning process were very hands-on experts in the organization, subject matter experts who were "doing the job."

You can understand operational planning as a sort of optimization to tactical S&OP. There was tight integration between those two processes ensured by especially aligned calendar of activities. At minimum once per month, outputs of operational planning were integrated into tactical S&OP. The operational process was executed typically on a single meeting where product, customer, demand, supply, and financial information were available to make short-term decisions. Even though this process was tightly connected to execution, you still can look at it as execution steering, way to get alignment with framework defined in tactical S&OP. We have seen that operational planning can be done within country on sales zone level or cross-countries but then driven by brand/product group tactics and specifics.

In Fig. 1.1, you can see a summary of observations about key characteristics linked to planning types, horizons, and levels. We have observed very often that many organizations struggle to connect those planning processes because of their differences and lack of focus on organizational and technology aspects.

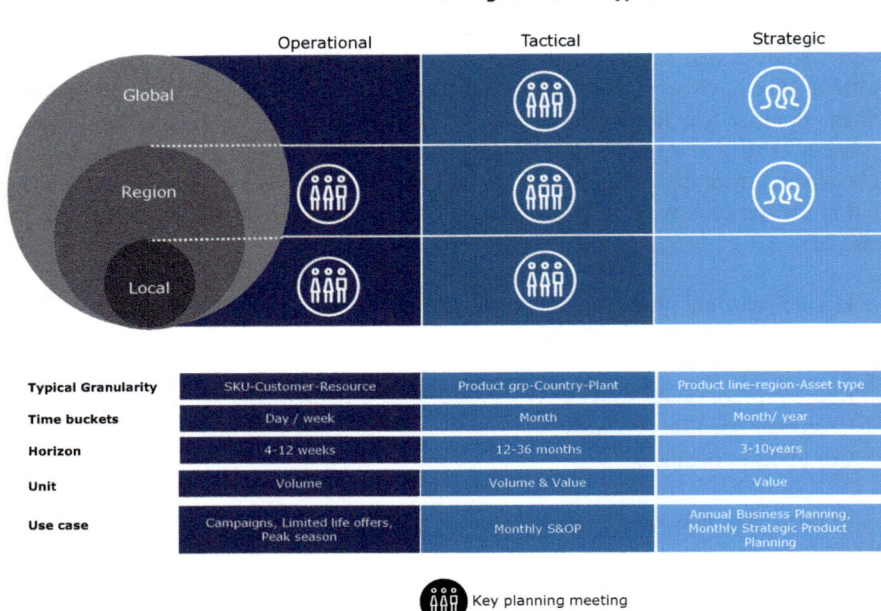

Fig. 1.1 Planning horizon-type levels and their key characteristics

What we have found very interesting is that activities in all planning types can be mapped against well-recognized sales and operations planning process dimensions. Just a reminder, S&OP has the following process dimension:

- Product
- Demand
- Supply
- Reconciliation (pre-S&OP)
- S&OP

Observations about planning types and S&OP process step were presented in Fig. 1.2. As we can see on the figure, activities across all planning types can be mapped against the same S&OP process dimensions, but they have different objective, focus, and stakeholders. We are bringing up mapping of activities across all planning processes, to illustrate that they have similarities. Those similarities

1.1 Summary

S&OP process dimensions		Planning horizons & types		
		Operational	Tactical	Strategic
	Product / Customers / Services Review	Order based changes in product packaging	New product launches and withdrawals Product transfers	New technologies introductions Technology transfers
	Demand Review	Order types Sensed demand Sensed forecast	Forecast on detail and aggregated level in volume and value	Demand trends New markets New sales channels
	Supply Review	Existing inventories Firm Supply	Planned safety stock Optimized supply plans Fair share / profitable allocations	Planned supply capabilities Internal & external manufacturing
	Reconciliation in volume and value (Pre-SO&OP)	Detail balancing and demand fulfilment prioritization	Volumetric and value E2E reconciliation & simulations Mid term financial risk & opportunities	Financials risks & opportunities CAGR, long term operating profits
	S&OP meeting (sign off authorization)	Experts	Managers	Senior Management

Fig. 1.2 Planning types versus S&OP process dimensions

should be leveraged when putting all of planning types into one coherent business management and planning environment called Integrated Business Planning.

1.1 Summary

- We have observed that very often planning horizons and types are not integrated; companies operate them in a very isolated way, on a not synchronized calendar of activities, without structures and capabilities which enable connection between planning types; and unfortunately processes are often operated on non-value-adding granularity levels and on wrong horizons.
- Operational, tactical, and strategic planning processes share the same S&OP process dimensions, but focus and importance of those steps are different per planning type.
- Furthermore, we have realized that organizationally and capability wise those processes are very often not integrated. Functions define their organization structures and required capabilities to operate in their own silo process but not in a purpose to "act as one."
- We have recognized that many companies struggle to define the right level of detail for strategic, tactical, and operational planning. The figure below gives a hint on what to consider in process design (see Fig. 1.3).
- Last but not the least, companies operate those planning processes on fragmented planning solutions, which require enormous amount of time to integrate and reconcile data.

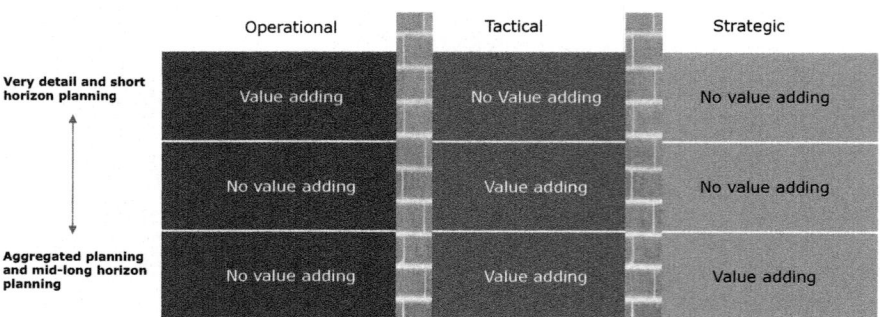

Fig. 1.3 Disconnect of panning horizons and granularity

Reference

Dougherty, J., & Gray, C. (2006). *Sales and operations planning – Best practices. Partners for excellence*. Belmont: Trafford Publishing.

Why Move to Integrated Business Planning 2

2.1 Value of IBP Process and Organization Transformation

IBP can bring tangible value from process and organizational perspective.

2.1.1 Process Value

Let's bring some examples of the value gained from Integrated Business Planning transformation programs (see Fig. 2.1):

Why should you consider transformation of your planning processes into IBP? Because if done properly, they can bring substantial benefits, e.g.:

- Increasing revenue 52%
- Improving forecast accuracy 31%
- Improvements in the perfect order and customer service 31%
- Better supply planning and schedule adherence 31%
- Improving new product launch 28%
- Reduction of inventory 27%
- Improve translation of demand into procurement requirements or buy-side contract needs 21%
- Capital planning and asset management 21%
- Developing and executing demand-shaping programs 20%
- Improving logistics planning 19%
- Improving asset utilization 17% (Palmatier & Crum, 2013)

Companies implementing IBP not only experience benefits in costs reduction but also increase in sales revenue and market share. This is because IBP can be used as a strategic management process (Palmatier & Crum, 2013).

Planning horizon	Value add metrics examples
Operational	• 35 % short term forecast accuracy improvement • Lower re-distribution costs • Lower change over costs & time • Higher order fulfilment
Tactical	• 15 % forecast accuracy improvement, 66 % process efficiency improvement • Up to 30% inventory optimization • 4% increase in profitability • Reduced supply cost
Strategic	• Improved strategic initiative planning and simulation

Improved collaboration, transparency, visibility. Single source (set) of data to manage business. End to end risk & opportunities with "what-if" scenario planning.

Fig. 2.1 SAP IBP example of value delivered per planning horizon

Let us bring some examples of benefits linked to S&OP process which incorporates IBP value drivers (see Fig. 2.2).

IBP can bring substantial efficiency and focus value if planning processes are aligned to granularity, frequency, and horizon (see Fig. 2.3).

One of the substantial values Integrated Business Planning brings to companies is it does enable improvement to manage business through connection of operational planning, tactical S&OP, and strategic planning. This connection as described at the beginning of this book has process, organization and capability, and SAP IBP technology dimensions.

2.1 Value of IBP Process and Organization Transformation

PRODUCT REVIEW (P)	DEMAND REVIEW (D)	SUPPLY REVIEW (S)	Integrated Reconciliation (IR)	Management Business Review (MBR)
• Improved integrated E2E Product Launch risk & opportunity "what if" assessment in volume, value (incl. registrations)	• Significantly improved process efficiency (workload) and effectiveness (accuracy) with introduction of differentiated forecasting & demand planning, statistical forecasting	• Improved unconstrained supply planning cross network, BOM, lead-times for strategic and tactical horizon		• Improved demand-supply-finance reconciliation in volume and value between Market-Sites-Regions
• Improved process efficiency with use of Product segmentation	• Demand planning enriched on level aligned to best insights of business stakeholders	• Improved integration of supplier collaboration in constrained and unconstrained planning (ARIBA)		• Improved integration between strategic-tactical-operational planning incl. budgeting
• Improved process efficiency with product/customer/market (or combined) segmentation	• Transparency of value and non value add activities	• Improved cross the levels (Market-Regions-Sites) bi directional propagation of demand and constraints enabling unified, feasible plans shared cross organization leading to reduction of supply & distribution costs		• Improved Market-Site-Region transparency and visibility of target realization, gap identification on any level, improved management of gap closure with JAM collaboration and shared data
• Rationalization of portfolio, services, customers, and analysis of markets from profitability, revenue, cost perspective	• Demand sensing enabling improvement of late customization decisions, transportation costs, replenishment	• Improved cross network/bom simulations for assets extensions, alternative transportation routes, production efficiency improvements, events		• Improved visibility of performance vs KPI targets
	• Exception based management of uncertainties and market events in what if mode realized in volume, value	• Improved modelling of network, BOM, costs, revenue for strategic & tactical planning		• Improved collaboration, tasks mgmt., escalations, process adherence, orchestration, process management with JAM
• Correlation of measures enabling E2E decision with inventory forward cover, budget realization, profits against ABC/XYZ	• Improved price changes (and other variables) impact simulations	• Improved safety stock planning and reduction of inventory with multi-echelon optimization		• Improved visibility of non standard revenue sources
				• Substantially reduce focus on "fire fighting"
		• Improved integration of short term optimized scheduling and sequencing (PP/DS)		• Enabled fact based decisions with single set of E2E volume and value data

Fig. 2.2 IBP example of process step value

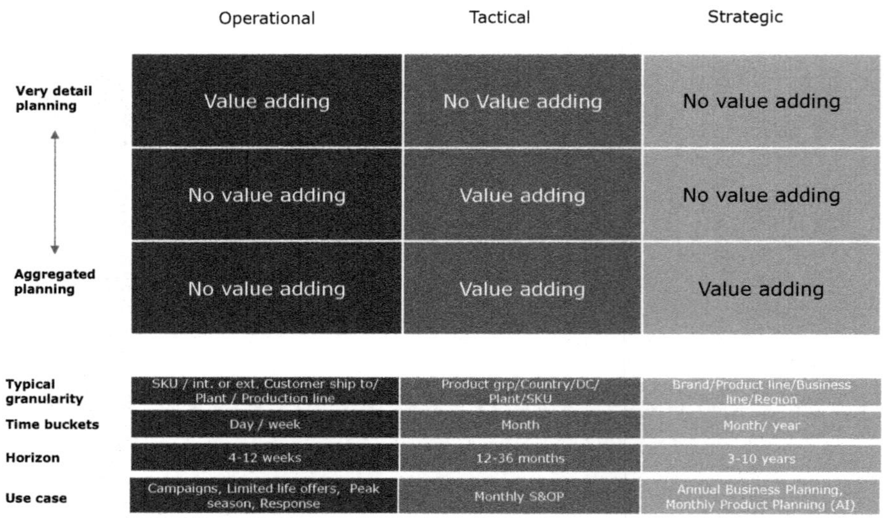

	Operational	Tactical	Strategic
Very detail planning	Value adding	No Value adding	No value adding
	No value adding	Value adding	No value adding
Aggregated planning	No value adding	Value adding	Value adding
Typical granularity	SKU / int. or ext. Customer ship to/ Plant / Production line	Product grp/Country/DC/ Plant/SKU	Brand/Product line/Business line/Region
Time buckets	Day / week	Month	Month/ year
Horizon	4-12 weeks	12-36 months	3-10 years
Use case	Campaigns, Limited life offers, Peak season, Response	Monthly S&OP	Annual Business Planning, Monthly Product Planning (AI)

Fig. 2.3 IBP characteristics aligned to value add

2.1.2 Organizational Value

On the other hand from organizational perspective and process efficiency perspective, there is impact which may consider (see Fig. 2.4).

2.2 Value of SAP IBP on HANA in Cloud

SAP IBP is a cloud-based solution driving faster time to value for customers. Offered as software as a service from SAP Cloud, IBP solution is readily available to customers upon subscription and provides faster onboarding. Customers benefit from lower total cost of ownership, faster implementations, and regular product innovations.

The up-front capital expenditures are no longer required. SAP handles ongoing maintenance of the solution without the need for customer to have an IT support organization and infrastructure teams for time-consuming and expensive upgrades. SAP takes care of data security, SOX compliance and certifications, up-to-date software, and latest technology to ensure smooth running of the systems.

There are several benefits of IBP that we explore in detail in the follow-up sections. These include:

1. Faster time to value
2. Reduced total cost of ownership
3. Faster innovations

2.2 Value of SAP IBP on HANA in Cloud

Organization / Process step	Optimization examples
Forecasting & Demand planning	• Opportunity to maximize time being spend by sales & marketing on forecasting with use of exception based process, differentiated forecasting • Opportunity to optimize Country– Regional – Global demand planning workforce with increase of automatization and process efficiency • More time for sales organization to sell
Supply Planning	• Opportunity to optimize Regional / Global supply planning workforce with increase automatization and process efficiency • Opportunity to optimize Site supply planning workforce and combine some functions with scheduling and sequencing
Integrated Reconciliation	• Opportunity to optimize Finance workforce through embedding roles in integrated process supported on fully integrated data
All S&OP process steps	• Significant (even 90%) time reduction to integrate and reconcile data either to be used for analysis or to be optimized • More focused and efficient roles & responsibilities • More time to analyse business risk & opportunities • Team prepared for business changes • Roles & responsibilities enabling process integration improving management of the business

Fig. 2.4 IBP example of organizational value

4. Operations support for infrastructure and system maintenance
5. Security of data
6. Application support

SAP IBP is only available as a cloud-based solution. It comes with a robust cloud-based data integration platform CPI-DS which is purposely built for cloud integration. It integrates data from on-premise, Cloud landscapes, and other heterogeneous landscapes of customer to SAP IBP. SAP JAM is a cloud-based collaboration platform that is well integrated with SAP IBP to provide collaboration for cross-functional teams in IBP. Further SAP IBP uses SCI for secure user access.

1. Faster Time to Value
Instant Access to the Solution

SAP IBP is a reliable, scalable, secure, and performant software application deployed on the cloud which is instantly available upon subscription. SAP provides a SLA of 99.5% for SAP IBP which means the systems are reliable and available for users always. The software installations and infrastructure for the application are taken care by SAP as a service provider, and customers are provided with system access, onboarding guidance, and support structure. Further customers can subscribe to test and production instances or starter edition which allows them to do proof of concepts and self-testing before making a buy decision.

Faster Adoption by Users

SAP IBP is designed keeping in mind the usability needs and faster adoption by the business users. With rich user interface based on Excel Add-In and Fiori UIs and best practice content to run business processes, end users should be able to easily adopt the solution without high training efforts and involvement with IT.

SAP IBP provides high flexibility to customize solution based on customer's business process. It allows business and IT to be self-serviced while using the application. For example, the business users can instantly access SAP IBP using single sign-on and create their own analytics and customized dashboards without the need for IT to be involved. They can further share charts and dashboards and work in a collaborative manner.

The cloud-based integration: CPI-DS used by SAP allows for harmonized data integration across multiple data sources so that the right information is available for business users at their fingertips, without the need to log in to different systems for data gathering and deriving actionable insights from data.

Best Practice Content for Faster Implementations and Learning

SAP IBP comes pre-built with sample business planning models and best practice content which allows the users to be self-sufficient to jump-start their implementation or use the content for internal training and learnings. The best practice content provides the analytics, planning views, business process flows, test scripts, and detailed documentation to run business processes in IBP.

Reduced Total Cost of Ownership

In contrast to the license-based traditional software buying and deployment in on-premise landscape by customer, SAP IBP is a subscription-based SaaS application which means the infrastructure, deployment, monitoring maintenance, and support are handled by SAP.

Figure 2.5 shows the difference between cloud-based application vs on-premise installation. The SaaS model benefits from the overall reduced TCO compared to on-premise initial setup costs and ongoing costs for maintenance and support, IT teams, and training.

2. Faster Innovations and Release Cycles

Cloud-based applications like SAP IBP complement customer's on-premise installation providing the flexibility and agility for business to deploy faster new business processes and benefit from the faster innovations cycles that are provided by IBP. However, to benefit from Cloud solutions, it will be beneficial for customers to have a Cloud strategy and the overall solution strategy for coexistence of both customer's on-premise and cloud-based applications in place.

IBP provides very high level of configuration to be able to model customer's unique business process. However, with cloud-based application, there is no custom

2.2 Value of SAP IBP on HANA in Cloud

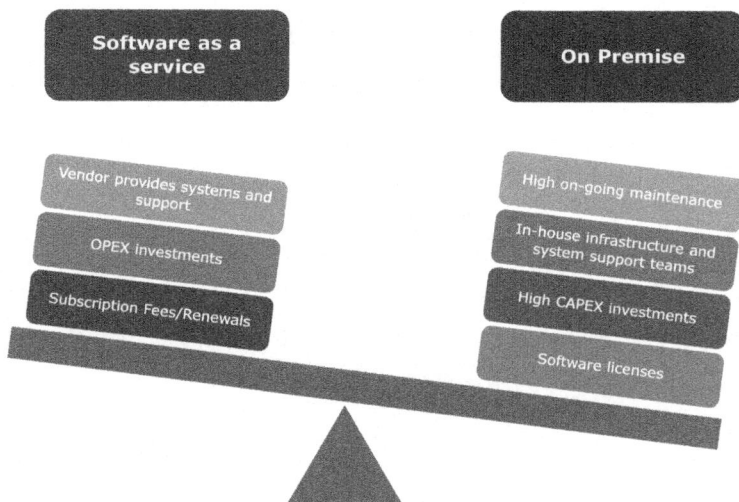

Fig. 2.5 SAP Cloud versus on-premise system

development or specific extensions of the software. Some extensions can be done through LCODE which is a proprietary L-based language script for complex key figure calculations. To keep up with the different customer requirements and market edge, SAP IBP innovates rapidly providing new functionality and enhancements every quarter.

IBP follows a quarterly release cycle. Further hotfixes and patches contain fixes for the current release which are deployed in the regular maintenance windows agreed with customers.

3. Infrastructure, System, and Security

SAP IBP system is provisioned in SAP Cloud landscape after executing the contract agreement. Based on the application modules licensed, size of HANA system, type of system—test, production, or starter edition—and the relevant system are made available to the customer. Most customers typically run a 2-tier Cloud instance with test and production instance. Customers can also choose to run a 3-tier landscape of development, test, and production instances. SAP provides single tenant per productive landscape with a secure and isolated instance. The cloud systems are provisioned in the customers' regional data center.

The SAP Cloud Platform runs a secure, certified, and industry standard complaint infrastructure. SAP runs seven worldwide data centers. To ensure the systems and data are secure, the data centers are certified for all standard certifications and audits. For example, IT operations are ISO 27001 certified which is a regulation on how to manage information security in a data center (SAP, n.d.-b).

SAP data centers are tier 3/tier 4 certified meeting several requirements for physical security of the buildings using surveillance cameras, digital recording,

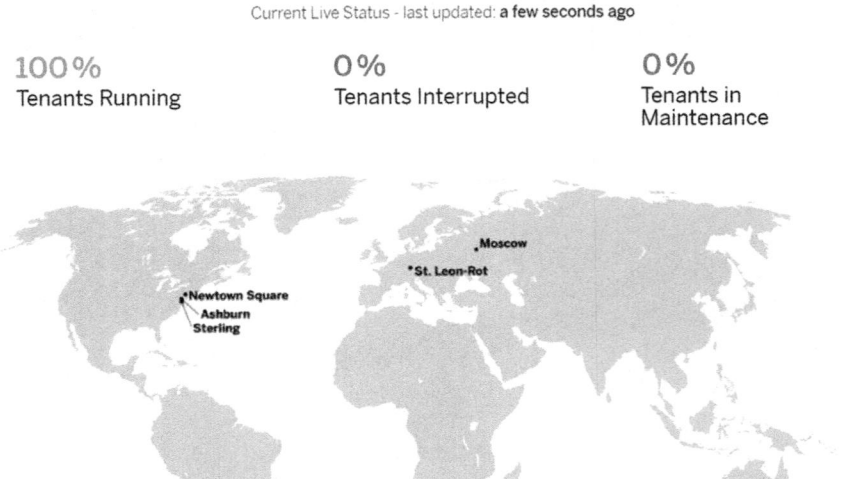

Fig. 2.6 SAP Cloud operations

biometrics access, on-site 24 × 7 security and facility support, redundant power supply, fire and flood protections, auxiliary cooling systems, etc.

Typical operations involved during system provisioning are hardware procurement and installation, system build, software installations, network and application security, whitelisting, transport setup, system connectivity tests, and technical onboarding.

Customers can see live IBP cloud service from SAP Cloud Trust Center which provides information on the cloud service status and is an entry point for various security topics (SAP, n.d.-c).

Figure 2.6 shows a snapshot of cloud service status for IBP.

4. System Operations Support

The system operations support ensures the availability and reliability of the deployed cloud systems and the regular maintenance activities. Service level agreements are defined for SAP Cloud with regard to system availability and maintenance windows (SAP, n.d.-a).

Some of the services supported are:

- Application availability SLA
- Planned maintenance for system downtime
- Backups and recovery

2.2 Value of SAP IBP on HANA in Cloud

- Primary storage on production data center and secondary in backup location off-site. Retention policies on the number of snapshots to be kept and retention periods
- Full daily backups and log files incremental backups
- System monitoring, performance checks, networks monitoring
- Data refresh and copy
- Regular maintenance for releases, hotfixes, and emergency patches
- System access support: access to CPI-DS, SCI connectivity, and JAM tenant

5. Upgrades, Notifications, and Communications

As part of the service agreement, the maintenance windows for weekly upgrades and quarterly releases are planned. Weekly upgrades include deployment of hotfixes, patches, and regular maintenance activities. The quarterly releases are first applied to the test instance followed by production instance with about 2 weeks' time in between. Customers need to run smoke tests and basic regression tests to ensure that their main use cases are working as before. The releases include new functionality which can optionally be adopted by customers. It further ensures that there are no incompatible changes between releases or, in case they are, they are clearly communicated.

Communication emails are sent to customer prior to upgrade to quarterly releases to ensure that the timelines fit with customer project activities. The key contacts identified in the customer contract are sent communication about upgrades and other planned maintenance activities. In case of unforeseen downtime, notification emails are sent to the customers informing the reason for the technical issue, its impact, solution, and root cause analysis.

6. Onboarding Guidance and Initial Setup by System Admin

After successful system provisioning, a welcome email with onboarding checklist will be sent to customer to ensure their cloud readiness. Welcome email with URL links is sent to system administrator with access information for:

- SCI
- IBP
- CPI-DS

Further, the onboarding instructions for self-service on setting up IBP by the customer are listed. These include:

- How to log in and set up users
- Setup integration with JAM
- Setup integration with on-premise systems (CPI agent)
- Install Excel Add-In
- Submitting tickets for support

7. Application Support, Learning, and Customer Success

To ensure smooth operations and timely resolution of issues, SAP IBP has the application support team consisting of primary product support, active global support, and development teams. This incident management team has different levels of support to solve customer issues based on the ticket resolution SLAs. Customer logs tickets through the ticket system.

Customers are provided with tools to make them self-sufficient for learnings and trainings on IBP. These include the following to name a few:

- Application help
- Product videos
- Solution and product updates webinars
- SCN Community
- SAP education for training
- Best practice content

To ensure strong collaboration between SAP and customer and for customer to benefit from SAP investments, faster time to value, mitigate risks, and adopt solution successfully, a customer success team is defined for strategic accounts. SAP supports customer on different phases of the project from pre-subscription to go-live by providing RFE support, presales engagement, and answers to security questions, providing onboarding checklists, defining customer engagement teams, and providing development angel support for strategic customers and key implementations and customer office support to ensure there is an escalation path, to mitigate risk, and to ensure success of IBP implementations.

8. SAP IBP on HANA

SAP IBP is run natively in HANA within the planning and calculation engine. This allows for faster calculations where the data and calculations are run in-memory. This gives users speed and agility to run complex supply chain planning processes in one data model (Fig. 2.7) covering strategic, tactical, and operational process across multiple simulations and scenarios.

In SAP IBP, the key figures are stored and/or calculated. The calculated key figures have calculations on the stored key figure with several intermediate

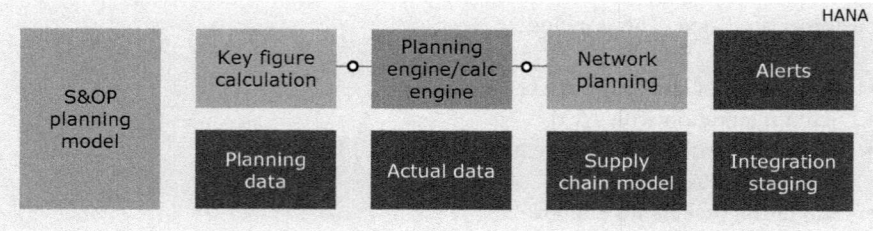

Fig. 2.7 SAP IBP planning model on HANA

calculations at different levels of hierarchies. Only the stored key figures are stored in the HANA in-memory database, and the calculations behind the calculated key figures are executed on the fly whenever user queries such key figures from Excel, analytics, planning operators, etc. On the fly aggregation is performed on the stored data and in-memory utilizing the power of SAP HANA, so there is no need to store aggregates or intermediate calculation results.

SAP application modules mapped to strategic, tactical, and operational planning.
What makes SAP IBP unique:

1. Connected planning processes in a unified planning model
2. Simplified user experience with Excel and Web UI
3. Advanced planning algorithms for special functions like demand sensing, supply planning, response planning, etc.
4. Embedded social collaboration using SAP JAM
5. Real-time planning, simulations, and what-if analysis
6. Embedded end-user analytics, alerts, and dashboards
7. Best practice content for integrated business processes across all application modules
8. Speed and agility of SAP HANA
9. Simplified deployment on cloud

Figure 2.8 shows overview of IBP with system integration, HANA planning platform, data management, planning algorithms, and user layer including Excel UI, Web UI, and JAM Collaboration.

2.3 Value of SAP IBP Pre-configured System

SAP delivers out-of-the box standard planning models and best practice content for business processes covering S&OP, demand planning, supply planning, inventory optimization, response planning, and control tower.

SAP delivered planning areas contain data model for master data, planning hierarchy levels, and key figures and calculations behind a business process, the purpose of which is to give a depth of functionality covering each business process. These can be used as a good starting point to jump-start customer's implementation projects and to gain an understanding of the system and connected processes. They can be used as a baseline configuration and further adjusted to meet the business process of the customer. The models come with predefined planning elements covering all the functions relevant for a planning process. For example, demand model (SAP6) has a sample content for typical demand planning key figures. These can be further extended to meet the planning hierarchies and key figures of the customers.

The life cycle of planning areas is represented in Fig. 2.9. Customers typically start their projects by taking a copy of SAP delivered models to their customer usage area. After the copy is performed, the SAP delivered models and customer's models

2 Why Move to Integrated Business Planning

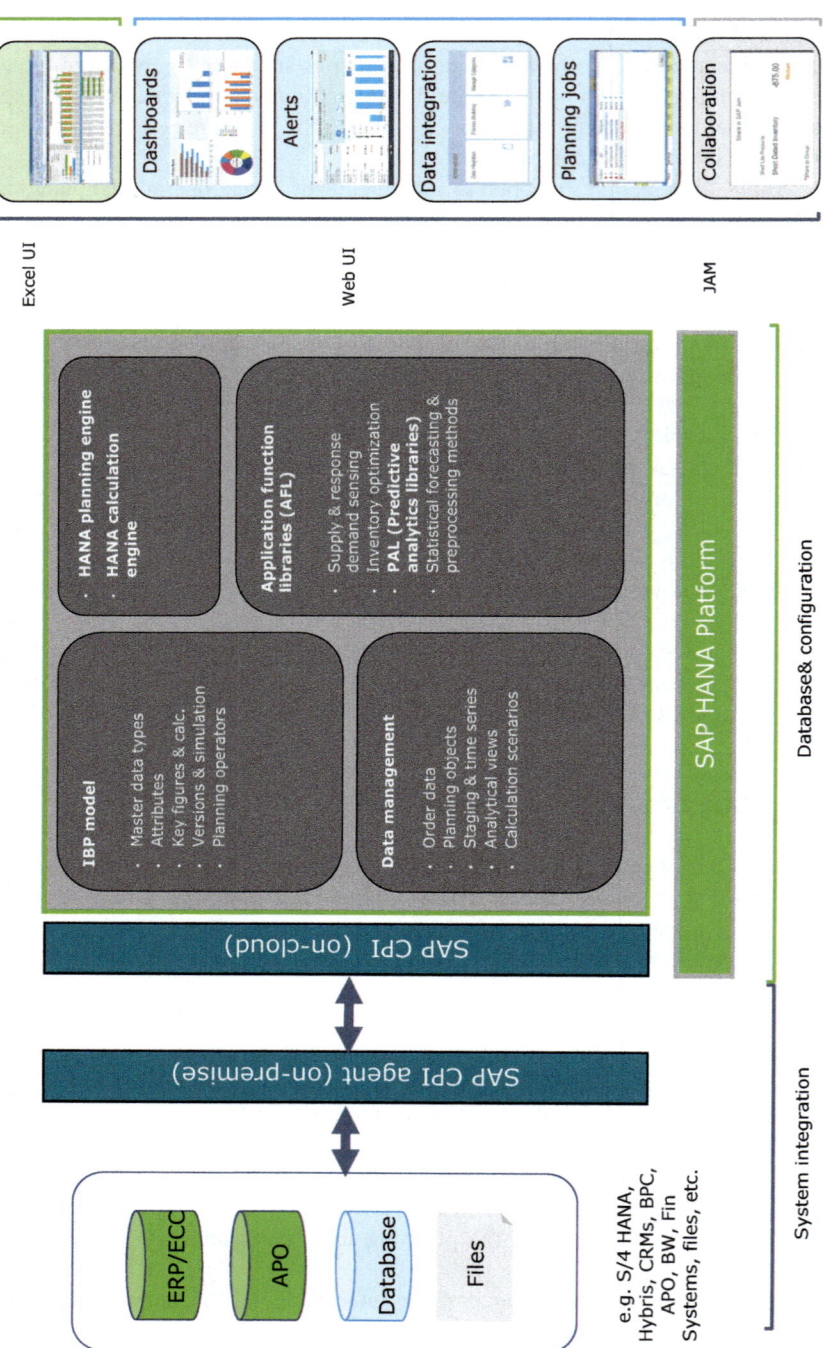

Fig. 2.8 SAP IBP system overview from data integration to user interface

2.3 Value of SAP IBP Pre-configured System

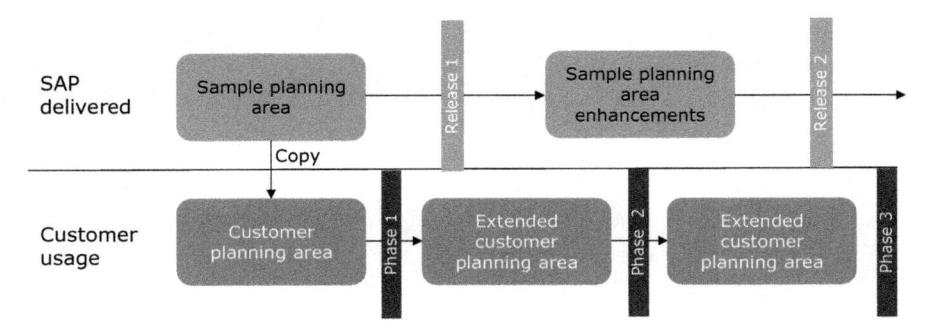

Fig. 2.9 SAP IBP how to leverage pre-configured SAP IBP planning area

run independently and have their own life cycle. The customer planning areas can be extended based on the project phases identified and the overall rollouts. For each release, SAP updates the sample planning areas covering the new features and functionality released. Customers can adopt their existing models taking the new features available in the delivered models.

The model covers a breadth of functionality that is most common for all industries. It has a fixed semantic part which is used by the underlying planning algorithms along with highly flexible configuration which can be used as an initial template upon which additional customer-specific business processes and modeling elements can be added. For example, the demand plan for some customers may be at month/product/customer level, whereas for other customer could be at week product/customer/sales area level, yet some other customer could have by week product/customer/location level. IBP allows customers to define these flexible planning hierarchy levels along with custom key figures and calculations.

When IBP is implemented at a customer for a single application like S&OP or inventory or demand, etc., the individual planning areas can be used (Fig. 2.10).

All the SAP delivered planning areas are aligned on a unified set of planning attributes and master data types. For example, there is one product master data type used across all planning areas in IBP. The attribute usage depends on the assignment of attributes to the planning area.

In addition, SAPIBP1 planning area (Fig. 2.11) is a unified planning area that enables integration across application modules in a single data model and providing best practice sample business process and planning content like planning views, dashboards, analytical charts, process guides, sample data, and test documents.

Further SAP74 planning model (see Fig. 2.12) provides a combined planning area for response and supply planning based on order-based direct integration to SAP ECC. SAP provides best practices and content for planning processes like supply and allocation planning.

Application	Planning Area	Purpose	Planning Periodicity	Planning Process	Process Type
IBP Sales and Operations Planning	SAP2	Tactical Consensus Demand Planning, Finance Integration, Demand/Supply balancing	Monthly	Mid to Long Term Tactical	Time Series
IBP for Inventory Optimization	SAP3	Multi Stage Inventory Optimization, Single Stage IO, Inventory Components	Weekly	Mid to Long Term Operational	Timer Series
Supply Planning	SAP4	Time Series based Heuristics and Optimizer	Monthly (can be adapted to other levels)	Mid to Long Term Tactical	Time Series
Supply Chain Control Tower	SAP5	Supply Chain KPIs, Score Metrics	Daily	Short to Mid Term	Time Series and Orders
IBP Demand	SAP6	Mid-Long Term Demand Planning and Short Term Demand Sensing	Weekly and Daily	Short Term and Mid Term Operational	Time Series and Orders
Supply and Response Panning	SAP7	Order based planning for Supply and Allocations Planning, Response Planning, Deployment, Integration with ECC	Daily, Weekly	Short Term and Mid Term Operational	Order based Planning

Fig. 2.10 SAP IBP pre-configured specialized systems

Planning Area	Purpose	Planning Periodicity	Planning Process	Process Type
SAPIBP1	Unified Planning across IBP Business Processes covering S&OP, Demand, Inventory Optimization, Supply and Supply Chain Control Tower	Daily, Weekly (incl.Technical Weeks),Monthly	Short Term Operational, Mid to Long Term Tactical.	Time Series and Order based.

Fig. 2.11 SAP IBP pre-configured unified planning area

Planning Area	Purpose	Planning Periodicity	Planning Process	Process Type
SAP74	Unified Planning across Tactical Supply Plan and Operational Order based Response Planning based on external integration with ECC	Daily, Weekly	Short Term Operations, Mid-Long Term Tactical	Time Series and Order based.

Fig. 2.12 SAP IBP pre-configured unified planning area

2.3 Value of SAP IBP Pre-configured System

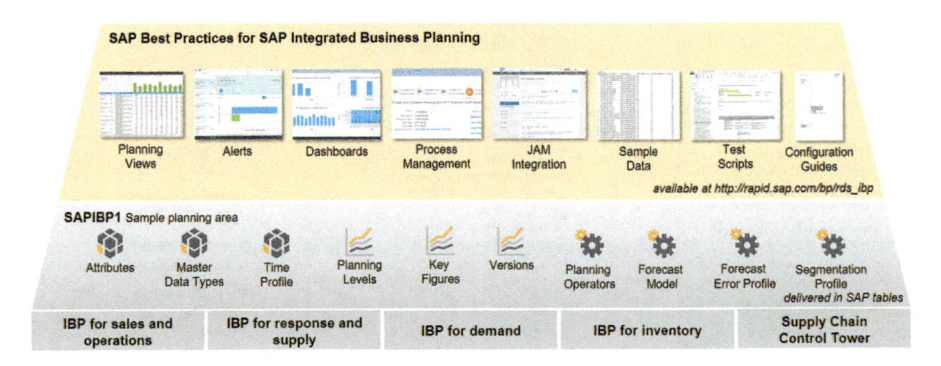

Fig. 2.13 SAP IBP best practices embedded in Rapid Deployment Solution. This figure is based on IBP SAP (2016)

Best Practice Content

Together with the delivered models, IBP also provides a best practice content for the unified planning area (SAPIBP1) covering an end-to-end sample business process along with detailed business process maps and content that can be readily used and adapted further. This helps customers with faster onboarding, easy to learn, train, and consume the newer functionality and innovations from SAP IBP. The pre-delivered content including Excel-based planning, dashboards, planning profiles, alerts, process models, sample data, etc. shows how to run an integrated process (see Fig. 2.13).

When customer test systems or starter editions are provisioned, it comes with preinstalled and ready to use planning model and best practice content together with sample data. Further, the content is easily available for download. With the best practice content, customers can get a clear understanding of how processes across different planning hierarchy levels, data at different granularity, and different horizons integrate with each other, for example, how to connect tactical, operational, and execution processes across different horizons—short, mid, and long term. For example, how does safety stock recommendations from inventory optimization can feed to tactical S&OP planning process and how short-term demand sensing can be an input to inventory optimization.

Business Process Flows Covered in Best Practices

Figure 2.14 shows some of the business processes and the integration of processes across different IBP applications covered by the unified planning process. All these underlying processes work on one data model with one set of master data and harmonized key figures across several planning hierarchical levels covering tactical, operational, and execution processes.

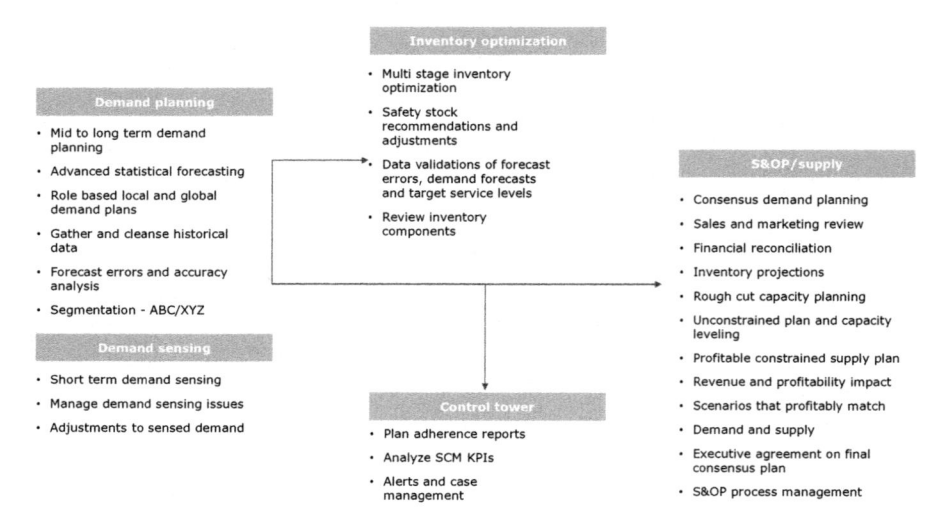

Fig. 2.14 SAP IBP example of processes in Rapid Deployment Solution

Demand planning
- Mid to long term demand planning
- Advanced statistical forecasting
- Role based local and global demand plans
- Gather and cleanse historical data
- Forecast errors and accuracy analysis
- Segmentation - ABC/XYZ

Demand sensing
- Short term demand sensing
- Manage demand sensing issues
- Adjustments to sensed demand

Inventory optimization
- Multi stage inventory optimization
- Safety stock recommendations and adjustments
- Data validations of forecast errors, demand forecasts and target service levels
- Review inventory components

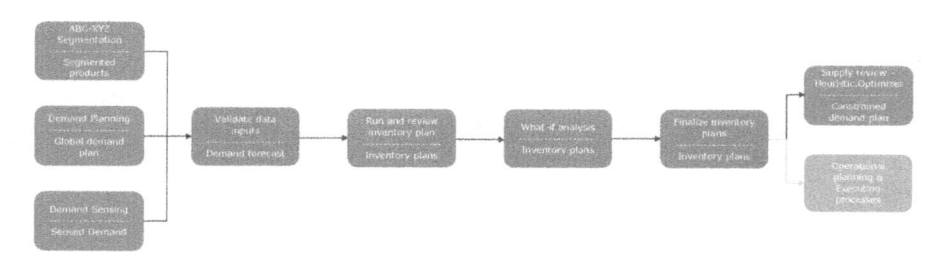

Control tower
- Plan adherence reports
- Analyze SCM KPIs
- Alerts and case management

S&OP/supply
- Consensus demand planning
- Sales and marketing review
- Financial reconciliation
- Inventory projections
- Rough cut capacity planning
- Unconstrained plan and capacity leveling
- Profitable constrained supply plan
- Revenue and profitability impact
- Scenarios that profitably match Demand and supply
- Executive agreement on final consensus plan
- S&OP process management

Fig. 2.15 SAP IBP RDS example of best practice process. This figure is adjusted and based on IBP SAP (2016)

The best practice includes 13 integrated planning processes in all 5 IBP applications (Fig. 2.14). The below example shows one such process for running inventory optimization where we start with inputs from short-term demand sensing and mid- to long-term demand plan along with segmented products for customer segmentation and forecast errors to run multistage inventory optimization, perform what-if analysis, review generated inventory components, and finalize an inventory plan that can be sent to tactical-monthly S&OP process and to execution processes in ECC.

Customers can follow this sample process (see Fig. 2.15) as a starting point and walk through the process using the content provided for each process.

In addition, the best practices contain detailed process flows (Fig. 2.16) which go deeper into each of the high-level process flows and outline what are the inputs, outputs, and processing steps carried out in each phase. This helps customers to understand clearly the business process and also how to run it.

2.3 Value of SAP IBP Pre-configured System

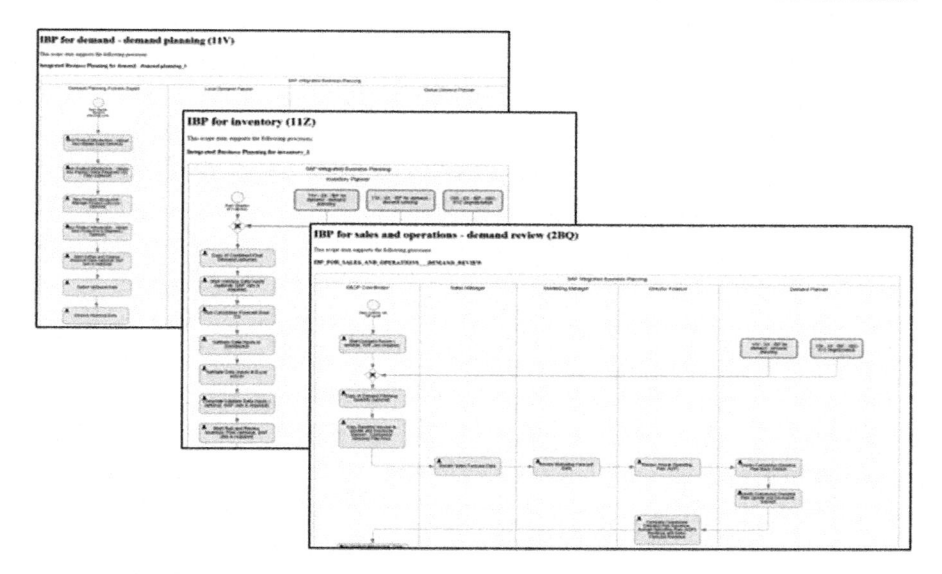

Fig. 2.16 SAP IBP RDS example of best practice process model. This figure is based on IBP SAP (2016)

Best Practice Content Covered

As previously mentioned, the artifacts in SAP IBP to run a business process are the planning view templates, dashboards, process scripts, alerts, collaboration content, etc. The unified planning best practice content contains on top of SAP delivered planning areas: SAPIBP1 and SAP74 including:

- 15+ planning view templates
  For example, planning view template below shows a supply planning view with detailed views on capacity, production, transportation, and supply chain costs (Fig. 2.17).
- 15+ dashboards with 75+ predefined charts
  The dashboard and charts cover key analytics supporting a business process and can be shared with different users collaborating in the planning process. For example, the dashboard below shows a control tower global visibility of the inventory position across different product categories and geographies (Fig. 2.18).
  The chart can show results of inventory optimization run (Fig. 2.19).
- 5+ custom alerts and cases covering most important business alerts that need to be tracked, for example, over capacity alert, incoming orders over forecast (see Fig. 2.20), etc., further three process management templates cover the business

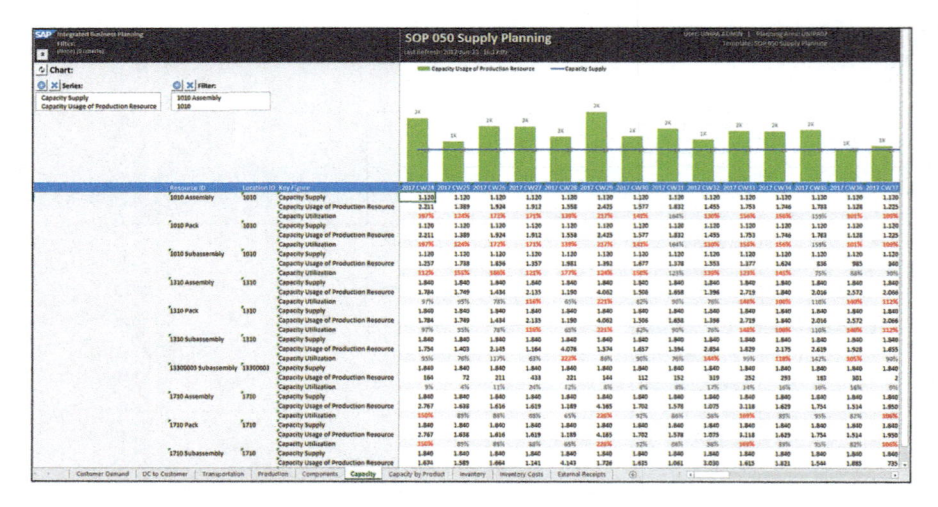

Fig. 2.17 SAP IBP example of RDS—Excel UI template

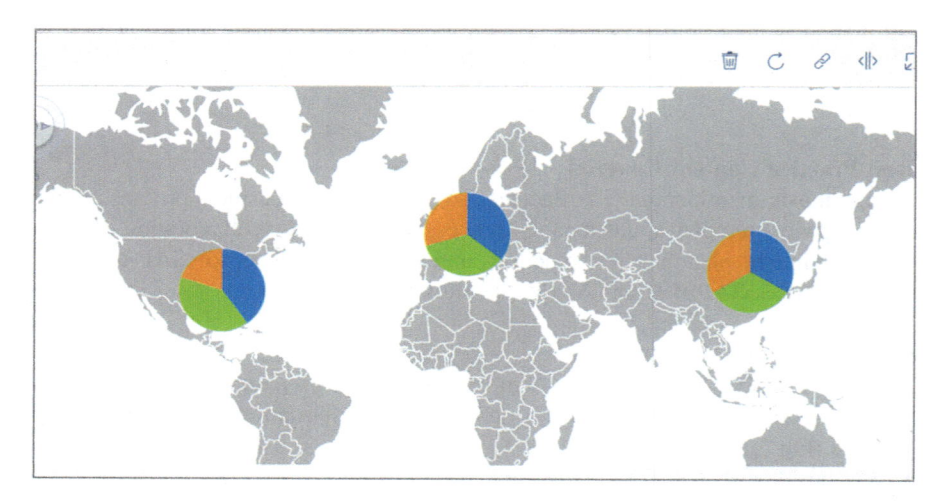

Fig. 2.18 SAP IBP example of RDS—Geo Product line inventory levels pie chart

process flow and orchestration of processes across several cross-functional teams involved in a process.
- Detailed documentation with 30+ configuration guides and test scripts

In addition to the above content, the best practices for SAP IBP also include extensive documentation for setting up these contents from scratch; preparing the required steps like data loads, planning profiles, etc.; and step-by-step test scripts to run end-to-end IBP process.

2.3 Value of SAP IBP Pre-configured System

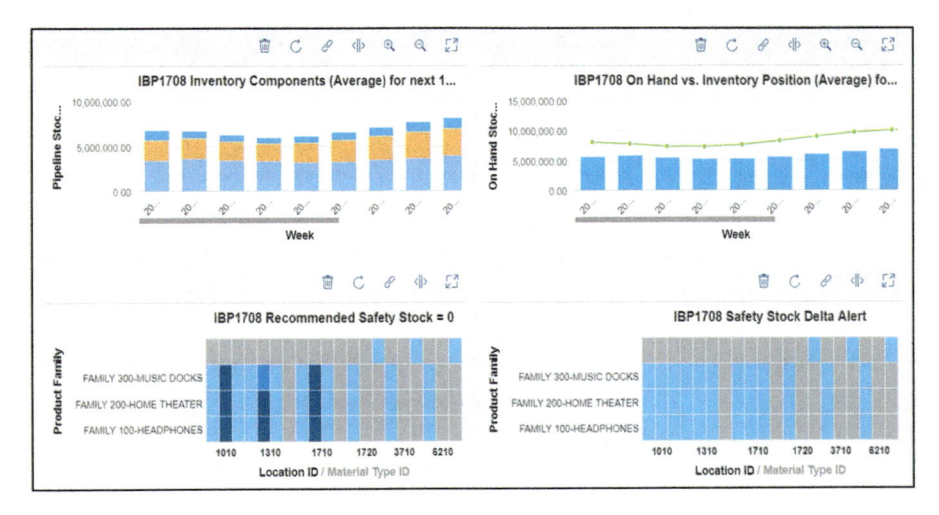

Fig. 2.19 SAP IBP example of RDS—optmized inventory dashboard

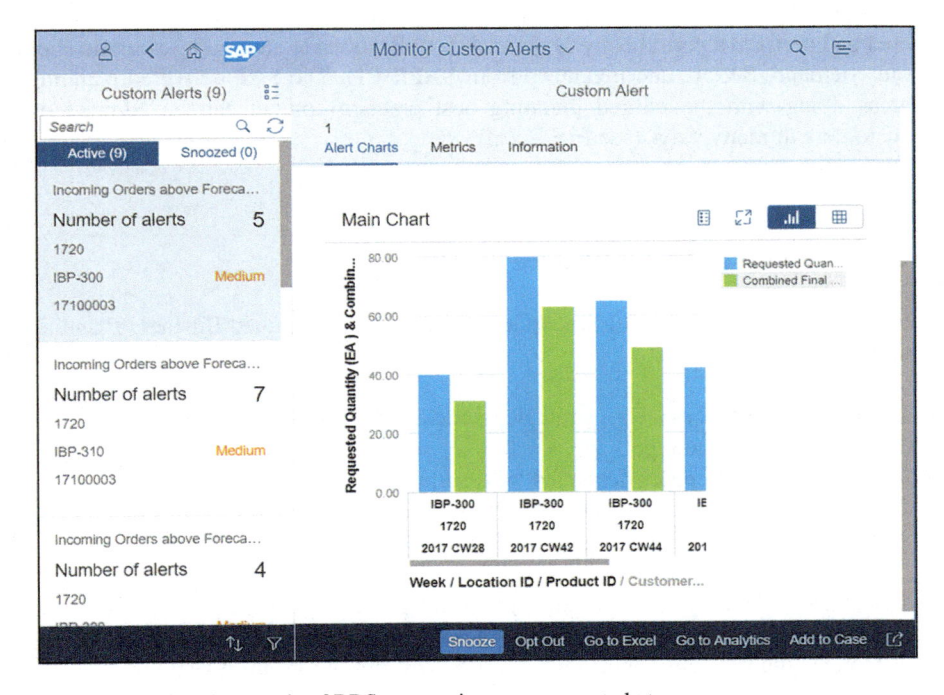

Fig. 2.20 SAP IBP example of RDS—exception management alerts

Use case	Study description
• Study	• Educate yourself and use as reference material
• Training	• Educate project members, key users and end users
• Demonstration	• Sell it to your clients and demonstrate IBP capabilities in a business process-oriented way
• Proof-of-Concept or Pilot project	• Evaluate IBP and build solution that fits to your client's requirements
• Implementation project	• Roll out IBP in your client's organization and set it into productive use by extending to your business processes

Fig. 2.21 SAP IBP RDS use cases

How to Use the Pre-delivered Content

Based on the customer's scope and their business process, customers can choose to start with SAP delivered planning areas to reduce the manual work re-creating a model from scratch. Customers can choose to start with individual planning areas and add further configuration as they expand scope or start with a unified planning area and perform a partial copy to get to the applications to start with (example slice only demand, S&OP, and inventory from SAPIBP1). The SAP delivered planning areas along with the unified planning best practice content can be adopted by customers in many ways (see Fig. 2.21).

2.4 Value of Operating IBP in Holistic Way

Figure 2.22 was made to illustrate that at the end with Integrated Business Planning we connect:

1. All planning process, e.g., strategic, tactical, and operational
2. Volume and value inputs
3. Risk and opportunities described by assumptions
4. All levels from local market, production, distribution in regional to global level.
5. All dimensions of operating model (process, people, technology)

> Connecting strategic, tactical, and operational process will **improve your business**.
> Connecting volume with value will **make planning important**.
> Connecting risk and opportunities in IBP will **make planning real**.
> Connecting local, regional, and global level will make **IBP stakeholders as a team**.
> Connecting operating model dimension will help you **make IBP happen**.

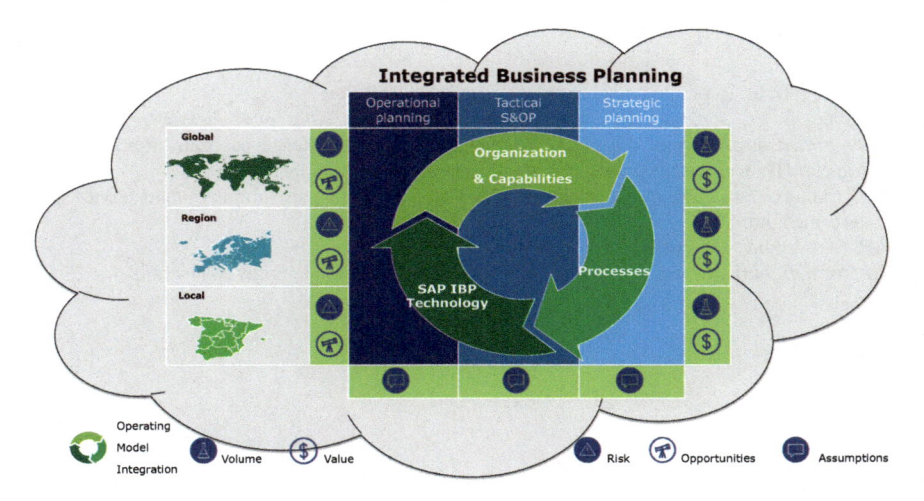

Fig. 2.22 Holistic way to operate Integrated Business Planning enabled on SAP IBP

2.5 Summary

- Integrated Business Planning framework generates tangible benefits when all aspects of operating model are addressed, meaning processes/organization and capabilities/technology.
- Transformation of business processes into coherent IBP brings benefits in:
  - Forecast error reduction up to 35%
  - Process efficiency gain up to 66%
  - Optimization of inventory levels up to 30%
  - Service level improvement up to 31%
  - Capture sales upside up to 52%
  - Improvement in managing profitable decisions 4%
  - Improvement in supply chain and operations cost management 17–21%
- Business process transformation brings substantial efficiency gains to how company operates, prepares for growth with same resources, and leverages digitalization.
- Organizational and capability adjustments enable "people integration" on structural and capability level to cope with increasing complexity and need for responsiveness.
- SAP IBP cloud system enables companies to focus on their core business and core competencies letting technology provider ensure system availability and lower cost of ownership.
- SAP IBP offers pre-configured system which enables easier adoption and faster time to value.
- SAP IBP is enabled on single HANA database for all applications, which reduced data latency and data integration requirements.

References

IBP SAP. (2016). Rapid deployment solution for IBP. *SAP Blog*.
Palmatier, G. E., & Crum, C. (2013). *The transition from sales and operations planning to integrated business planning*. New London: Oliver Wight. Retrieved from https://www.amazon.com/Transition-Operations-Planning-Integrated-Business/dp/1457518252.
SAP. (n.d.-a). http://www.sap.com/corporate-en/about/our-company/policies/cloud/service-level-agreement.html
SAP. (n.d.-b). http://www.sapdatacenter.com
SAP. (n.d.-c). https://www.sap.com/about/cloud-trust-center/cloud-service-status.html

What Makes Integrated Business Planning 3

3.1 Integrated Design

In the previous chapter, we have highlighted that different planning types are often not integrated; therefore, companies have big challenges to:

- Operationalize their strategies.
- Connect strategic, tactical, operational planning with execution.
- Anticipate and/or react on changes in performance or business environment.
- Understand business risk and opportunities.
- Allocate and leverage right investments in processes, people, and technology to maximize company profit.

To understand what IBP is and to address those pain points, we wanted to share some hints about integrated design, enabling connection to what drives and enables successful IBP transformation.

The word which makes a difference in term Integrated Business Planning is "integrated." In this chapter we will define key dimensions of integrated design (see Fig. 3.1).

What makes integration so important and challenging is that all above dimensions co-exist and co-function like in living ecosystem. Connecting them and finding right trade-offs are what make a difference to change, aiming to improve your business performance and to expand competitive advantage to your business in the digital era.

Business priorities—Knowing your pain points and inefficiencies is undisputable value for an organization which want to do something with it. We have faced misinterpretation of pain caused by organizational unit pushing for change. An example was that company wanted to improve supply planning, but true pain point was lack of integration between functions, lack of sales engagement in S&OP process, and lack of transparency in regard to financial information, resulting in huge variations and firefighting in supply. Some say knowing business priorities is

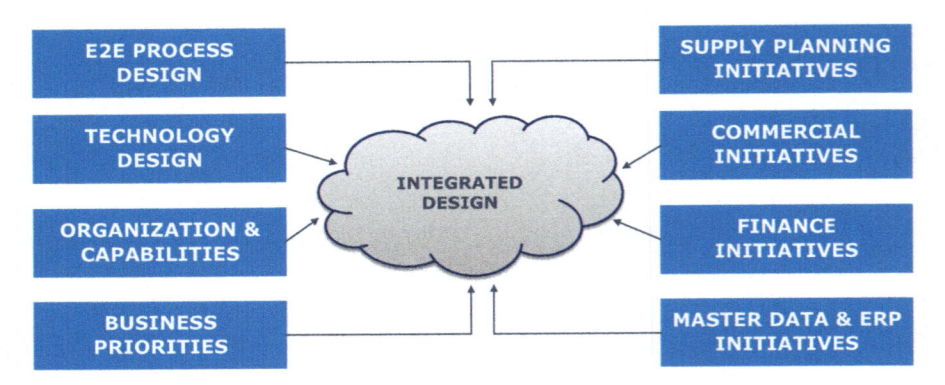

Fig. 3.1 Integrated design for IBP

like knowing your enemy; if you know them, you have a chance to make a successful change.

Organizational design and integration—We can define organizational design and integration as:

- Organizational structures
- Roles and responsibilities
- Competencies and skills
- Capability to influence and change way of working to enable integration between processes, to remove walls and obstacles, which are needed to make IBP happening on local (market), production sites, and regional and global level for strategic, tactical, and operational planning

There are two major organizational integration flows:

- Horizontal integration between S&OP process dimensions which exist in every planning type (see Fig. 1.2)
- Vertical integration cross organizational levels and processes

We have realized that "people factor" in IBP is very challenging. Finding and retaining right people, with right functional and soft skills to ensure Integrated Business Planning works not only on power point but in reality, is critical. We have seen organizations where "people factor" was not a challenge but a driver and enabler to transform IBP processes and put in place missing IBP technology. Those two starting points require different approach in transformation; therefore, please have a look on role of transformation path.

We worked for and in various companies, but what we have found very symptomatic is that the same two types of roles were understood as key enablers in organizational design and integration. They were role of demand planning/demand management and role of finance. Those two roles helped to ensure removal of bias coming from too strong sales- and marketing-driven organizations or too strong supply chain-driven organizations. It is essential to achieve state of equilibrium between various IBP stakeholders like in our experience with demand planning and management and finance. Again what makes it so important is that right people in right roles, their passion for topic, and their functional and soft skills make a difference. Everybody knows about role "people factor" can play, but who takes it to reality and to functioning makes an impact. We see IBP champion and IBP Center of Expertise to make an impact and find and retain the right champion and team.

To help demand planning and management, finance run horizontal and vertical integration you should consider to

- Define global organizational structure which ensures country and regional and global levels are connected by reporting lines and positions.
- Introduce differentiated seniority and differentiated competencies to ensure connection between strategic, tactical, and operational processes on various levels (country, site, regional, global).
- Embed differently focused demand planning and demand management to ensure certain competencies are in place to execute tasks with various functions like product, sales, marketing, finance, supply, IT, and management.
- Embed finance role that crosses all S&OP process dimensions with clear background in controlling and not accounting.
- Build and extend existing capabilities to shift from supply chain-driven volumetric process to cope with financial elements as integral part of IBP process framework.

Under organizational integration we should understand change management and change governance implications on transformation. When driving change you will need to find out what responsibilities/authority transformation "project" and "line" organization should have. Does configuration, where "line" organization owns a change and results, but "project" organization owns design and enables transformation, sound logical to you?

You should define a governance and accountability in transformation program which will reflect the interests/goals of both "project" and "line" organizations. You may think of looking at it from the early beginning of the transformation journey.

Why so early you may ask? When you initiate transformation or change, you should identify how you will sustain it. Who will run, who will improve it are those the same people or maybe not but shifting over time their responsibilities. It is not only about the drive for change but how to enable change sustainability and further improvements of the change. What is constant is change, which needs to be adapted. This needs to be thought through, and that is why we raise to your attention concept of cross-functional Integrated Business Planning Center of Expertise team and champion.

The way you set up "project" organization should help new knowledge to be kept, leveraged in the company to generate further value. Is it about how the company will be able to ensure value realization of the new process, new capability, and new technology when having "project" and "line" organization in place? How to ensure flow of people and expertise between those organizations? Those two organizations may have different needs, ambitions, and competencies, which should be understood before change starts.

On the other hand, let us not forget that need for adaptation of organization structures, roles, and responsibilities would be potentially and naturally exposed with Integrated Business Planning. Connecting human capital (HC) and human resources (HR) into IBP transformation "project" will help. Looking in our experience and leaving this aspect only to functional leads was not always a good choice. Looking on leading practices and involving HC/HR in IBP transformation program will set emphasis on understanding "people factor" and right attention to "people factor." We have seen companies struggling with defining proper structures, roles, and responsibilities and building or finding right competencies to deal with cross-functional nature of the IBP transformation.

When bringing improvements to organizational structures, roles, responsibilities, processes, and technologies, we should not forget to assess key performance indicators which drive behavior of the individual teams.

Take it as a friendly hint based on many "grey hair" experiences and invest appropriate amount of efforts into "people factor."

E2E process design and integration can be understood as:

– Set of activities to achieve expected and agreed IBP outcomes (e.g., unconstrained forecast and constrained plan in volume and value, "top line" revenue, "bottom line" profit, risk and opportunities with verified assumptions on each level of the organization)
– IBP outputs which need to be leveraged in other adjacent processes (e.g., Integrated Business Plan in value used in financial processes and system to project P&L)
– IBP inputs from adjacent processes (e.g., average sales price, shipments, invoices)
– Design principles (e.g., demand review meeting is about signing off realistic unconstrained, free from supply constraints forecast for current and next year which need to be available globally on work day 5 or integrated business plan which represents actuals in the past and constrained volume and value projection until end of current year plus one, with incorporated risk and opportunities available on work day 10)
– Globally aligned and synchronized calendar of activities cross strategic, tactical, operational planning processes (e.g., in tactical planning in week 2, integrated business plan has to be defined with input with recent updates from operational planning)

- Globally aligned and synchronized calendar of milestones of activities, e.g., consensus forecast being agreed by working day 5
- Understanding how strategic process outputs will influence and connect in bidirectional way tactical processes
- Understanding how tactical process outputs will influence and connect in bidirectional way operational planning processes
- Understanding how financial, commercial, supply, and demand processes will interact in order to generate integrated business plan
- Finally understanding how operational planning processes should be linked to execution processes

Enabling process integration in a large-scale company is not a trivial task, mainly due to fact that those companies do not have a homogeneous business models. What makes it hard to do is to find balance and trade-offs between flexibility expressed in process variants linked to different business models and process standardizations/harmonizations required to manage them on global level.

We did see that in one company there were several business lines. Each business line had very different business models/drivers which determined different focus horizons, different granularity and frequency of main stakeholders meetings. In this particular case, putting "one size fit all" approach to end-to-end process design and wish to achieve 100% single process would be an approach designed for failure. If there is such a fundamental justified difference in business models, you could align design principles, common milestones, and outcomes but maybe not in detail all process steps. We wanted to achieve common process integration points and common calendar of integrations. Process framework was valid for all process variations in all business models.

Let us try to explain this problem further. Would you apply the same rules and the same process step timelines to countries which are small in your revenue portfolio, which do not have sophisticated capabilities and skills in place, versus the countries with big revenue and complex and demanding process, which requires sophisticated competencies? This is what we meant when we talked about balancing flexibility with standardization; this is when we think alignment on process milestone, design principles, and objectives are sufficient. More tailored approach in process design is needed then. In highly heterogeneous conglomerates of business models, alignment on having key milestones in the process is crucial, but experience says that "one size does not fit all." Do not try to control everything; it does not make sense these days. Size, importance, maturity, and degree of integration of a specific business model in the whole operating model could make a difference in the definition of end-to-end process design, transformation, and implementation approach.

We just discussed differences in business models but for the same tactical S&OP process. Another set of differences come from the fact that we experience operational, tactical, strategic planning. Those processes have different stakeholders, calendar of activities, and inputs and outputs. The IBP operating model design should address all of those differences and make alignment which make sense only. Exactly this makes it hard to integrate:

- Highly granular, high-pace operational planning
- Through monthly, centric to IBP tactical S&OP
- Business growth-oriented strategic business planning

End-to-end IBP design should take care of touchpoints with adjacent processes. Let us bring few examples of those touchpoints and decisions which need to be reflected in IBP design principles.

- When and how to integrate sales prices for forecast valuation?
- What currency exchange rates should be used?
- When and how to integrate costs for profit calculations?
- When supply systems in short horizon will deliver reliable optimized 3 month schedule?
- When and how data should be bidirectionally exchanged with ERP system for detail supply scheduling and supply execution?
- Does sales community need to update account plans or forecast in SAP IBP or CRM system?
- Will Integrated Business Plan be on "net" level?
- What should be the source system of material master data attributes and how and when in the process they should be integrated?
- What should be the source system of customer and commercial hierarchy master data attributes and how and when they should be integrated in the process?
- What should be the source system for financial master data attributes and how they should be integrated?

Initiative integration could be understood as set of activities leading to understating interactions required between IBP and finance, commercial, supply, master data, or even ERP initiatives. Connecting with other initiatives at least on design principles and integration principles is a minimum. In large organization knowing what the "left" and "right" hand is doing is not that easy. Initiative integration will help you to:

- Avoid duplication of work in process design.
- Make integration between processes coherent.
- Get understanding of complexity and importance of each function input.
- Define required inputs and align implementation timelines.
- Sequence design and implementation plans.
- Understand and address initially contradicting designs.
- Understand cost and value realization impact potentially caused by lack of alignment between process areas and initiatives.

Technology design and integration—These days' business models are complex, data availability grows exponentially, and system landscapes are not homogeneous anymore. The Integrated Business Planning platform should enable data and system integration. You should understand what you have and define what is needed already as part of preparation to transformation or initial phase of it. System integration may form even up to 30% of implementation costs.

Technology design and integration should be defined in two steps:

- In the first step, you should understand technology landscape affecting Integrated Business Planning, define systems which need to be integrated and platforms on which they operate now and in the future, and understand improvement initiatives affecting systems to be integrated as part of IBP solution. This activity normally should happen before or in the initial phase of the transformation program.
- In the second step, you should be able to define data model and detail data integration requirements to support end-to-end process design. This activity normally happens in process design phase of the transformation program.

In some companies due to poor quality of data or very heterogeneous IT landscape, special project stream was formed to address not only master data but transactional data challenges. You may consider to position such stream as part of technology.

We have heard that paraphrasing the quote "DESIGN IS NOT A WORD DOCUMENT OR POWER POINT BUT THE WAY PROCESS, ORGANIZATION, SYSTEM OPERATES IN BUSINESS" makes a lot of sense to many of our customers. The organizational unit co-responsible for design (normally part of "project" organization) should be at least co-responsible for how it works in business (with "line" organization) and maybe co-accountable for business case delivery (see Fig. 3.2). Let us connect this back to integrated design:

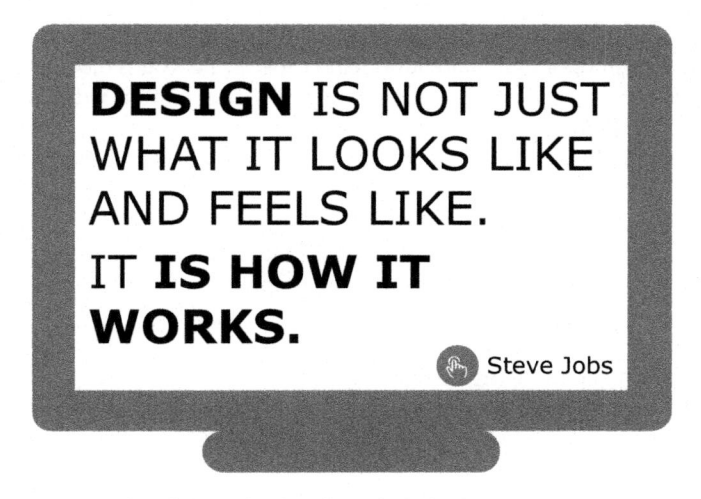

DESIGN IS NOT JUST WHAT IT LOOKS LIKE AND FEELS LIKE. IT **IS HOW IT WORKS.**
— Steve Jobs

Fig. 3.2 Design is not how it looks but how it works in business

- Integrated design approach will help you make IBP happen and navigate via inevitable changes in scope, focus, stakeholders, and business environment and address key pain points of disconnected planning.
- Integrated design helps to find out what Integrated Business Planning can mean for your company.

3.2 Connect Planning Processes: Strategic, Tactical, and Operational

One of the crucial aspects of IBP is to connect planning processes. Connection between them should happen in most suitable integration window. We will try to explain those integration windows and their purpose.

3.2.1 Strategic Annual Business Planning and Tactical S&OP Integration

Why?
Have you ever experienced a situation in which your long-term growth plans went out of sync already for the next year with the next year tactical S&OP projections? Do you remember the management confusion when they looked on the next year projections and saw very different volumetric and financial projections from these two sources? Do you recall their faces when they understood that the assumptions behind plans were different? Do you recall a situation where strategic investment initiatives were planned on a global level and were not embedded and planned for operationalization on a regional and a market level? Do you remember a situation when you asked yourself a question on why you were not informed or not involved and how come it did happen?

Summing up, the rationale behind the alignment and integration are:

- Next year plans are out of sync.
- Lack of alignment on priorities, initiatives, and investments.
- Lack of transparency and alignment of assumptions.
- Multiple set of figures driving next year business plan.
- Senior management has a perception that plans are clear to all stakeholders and under control across all organizational levels.
- Lack of organizational integration.

When?
You do not have to invent a special integration time frame but rather leverage an existing one. In many companies tactical S&OP can feed information to budgeting process: in the example below, it happens once per year around August/September.

3.2 Connect Planning Processes: Strategic, Tactical, and Operational 39

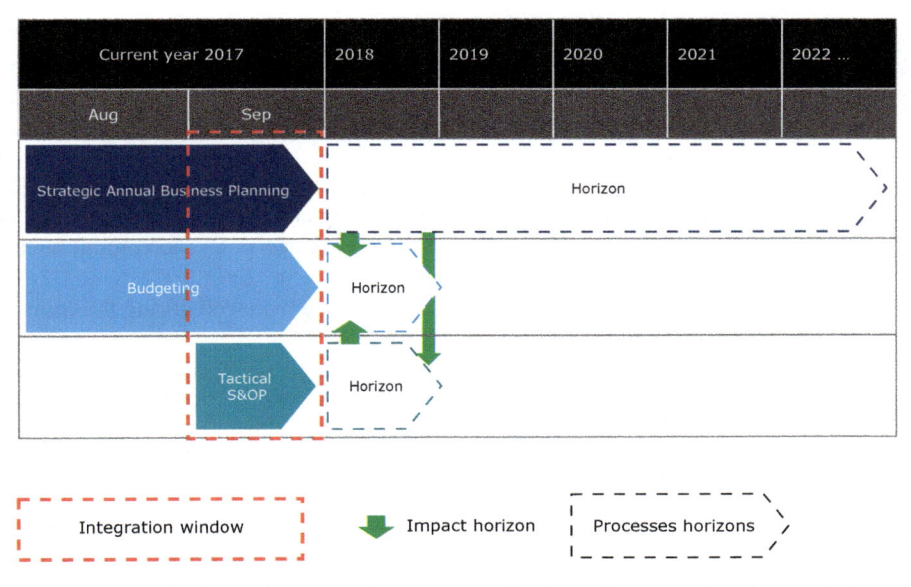

Fig. 3.3 Strategic annual business planning, tactical S&OP, and budgeting integration window

Some companies go even further and update their budget figures from tactical S&OP more often. The process of aligning tactical S&OP and budgeting requires a certain degree of maturity and stakeholder's awareness, but it is common in many industries and companies.

You should leverage those integration points to align your strategic annual business planning outputs to the tactical S&OP and budget process. Tactical S&OP covers the current year and the current year plus one (maybe two), while budgeting covers current year plus one. That point in time is a great opportunity to provide input from a strategic level to a tactical one and influence as well as reconcile the next year budget (see Fig. 3.3).

3.2.2 Monthly Strategic Product Planning and Tactical S&OP Integration

Why?
Have you ever experienced a situation when global team anticipates constraints on key active ingredient and steel and raw materials where you were not aware of its impact on your in market/country tactical S&OP? Do you remember the market management confusion when they recognized that they could not deliver their full year commitments because of key raw material shortages while the other market could? Do you recall the sales people frustration when they made midterm commitment to the customer and realized that they could not be kept? Have you experienced a lack of information about extra supply or a different form of the product, which could have helped you to realize country or market plans and objectives? Have you

been faced as global supply team member with the problem that bottom-up short-term forecast or short-term sales increased and led to unexpected midterm shortages on key active ingredients and steel and raw materials?

Summing up, the rationale behind the alignment and integration are:

- Lack of "translation" between global strategic products (active ingredient, steel, seeds variety) and market forecasting and planning activities
- Lack of transparency, assumptions leading to wrong decisions and commitments that cannot be fulfilled
- Lack of information about how supply gaps could be managed during the course of the year to match your demand patterns
- Lack of both ways of process integration leading to unexpected shortages or expensive changes of priorities
- Lack of organizational integration which should be provided by demand planning and management and finance

When?

The monthly strategic product planning needs to be integrated with the tactical S&OP process once per month (see Fig. 3.4). Both processes "have to talk to each other" both ways. Integration of processes does not mean that every time an impact can be captured and understood in the same monthly period. Normally, tactical S&OP will fully react to monthly strategic product planning inputs only in next cycles. The budgeting process may leverage information for the next year supply constraints coming from the monthly strategic product planning.

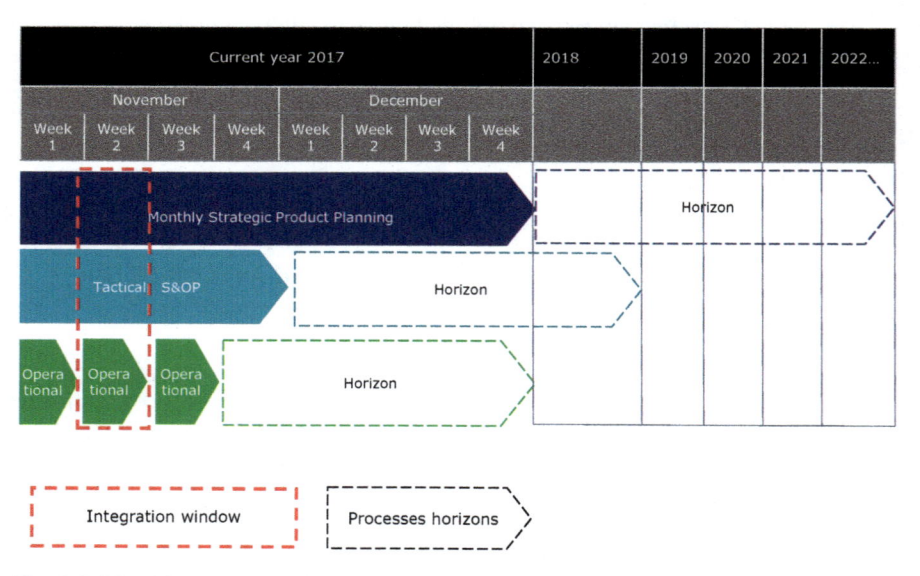

Fig. 3.4 Monthly strategic product planning, tactical S&OP, and operational planning integration windows

You may ask yourself why integration between operational planning and tactical S&OP should happen in week 2 every month. Integration should happen when process tactical S&OP is supposed to conclude constrained Integrated Business Plan with most recent inputs. It does not make too much sense operational planning inputs when in week 1 of tactical S&OP unconstrained forecast is being defined. Touchpoint between the two should happen in process area which overlaps in this case in utilization of assets (product inventories, firm supply, firm orders).

As you see from the diagram above:

– Integration between monthly strategic product planning and tactical S&OP happens once per month in the same week.
– Operational planning provides input for tactical S&OP.

3.2.3 Operational Planning and Tactical S&OP Integration

Why?
Have you been faced, as sales lead, with the fact that you did not have feedback about what you will be able to sell to increase customer satisfaction? Have you experienced that your portfolio of products and customers, even though profitable, did not receive the right focus and service? Have you been informed about business risks and opportunities agreed in the monthly S&OP process affecting your area of responsibility? Have you ever learned after operational planning meeting that you did not consider all the data, since it was not available on time? Have you ever made decisions based on your "gut feeling" because the financial information needed to take those decisions were not available at the right moment? Do you remember a situation where the monthly plan/objective agreed with the management was not known to all stakeholders on the operational level? Have you seen a situation while based on "order book" you had a hunch, but not a prediction that you will sell much more than planned now and how next month potential issues should be addressed? Have you ever seen in your operational meeting anybody from marketing, demand management, and finance to support the decision-making process?

Summing up, the rationale behind the alignment and integration are:

– Ensure that the execution will be aligned to tactical plans approved by management.
– Profits (or highest availability) and not who shouts the loudest will take the lead in the short-term decision-making process.
– Remove from tactical S&OP very short-term-oriented escalations and bias.
– Keep short-term focus but provide key insights to better constrain tactical S&OP inputs.
– Enable insightful learning about tactical S&OP assumptions and performance executed in operational planning.
– Enable data-driven decisions supported by demand management and finance.

When?

The outcome of operational planning needs to be fully integrated into tactical S&OP at least once per month (see Fig. 3.5). It means that all decisions in volume and value would need to be recorded and fully transparent between those two processes. The alignment should happen at the latest in the week when tactical S&OP generates integrated business plan on market/country level. In this week reconciliation between demand, supply, and finance should happen.

The effective integration between tactical S&OP and operational planning should happen on multiple dimensions:

- Organizationally ensured by demand manager and finance manager
- Process-wise ensured by a once per month alignment to tactical S&OP
- System-wise enabled via a robust data model, exception management, and segmentation

3.2.4 Summary

Planning process has obvious and natural integration windows, where dedicated roles like demand planning and management and finance can connect key outputs, assumptions, and insights. When using integrated design approach to introduce IBP framework, those integration windows should be identified and leveraged.

Leverage following integration windows:

- Use budgeting period to connect strategic and tactical planning.
- Use normally second week of S&OP when constraints are being discussed and final plan generated to connect operational planning with tactical.

Main objective to keep strategic, tactical, and operational planning processes connected is to define coherent IBP planning framework, which can be used to:

- Steer how strategic decisions are understood and deployed in tactical and operational horizon.
- Introduce end-to-end transparency, monitor progress, and loop back feedback to strategic planning from tactical and operational team.
- Improve decision-making process from strategic to tactical and tactical to operational while inheriting objectives, assumptions, and decisions between planning types.
- Improve ability to react and plan in constantly changing business and planning environment with differentiated granularity and focus cross various planning.
- Drive decisions based on facts and information exposed cross planning types.

3.2 Connect Planning Processes: Strategic, Tactical, and Operational

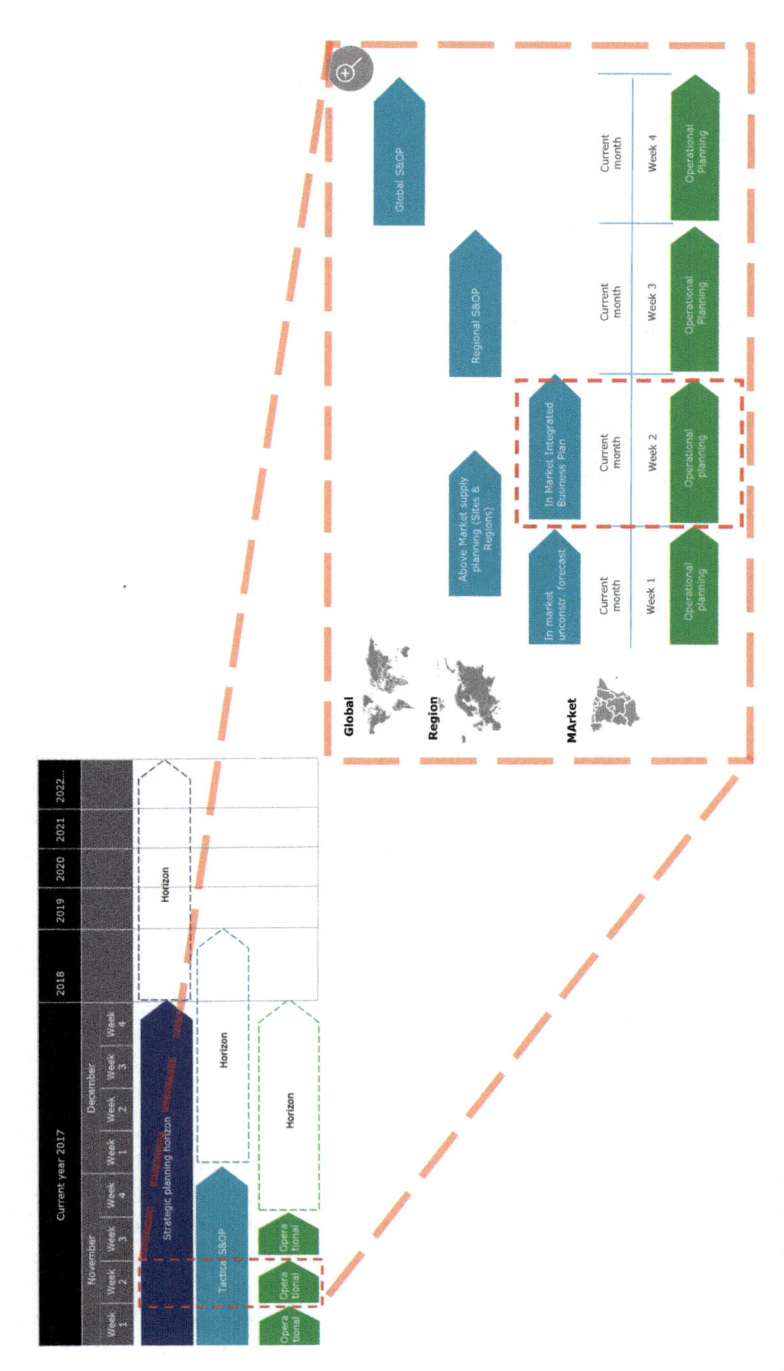

Fig. 3.5 Tactical S&OP and operational planning integration window

3.3 Extend S&OP

S&OP operating without integration to other planning processes and without value-added extensions like financial integration or end-to-end "what-if" business risk and opportunities simulations could hinder possibility to achieve competitive position in a dynamic, complex marketplace. More tailored products and more sophisticated services require higher adaptability and flexibility in planning processes, all based on richer sets of source data and larger number of source systems. Clear rationale behind maturing S&OP and extending it is to cope with market dynamics and constant changes.

Integrated Business Planning transformation can be understood as:

- Maturing and extending S&OP with IBP value drivers
- Embedding matured S&OP into IBP operating framework which connects strategic, tactical, and operational planning processes
- Enabling organizational and capability connection between processes into IBP coherent organization
- Enabling with SAP IBP technology integration of various data sources into one data model for discussed planning processes
- Enabling management of volume and financial information in one framework
- Enabling end-to-end "what-if" business risk and opportunity simulations in volume and value

Why do we highlight IBP transformation in this chapter? We wanted to explain that making your S&OP process more mature with new value drivers is one of the major but not the only element in IBP transformation.

For the purpose of this book, we wanted to characterize IBP as follows (this does not mean we want to challenge existing terminology):

INTEGRATED BUSINESS PLANNING IS A BUSINESS MANAGEMENT PROCESS WHICH AIMS
TO CONNECT STRATEGIC, TACTICAL AND OPERATIONAL PLANNING,
ON LOCAL (MARKETS, SITES), REGIONAL (INCL. PRODUCTION SITES) AND
GLOBAL LEVEL,
TO ASSESS RISK AND OPPORTUNITIES, VERIFY ASSUMPTIONS
AND GENERATE WITH CROSS FUNCTIONAL COLLABORATION
A FEASIBLE INTEGRATED BUSINESS PLAN IN VOLUME AND VALUE.

We see quite a confusion or freedom in interpreting what is Integrated Business Planning, is this just a new term for S&OP, is this S&OP with financials, etc. As highlighted in the IBF article by Bowe, some of the above value drivers should have been accelerating well-established and mature S&OP process. Unfortunately, transformation projects often poorly address these. Also, there is no institution to define S&OP reference standards like SCOR/APICS (Bower, 2012).

Let us keep Integrated Business Planning as term in the business, let us not throw it away, and do not neglect value it did create for companies needing second chance for their S&OP and especially for those who see that IBP can help them to connect

3.3 Extend S&OP

- Projection of price, costs, margins embedded in processes & accountabilities
- Alignment & integration between strategic, tactical and operational processes
- Tight integration of product, customer, services planning
- What-if business scenario planning to model risks & opportunities in product/demand/supply/finance.
- Budget, Forecast, Plans gap identification and management
- Granularity, frequency aligned to process horizon. Ways of working and level linked to best insights.
- Fit for purpose organizational structures, roles & capabilities

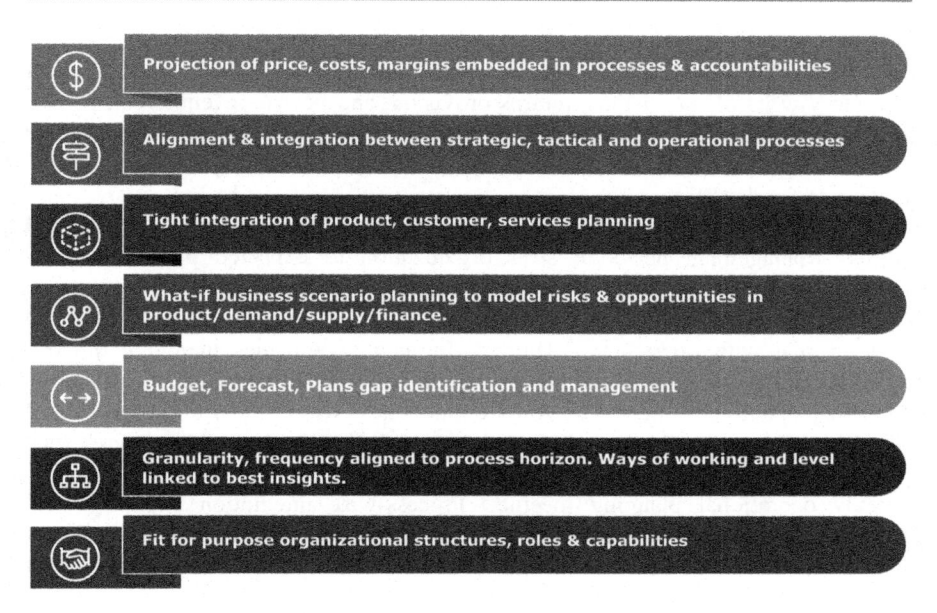

Fig. 3.6 S&OP value drivers enabling step change into IBP framework [revised based on Palmatier and Crum (2013)]

strategic, tactical S&OP and operational planning process on organizational and technology dimension.

Based on the discussions with customers, prospects, our colleagues, and our own experience, we have listed key value drivers which should be considered when maturing your S&OP process to make it fit into IBP holistic business management process framework (see Fig. 3.6).

Let us shortly describe value drivers.

Price, cost, and margin projections—They serve as vital component to enable monetization of the forecasts and plans in terms of top-line revenue, bottom-line profit, and gap exposure to budget. Finance needs to perform required activities linked to prediction of prices, costs, margin, and currency exchange rates with other stakeholders like demand management, marketing, supply chain, production as per defined calendar of activities to meet objective of having financials fully embedded in matured S&OP process. Some may say correctly that selected financial activities should be moved from isolated and not fully on time integrated finance solutions and processes into cross-functional and transparent mature S&OP which acts as foundation of IBP. Essentially, finance will help other IBP stakeholders to predict future sales prices and to understand it you can see use cases on how companies assess impact of price change on volume, revenue, and profit if needed. We have seen simplified planning of unit costs and margin being part of IBP and used as instrument to plan bottom-line profits as part of monthly rolling process. Embedding financial elements as being planned and analyzed in IBP open doors to manage risk and opportunities in integrated way. Apart from projections of price, costs, and margin, there are other financial components which we have seen fully integrated in IBP process framework like projections of currency exchange rates or planning of inventory write-off provisions, returns provision, and license revenue fees. In IBP finance controllers can monetize critical business drivers. We see highly mature IBP when finance activities are embedded, not just integrated in an operational, tactical, and strategic planning.

Alignment and integration between strategic, tactical, and operational plans—Management needs to steer organization to expected performance by connecting strategic-tactical-operational planning processes. It becomes essential to define what, when, how, and who will integrate firstly strategic with tactical and then tactical with operational planning. In many companies there are obvious integration windows like budgeting time when you could connect strategic planning to tactical planning for next year. Another integration window is the second week of S&OP calendar of activities when in the country S&OP process, you agree final integrated business plan which needs to be enriched with insights from weekly/bi-weekly operational planning meeting. Process-wise integration and alignment should be supported by defined calendar of activities, plans being shared on different levels, and assumptions which explain plans and, finally as discussed further in more detail, integrated by demand management and finance.

Planning products, customers, and services—Product planning and review are in many companies not always integrated into S&OP. Product planning has an impact mainly on tactical and strategic planning. Inputs being discussed can take various forms depending on planning type, e.g., in strategic annual business planning, we may talk about impact of new technology or impact of major technology changes. In tactical S&OP we may talk about product packaging, midterm substitutions, country-specific labeling, launch and product registration dates or withdrawal dates, and cannibalization of demand. In monthly strategic product planning, we may talk about new active ingredient, new steel quality, or new seed varieties. As part of this value driver, we have seen discussions happing about product portfolio rationalization and profitability of products. In same process we have seen (maybe not common but still) review of customer portfolio or service portfolio. In some companies decisions to whom to give product which is in shortage was supported by customer segmentation. Customer segmentation helped as well in rationalization of customer base. We have seen a case driven by strategic objective set by the vice president to optimize customer portfolio based on profit. The most advanced but highly valuable form of segmentation is when portfolio and customer segmentation are combined and weighted. In annual business planning, customer review takes often different form, and then markets or channels are being discussed. Review of products, customers, and services with use of segmentation can help you to introduce differentiated forecasting, planning, and replenishment.

"What-if" business scenarios to model risks and opportunities—How shall we understand it? First of all, business risks and opportunities are connected to all process steps of tactical S&OP process. There are risks and opportunities in product, demand, supply, and reconciliation executed in pre-S&OP, finally in decisions taken in S&OP meeting. Uncertainty and internal and external interdependencies are everywhere; therefore, we should think of it as normal in the process. We should define ways to capture, assess, and validate risk and opportunities based on documented assumptions. Making scenario planning transparent, quantifiable, comparable, and able to go end to end until final impact substantially can increase quality and value of decision-making process.

Quote from *Heraclitus* "The Only Thing That Is Constant Is Change" adheres perfectly to fact that change should be modeled with use of end-to-end what-if scenario planning.

Here are some examples of risks and opportunities which may be mapped and supported through what-if scenario planning:

- Opportunity introduction of new e-commerce sales channels and impact on long-term capacity linked to impact on long-term projection of operating margin
- Opportunity to acquire new big customer or company that will complement your service offering against the competition
- Opportunity to run plant extension or external manufacturing network to copy with increased long-term demand
- Risk of delayed product registration and its impact on revenue and profit in current calendar year
- Risk of keeping nonprofitable customers in the portfolio
- Risk that a local currency for a big market (e.g., Brazil, Russia) will drop down and seriously damage your current year performance
- Risk of supply shortages not being exposed and not planned to optimize either profit or availability
- Opportunity to sell out extra stock with special discounts as demand-shaping activity during short-term horizon in the peak season

Risk and opportunities are very often cross-functional and have financial implications. You may consider to focus more effort and time on risk and opportunities, uncertainty areas, and then on the stable part of your business. Differentiate degree of automatization and skill sets to manage one or the other.

Budget vs forecast vs plan gaps identification and management—Management of gaps to budget and forecasts or integrated business plan become value driver for local (country, site), regional, or global management. In various forms they want to understand how this or the other what-if scenario helps them to manage budget gap or surplus. Here you will find just few examples of key gaps:

- Consensus unconstrained market potential in volume and value versus constrained integrated business plan
- Consensus unconstrained market potential in volume and value versus budget
- Constrained integrated business plan versus budget in volume and value

What makes it hard is how to expose the gaps on actionable level. What do we mean by that? Try to assess what is the value of information that in Germany they have 15 million gap to the budget. We were asking ourselves on many S&OP meeting how actionable is this information. In such a case, SAP IBP technology can play a vital role to enable gap exposure on any level of material, location, customer, and organizational dimension. System functionality will facilitate the development of corrective actions which are actionable, on which defined team can collaborate, assess pros and cons to find consensus, set actions, and follow up on them.

Granularity and frequency aligned to horizon: ways of working aligned to best insights—Considering right process granularity as value driver plays an important role since many times we have seen that a long-term process is executed on very granular level, e.g., production line capacity utilization in 5-year horizon is rather non-value-adding information, and looking on the same capacity utilization but rather on plant level for long-term planning horizon would make sense. Granularity and frequency of the planning process should be aligned to planning type and its horizon. Those process characteristics should tell us we should differentiate. What do we really mean by differentiation of granularity and frequency to horizon in which process operates? We mean to differentiate granularity on which strategic, tactical, and operational planning processes are executed. The same applies to frequency.

The strategic annual business planning process operates in horizon of 5–10 years, requires annual or half-year frequency, and is typically executed on business/product line level opposed to operational planning in case of management of promotional campaign where we talk about next few weeks of time horizon; therefore, process is executed very frequently and sometimes even daily. The same applies for granularity of the data being used and analyzed; further in the future, we plan it should be more aggregated.

Another dimension of this value driver is how to align level on which function normally works to their best insights. Let us illustrate that with few examples:

- Marketing should be able to provide forecast on their accountability level, e.g., product group and product line.
- Supply should be able to define their plans on resource level.
- Finance should be able to define financial elements on level which makes sense for business models, e.g., ex-rate on country/currency level, and future price may be even on SKU/sales zone level.
- Demand manager should be able to help organization to balance demand, supply, and financial information on level tactics in pre-S&OP meeting being defined.

Some of the information would need to be aggregated and disaggregated based on rules you define to enable comparisons and analysis. Data can imported but stored in your SAP IBP system on different levels if it makes sense for IBP process. You may need to consider to display information on aggregated level and still work on detail. Technology should not be a constraint but a facilitator.

Fit for purpose organizational structures, roles, and capabilities—We often have seen that "people factor" was set aside in transformation programs and was set as second priority to be addressed later. We have seen programs which were initiated, but there was no idea how change will be sustained, who will take care of further improvements or very fundamental decision, and who will sign off design. We have seen on many occasions that organizational and competency design was not done. It should be indicated in the initial chapter where we talked about integrated design.

3.3 Extend S&OP

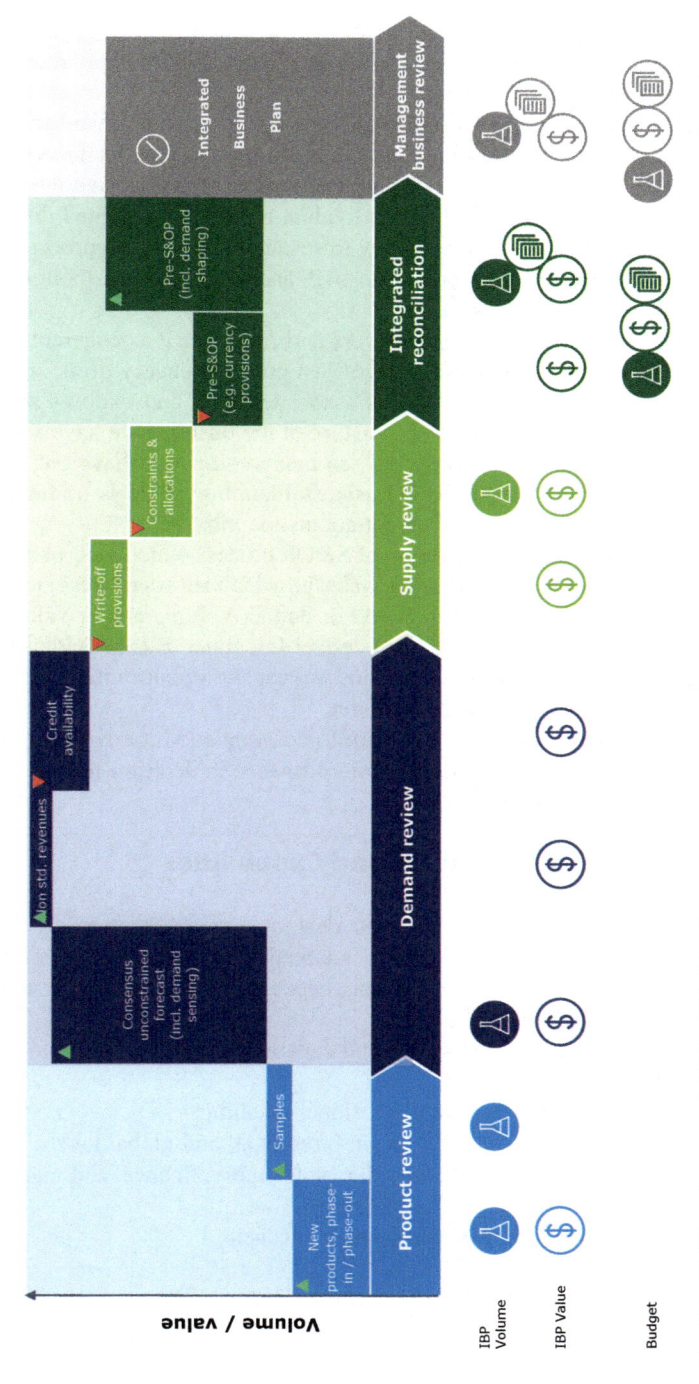

Fig. 3.7 S&OP on "energy drink" fits IBP objectives

Integrated business planning exposes high requirement for competencies and skills which one of our friends used to call "ability to connect dots." Abilities to understand, analyze, and foresee potential impacts in cross-functional process are on demand for IBP process.

Right granularity of the process considered as value driver is linked with differentiation of competencies cross levels and types of process. This seems obvious but we have observed that functional leadership roles were often allocated not based on balanced set of skills and experience of individual but budget assigned to role.

This value driver approach is about how to sustain change in the process, how to prepare for new, which roles are critical to IBP, and what to think about Center of Expertise for cross-functional process.

As we look on above S&OP value drivers and role of IBP as coherent planning environment, we clearly understand it is not just gulp of "energy drink" to already existing S&OP. It takes what S&OP was associated with and exposes some new complementary solutions exposed due to nature of the business we have seen at our customers, prospects, and employers. We see many companies have put roles and functions and named them Integrated Business Planning; there is nothing wrong with it. It works for them, and this is what counts the most.

In Fig. 3.7, you will find visualization of S&OP process which incorporates main value drivers in the following way. It is a waterfall which shows process steps on the bottom, bars represent activities which add or deduct volume and/or value toward final pre-S&OP, and S&OP meeting steps deliver Integrated Business Plan with e2e "what-if" scenario planning reflecting business risks and opportunities explained in verified assumptions and compared to budget.

We have seen significant improvement of forecasting and improvement of profitability achieved mainly based on integration of finance in decision-making process.

3.4 Connect Org. Structures and Capabilities

As we have highlighted in the integrated design approach connecting planning process through organizational structures, adaptation of roles and responsibilities and introduction of new or exposing existing capabilities will make a big impact on how process is being operated.

Why do put organizational structures and capabilities together?

- To connect strategic, tactical, and operational planning
- To connect local (market, production site), regional, and global level
- To connect product, sales, marketing, demand, supply, finance, and management functions
- Ultimately to improve the way you manage business

We have observed that most of the challenges occur between sales and supply organization (if sometimes even not "fights"), product and finance are not well connected, and middle and senior management has their own priorities. In the IBP

3.4 Connect Org. Structures and Capabilities

framework, we should achieve point of equilibrium between different functions, point where organizational design helps to manage business. To address purpose of organizational integration, we propose demand planner, demand manger, and finance controller as roles which will act as referee, facilitators, and enablers to drive IBP.

3.4.1 Connect Functions

Once we have selected key roles which can integrate various functions, we need to position which function integrates the best to the others (see Fig. 3.8, three proposed roles which can connect whole IBP together).

We used following rationale:

- Demand planner works on development of consensus forecast and understands through work with sales and marketing what happens in marketplace.
- Demand manager works on translation of supply constraints to maximize business return.
- Finance manager works on connecting management and align with finance and pricing.

Those three roles connect all other functions into Integrated Business Planning through activities and perform together as part of S&OP process and according to S&OP calendar of activities. We want to leverage those touchpoints and make it

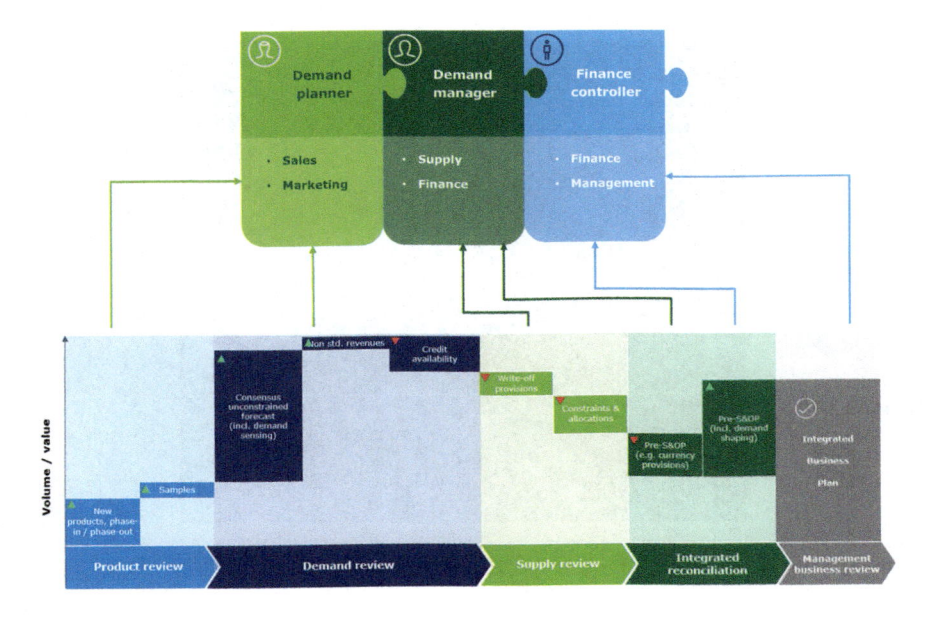

Fig. 3.8 Three proposed roles which can connect whole IBP together

even stronger and tighter integrated under IBP framework; therefore, we see demand planners connecting sales organization and marketing organization, demand manager connecting supply organization and finance representatives, and finally finance controller connecting broader finance organization and management.

3.4.2 Connect Organizationally Planning Processes and Levels

Once we have defined roles which will connect all relevant IBP functions, we have to define per planning process which "integrator function" needs to be in place and which particular role and maturity need to be in place (see Fig. 3.9). From functional focus we need to get to planning type focus. It means we need to select right skill set and experience to facilitate to run and to connect planning types. Even though the same processes are executed in market- or product-driven organizations, there are some differences as shown in Fig. 3.9.

Operational planning is very close to execution, often even confused with it. We see demand planner and demand manager in local (country or market) organization well positioned as roles still "down to earth" but enabling connection to tactical S&OP. Those roles have to balance very short-term-oriented stakeholders with objectives given by tactical S&OP. This connection has to ensure framework defined in tactical S&OP is respected but optimized in short-term horizon.

Tactical S&OP is a heart of Integrated Business Planning. We need to have demand manager and finance controller with right seniority and with strong business acumen. Those two roles can drive process adherence, right set of deliverables, right

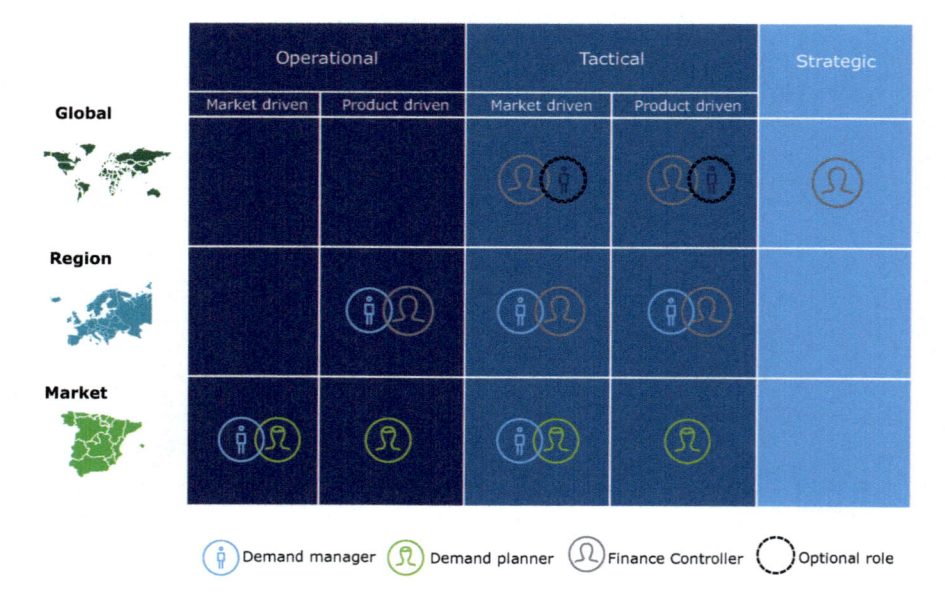

Fig. 3.9 Minimum representation of roles to connect planning processes and levels

3.4 Connect Org. Structures and Capabilities

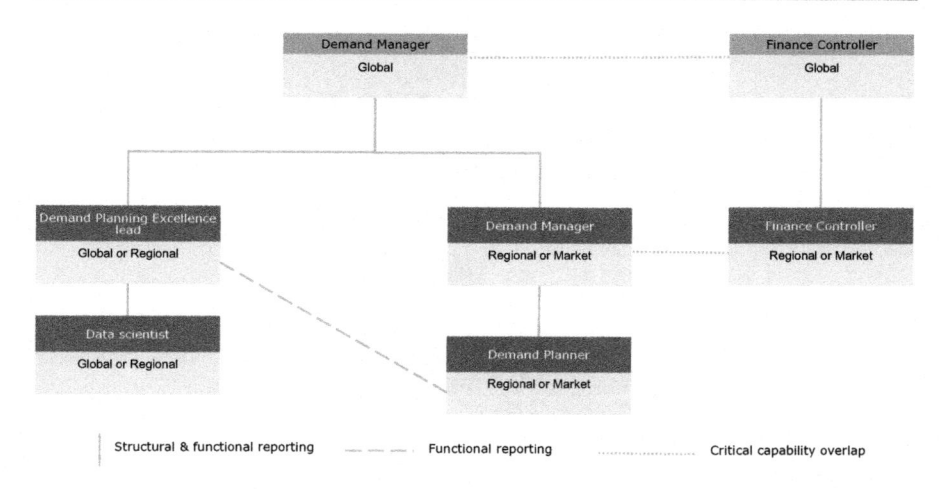

Fig. 3.10 Structural connection between IBP facilitator's roles

granularity of discussion and conclusions, and consensus to be achieved as per IBP process.

Strategic planning is tightly connected to development of strategic long-term decisions. Enabling senior stakeholders to see financial and business risks and opportunities is essential in this process. We see finance controller as a facilitator of strategic planning and connector to tactical S&OP.

If we put the above into organizational structure, we see that for product-driven or market-driven organization, connection between demand manager and finance controller becomes essential (see Fig. 3.10).

The above structure will address most of the process part, data, and systems (with excellence team), but gap will exist if we will not connect finance. What would be the way to address connection between finance controller and demand manager? We propose to investigate it on a softer level, level of capabilities and seniority. Create overlap of capabilities and mutual understanding. Bring it from structures to individuals.

3.4.3 Create Overlap of Capabilities

Organizational structure will not make connection between people working. We have identified missing chain in connection between demand manager and finance controller. We have found out that in practical terms, this can be addressed by creating overlap of capabilities. There should be an overlap of capabilities, skills, and experiences which will keep finance controller and demand manager work seamlessly cross structures.

One way of looking on overlap of capabilities is visualized in Fig. 3.11.

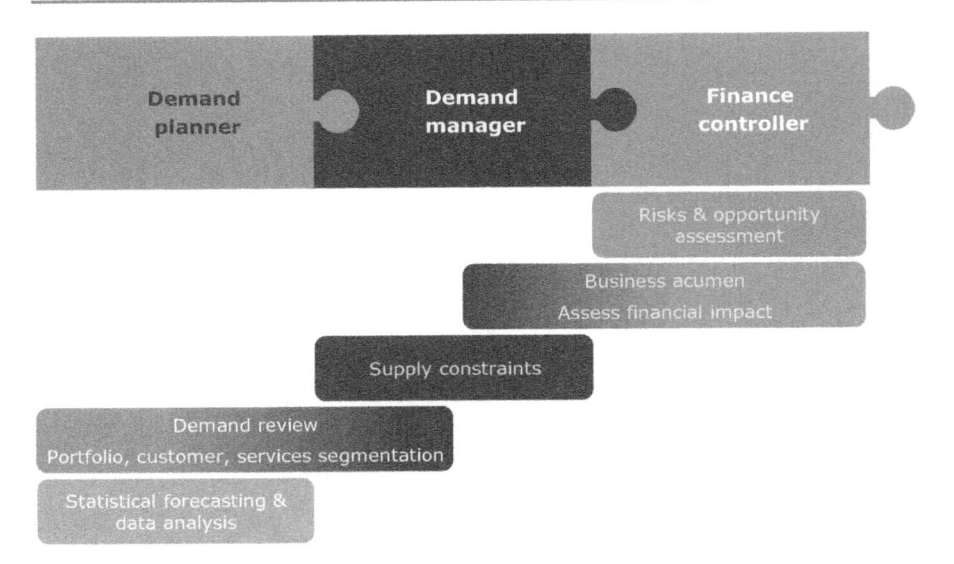

Fig. 3.11 Overlap of selected competencies improves integration

Overlap of capabilities creates an opportunity to generate common understanding, shared objectives, and goals through experience. In every business we have business risks and opportunities. If we map risks and opportunities to S&OP process, we will acknowledge that they exist in each process step (see Fig. 3.12). Therefore, overlap of capabilities will help to understand them better and simulate impact in more business coherent manner.

End-to-end scenario which leverages overlap of capabilities happens as you should segment the planning strategy according to product variability/volume. Probabilistic estimates and decision points should be also used to manage high-variability items (e.g., project driven) with a risk-based approach. You should also consider to use postponement strategies/modularity to mitigate uncertainty (Crum & Palmatier, 2003).

In Fig. 3.13, we tried to visualize key process steps and responsibilities of demand planner, demand manager, and finance controllers enabling process and organization integration under Integrated Business Planning framework.

Demand planners should drive the development of unconstrained forecasts that takes into consideration Product Review, as well as qualitative and quantitative inputs. Demand planners should ensure that the development of the forecast starts from volume and is then monetized. In no case, the forecast should start from a value forecast. The development of the forecast should aim to be efficient and focused which means we should have the same ways of working for all products in the portfolio. Development of the unconstrained forecast should aim to deliver realistic predictions.

Demand planning is about developing an unconstrained forecast that needs the S&OP finalization. If this process reaches mature levels, it evolves into the sophisticated modeling of segmented channels. Very often this is combined with demand sensing which requires advanced techniques. When enhanced further to VMI,

3.4 Connect Org. Structures and Capabilities

Supply
- Product availability
- Manpower, Machine, Material constraints and extra availability
- Internal & External manufacturing and operations

Product
- Registrations
- Phase-ins & -outs
- Long term substitutions
- Operational substitutions

Finance
- Credit availability / exposure
- Currency fluctuations
- Provisions for inventory write-offs, returns
- COGS fluctuations

Demand
- Price tactics
- Promotions / campaigns
- New business gains
- Business lost
- Competition activities
- Profitability optimization

What if scenario planning for business risks & opportunities

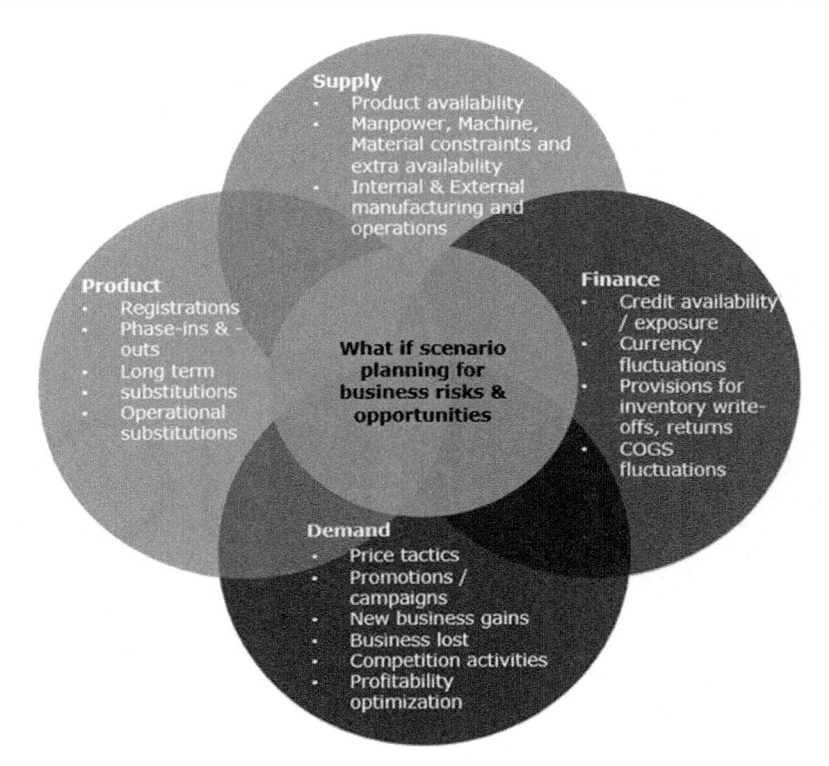

Fig. 3.12 Overlapping capabilities improve modeling of cross-functional business risk and opportunities

demand is made transparent and visible through the use of collaboration (Steutermann, Salley, & Lord, 2012).

Demand managers should drive the development of allocation plans based on supply signals and jointly with finance controller drive development of integrated business plan in volume and value. Both roles should ensure monetization of forecasts and plans.

Demand managers should be responsible for demand shaping, which is specific to industry and business strategy (consumer products, commodity products, and medical device products), and it requires synchronization with the decision-making processes and agility throughout the internal processes (Steutermann et al. 2012).

Demand planning and demand management role(s) should be FTE role(s) and not ad hoc activities. They should be given the power to communicate agreed forecasts and plans, coordinate changes, and become main go-to person for sales and marketing and supply and finance topics (Crum & Palmatier, 2003).

Finance controller should be responsible to lead monetization of forecasts and plans. Controllers and financial elements which they ensure should not only be integrated but embedded in the process. Finance controllers should help organization

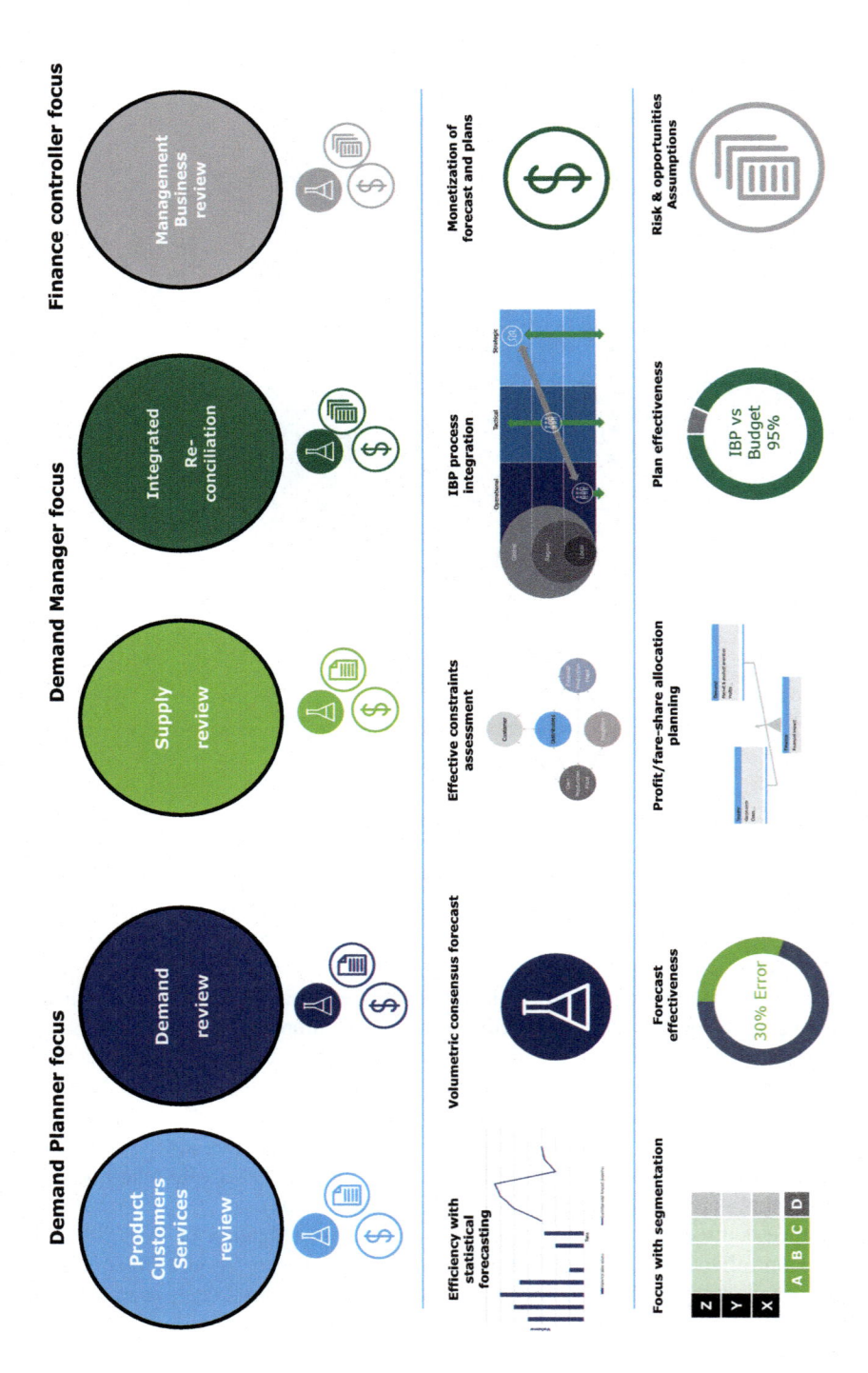

Fig. 3.13 Demand planner, demand manager, finance controller IBP focus areas

to develop what-if scenario planning which covers end-to-end risk and opportunities and should help organization to validate assumptions and clearly expose financial impacts. Controllers should not stay aside but play active role and contribute in S&OP meetings.

We fully agree with Mark A. Moon (Moon, 2013): Demand planners and demand managers play a vital role in making integration between demand (sales and marketing) and supply organizations possible. We would like to build on this and enhance it with role of finance controllers.

3.5 Connect Data and Systems

One of the biggest strengths of SAP Integrated Business Planning is the ability to integrate data from various data sources, SAP/non-SAP systems, on premise/cloud applications and systems. In Fig. 3.14 we wanted to illustrate how IBP process may drive requirement to integrate data from dedicated systems/solutions in order to bring key and relevant planning data to make holistic decisions. We created this figure as extract from few projects. Common link between those projects was that we did not bring all data from those connected system but only these which were relevant to make integrated decisions in IBP. Another aspect which was common in projects we were involved, was that we did bring data with various granularities, volumes, frequencies, and horizons into IBP and use built-in instruments to aggregate, disaggregate, split, and manage data flows to make best out of it.

Often we had to deal with non-harmonized data sources, e.g., multiple ERP. We used to make a joke that non-harmonized data sources were as common as rain in England. It was our challenge to put solution in place to map those sources versus target IBP data model and link IBP project planning to pace and need to harmonize data directly at source (e.g., ERP).

Let us elaborate a bit on next figure. We have brought data which was relevant for IBP process steps, we have defined data integration requirements, we have defined "master and slave" system for every data object, and we have assessed data quality in source system before we started integration. Data quality assessment which aims to define how to deal with non-harmonized data and non-standardized data should be considered if needed.

We have already seen in the previous chapters that an integrated business planning framework brings together various processes that are part of the extended supply chain management to facilitate the cross-functional alignment and collaboration.

Behind these processes we have data and technology. Connecting systems and information efficiently will enable organization to understand and leverage data in business decisions, driving the organization to a competitive advantage. Connection of data will happen with different options depending if its strategic, tactical, or operational planning.

The integration needs are very different from one company to another, depending on the organizations' size, the degree of processes, and technology standardization across locations or division and industry specifics. When it comes to SAP IBP, the

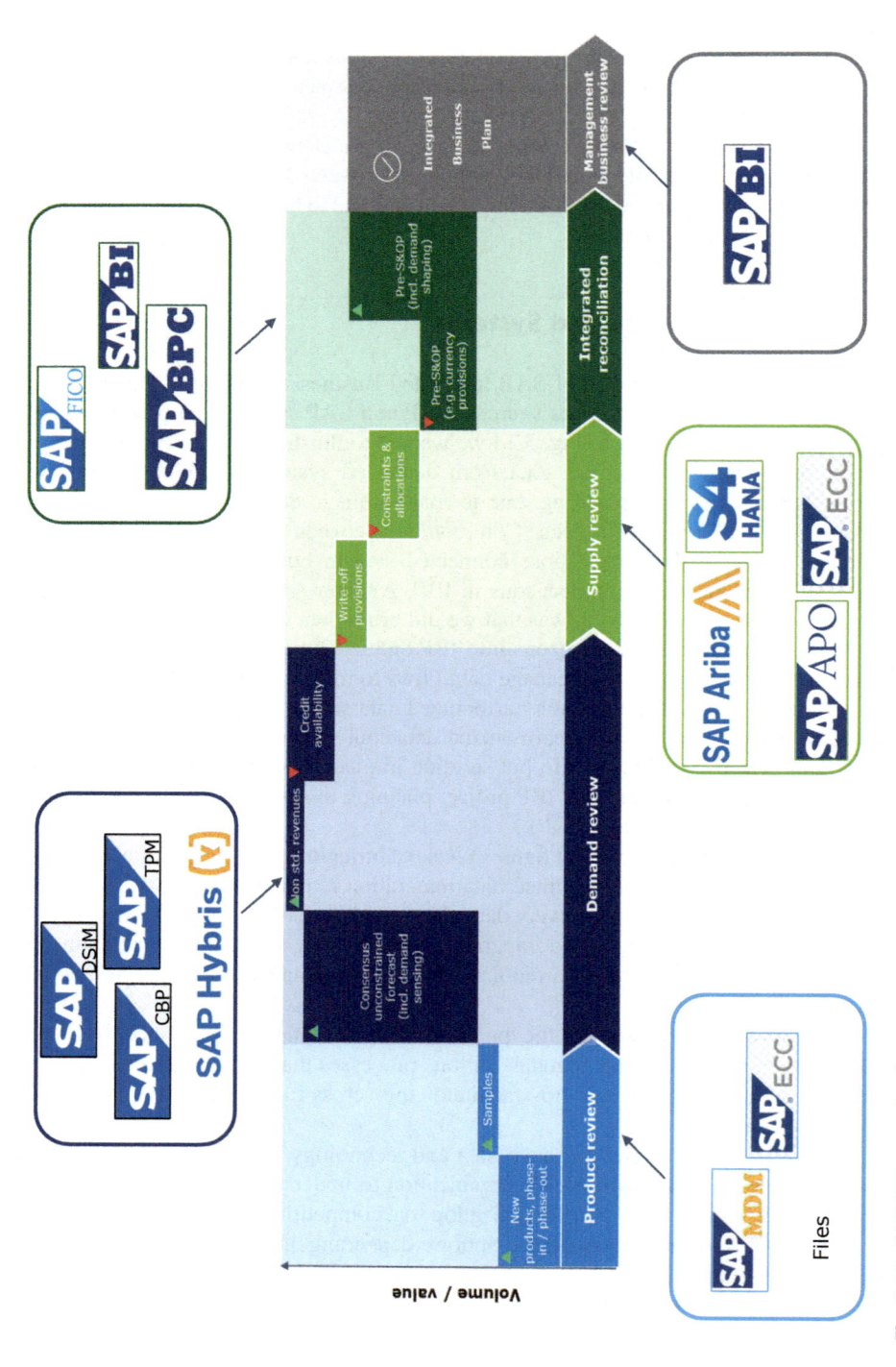

Fig. 3.14 SAP IBP example of system integration from process perspective

3.5 Connect Data and Systems

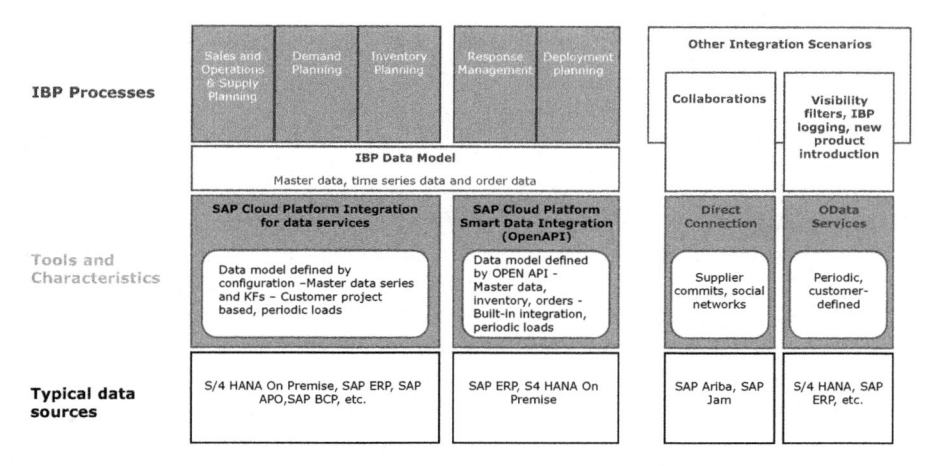

Fig. 3.15 SAP IBP integration options

	IBP Processes						Other Integration Scenarios	
	Sales and Operations & Supply Planning	Demand Planning	Inventory Planning	Response Management	Deployment planning		Collaborations	Visibility filters, IBP logging, new product introduction
	IBP Data Model Master data, time series data and order data							
Tools and Characteristics	SAP Cloud Platform Integration for data services		SAP Cloud Platform Smart Data Integration (OpenAPI)			Direct Connection		OData Services
	Data model defined by configuration –Master data series and KFs – Customer project based, periodic loads		Data model defined by OPEN API - Master data, inventory, orders - Built-in integration, periodic loads			Supplier commits, social networks		Periodic, customer-defined
Typical data sources	S/4 HANA On Premise, SAP APO, SAP BCP, etc.		SAP ERP, S4 HANA On Premise			SAP Ariba, SAP Jam		S/4 HANA, SAP ERP, etc.

integration content is also driven by the licensed modules that are under the implementation scope.

To reduce the complexity that is usually associated with the data integration, SAP Integrated Business Planning solution comes with complementary integration technologies that will facilitate the organizations' journey in collecting/sending data from/to multiple sources. We will review these integration technologies presented in Fig. 3.15 to explore which one makes sense for your IBP.

3.5.1 Time Series Integration

SAP Cloud Platform Integration for data services (CPI-DS) is a solution which is used for the integration of the time series data. It is the most relevant for IBP applications such as IBP for demand, inventory, sales and operations planning, control tower, or supply.

It means that time series data integration is used mostly for strategic planning and tactical S&OP process steps but less for operational planning.

CPI-DS (formerly known as SAP HANA Cloud Integration for data services or HCI-DS) is a multi-tenant cloud solution that enables organizations to safely extract, transform, and load (ETL) data from source systems to IBP tables via HTTPs protocol. It comes with a simplified and intuitive Web-based user interface that allows to drag and drop objects in order to define data mappings and create transformation flows.

To meet the most common requirements of an IBP implementation project, SAP provides flexible integration content based on SAP CPI-DS, ready-to-use interfaces that serve as a starting point for the creation of their own content, inbound (data is loaded to IBP) or outbound (data is extracted from IBP). These integration prepackaged scenarios for periodic data exchange can be classified in the following groups:

- Master data templates that provide content to transfer master data from the leading system that can be SAP ERP or APO. The template content covers various master data objects such as product, location, customer, product-location, or resources.
- Key figure content that is used to transfer transactional time series data needed as input to various processes executed in IBP. We list here key figures like initial inventory, actuals/shipment history, open orders, capacity limit and consumption, demand plan, sales opportunities and revenue, aggregated point of sales, and point of stock data. The sources from where these KFs are extracted vary: SAP ERP, SAP APO, SAP Hybris Cloud for Customer (C4C), and SAP DSiM (Demand Signal Management). The integration also covers the outbound from IBP.
- General-purpose templates contain some global variables that are required by IBP to process data after it reached the staging table.

Let's see some examples where the data that is required to feed the integrated business planning is available in different source systems and how integration into IBP can be automatized using CPI-DS, with or without prepackaged integration content.

Integration with SAP Hybris Cloud for Customer
One of the standard integration scenarios for transactional data covers the integration to IBP from Hybris Cloud for Customer and SAP's cloud solution for customer relationship management.

SAP Cloud for Customer (C4C) solution comes with a suite of applications that can help organizations to better know and engage their customers to increase the sales and achieve a better customer service. One of the application parts of SAP C4C is Cloud for Sales, whose features provide the framework for transforming the selling process and align it to the buying patterns of the consumers:

- Opportunity management and insight
- Sales performance management
- Account management and intelligence
- Mobility

The integration content from SAP C4C to IBP covers the opportunity management, an important pillar that can drive the effectiveness of the selling by gaining better pipeline visibility.

In the screen shot, we see the individual opportunities existing in SAP Hybris Cloud for Sales, but this is less likely to be the level of granularity required for the consensus demand planning process (Fig. 3.16). In the pre-delivered integration content, the opportunities get aggregated to a time series (time bucket) based on a

3.5 Connect Data and Systems

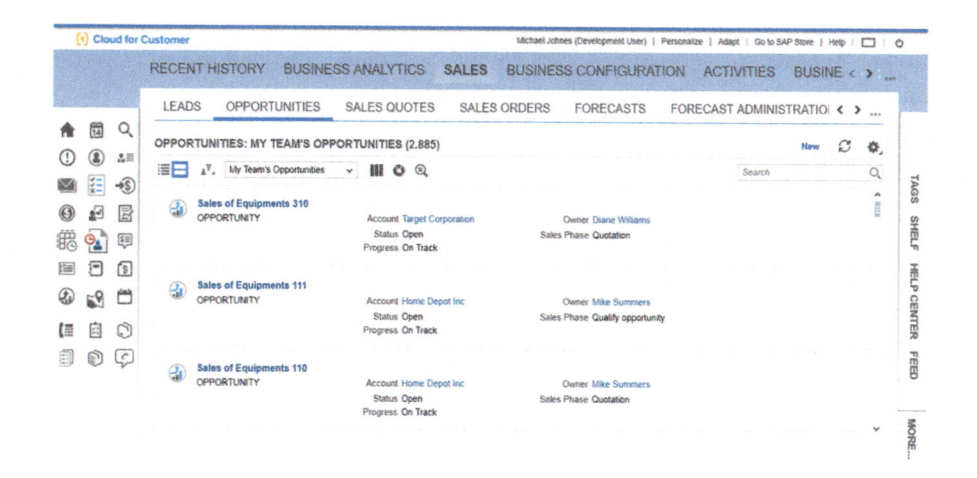

Fig. 3.16 SAP C4C opportunities—card view

selection of the opportunity status, probability to close, sales forecasted opportunity, and the forecast horizon. Integration level of granularity can be further adjusted to meet the requirements of each organization.

Visibility over the opportunities' pipeline and their probability can be a key driver of the monthly process of consensus demand planning, serving as a basis for what-if analysis to reach the most profitable decisions.

In this example, we see how opportunities can be analyzed as an input during the consensus demand plan process. Depending on the closure probability, they will be or not be included in the final volume plan. The probability divides these opportunities in two categories that are modeled in IBP as two different key figures (Fig. 3.17):

– Opportunities with a chance higher than 30% but lower than 70%. These opportunities are available for analysis, and they can be considered during consensus plan review, perhaps part of an optimistic plan.
– Opportunities higher than 70% that are automatically added on top of consensus demand plan.

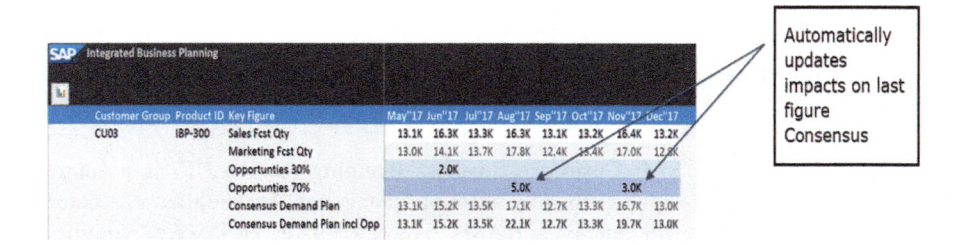

Fig. 3.17 SAP Hybris opportunities integrated with SAP IBP

Having opportunities part of the consensus demand plan will enable the demand and supply planners to run multiple what-if analysis and anticipate the outcome of opportunities happening probability:

- In case that opportunities get confirmed, how will they impact the delivery capacity? Do we have enough stock and/or capacity to fulfill the related demand or do we need to pre-produce and increase capacity by adding an additional shift, etc.?
- If opportunities are lost, how will this impact projected revenue?

Integration with SAP Trade Management
SAP Global Trade Management solution comes with innovative functionalities that accompany the organizations in their journey from planning to execution by providing support to streamline the sales and budgeting, customer, and promotion planning activities.

The solution combines three functional areas with the aim to build one integrated process driven by real-time visibility, prediction, and optimization capabilities:

- SAP Trade Promotion Planning and Management (TPM)
- SAP Customer Business Planning (CBP)
- SAP Advanced Trade Management Analytics (ATMA)

SAP Trade Promotion Planning and Management (TPM) solution provides wide functionalities for planning and managing trade promotions. Mainly for the consumer products industry, the trade promotion effectiveness can be one of the most important pillars for long-term business growth and increased customer loyalty.

With the SAP software for promotion planning and optimization, the organizations are able to identify the most profitable and strategic promotions. Integrating and analyzing actual data coming from stores or syndicated data allows the promotion execution tracking. In case of a promotion that does not return the expected results, failing both retailer's and manufacturer's objectives, you can react on the moment and take corrective actions. Or if the promotion is outperforming, having visibility into promotion as it happens, it will help you to avoid lost sales due to out of stocks. SAP TPPM helps to:

- Get reliable recommendations for promotional activity by running what-if simulations based on order history, retail point-of-sale, and market research.
- Predict and optimize promotion outcomes, including revenue and profit, for both manufacturers and retailers through predictive analytics.
- Determine the best way to promote a given product, such as discounts, rebates, or premiums.

The other module SAP Customer Business Planning (SAP CBP) is a central management tool that supports the key account managers to handle their customers throughout the year. It will enable the KAMs to have a holistic view across volumes,

3.5 Connect Data and Systems

mix, revenue, margin, promotions, and trade terms planning and combine them into an integrated and collaborative business plan.

While SAP TPM is focused only on the promotional activities, SAP CBP application covers the non-promotional side as well, offering a complete view of the customer P&L.

Key features of CBP:

- Creation of customer-specific planning product hierarchies
- Assortment planning
- Customer P&L analysis
- Business-friendly, easy-to-use graphical tool to plan and track annual business with trading partners

These modules are complementary to each other, and blending them together will allow organizations to take the right decisions that balance the promotional and non-promotional volumes to drive profits and category growth while increasing the internal margin. Further, to enable the cross-functional collaborative planning between sales, marketing, supply chain, and finance, we will integrate trade management with SAP IBP.

In Fig. 3.18, we see the integration points between IBP and trade management. We see there is no one direction for the data to flow but a bidirectional data exchange.

- To CBP: integrate the baseline consensus volume projection from SAP IBP as planned during the budget exercise in connection with targets coming from SAP BPC.
- To IBP: integrate adjusted baseline and promotional volume uplift.

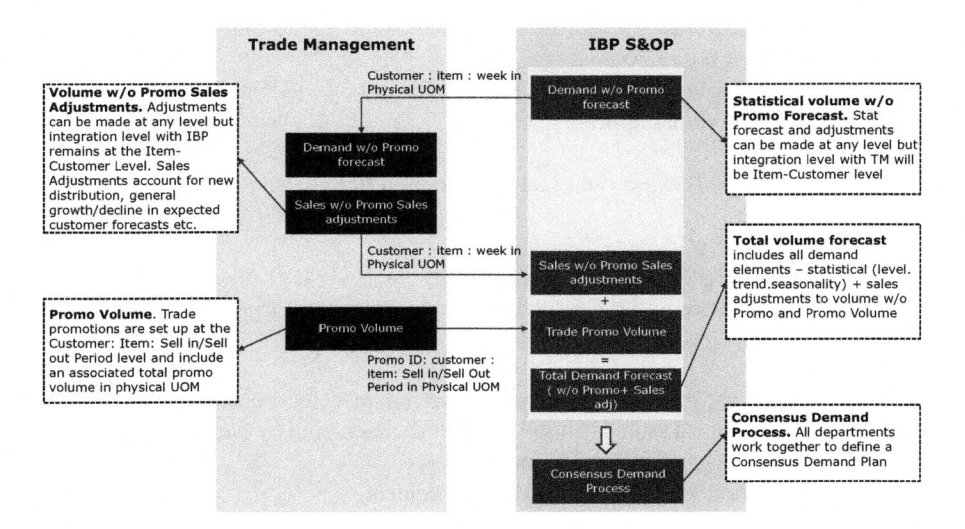

Fig. 3.18 SAP IBP and SAP trade management integration points

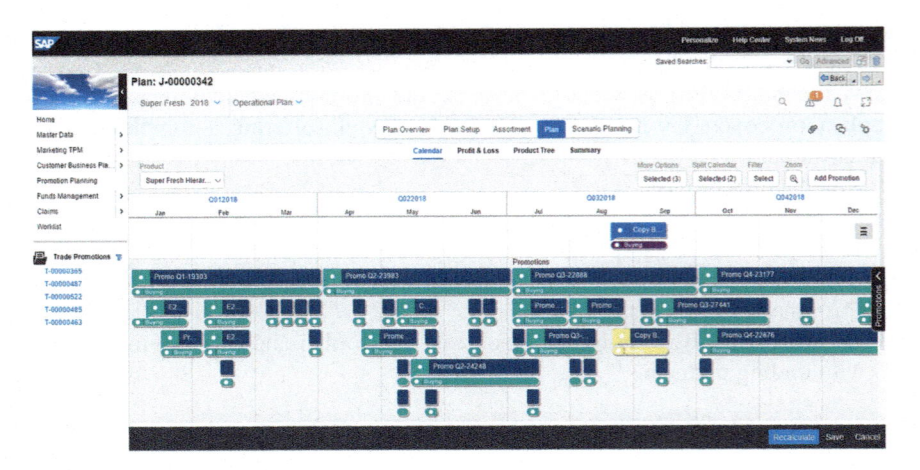

Fig. 3.19 SAP TPM—promotions overview

Let's have an example of the integration between these two solutions.

The scenario starts with the transfer of the baseline volume outlook for the next year from IBP into CBP (Fig. 3.19).

Once the data is available in CBP, the account manager is usually executing several activities that require tight integration with the trade promotion planning functionality. He will first review the non-promoted plan and adjust the baseline volumes to reflect the opening of two new stores. Next, he will need to plan the promotions and assess them in terms of volume, profitability, and trade budget spend. To do this, he checks what is already suggested from bottom-up trade marketing planning. He identifies which promotions to copy from previous years, the ones which have probability to be successful this year. While adding the promotions, he can easily keep an eye on the trade spend and ensure he is not overspending (see Fig. 3.20).

Once the total volume is completed, it will be sent into IBP at the level of regular forecast and promotional uplift:

- Baseline volume (key account manager opinion line)
- Uplift volume

Integrating the promotions expected uplift in SAP IBP does not only bring marketing intelligence in the demand planning process but also enables the supply chain side of managing promotions:

- Identify the right planning strategy to hedge against stock-outs.
- Ability to generate a more accurate baseline demand plan by identifying the uplift in demand connected with trade promotions.
- Allocate promotions down to distribution centers.

3.5 Connect Data and Systems

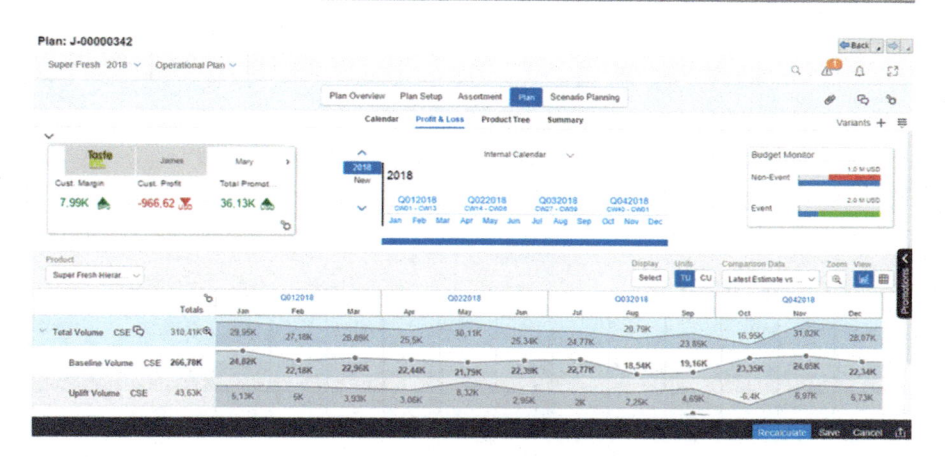

Fig. 3.20 SAP CBP baseline and promo uplift volumes

From a technical perspective, the promotion integration into IBP covers:

- Master data where we include promotions' characteristics such as promotion id, promotion description, buying periods, number of pre- or post-dip periods, start or end date, etc.
- Time series data that consists of promotion uplift quantities and the sales lift as planned in the promotion planning tool.

Visualizing and managing the promotions data at a glance is facilitated by SAP IBP Fiori Analyze promotions app which presents several functionalities:

- Customizable promotion display
- Calculation of maximum and average sales lift as well as of promotion success
- Overview of transferred promotions plus possibility to dig into details and display data as table or chart
- Notes creation that can be shared in SAP JAM
- Edit functionality for refinement of promotion allocation to locations

From the promotions overview screen where each user can define his own layout by adding or removing promotions characteristics, one can drill into the details behind each of the promotions by simply selecting the line with the mouse cursor (see Fig. 3.21).

From an integrated planning process perspective, incorporating the promotion uplifts into the S&OP planning cycle will lead to a robust unconstrained consensus demand plan (Fig. 3.22) based on which inventory and supply planning processes are triggered:

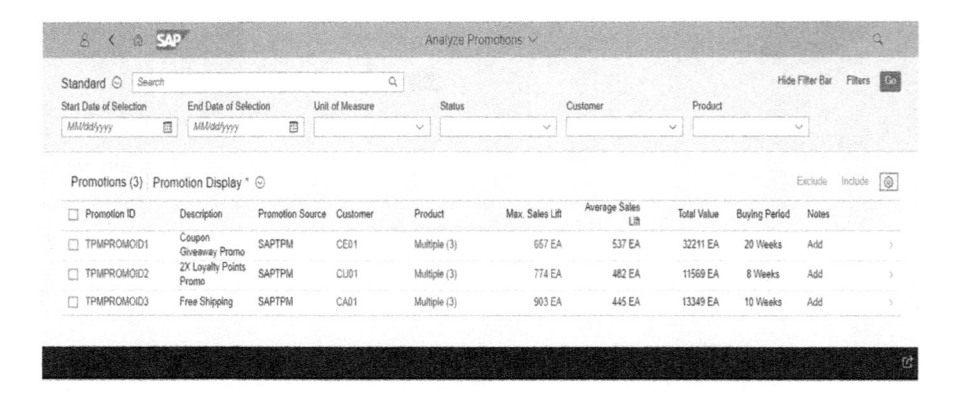

Fig. 3.21 SAP IBP—promotion overview app

Fig. 3.22 SAP IBP promotion uplift as part of consensus demand planning process

- Rough-cut capacity planning for early identification of potential capacity risks
- Explosion of the demand at the component level and integration with Ariba to see if the suppliers can commit on the forecast
- Inventory optimization
- Constrained supply planning

Integration with BPC

The next use case will show the integration with SAP Business Objects Planning and Consolidation (BPC) solution which supports the financial forecasting and consolidation process.

Many companies are using BPC to improve the annual and monthly financial planning and budgeting. BPC simplifies the annual planning process by providing step-by-step templates to assist and guide the business users in their activity, supports collaboration between finance and line of business managers, and helps improving forecasting accuracy.

The outcome of the financial planning, budget, or annual operating plan is an important metric that drives sales and operation planning process which identifies the needed action to enable the organization to achieve its budget targets. We identify at least two integration points between BPC and IBP:

SAP

Top Down Targets

TARGET
BestRun Corporation Input

	2018	2019	2020	2021
Net Revenue	450,000,000	540,000,000	648,000,000	777,600,000
Direct Costs	150,000,000	178,500,000	212,415,000	252,773,850
Profit After Direct Costs	300,000,000	361,500,000	435,585,000	524,826,150
Total Personnel Expenses	65,000,000	74,750,000	85,962,500	98,856,875
Other Dept Expense	110,000,000	126,500,000	145,475,000	167,296,250
Depreciation & Amortization	17,500,000	19,250,000	21,175,000	23,292,500
Total Operating Expenses	192,500,000	220,500,000	252,612,500	289,445,625
Operating Income	107,500,000	141,000,000	182,972,500	235,380,525

Fig. 3.23 SAP BPC top-down targets

- Inbound from BPC to IBP: budget/annual operating plan
- Outbound from IBP to BPC: monthly integrated business plan

Therefore, seamless integration between BPC and IBP is critical to drive cross-functional alignment between operations and finance.

Depending on each organization, the planning can be executed at different level of detail. In the figure, we see an example where targets are initially set on a highly aggregated level following to be allocated to each business unit (Fig. 3.23).

While maintaining the forecast, BPC provides tools that will allow the user to spread, trend, or weight the dataset or even to input his own formula. It will also provide flexible allocation methods so that multiple users will be able to fill in their bottom-up budget and data will be consolidated on the fly once information is submitted. During budget exercise, multiple versions can be computed based on different inputs. It is enough to change any input like units or cost and BPC will recalculate everything starting from sales revenue up to the net income.

We see below the profitability analysis of 2018 budget based on the forecast units and cost of sales data at the granularity of region and product line see Fig. 3.24.

Moving from BPC to IBP, we will integrate the budgeted volume, revenue, and profit. The integration usually takes place at an aggregate level like product line, country; brand, region; or even product family, customer group level that can vary from an implementation project to another.

Once the data is available in IBP, we will bring it on a lower granularity. This approach will allow us to track the sales performance at a more detailed level and identify risks and opportunities.

In Fig. 3.25 from an IBP planning view, we see the integrated annual budget for year 2018 filtered by the product line 01 and Italy as country.

SAP

Italy
Profit After Direct Costs
Budget V2
Local Currency

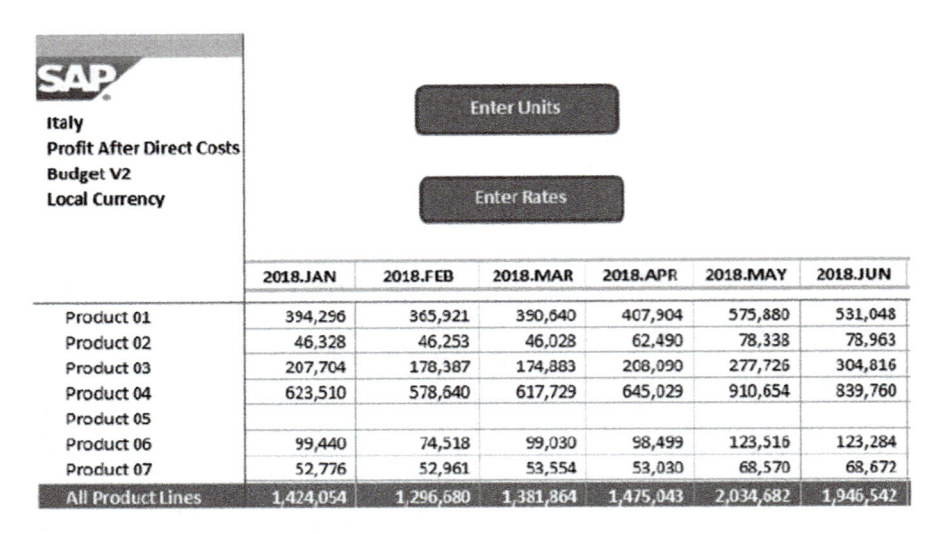

Enter Units

Enter Rates

	2018.JAN	2018.FEB	2018.MAR	2018.APR	2018.MAY	2018.JUN
Product 01	394,296	365,921	390,640	407,904	575,880	531,048
Product 02	46,328	46,253	46,028	62,490	78,338	78,963
Product 03	207,704	178,387	174,883	208,090	277,726	304,816
Product 04	623,510	578,640	617,729	645,029	910,654	839,760
Product 05						
Product 06	99,440	74,518	99,030	98,499	123,516	123,284
Product 07	52,776	52,961	53,554	53,030	68,570	68,672
All Product Lines	1,424,054	1,296,680	1,381,864	1,475,043	2,034,682	1,946,542

Fig. 3.24 SAP BPC profit target 2018 by product line

SAP Integrated Business Planning — Annual Budget

Product Line	Country	Key Figure	Jan'18	Feb'18	Mar'18	Apr'18	May'18	Jun'18	Jul'18	Aug'18	Sep'18	Oct'18	Nov'18	Dec'18	2018
Product Line 01	Italy	Agg Budget Qty.	3K	3K	3K	4K	7K	5K	5K	6K	5K	5K	4K	4K	55K
		Agg. Budget Rev.	867K	776K	833K	906K	1.3M	1.2M	1.2M	1.3M	1.2M	1.1M	1.0M	1.1M	12.7M
		Agg. Budget Profit	394K	366K	391K	408K	576K	531K	554K	589K	517K	478K	462K	478K	5.7M

Fig. 3.25 SAP BPC product line integrated budget into SAP IBP

SAP Integrated Business Planning — Annual Budget

Product Line	Country	Product	Customer	Key Figure	Jan'18	Feb'18	Mar'18	Apr'18	May'18	Jun'18	Jul'18	Aug'18	Sep'18	Oct'18	Nov'18	Dec'18	2018
Product Line 01	Italy	(None)	(None)	Agg Budget Qty.	3K	3K	3K	4K	7K	5K	5K	6K	5K	5K	4K	4K	55K
				Agg. Budget Rev.	867K	776K	833K	906K	1.3M	1.2M	1.2M	1.3M	1.2M	1.1M	1.0M	1.1M	12.7M
				Agg. Budget Profit	394K	366K	391K	408K	576K	531K	554K	589K	517K	478K	462K	478K	5.7M
		IBP-100	CA01	Budget Qty.	1K	1K	1K	1K	1K	1K	1K	1K	1K	1K	1K	1K	11K
				Budget Rev.	173K	155K	167K	181K	251K	232K	240K	270K	238K	213K	201K	216K	2.5M
				Budget Profit	79K	73K	78K	82K	115K	106K	111K	118K	103K	96K	92K	96K	1.1M
		IBP-110	CE01	Budget Qty.	2K	2K	2K	2K	4K	3K	3K	3K	3K	3K	2K	2K	27K
				Budget Rev.	433K	388K	416K	453K	628K	579K	601K	674K	595K	533K	504K	540K	6.3M
				Budget Profit	197K	183K	196K	204K	288K	266K	277K	295K	259K	239K	231K	239K	2.9M
		IBP-120	CU01	Budget Qty.	1K	1K	1K	1K	2K	2K	2K	2K	2K	2K	1K	1K	16K
				Budget Rev.	260K	233K	250K	272K	377K	347K	361K	405K	357K	320K	302K	324K	3.8M
				Budget Profit	118K	110K	117K	122K	173K	159K	166K	177K	155K	143K	139K	143K	1.7M

Fig. 3.26 SAP IBP budget disaggregation

From this aggregate level, the modeling can be continued to make the budget available on a more detailed level like product-customer using a disaggregation logic tailored to meet the business logic, e.g., based on the ratio of the actuals with an offset into year+1, see Fig. 3.26.

To close the loop, once the monthly sales and operation planning cycle is completed, we can integrate the latest plan from IBP to BPC. This will enable finance team to have a better overview of the expected realistic forecast and to develop rolling P&L.

3.5.2 Order-Based Integration

Moving from the tactical planning, we step into the short-term horizon where the operational planning happens. To support this perspective, detailed data like planned orders, production orders, sales orders, or purchase orders is needed. Orders suggest that we are on the border of planning and execution, which is a domain of operational planning. The module that supports this short-term projection and enables the planner to reach to short notice changes is called response and supply. And as the planning is driven by orders, it means we need a continuous integration of the order data into IBP response. So, using CPI-DS, which is a batch integration tool, will not support this need of a continuous push of the new orders.

To support the integration of data into the response module, SAP provides an integration enabler called **SAP Cloud Platform Smart Data Integration (SDI)** using the openAPI. As SDI is a native technology part of HANA database, the data movement happens in real time with high-speed and decreased latency due to in-memory processing.

When the integration is with SAP ERP, customers can use the SAP ERP supply chain integration add-on for SAP Integrated Business Planning. The add-on supports to gather, transform, and store the data in the database tables from where it can be accessed for integration with IBP. The add-on also supports the outbound integration from IBP and creates orders in ERP based on what is received from IBP.

One can transfer the following data types from ERP to IBP:

- Master data such as locations, transportation lanes, or materials
- Transaction data like storage location stock, vendor consignment stock, and orders (planned orders, production orders, sales order, etc.)

In Fig. 3.27 we have the material stock requirement list from ECC where we get an overview of the initial stock, sales orders, and transports requisitions created via IBP to ECC interface coming from response.

On IBP side, we have the projected stock app which displays the transactional elements including the sales orders originating from ECC, the open forecast, and the stock transport requisitions. Note that the orders from ECC appear with the ECC order numbers Fig. 3.28.

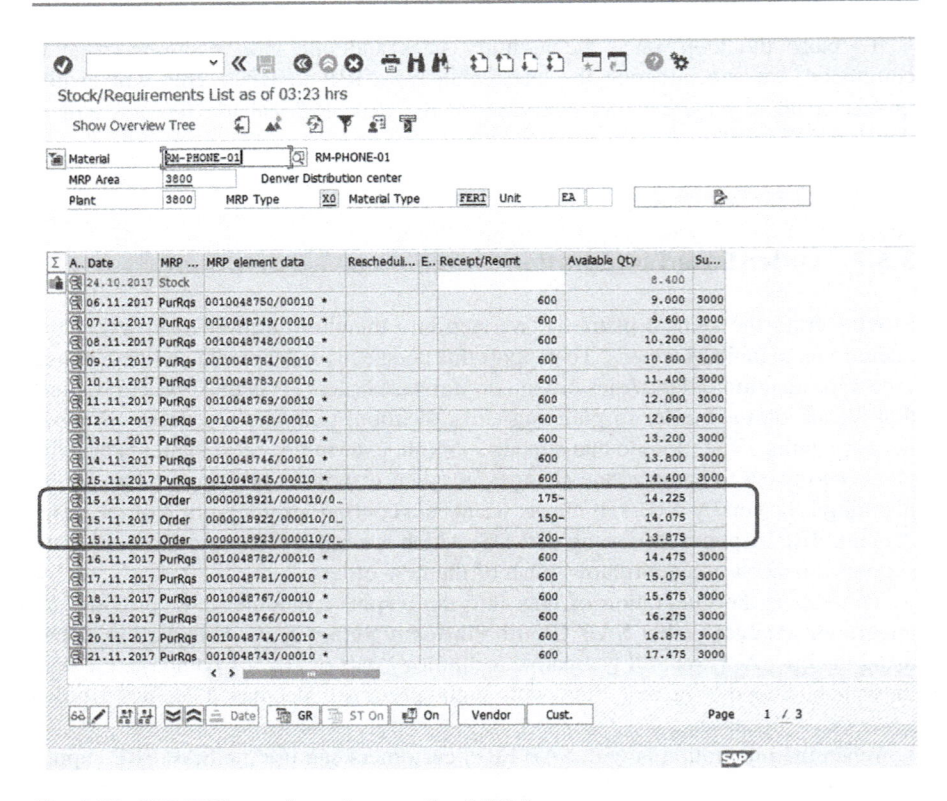

Fig. 3.27 SAP ECC—stock requirements list (MD04)

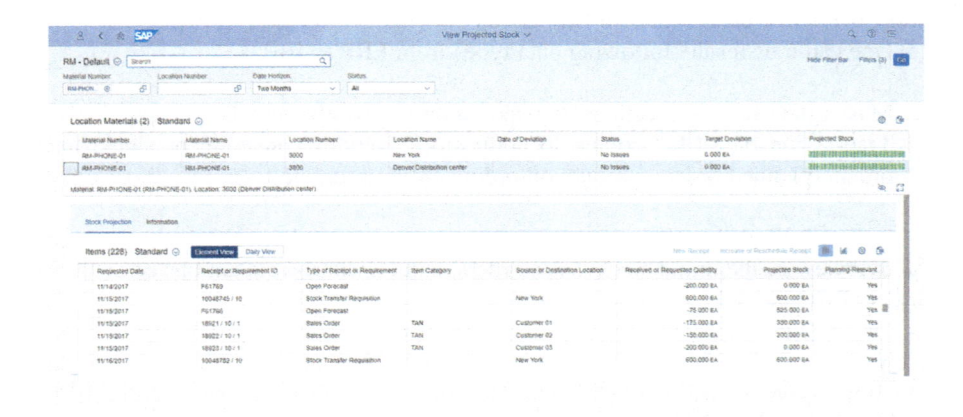

Fig. 3.28 SAP IBP—projected stock application

3.5.3 Other Integration Options

3.5.3.1 Direct Integration
Now that we have reviewed the two main integration technologies, let's go back to the Fig. 3.15 and focus on the right side of it where we have the integration with SAP JAM and SAP Ariba. These integrations are handled through the communication management app which enables you to establish direct communication with other systems.

3.5.3.2 Manual Integration with CSV files
When it comes to time series integration, one can choose not to go with SAP CPI-DS and use instead an on premise ETL tool. With this approach, they can extract data into flat files which are then loaded to IBP via HTTPS protocol using the data integration job app. However, we don't recommend this option for production environment, and we would restrict it for the beginning of an implementation project or for a proof of concept/pilot project where data load is limited to most representative samples. Moreover, SAP CPI-DS has the advantage of providing an end-to-end visibility over the integration flow which a different ETL tool cannot support as the integration would be split and intermediated by flat files.

3.6 Summary

- Connect planning processes by aligning their calendars of activities:
  - Once per year between strategic annual business planning and tactical S&OP planning, normally around budgeting period
  - Monthly between strategic product planning and tactical S&OP
  - At least once per month or bi-weekly between operational planning and tactical S&OP
- Enrich standard S&OP with following value drivers:
  - Incorporation of finance elements and finance controller into the processes enabled to improve pricing tactics and profitability of decisions were improved.
  - Alignment and connection between planning types tremendously improved transparency and steering of planning by management.
  - Portfolio, customer, and services rationalization brought substantial financial impact and improved process efficiency.
  - "What-if" business scenarios enabled better adoption to internal and external uncertainties.
  - Comparison of integrated business plant to budget on any level of commercial, material, and geographical hierarchy was an eye opener, enabled deliver of gap closing activities.
  - Granularity, aligned to horizon, introduced substantial reduction of time being spent on non-value-added activities.

- Organizational structures and capability models defined cross-functionally helped organization to be more focused and capable to work as one, break walls, and work cross boundaries.
- Leverage demand planning, demand management, and finance controlling functions as "connectors."
- Leverage overlap of capabilities to improve business risk and opportunity modeling.
- Integrate required systems and get specialized data to enable integrated decisions. Get sales and marketing, demand, product, supply and operations, finance, and targets information to IBP.
- Use time series integration in tactical S&OP and strategic planning.
- Use order-based integration in operational planning.
- Leverage integrated design approach by connecting
  - Process
  - Organizational and capabilities
  - Technology
  - Business priorities
  - Supply, commercial, finance, master data, and ERP initiatives when planning IBP since IBP design means how IBP works in business

References

Bower, P. (2012). Integrated business planning: Is it a hoax or here to stay? *Journal of Business Forecasting, 31*(1), 11–17. Retrieved from http://www.jaguar-aps.com/pdf/IBPisaHoax.pdf

Crum, C., & Palmatier, G. E. (2003). *Demand management best practices: Process, principles, and collaboration.* Boca Raton: J. Ross Publishing. Retrieved from http://books.google.at/books?id=6l3iWbGM-54C

Moon, M. A. (2013). *Demand and supply integration: The key to world-class demand forecasting.* Upper Saddle River: FT Press. Retrieved from https://books.google.com/books?id=2M9njA9JcMgC&pgis=1

Palmatier, G. E., & Crum, C. (2013). *The transition from sales and operations planning to integrated business planning.* New London: Oliver Wight. Retrieved from https://www.amazon.com/Transition-Operations-Planning-Integrated-Business/dp/1457518252

Steutermann, S., Salley, A., & Lord, P. (2012). Demand management elevates value network performance. *Gartner.*

How to Run IBP: Use Cases

4.1 Strategic Planning

4.1.1 Improve E2E Strategic Initiative Simulation

As part of strategic planning process, several metrics can be used to measure the organization performance against its strategic goals. One of these is the compound annual growth rate (CAGR), which helps to assess the company's annual growth over a defined horizon of time. The CAGR is a straightforward Key Performance Indicator which provides one number to explain growth rate. It does use as input for the calculation only few factors: the number of periods, a beginning and a final value. Final value could be expressing growth of profits, revenue, or units sold.

Process needs to answer the basic question "How much business growth can we expect if":

- We launch a new product, new technology?
- We choose to extend the sales in a new country or region?
- We plan to extend the packaging capacity by adding a contract manufacturer in the supply chain network?

Starting from Fig. 4.1, which depicts the as-is and to-be simplified network diagram of a company that plans to extend its business footprint by creating a new sales channel, we will see how Integrated Business Planning improves planning of strategic initiatives.

From a business perspective, we would like to model new sales channel, model growth associated to it, and translate this demand into capacity utilization for strategic horizon.

System-wise we will leverage one of the key functionalities available in SAP IBP, namely, the version planning capability which is frequently used to manage alternate plans, for example, a risk (pessimistic)- and an opportunity (optimistic)-driven plan. While the data stays intact in the current plan (baseline), the end users can change

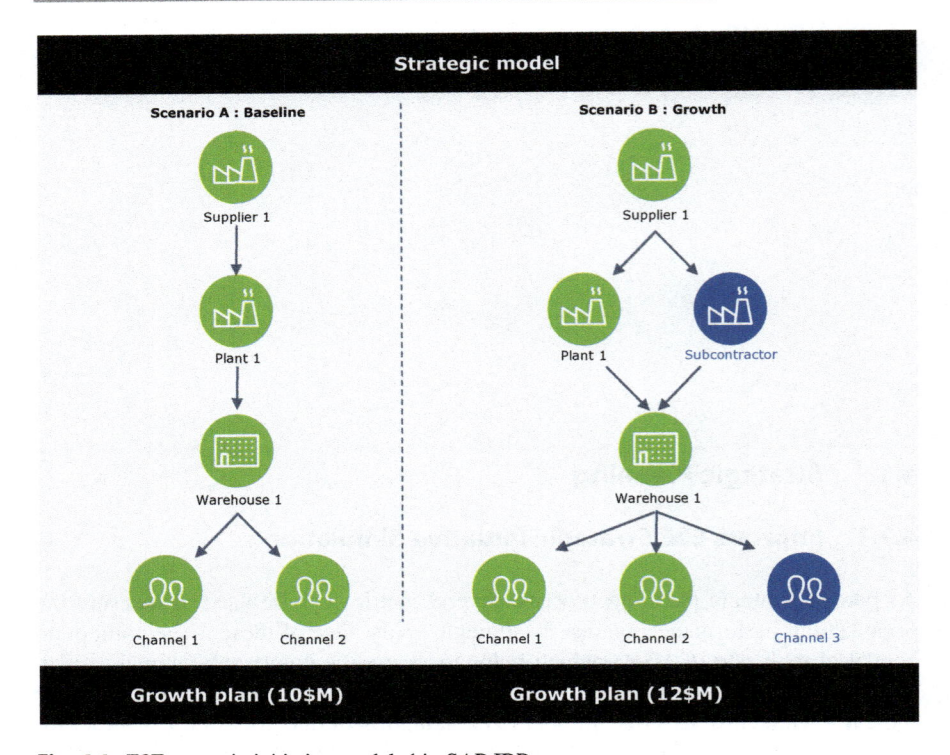

Fig. 4.1 E2E strategic initiative modeled in SAP IBP

and assess impact of various factors by running business process simulations in parallel versions. This parallel version can mirror or can be an extension of a business model, supply chain network stored in the baseline version (the version where usually the current plan is held).

There are two ways to leverage SAP IBP in strategic planning. One way is to modify data in parallel versions or scenarios to simulate business risk and opportunities and compare them. The other way is to model changes in business model, network, portfolio, etc. on the top of modification of assumptions captured in data.

More business comprehensive strategic planning will use a master data which is version dependent. To avoid issues with data consistency, we would leverage baseline master data and extend it with new nodes in parallel versions. Having a copy from baseline to the new version as a starting point will save considerable effort in preparing such a version. Then, we can extend the business model by adding master data for the new sales channel, new markets, new plants, new technology, etc.

The snippet below, taken from the "compound annual growth rate" planning view, highlights the baseline version revenue projection which is based solely on the existing B2B channel and shows an expected growth of 10.14% average annual rate.

4.1 Strategic Planning

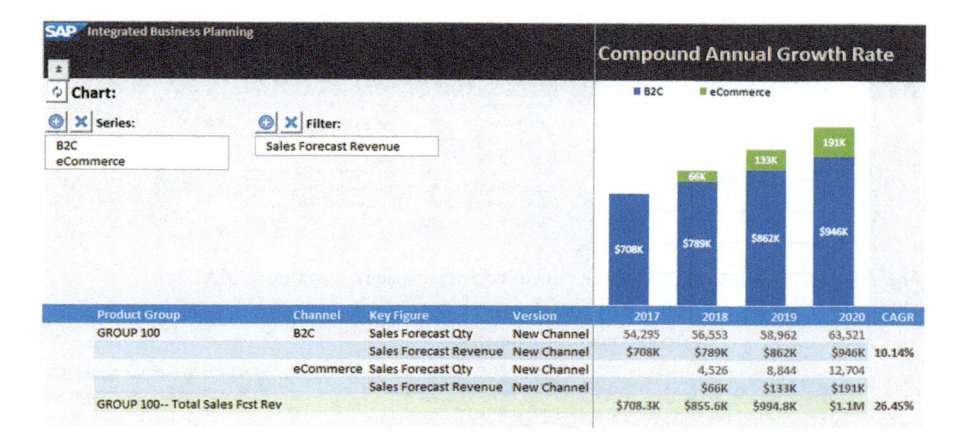

Fig. 4.2 SAP IBP—new sales channel CAGR calculation

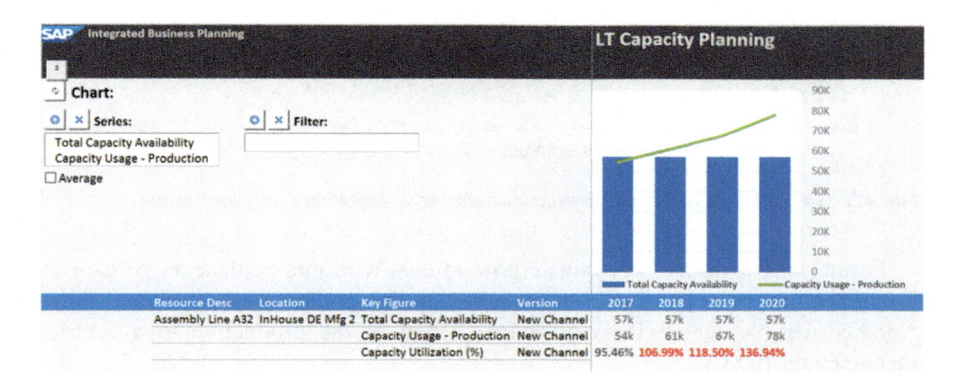

Fig. 4.3 SAP IBP—strategic long-term capacity utilization projection

Exposing the new channel—e-commerce in the CAGR calculation—shows an increase up to 26.45% for the same time horizon.

As SAP IBP interface is based on Excel, the calculation of CAGR is leveraging the excel flexibility of having ad hoc calculations based on the data retrieved from the backend (see Fig. 4.2).

But attaining a 26% CAGR resulting from the volume increase corresponding to the new channel can only happen if there are available resources to support the additional production. How is the 26% revenue CAGR translated in the extra capacity required? To answer this question, we are going to propagate the volume increase throughout the entire network by executing the supply planning heuristic operator in parallel version to baseline.

Results of unconstrained long-term supply planning run grab our attention by alerting a capacity overutilization that goes up to 137% by year 2020 in Germany, Manufacturing Location 2 as per Fig. 4.3.

Resource Desc	Location	Product Group	Key Figure	Version	Scenario	2017	2018	2019	2020
(None)	InHouse DE Mfg 2	GROUP 100	Average Unit Cost	New Channel	CMA Scenario	128	130	133	134
Assembly Line A32	InHouse DE Mfg 2	(None)	Capacity Utilization (%)	New Channel	CMA Scenario	95.46%	95.87%	96.22%	96.58%
			Total Capacity Availability	New Channel	CMA Scenario	57k	57k	57k	57k
		GROUP 100	Capacity Usage - Production	New Channel	CMA Scenario	54k	55k	55k	55k
(None)	Contract Mfr 101	GROUP 100	Average Unit Cost	New Channel	CMA Scenario		110	108	108
CMA101 Assembly	Contract Mfr 101	(None)	Capacity Utilization (%)	New Channel	CMA Scenario		79.15%	84.57%	91.94%
			Total Capacity Availability	New Channel	CMA Scenario		8k	15k	25k
		GROUP 100	Capacity Usage - Production	New Channel	CMA Scenario		6k	13k	23k

Fig. 4.4 SAP IBP—own and contract manufacturing capacity planning (CMA)

LT Operation Profit comparison

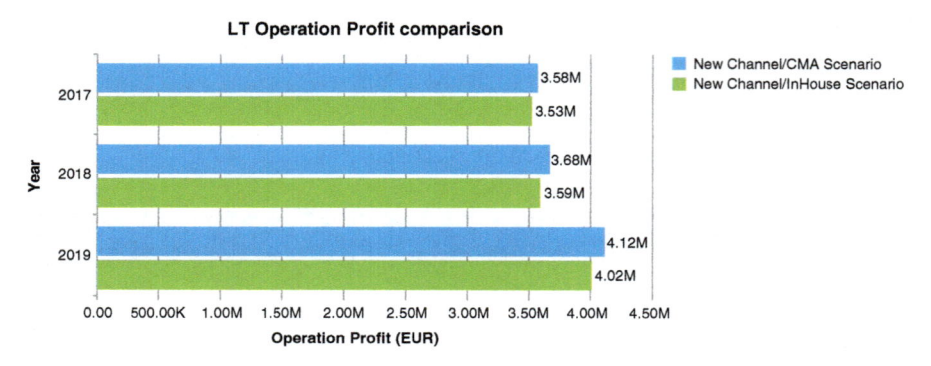

Year	New Channel/CMA Scenario	New Channel/InHouse Scenario
2017	3.58M	3.53M
2018	3.68M	3.59M
2019	4.12M	4.02M

Fig. 4.5 SAP IBP—in-house and contract manufacturing operating profit comparison

Further, the team has to evaluate how to deal with this bottleneck, perhaps an investment to increase the in-house capacity by adding night/weekend shifts. Another feasible option is to outsource a part of the production to a contract manufacturer (CMA).

Buyer has identified a CMA that can gradually increase its capacity and absorb the production that cannot be sustained in house, as the CMA is based in a country with lower more competitive labor costs but highly qualified staff. We see the expected average unit cost comparison between in-house production and outsourced production.

As we maintained the CMA in IBP as an own location, the planner can easily track what is the current load at the CMA against the available contracted capacity (see Fig. 4.4). We saved the CMA simulation as a scenario within the new channel version so that we can compare it against the baseline.

The CMA might seem a very good option, but there are also disadvantages associated with it: the company will lose from its flexibility to react to demand changes and will have to increase inventory levels as the contract manufacturer will come with greater lead times and lead-time variability. To have an assessment of the impact on the inventory levels, the simulation could be continued using the IBP inventory operators. But we keep this example for a later chapter.

Wrapping the analysis for the strategic planning can be done using the analytics app to highlight a comparison between versions and/or scenarios (see Fig. 4.5).

4.1 Strategic Planning

LT Operating Profit projection

- 2017: Base Version 283.61K
- 2018: Base Version 317.44K; New Channel/CMA Scenario 362.50K
- 2019: Base Version 348.24K; New Channel/CMA Scenario 427.44K
- 2020: Base Version 375.63K; New Channel/CMA Scenario 562.73K

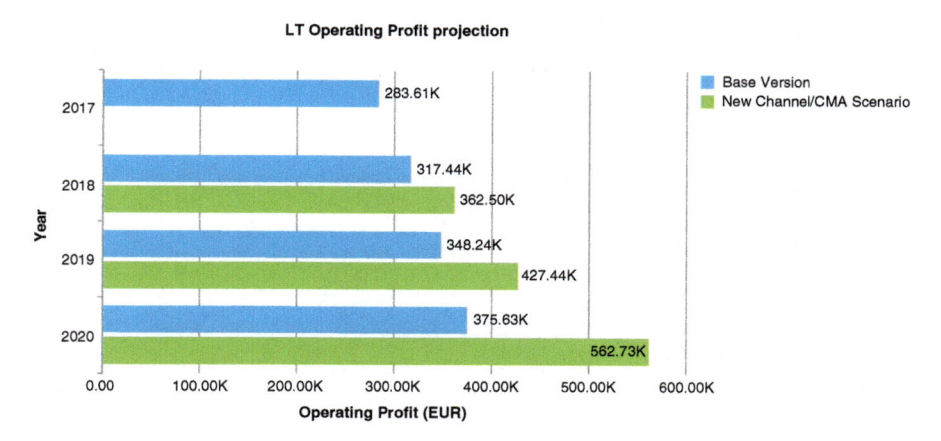

Fig. 4.6 SAP IBP—as-is versus to-be operating profit comparison

Looking at the comparison between the in-house and CMA as options for producing the extra volumes generated by the introduction of the new sales channel, we easily observe that the CMA scenario comes with a higher operating profit.

Bringing together the AS-IS plan which is based only on the growth generated by the current B2B channel and the TO-BE plan based on the channel extension, we see the operating profit growth potential the organization has planned for as per Fig. 4.6.

4.1.2 Improve Strategic Product Demand Planning

In another use case for strategic planning process, we see how SAP IBP can be used to facilitate the alignment between the local and global functions in building the long-term forecast for strategic product or even business line.

In Fig. 4.7, we see a consolidated view across inputs that are provided at different levels of granularity. On one hand, we have the opinion lines provided as top-down by the marketing and business planning global functions. On the other hand, we have the region-/country-specific projections which are provided by country/regional representation.

You should not expect the same opinion between stakeholders about long-term price or volume. Further we go into the futureless facts we have and more assumptions. This is the reason why managing bottom-up and top-down is done on separate inputs without overrides. Comparisons between inputs should expose difference on any level. This way of setting up the process will help you to keep required engagement from all functions providing input.

In Fig. 4.7, we see lines propagated on global (marked none or dark gray) or specific region level (see Region Column). Strategic long-term product planning can be linked to tactical S&OP in various forms as discussed at the beginning of this book.

Business Line	Region	Key Figure	2018	2019	2020
Basic resins	(None)	Global Marketing Qty	58.95K	60.75K	62.30K
	(None)	Global Business Planning Qty	58.26K	59.40K	61.10K
Basic resins	EMEA	Regional/Ctry Marketing Qty	19.10K	20.20K	20.60K
	APAC	Regional/Ctry Marketing Qty	18.00K	19.20K	20.30K
	NALA	Regional/Ctry Marketing Qty	24.00K	24.50K	24.90K
Basic resins --- Total Marketing Qty			61.10K	63.90K	65.80K
Basic resins	(None)	Global Marketing Price	20.0	21.0	22.0
	(None)	Global Business Planning Price	20.0	21.5	23.0
Basic resins	EMEA	Regional/Ctry Marketing Price	21.0	21.0	21.5
	APAC	Regional/Ctry Marketing Price	21.0	22.0	23.0
	NALA	Regional/Ctry Marketing Price	20.5	21.0	22.0
Basic resins --- Average Price			20.8	21.3	22.2
Basic resins	(None)	Global Marketing Rev	$1.18M	$1.28M	$1.37M
	(None)	Global Business Planning Rev	$1.17M	$1.28M	$1.41M
Basic resins	EMEA	Regional/Ctry Marketing Rev	$401.1K	$424.2K	$442.9K
	APAC	Regional/Ctry Marketing Rev	$378.0K	$422.4K	$466.9K
	NALA	Regional/Ctry Marketing Rev	$492.0K	$514.5K	$547.8K
Basic resins --- Total Marketing Rev			$1.3M	$1.4M	$1.5M

Fig. 4.7 SAP IBP—global and regional marketing forecast for strategic business lines

4.2 Tactical S&OP

4.2.1 Improve Focus with Segmentation

Segmentation can be used to improve focus and introduce differentiation of efforts being invested in the process.

Segmentation can be used to segment:

- Products or any attribute linked to it
- Customers or any attributed linked to it
- Services
- Any dimension of your data model which holds relevant data for segmentation purposes, e.g., formulations linked to products, sales representatives linked to customers, customer groups linked to customer, etc.

Let us take a business process use case where a specific company was using segmentation to differentiate their forecasting and demand planning with the use of product segmentation.

On the one hand, in this project, we wanted to differentiate products by the profit contribution it has. This particular measure was aligned to business strategy to enable profitable growth. On the other hand, we wanted to differentiate process by how hard it is to predict forecast or how variable forecast error is. This particular measure was aligned to one of the voices of the customer (internal one in that case) requirement to spend less time on predictable items.

4.2 Tactical S&OP

We have defined requirements for bidimensional product segmentation. In SAP IBP terminology, segmentation was based on two different key figures. In this segmentation approach, we used profit contribution classified in ABC and forecast error variability classified in XYZ measure.

Let us shortly discuss rationale of selecting measures for ABCD/XYZ product segmentation.

ABCD:

- Align your segmentation to forecasted SKU profit position for selected future horizon.
- Drive focus based on profits or revenue or volume.
- Incorporate new product positioning based on their forecasted profit.
- Leverage sales, marketing, demand planning, and finance insights and knowledge captured in your consensus forecasted profit.
- Enable selection of an appropriate horizon and time, which drives connection to your profitability.
- Enables tailored differentiation (different ways of working for different segments).

XYZ:

- Enrich your segmentation with forecast error variation which can describe process stability and process predictability.
- Enrich focus based on how good your process is in predicting future.
- Incorporate new product positioning based on their success rate.
- Leverage your process output maturity driven by process, people, and technology.

ABCD/XYZ matrix is visualized in Fig. 4.8.

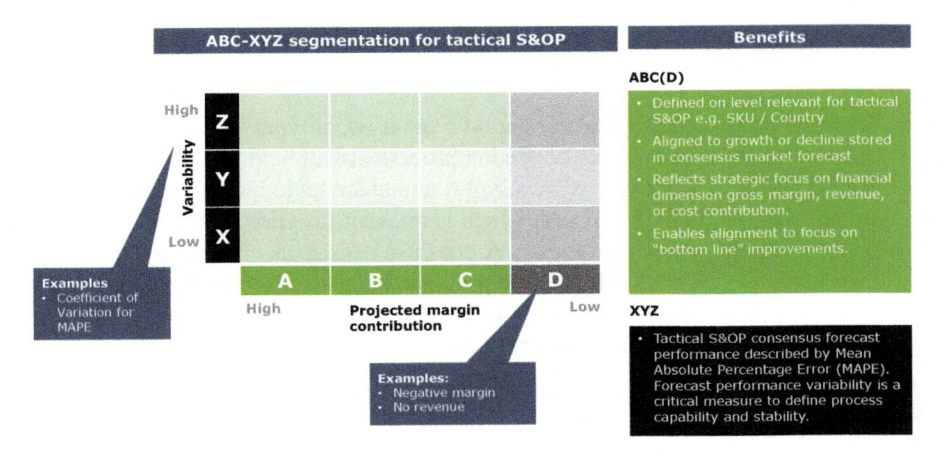

Fig. 4.8 ABC"D"/XYZ segmentation

Let us characterize parameters for ABCD/XYZ portfolio segmentation in more detail.

ABCD level:

- Geographical: Specific business unit/country.
- Example on country S&OP process: The objective will be to facilitate local process and improve country/market focus on profitability.
- Material hierarchy level: Sellable SKUs. Normally in company definition, there are SKUs which you do not sell; select the ones which you do sell and forecast. You may apply filters to select the right portfolio for your segmentation.

ABCD measure:

- Integrated business plan profit may be used as a measure to drive ABCD dimension of your segmentation.
- Integrated Business Plan Profit = Integrated Business Plan Volume * Forecasted Margin; assuming unit margin multiplied by volume equals profit.
- This measure needs to be configured in your system first.

ABCD thresholds: (for data sorted descending)

- A products: $0\% \leq A \leq 80\%$.
- B products: $80\% < B \leq 95\%$.
- C products: $95\% < C \leq 100\%$.
- D products: Non-moving products where the forecasted volume or forecasted margin is set to zero (or negative) or the ones decided by the marketing department to be withdrawn from your offering. In this segment there might be SKUs popping up where you lose money (expressed by negative margin). This segment requires special attention especially from your company's overall product offering perspective.

ABCD timing:

- It would make sense to select a period around which your forecasting might be used as input for next year's budgeting process. It will help you to align in some way portfolio positioning between your annual strategic budgeting process and monthly tactical S&OP, in cycle which is relevant for your business.
- Example: In September, Company A does use consensus unconstrained forecast as primary input for their budgeting process. Agreed consensus forecast is being integrated with their budgeting application.
- Example: You may think as well to run portfolio before and after the main season.

ABCD horizon:

- It needs to fit the purpose of reflecting forward looking but not the short but view which is aligned as much as possible to your strategic view.

4.2 Tactical S&OP

- Example: If you are starting your budgeting period in August/September and use forecast as a baseline input, it would make sense to use forecast from September of the current year until the end of the next year at minimum.
- Example: You may think as well to run portfolio before and after the main season with horizon linked to in season and after season. You could select your season months and run product segmentation to support strategies and tactics defined for it and then after the season recalculate to change the focus.

XYZ level:

- Commercial or geographical hierarchy level: Alignment to process measurement level.
- Material hierarchy level: Sellable SKUs. Normally in company definition, there are SKUs which you do not sell and select the ones which you do sell and forecast. You may apply filters to select the right portfolio for your segmentation.

XYZ measure:

- You have quite a few options here, since there are plenty of measures which will help to assess variability or in statistical terms capability of your process. You may use specific measure and run coefficient of variation (CoV) for it.
- Let's briefly discuss two measures used in segmentation wMAPE.
- wMAPE is a well-known and an established measure described in the following formula:

$$\text{weighted\_MAPE} = \left(\frac{\sum |\text{Forecast} - \text{Sales}|}{\sum \text{Sales}}\right) \text{ or }$$
$$\text{weighted\_MAPE}\left(\frac{\sum |\text{Absolute Error}|}{\sum \text{Sales}}\right).$$

XYZ thresholds:

Your wMAPE can be used as input key figure for calculation of variability of this measure. If wMAPE is more variable, then it means your forecasting process is very unstable and delivers results that are not reliable. From a process improvement perspective, it is better that errors may be high but are not jumping up and down compared to medium but very erratic. CoV is a measure which is defined as standard deviation to mean of selected input.

XYZ timing should be aligned to ABCD timing of product segmentation process execution.

XYZ horizon and input:

- Recommended 1 year or horizon between product segmentation cycles
- Integrated business plan performance measured with wMAPE

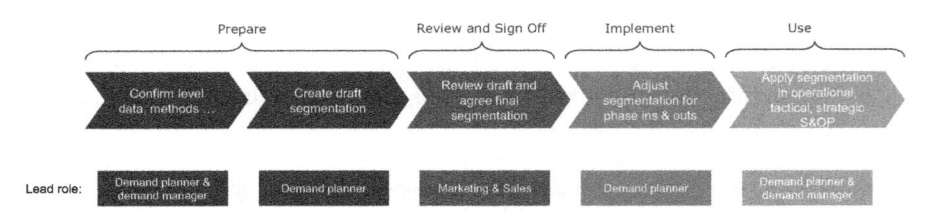

Fig. 4.9 ABC/XYZ segmentation process framework

Fig. 4.10 SAP IBP—ABC segmentation (1)

ABCD/XYZ process is visualized in Fig. 4.9.

Process framework for ABC/XYZ can be defined with the use of collaboration features in SAP IBP. Based on the calculated values, there must be review and sign off process; but it should only be linked to ABCD, you should not change value for XYZ. We strongly recommend not to overwrite any values coming from your measurement used as proxy for XYZ, except for new products for which we would assign automatically to Z and review calculation after a few months. Once agreement is achieved, it would need to be recorded in attribute which you would like to make editable for that purpose. Prepared segmentation should be treated as an input to define differentiated ways of working.

SAP IBP segmentation profile provides definitions for ABC and XYZ.

You can define ABC input key figure as revenue, profit, or volume or any other which makes sense from a business perspective (see Fig. 4.10).

Then you define thresholds for ABC.

Thresholds will help to make appropriate focus (see Fig. 4.11). D classification has to be defined manually by user.

In a similar way, XYZ is being defined. Segmentation measure can be consensus forecast, integrated business plan, or key figure which expresses performance, e.g., wMAPE (Fig. 4.12).

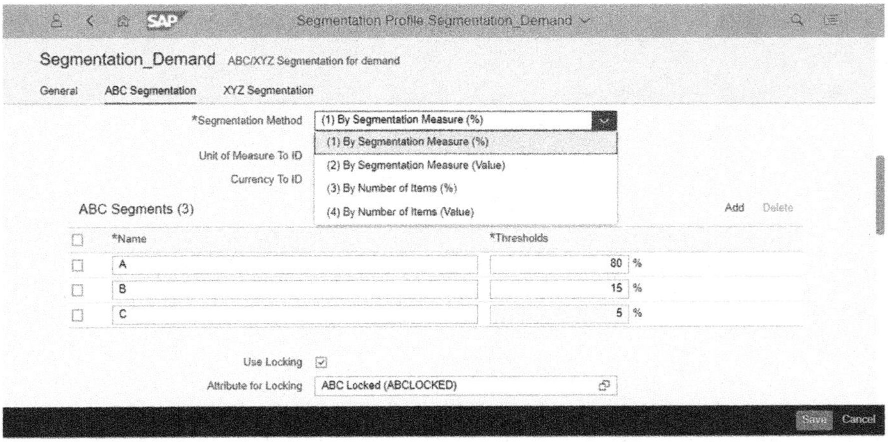

4.2 Tactical S&OP

Fig. 4.11 SAP IBP—ABC segmentation (2)

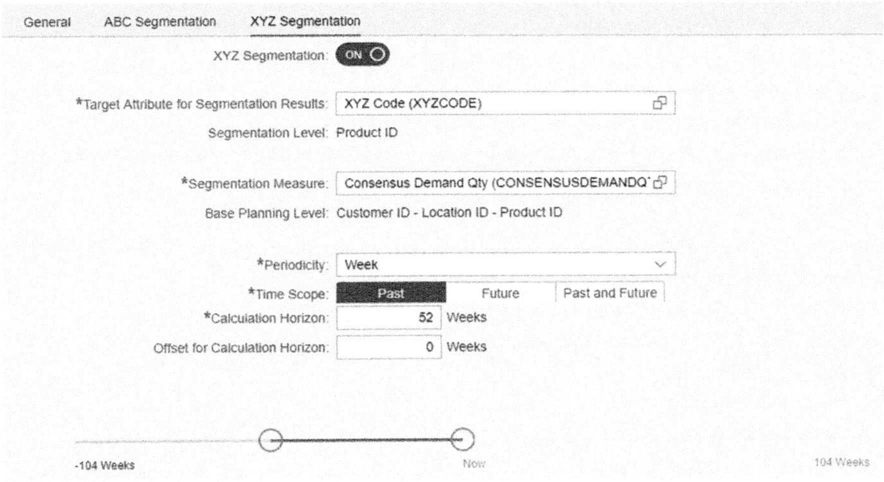

Fig. 4.12 SAP IBP—XYZ segmentation configuration (1)

While in ABC we had various classification methods to choose from, XYZ is using only one measure, namely, the coefficient of variation (CV), also known as relative standard deviation. Coefficient of variation is a measure calculated as standard deviation divided with mean of data series. For CoV you would need to define thresholds (Fig. 4.13).

ABCD/XYZ product segmentation may serve you as basis for correlation of measures which describe situation in broader IBP context.

It would make sense to correlate different supply chains or display measures aggregated to year to date or year over year. Matrix could be used as an instrument to assess specific point in time situation but not how situation did develop over time.

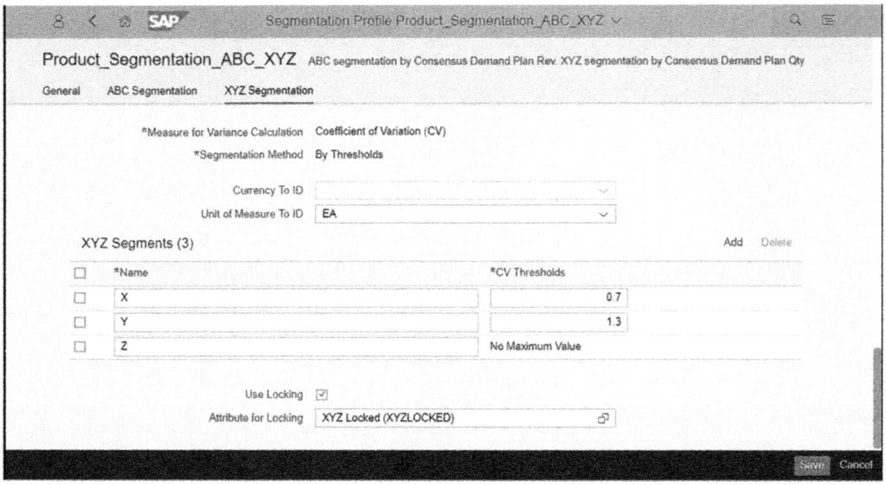

Fig. 4.13 SAP IBP—XYZ segmentation configuration (2)

SAP IBP unified planning area opens doors for much easier access to key performance indicators. Some say more is not always better, but in this case, more accessibility and more data give you a better view.

Here are some hints on how to design your cross-functional dashboards and move from alert to action.

Step 1: Display measures which bring demand, supply, and finance together and display them against ABCD/XYZ matrix, e.g.:
– Inventory forward cover
– Full year IBP vs full year budget realization projection
– No. of stock outs
– Forecast wMAPE
– Forecast bias
– No. of forecasted events

Step 2: Correlate measure values even with simple "visual stacking"; try to find a pattern or logical connection between values and segments. Some correlated values of performance indicators may give you logical meaning, while some may not always fit, but the most important is to find a pattern.

Step3: Define actions to be taken.

ABC/XYZ matrix visualization could be as per Fig. 4.14.

Let's shortly analyze the example of correlation of measures presented against ABCD/XYZ matrix.

Segment X: Good forecast error and low inventory forward cover vs low full year prediction of budget realization and low no. of events coordinated by sales/marketing suggest that we might have been good in the past, but recently stock outs went up, and forward-looking picture requires more demand-shaping activities since gap to budget is significant.

4.2 Tactical S&OP

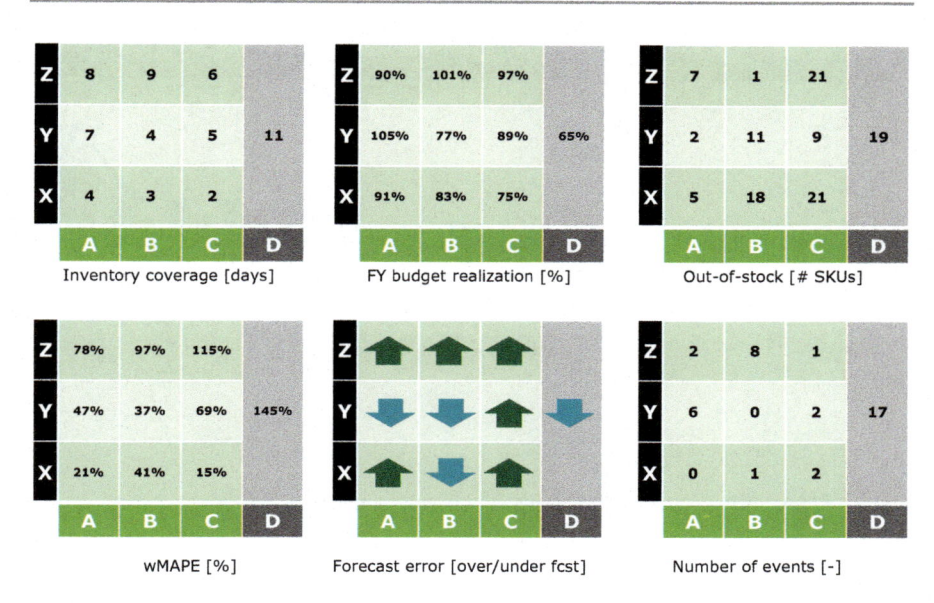

Fig. 4.14 ABC/XYZ used to correlate metrics

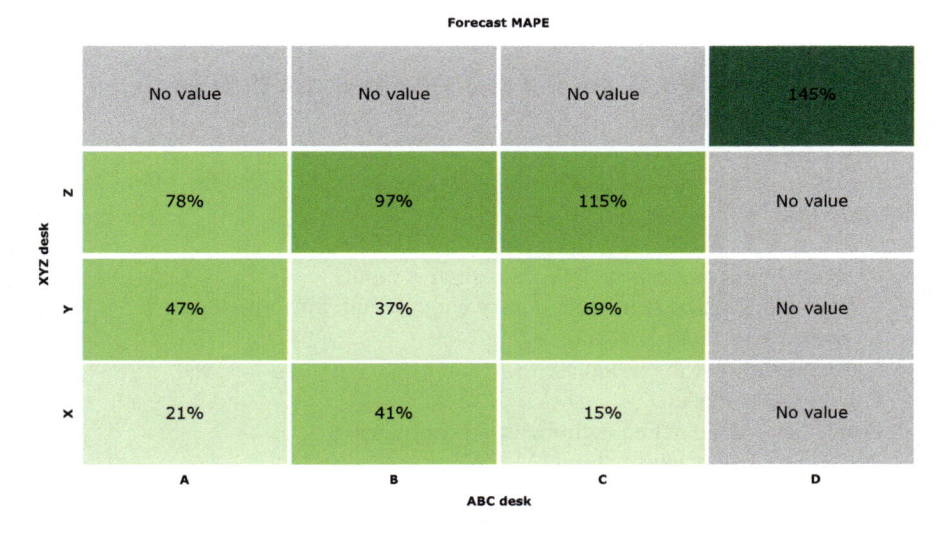

Fig. 4.15 SAP IBP—ABC"D"/XYZ matrix for MAPE

You will find SAP IBP representation (Fig. 4.15) which does leverage the heat map capability of analytics app on WEB UI; it does show forecast MAPE displayed against ABC/XYZ product segmentation attribute values.

There are many more use cases for ABC/XYZ; one very common is to use segmentation to prioritize demand review meeting like per Fig. 4.16.

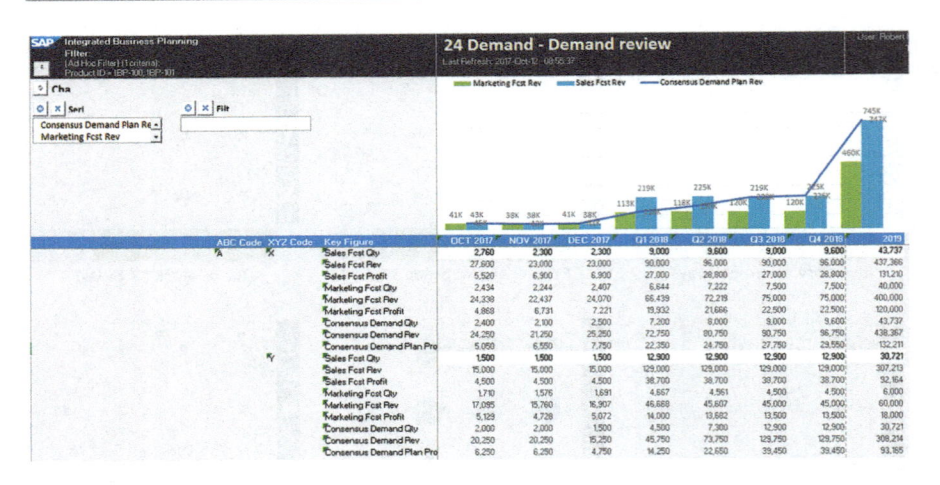

Fig. 4.16 SAP IBP—ABC/XYZ segmentation in demand review

You can define review process which results in consensus forecast per ABC classification with subcategorization by XYZ.

4.2.2 Improve Efficiency and Effectiveness with Differentiated Forecasting

Many of us experienced that forecasting and demand planning often can be characterized by:

- Workload intensive especially for qualitative inputs.
- Sales and marketing team do not have enough time for forecasting.
- Overrated basic statistical forecasting.
- Large portfolio of the products.
- Few business models.
- Problematic since not enough focus was introduced.
- Performing below expectations.

Many have faced challenges on how to:

- Distinguish promotion signal from baseline demand and product mix shifts in volume.
- Find the right balance between statistical forecasting and collaborative bottom-up inputs from demand organization.
- Make stakeholders more accountable for forecast accuracy (Steutermann, Scott, & Tohamy, 2012).

4.2 Tactical S&OP

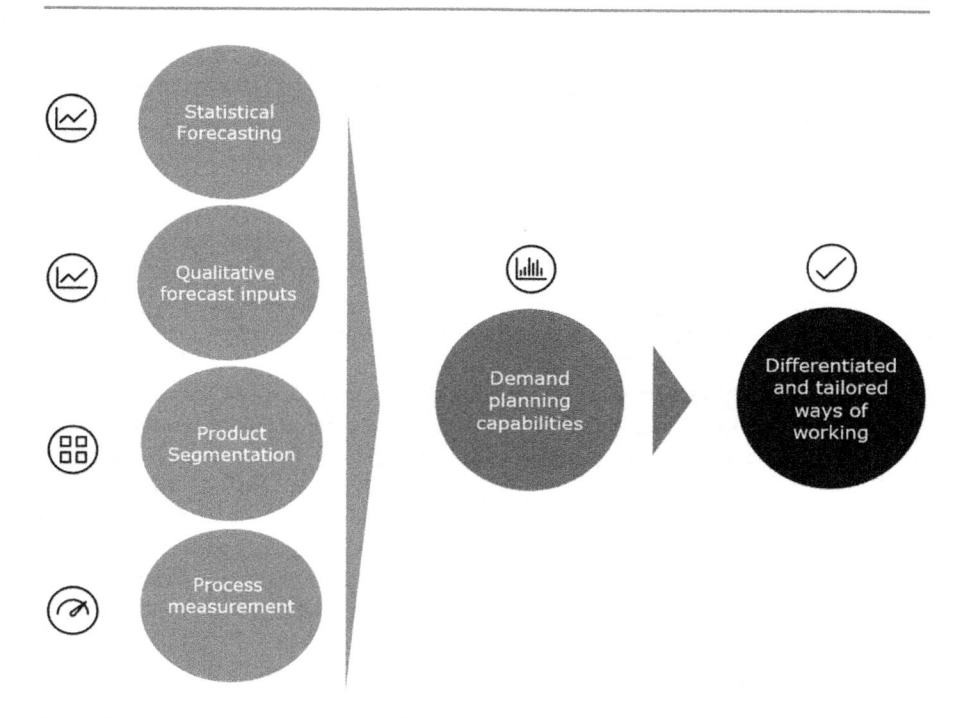

Fig. 4.17 Differentiated forecasting building blocks

How to turn it around and how to become more efficient and effective in your forecasting and demand planning process? To increase process efficiency and effectiveness, you should walk away from "one-size-fits-all" forecasting and build "differentiated forecasting and demand planning" which is really about introduction of tailored ways of working for different product segments.

Differentiated forecasting consists of elements as per Fig. 4.17:

- Qualitative input provided by various functions: sales, marketing, demand planning, and sometimes business development should provide forecast input aligned to best insights.
- Statistical forecasting: functional system capabilities of basic and advanced statistical forecasting supported by demand planners or data scientists.
- Product segmentation: instrument which will help you to introduce focus on right materials, in a way to be aligned to your strategic objectives (e.g., revenue or profitable growth).
- Process measurement: measurement of all forecasting inputs (qualitative, quantitative) and consensus unconstrained forecast with agreed parameters aligned to S&OP characteristics.

- Demand planning capabilities: analytical and communication skills; for full set of capabilities and skills, please refer to relevant chapter at the beginning of the book.

Segmentation of product portfolio by criteria such as "volume, predictability, channel/customer, promotional and seasonal items" with assigned forecasting type accordingly seem to be very important. Combination of collaborative approach and statistical forecasting is key (Steutermann, Scott, & Tohamy, 2012).

Rationale for differentiated forecasting, tailored ways of working:

- Balance which function you ask for what type of input. Does it not sound like a waste of time to ask marketing and sales to provide input for extremely easy-to-forecast stable portfolio which has minor impact on revenue or profitable growth? Can demand planning be responsible for forecasting low value contribution/high predictability product segments? Demand Planners should be doing this but sales and marketing should review it on aggregated level to make process efficient.
- Sales team does not need to provide input for all SKUs/customers. Why not leave in their forecasting portfolio those forecasting combinations which are critical to the business?
- Sales or marketing should own sales forecast, but process design and process improvement should be done by demand planning. Sales and marketing could focus on their core activities and gain time for selling.
- Time being gained from transformation to "differentiated forecasting" can be leveraged for selling, analytical support, development of business risks and opportunities, etc., in other words in more value-adding activities. Demand planning plays a crucial role in optimizing time being spent on forecasting. This function has to make this change happening.
- Once you have most of the building blocks in place, it is most probably inevitable to consider introduction of target setting. Target setting should be done based on a segment or at least groups of segments, so-called blended targets.

ABC/XYZ visualization matrix shown in Fig. 4.8 is a foundation of differentiated forecasting and can make an impact on how you organize your demand review process, e.g., bottom-up, top-down qualitative forecast inputs, statistical forecasting, and demand review preparation.

In Fig. 4.18, there is an example on how you can leverage differentiated forecasting concept:

1. Define leading and supplementary techniques, e.g., input from sales and marketing (S&M), statistical forecasting (STAT), and input from marketing (M).
2. Set forecast performance targets in a more tailored way.
3. Share responsibility across different functions to provide forecast.

4.2 Tactical S&OP

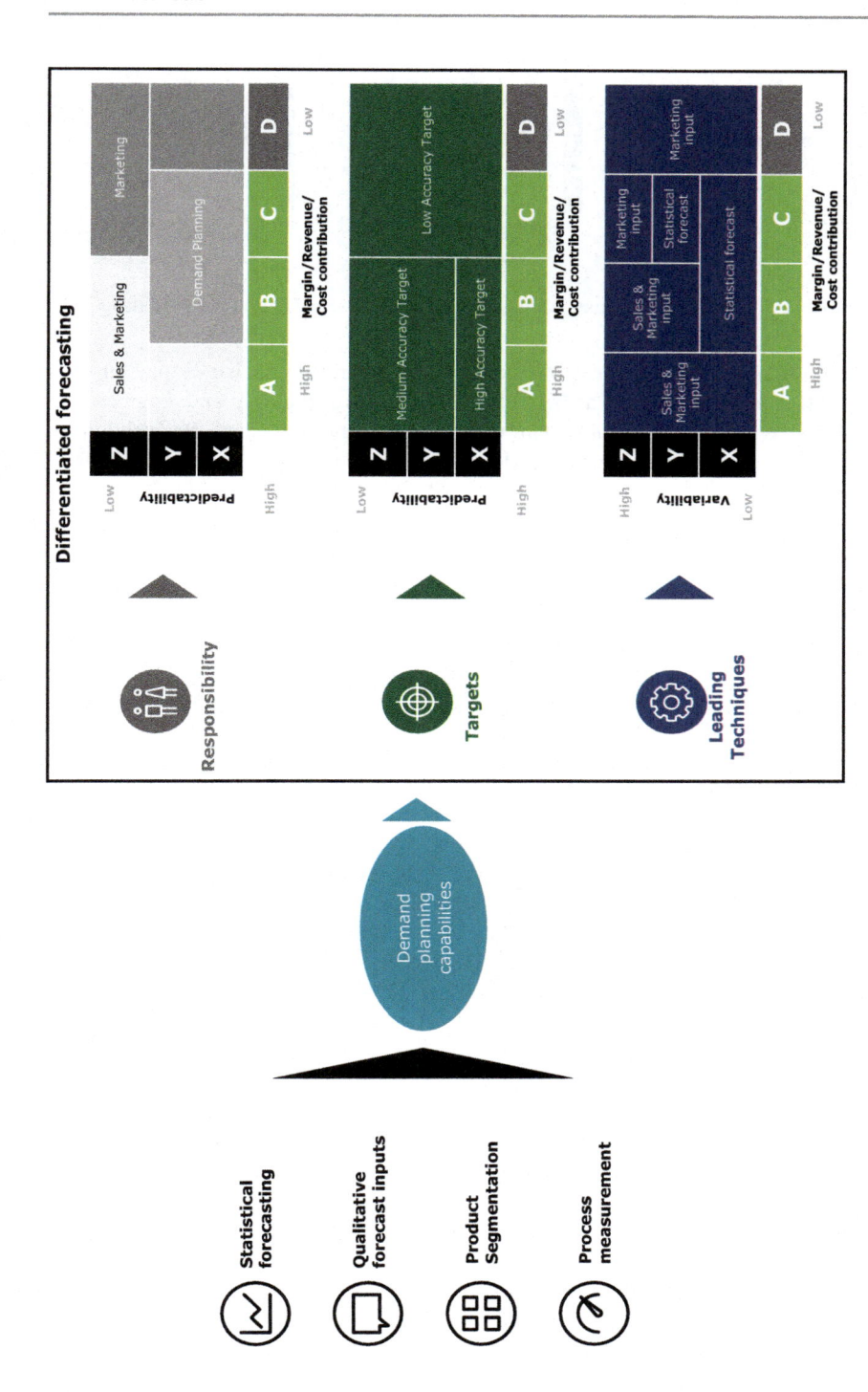

Fig. 4.18 Differentiated forecasting deep dive

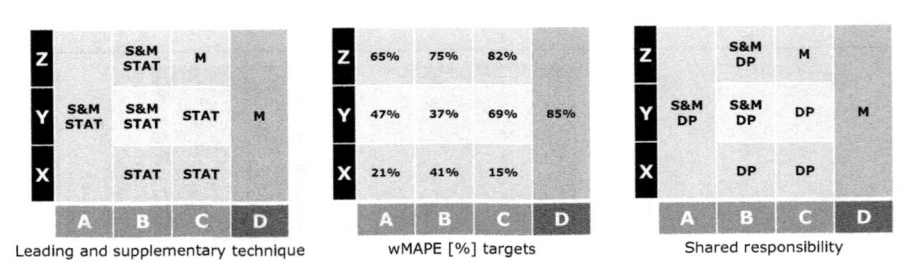

Fig. 4.19 Differentiated forecasting leading techniques, targets, and shared responsibilities

Definition of leading forecasting technique should result in a list of qualitative or quantitative methods agreed as being the leading one or the only one. Segment BX and CX may be forecasted only with the use of statistical forecast, but it should be reviewed maybe even on aggregated level in demand review.

Shared responsibility should result in a better balance of workload for input, review, and analysis of the forecast between sales, marketing, and demand planning. It would make sense to allocate forecasting of certain group of products to demand planning but still keeping those segments under review in demand review meeting.

Last but not least is the topic of forecasting performance targets. Targets in differentiated forecasting should be established with a lot of sensitivity, and they should be shared between stakeholder group of sales, marketing, and demand planning. Targets should be challenging but realistic; therefore, you should start your target preparation with data analysis of your past performance. Do not start from visionary target without knowing your current performance. Performance targets need to be prepared based on historical performance with identification of ABC/XYZ; you should analyze time series and full year view. Differentiated error targets should be set across portfolio.

Once all of the differentiated forecasting building blocks are in place, you will be able to map the whole solution against ABC/XYZ matrix as per Fig. 4.19.

Let's see how we can leverage the above concept in SAP IBP.

We have learned in the previous use case who can build segmentation. With the use of segmentation, we will define different ways of balanced workload efforts, product importance, and demand patterns. Let us extend this to the other components of differentiated forecasting.

4.2.2.1 Effective Forecasting Strategies

In this use case, we will generate consensus forecast based on forecasting strategies.

The forecasting strategy will be defined as a characteristic (attribute) of the product/country and will be maintained against ABC/XYZ segmentation (as per Fig. 4.20).

We have defined the following strategies (see Fig. 4.21):

4.2 Tactical S&OP

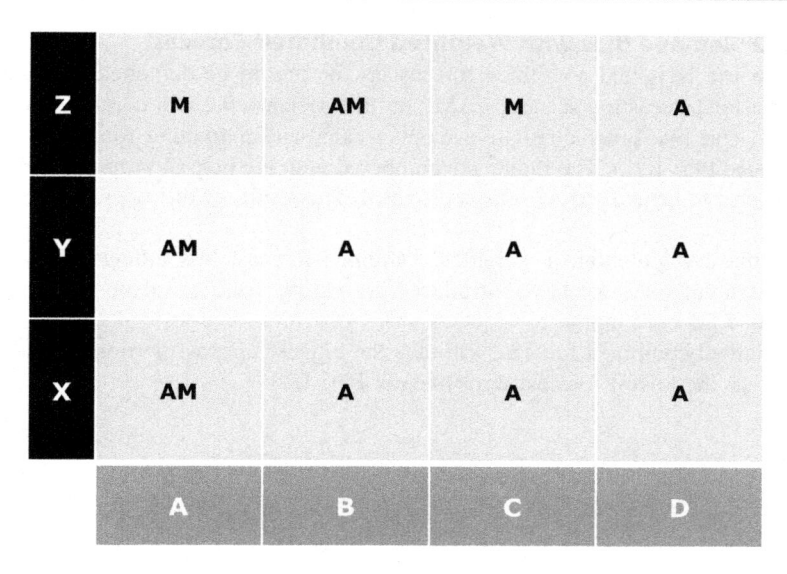

	A	B	C	D
Z	M	AM	M	A
Y	AM	A	A	A
X	AM	A	A	A

Fig. 4.20 Forecasting strategies of matrix visualization

Product ID	Customer ID	ABC Code	XYZ Code	Planning Strategy	Key Figure	17-Jan	17-Feb	17-Mar	17-Apr	17-May	17-Jun	17-Jul	17-Aug	17-Sep	17-Oct	17-Nov	17-Dec	2017
IBP-100	CA01	A	X	AM	Statistical Fcst Qty	127K	125K	132K	129K	143K	143K	143K	143K	143K	143K	143K	143K	1.7M
					Demand Planner Input	141K	120K	116K	131K	136K	116K	146K	117K	114K	147K	116K	132K	1.5M
					Demand Planning Fcst Qty (Computed)	134K	123K	124K	130K	140K	130K	144K	130K	128K	145K	129K	137K	1.6M
IBP-110	CE01	B	X	A	Statistical Fcst Qty	220K	203K	228K	222K	240K	240K	240K	240K	240K	240K	240K	240K	2.8M
					Demand Planner Input													
					Demand Planning Fcst Qty (Computed)	220K	203K	228K	222K	240K	240K	240K	240K	240K	240K	240K	240K	2.8M
IBP-120	CU01	A	Z	M	Statistical Fcst Qty	273K	231K	257K	272K	282K	282K	282K	282K	282K	282K	282K	282K	3.3M
					Demand Planner Input	296K	224K	224K	274K	244K	238K	287K	220K	242K	274K	235K	260K	3.0M
					Demand Planning Fcst Qty (Computed)	296K	224K	224K	274K	244K	238K	287K	220K	242K	274K	235K	260K	3.0M

Fig. 4.21 SAP IBP—forecasting strategies in differentiated forecasting concept

- "A" (Automatic): Consensus forecast defaulted from Statistical Fcst Qty. For "CX" products with small volatility and low profit contribution, consensus forecast will be defaulted from statistical forecast.
- "AM"—(Automatic and Manual): Consensus forecast is calculated based on statistical Fcst Qty and the manual input(s). In our example, we combined statistical forecast with demand planner input, but you can combine statistical forecast with many inputs (sales, marketing, demand planning) and use weighted combined forecast concept to combined methods. For "XY" products due to its importance, we decided to combine quantitative and qualitative inputs.
- "M" (Manual): Consensus forecast in our example will be defaulted to demand planner input but can as well be defined as other or combination of inputs.

4.2.2.2 Remove Bias with Weighted Combined Forecast

We can use weighted combined forecast as the one to be defaulted to consensus forecast for forecasting strategy "AM." In this scenario we will combine statistical forecast and two other qualitative inputs—sales and marketing forecasts, respectively (see Fig. 4.22). The inputs are combined with the help of purpose-configured key figures to generate a consensus proposal. The results of this scenario are shown below.

To make calculation of weighted combined forecast less influenced by single forecast input bias, we have introduced weighting done based on forecast error calculated for each input.

Weighted combined forecast will take the biggest forecast portion from the one which has the lowest forecast error like per Fig. 4.23.

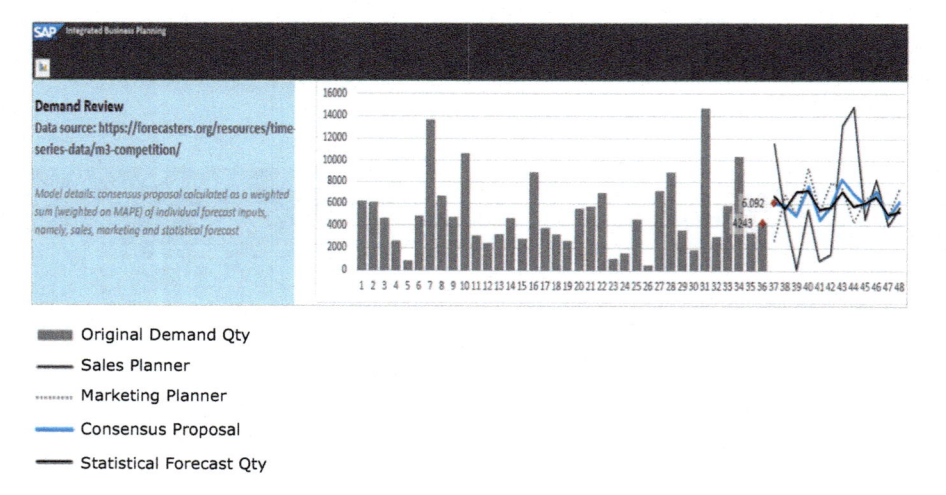

Fig. 4.22 SAP IBP—consensus forecast calculated as weighted combined forecast

Product ID	Customer ID	Key Figure	JUN 2017	JUL 2017	AUG 2017	SEP 2017	OCT 2017	NOV 2017	DEC 2017	JAN 2018	FEB 2018
IBP_P003	IBP_C001	Original Demand Quantity	10380	3360	4243	2542	5512	9277	7113	4367	16477
IBP_P003	IBP_C001	Cleaned Demand Quantity	10380	3360	4243						
IBP_P003	IBP_C001	Ex-post Forecast Qty	7008	6948	6314						
IBP_P003	IBP_C001	Statistical Fcst Qty				6700	5513	7096	7125	5395	5622
IBP_P003	IBP_C001	Sales Planner				11495	4700	106	5408	907	1410
IBP_P003	IBP_C001	Marketing Planner				2717	6764	4825	9290	5220	7937
IBP_P003	IBP_C001	MAPE Statistical	55,59	55,59	55,59	55,59	55,59	55,59	55,59	55,59	55,59
IBP_P003	IBP_C001	MAPE SALES				80,00	80,00	80,00	80,00	80,00	80,00
IBP_P003	IBP_C001	MAPE MARKETING				60,00	60,00	60,00	60,00	60,00	60,00
IBP_P003	IBP_C001	MAPE TOTAL				104	104	104	104	104	104
IBP_P003	IBP_C001	WMAPE STATISTICAL				42,54%	42,54%	42,54%	42,54%	42,54%	42,54%
IBP_P003	IBP_C001	WMAPE SALES				19,15%	19,15%	19,15%	19,15%	19,15%	19,15%
IBP_P003	IBP_C001	WMAPE MARKETING				38,31%	38,31%	38,31%	38,31%	38,31%	38,31%
IBP_P003	IBP_C001	Consensus Proposal				6092	5837	4887	7625	4468	5702

Fig. 4.23 SAP IBP—automatic MAPE weighting in weighted combined forecast

4.2 Tactical S&OP

Demand Planner	SKU	Country	Planning Strategy	Key Figure	17-Jan	17-Feb	17-Mar	17-Apr	17-May	17-Jun	17-Jul	17-Aug	17-Sep	17-Oct	17-Nov	17-Dec	2017
Amparo Rippolles	IBP-100	Spain	SM	Sales Fcst Qty	127K	125K	132K	129K	143K	143K	143K	143K	143K	143K	143K	143K	1.7M
				Weighting factor - Sales Fcst Qty	0.6	0.6	0.6	0.6	0.6	0.4	0.4	0.4	0.4	0.4	0.4	0.4	0.4
				Marketing Fcst Qty	141K	120K	116K	131K	136K	116K	146K	117K	114K	147K	116K	132K	1.5M
				Weighting factor - Marketing Fcst Qty	0.4	0.4	0.4	0.4	0.4	0.6	0.6	0.6	0.6	0.6	0.6	0.6	0.6
				Consensus Demand Qty	133K	123K	125K	130K	140K	127K	145K	127K	125K	146K	126K	136K	1.58M
				Ovr Consensus Demand Qty						132K		142K					274K
				Final Consensus Demand Qty	133K	123K	125K	132K	140K	127K	142K	127K	125K	146K	126K	136K	1.58M

Fig. 4.24 SAP IBP—manual weighting in WCF with overrides

The other way to address same solution for "AM" forecasting strategy is to combine inputs based on manually provided weighting. In the example below, demand planner should ensure we have weights of specific forecast input (sales, marketing) maintained. Based on forecast inputs from sales, marketing, other functions, statistical forecast, and weights, consensus forecast can be automatically calculated. As part of the process, you may want to introduce some special adjustments which can influence final consensus demand qty (see Fig. 4.24).

4.2.2.3 Make Process Effective with Statistical Forecasting

Effective and efficient differentiated forecasting depends in large extent on how we will use statistical forecasting. Statistical forecasting methods and algorithms are associated with different costs but as well with different values they bring.

See Fig. 4.25 for trade-offs between cost of inaccuracy and cost of sophistication (forecasting costs).

On one end of the spectrum, we have advanced models that impose high forecasting costs, but incur low inaccuracy costs. On the other end are models that are fairly simplistic and therefore are inexpensive to use (easier to set up and maintain), but incur higher inaccuracy costs. A key cost driver when it comes to model choice is the data requirements. For example, causal models require data for independent variables or causal factors that influence the dependent variable or the fact that is being estimated. The right choice involves optimizing total relevant costs—a choice that should land us in the region circled in Fig. 4.25. The first rule of forecasting, which is often repeated, is that forecast is always an error. It is important to remember this and to not be dazzled by sophistication and also to not confuse sophistication with automation. The focus should be "acceptable accuracy" (Mulllick Satinder, 1971).

Forecasting models which are available in SAP IBP are listed in Fig. 4.26. A qualitative estimation of forecasting cost is also provided.

SAP plans to extend forecasting models and techniques, e.g., with ARIMA; see official SAP IBP roadmap.

In Fig. 4.27 you will find correlation of statistical forecasting and analytics sophistication with service level, inventory level being improved. This particular transformation project was focused on making forecasting market-driven, with usage of statistical forecasting and analytics (Desmet & Sterckx, 2012).

As you can see from the above, adding sophistication to your forecasting methods and building new capabilities and skills pay off.

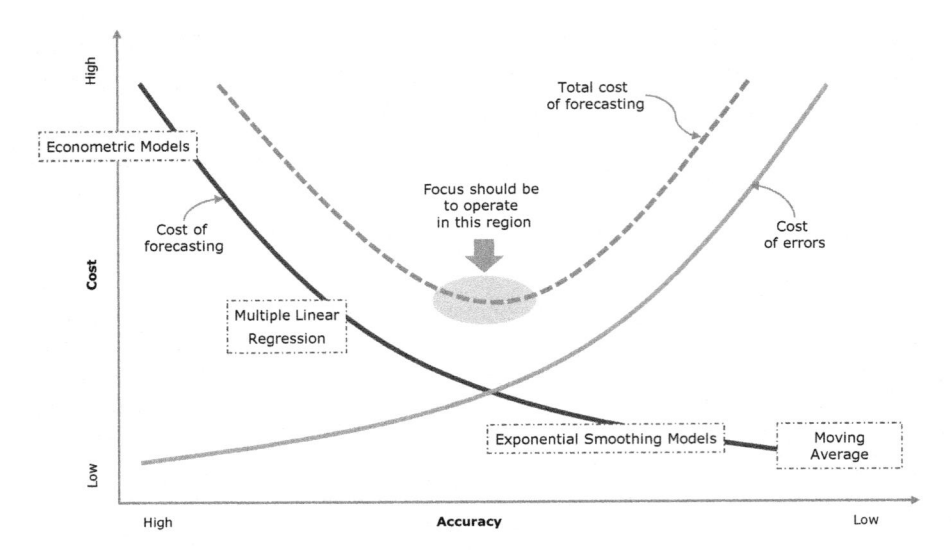

Fig. 4.25 Select an appropriate statistical forecasting model

IBP Algorithm	Algorithm Type	Forecasting Cost
Simple Average	Time-Series / Constant	Low
Simple Moving Average	Time-Series / Constant	Low
Weighted Average	Time-Series / Constant	Low
Weighted Moving Average	Time-Series / Constant	Low
Single Exponential Smoothing	Time-Series / Constant	Low
Adaptive-Response-Rate Single Exponential Smoothing	Time-Series / Constant / Adaptive	Low
Double Exponential Smoothing	Time-Series / Trend	Medium
Triple Exponential Smoothing	Time-Series / Seasonal	Medium
Automated Exponential Smoothing	Time-Series / Automatic Detection / Adaptive	Medium
Croston Method	Time-Series / Intermittent	Medium
Multiple Linear Regression	Causal	High

Fig. 4.26 SAP IBP—algorithms in 2017 release

4.2 Tactical S&OP

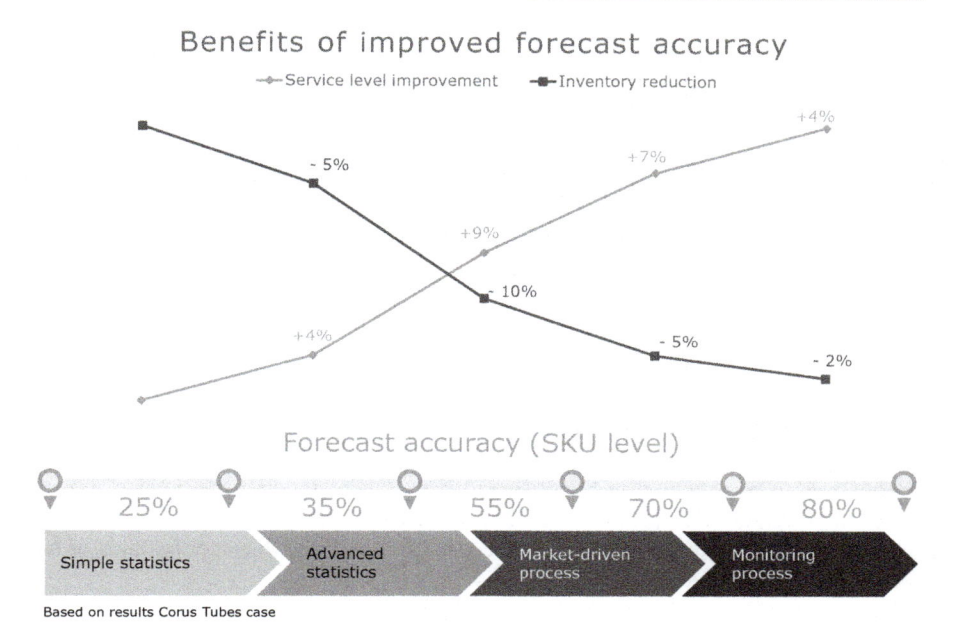

Fig. 4.27 Statistical forecasting methods vs impact of service and inventory level

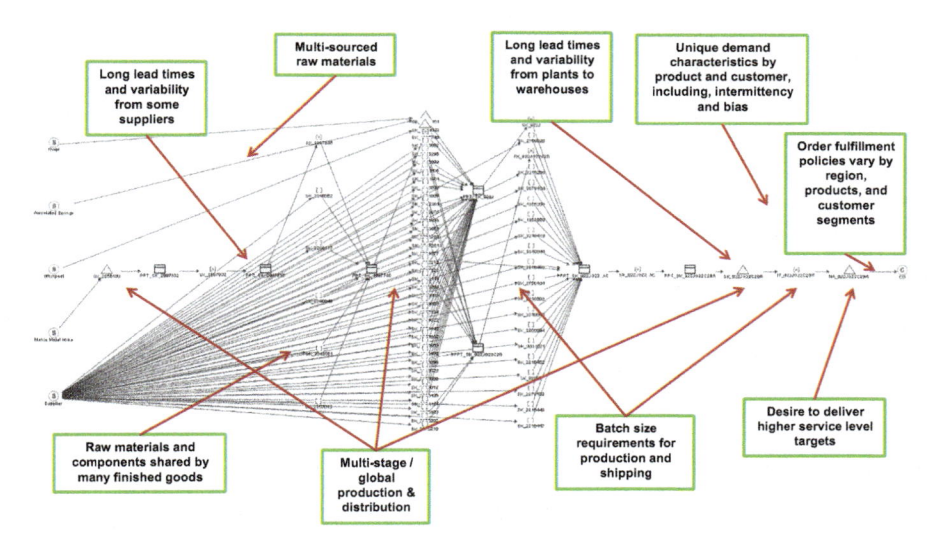

Fig. 4.28 Supply chain network and typical inventory optimization touchpoints

4.2.3 Improve Availability with Safety Stock Planning

When we look at Fig. 4.28, it becomes quite obvious why inventory optimization is needed and why it is more and more difficult.

Fig. 4.29 Types of inventory

Supply chain networks become more complex and sometimes evolve from one large network to set of connected subnetworks. Taking into consideration demand and supply variability which exist across the entire network(s) is an exercise which is impossible to be executed in Excel spreadsheet. Understanding the types of inventory, their drivers become non-Excel spreadsheet exercise; their coexistence and corelation should become a key task not only of the supply manager but also of the demand manager and finance controller.

Let us briefly define types and drivers of inventory visualized in Fig. 4.29.

Safety stock is:

- Maintained to avoid stock-out conditions due to demand and supply uncertainty
- Aims to provide a cushion for the exceptional scenario and not to be used as replenishment strategy

Safety stock drivers are:

- Demand
- Demand uncertainty
- Lead times
- Lead-time uncertainty
- Review frequency
- Service level targets
- Service times

Cycle stock is:

- Average amount of inventory required to meet customer demand
- Decreases with consumption against demand

Cycle stock drivers are:

- Demand
- Review frequency

4.2 Tactical S&OP

- Batch sizes
- Production rules

Pipeline stock is:

- Stock in-transit
- Increases with the additional sales volume and with longer lead times

Pipeline stock drivers are:

- Order processing lead times
- Transit times
- Demand

We see now how those types of inventory are connected to each other. Technology solution will help to cope with complexity of it. SAP IBP helps you to run inventory optimization in two distinct modes.

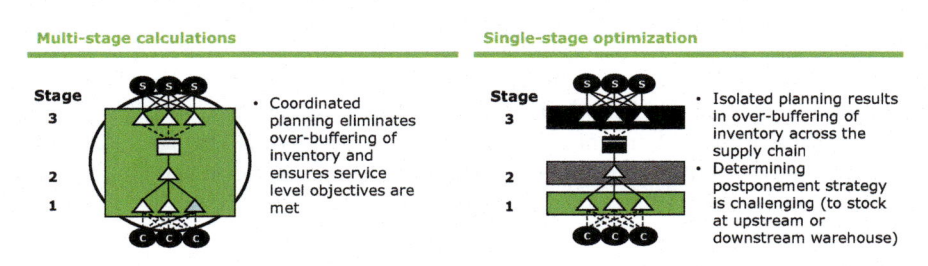

Two types of inventory optimization algorithms are illustrated in Fig. 4.30.

One mode of optimization will check whole network and propose you optimal inventory level considering demand and supply variability mentioned above. This mode is called multistage. The other mode is single-stage optimization which does focus its calculations and proposals for desired level on bill of material (e.g., finished goods only). As the outcome of both calculations, we will see projections of pipeline, cycle, and safety stock for given drivers. Inventory optimization can be done on existing set of parameters or as well with consideration of simulated improvements of IO drivers.

Let us go through how to plan the work with inventory optimization. Typically journey in inventory optimization consists of two steps like in the Fig. 4.31.

4.2.3.1 First Step: Hitting the Curve (Move from A to B)

- Have a correct product segmentation strategy and policy and stick to it.
- Implement inventory visibility/monitoring.
- Identify and reduce current excess.
- Rationalize slow moving/obsolete SKU.
- Optimize targets by SKU/location.
- Optimize customer service levels.

Multi-stage calculations

Stage 3, 2, 1
- Coordinated planning eliminates over-buffering of inventory and ensures service level objectives are met

Single-stage optimization

Stage 3, 2, 1
- Isolated planning results in over-buffering of inventory across the supply chain
- Determining postponement strategy is challenging (to stock at upstream or downstream warehouse)

Fig. 4.30 SAP IBP—inventory optimization algorithms

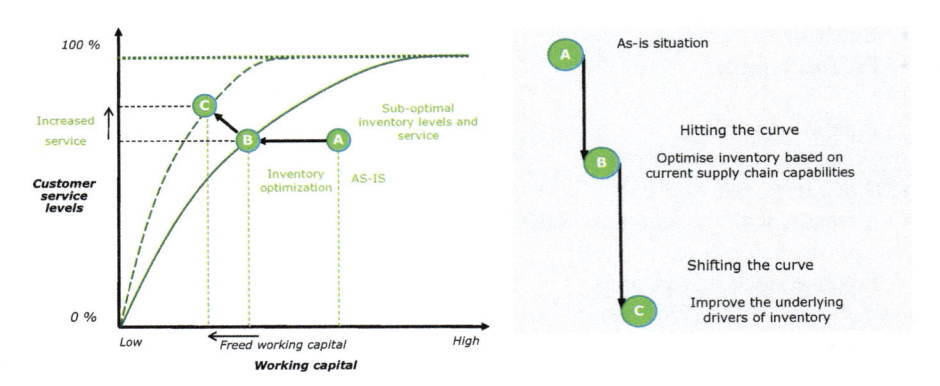

Fig. 4.31 Two steps in inventory optimization

We have recognized that inventory optimization and safety stock planning are very iterative processes, required due to risk and opportunities adjustments in what if scenarios. Behind each of the scenario, normally there are different assumptions like change of service level, change of lead time, change of demand, change of supply variability, etc., all impacting recommended types of stock and proposal of safety stock. Very often, the initial stage of optimization is more about understanding where you are and where the quantifiable and the most obvious and short-term areas of improvements are.

Once you have realized the first step, moving to the second one will be easier from an understanding point of view but not from realization. The second step requires introduction of changes in your processes, network, and supply chain parameters.

4.2.3.2 Second Step: Shifting the Curve (Move from B to C)
- Improve forecasting accuracy.
- Reduce sources of supply variability.
- Reduce lead times, incorporating total cost.
- Refine production run-strategy/shipping.
- Optimize supply network configuration.
- Implement postponement/white stock strategy.

We see that inventory optimization is a cross-functional process. Demand fulfillment is linked to the right positioning of inventory depending on the selected replenishment strategy: MTO, MTS, CTO, ETO, and ATS. Demand management should be involved when defining these strategies (Steutermann, Salley, & Lord, 2012).

We should connect inventory planning to replenishment strategies. Demand managers should drive the definition of replenishment strategies toward the following configurations:

4.2 Tactical S&OP

- MTS: High volumes and low variety. Attention is focused on the finished product.
- MTO: Low volume and high variety.
- ATO: Great number of end items with a possibility of limited components.
- Late customization: To manage all the possible product options and to guarantee flexibility for product mixes and availability (APICS—module 3.D—Implementation of Demand Plans, 2015).

Now let's see some use cases that will showcase not only the capabilities of the IBP inventory module but also the benefit of using a collaborative approach between demand and inventory processes.

We will start this example with two questions that can be answered by running the segmentation analysis at the product-location level:

- What are the top products that drive the inventory costs?
- How to differentiate inventory management and control by product segmentation?

Using the analytics app, we compare the recommended safety stock value for 2018 in connection with an initial flat service level target of 96% across all ABC segmentation categories (Fig. 4.32).

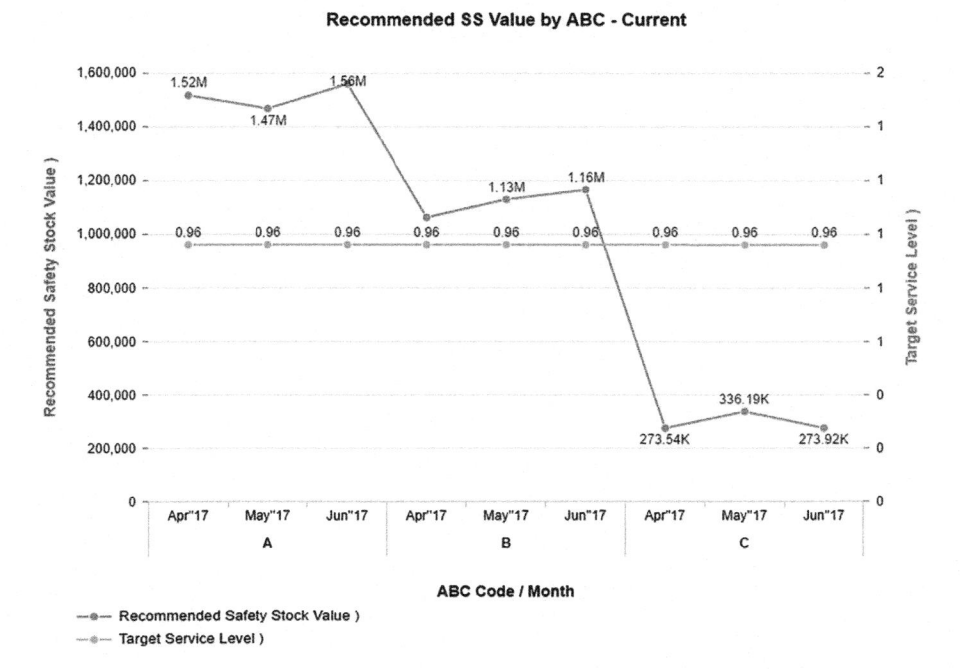

Fig. 4.32 SAP IBP—recommended safety stock value driven by 0.96 service level

We would like to further analyze how differentiating the end customer target service level by the segmentation class will help the organization to reduce the inventory costs. To facilitate this, we will use the real-time simulation capability for running the multistage inventory operator with a smaller target level and save then the results in ad hoc created scenario. While running, the operator performs a safety stock optimization across the entire network using several inputs like demand uncertainties, supply uncertainties, supply quantities, lead times, costs, and service levels.

Two simulations are carried out to recalculate the recommended safety stock for a service level reduction of 1% and 2% from the baseline. The results can be easily analyzed by bringing in the same planning view the baseline along with the two scenarios: target SL@95% and target SL@94%, respectively (as per Fig. 4.33). We see the projected inventory reduction in terms of safety days of supply, recommended safety stock qty, and value.

Before continuing the simulation with the calculation of various types of inventory that form the total inventory, we will stop to raise a question that might come into your mind while seeing the scenario comparison screenshot: What are behind the numbers that were computed for the recommended safety stock? To answer this, we will bring into the picture three key figures that are the outcome of the inventory optimization and provide visibility into the root causes of the recommended safety stock.

At a glance (Fig. 4.34), we can observe what uncertainty variables are accountable for the recommended safety stock volume across distribution centers:

- Quantity of stock due to demand variability
- Quantity of stock due to supply variability
- Quantity of stock due to service variability

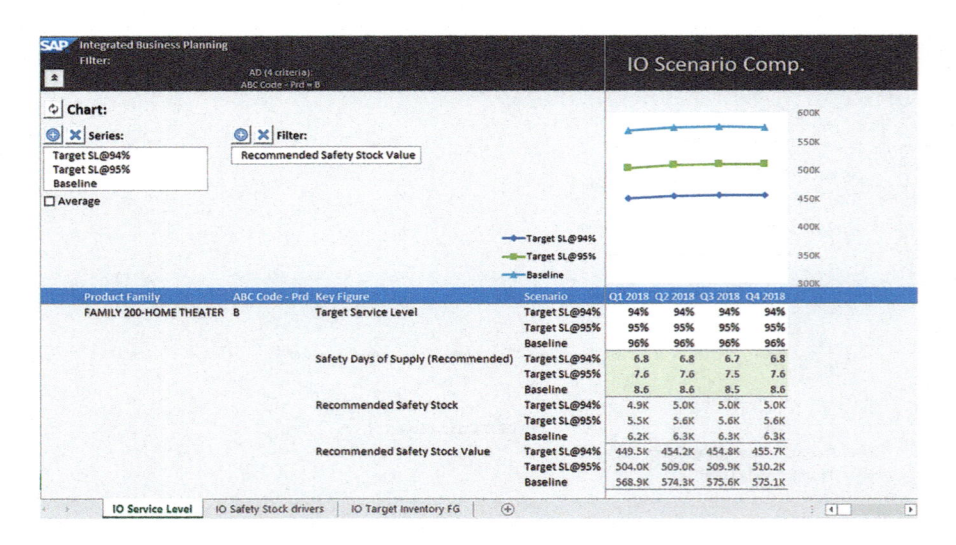

Fig. 4.33 SAP IBP—service level simulation scenario comparison

4.2 Tactical S&OP

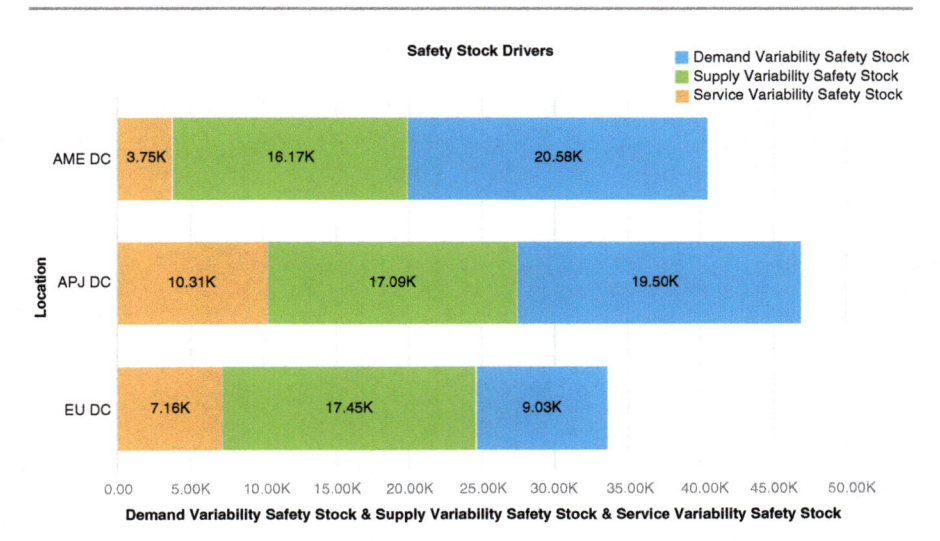

Fig. 4.34 SAP IBP—safety stock driver analysis

Fig. 4.35 SAP IBP—forecast error variability in scenario simulation

Let's focus on the blue segments that represent the demand variability. To estimate the variability of the demand, we need to identify the forecast error coefficient of variation (CV), which is the difference between what was forecasted and the actual demand. The computation of this statistical measure plus some many others can be easily handled using the IBP manage forecast error calculation apps. This will give both demand and inventory planners the right insight into the forecast accuracy.

What if our demand planning strategy will manage to generate lower variability of forecast error? What will be the recommended safety stock drop driven mainly by the demand variability safety stock? To answer these questions, we will run another multistage inventory optimization simulation which is triggered, this time, by a manual change of the forecast error CV. Once the simulation is done, saving it as ad hoc scenario allows the comparison against the baseline in order to assess the reduction in volume of the safety stock (Fig. 4.35).

Inventory optimization is more than safety stock planning, since it has to to hedge against risk and uncertainty in demand and supply. That is why we will introduce the

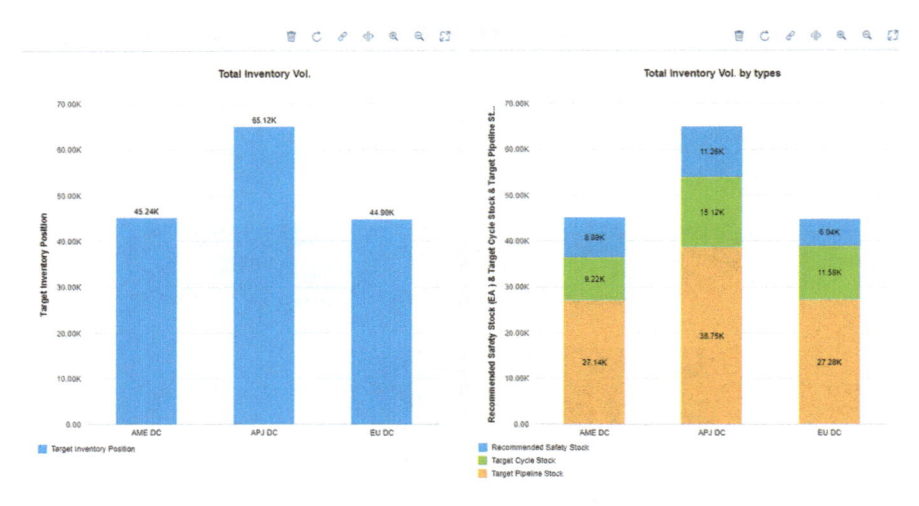

Fig. 4.36 SAP IBP—total inventory volume (left), total inventory volume by type (right)

calculation of target inventory with use of special planning operator. This operator computes the target inventory position which consists of the needed inventory to fulfill current period demand (cycle stock), the inventory for the future period demand until the next order is received (pipeline stock), and the buffer for uncertainty (safety stock) (see Fig. 4.36).

4.2.4 Improve Supply Chain Costs with Optimizer

It makes a huge difference how you make supply planning, how you constrain your supply projections, what criteria and what drivers will influence your calculation, or the way you adjust your optimized plans.

Taking consensus forecast which is an outcome of demand review process will be the starting point. Demand needs to be propagated and should consider:

- Levels in the bill of material
- Consumption factors in BoM
- Batch sizes
- Supply network
- Lead times
- Stock

As part of the demand propagation, utilization of assets (various types of production plants) will be calculated, availability of materials required will be calculated considering netting of stocks and in-transits, and collaboration with supplier via SAP Ariba can be triggered. In the next step, you will run supply planning and supply propagation which will enable communication back of supply plan to demand location (distribution centers, countries, markets) or demand entities (customers,

4.2 Tactical S&OP

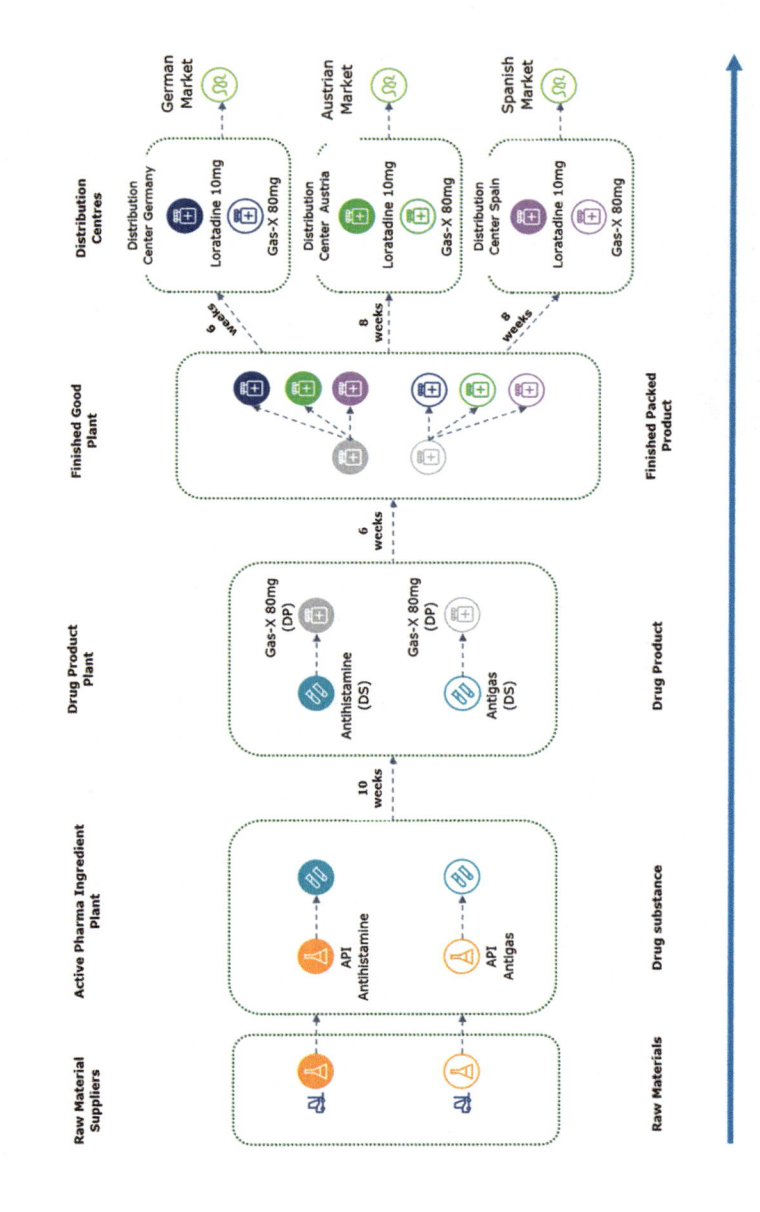

Fig. 4.37 Example of pharmaceutical supply chain network in SAP IBP

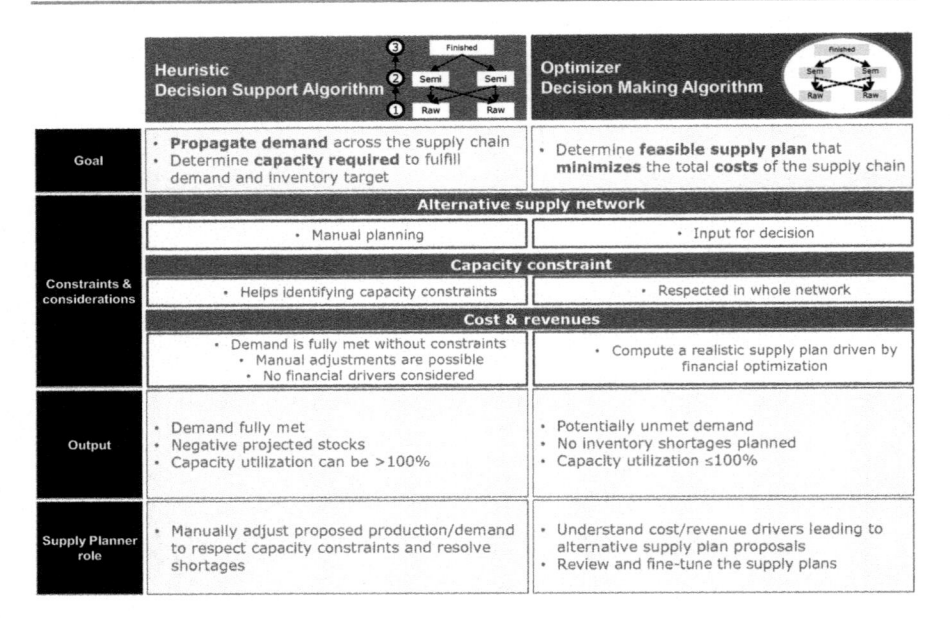

	Heuristic Decision Support Algorithm	Optimizer Decision Making Algorithm
Goal	• **Propagate demand** across the supply chain • Determine **capacity required** to fulfill demand and inventory target	• Determine **feasible supply plan** that **minimizes** the total **costs** of the supply chain
Constraints & considerations	*Alternative supply network*	
	• Manual planning	• Input for decision
	Capacity constraint	
	• Helps identifying capacity constraints	• Respected in whole network
	Cost & revenues	
	• Demand is fully met without constraints • Manual adjustments are possible • No financial drivers considered	• Compute a realistic supply plan driven by financial optimization
Output	• Demand fully met • Negative projected stocks • Capacity utilization can be >100%	• Potentially unmet demand • No inventory shortages planned • Capacity utilization ≤100%
Supply Planner role	• Manually adjust proposed production/demand to respect capacity constraints and resolve shortages	• Understand cost/revenue drivers leading to alternative supply plan proposals • Review and fine-tune the supply plans

Fig. 4.38 SAP IBP—supply planning algorithms

distributors). This will be called supply propagation. Demand and supply propagation will be explained on pharmaceutical example (Fig. 4.37).

Supply planning could be executed in unconstrained or constrained mode. In Fig. 4.38 you will find major differences between two methods.

As we see from the characteristics describing those two algorithms, we can expect significantly different results of supply planning. One highlights what needs to be done and the other makes proposal of decisions for you automatically. There is a huge value of using both types of supply planning algorithms, but we want to focus more on making optimization of your supply chain.

Optimizer works in two modes:

- Profit maximization—where profit is the difference between the revenue and total costs. The revenue is calculated by multiplying the nondelivery cost rate with the volume shipped to the customers, while the total cost is computed based on the costs that are generated during production, holding, and transportation activities. If the total cost is higher than the sales price, the optimizer will classify this demand as unprofitable and choose not to fulfill it.
- Delivery maximization—the goal is to identify the customer demand that can be fulfilled in the presence of various constraints that exist in the supply chain but without taking into consideration the profitability of each product, as profit maximization does.

4.2 Tactical S&OP

The constraints that are considered by the optimizer can be classified in three categories, based on the impact they have on the MILP solver:

- Hard constraints—conditions for variables like resource capacity, stock balance, or maximum inventory that are required to be satisfied.
- Soft constraints—failing to satisfy conditions for variables such as safety stock violation, inventory holding, or transportation cost is penalized by the objective function. The optimizer will try to keep the constraint violations as small as possible.
- Pseudo hard constraints—restrictions like adjusted or minimum values that have a very high penalty costs if not fulfilled. Given this, they usually get fulfilled unless there is a limitation like component unavailability.

As the optimizer is driven by costs, the objective of running this planning operator is to find a solution that minimizes all types of costs that are available in a supply chain, from production to distribution. The costs can be fixed or variable/per unit of quantity and are represented by key figures:

- Nondelivery costs rate (variable)
- Late delivery costs (variable)
- Transportation costs (fixed and variable)
- External procurement costs (fixed and variable)
- Production costs (fixed and variable)
- Inventory holding costs (variable)
- Safety stock violation costs (variable)
- Maximum inventory violation costs (variable)

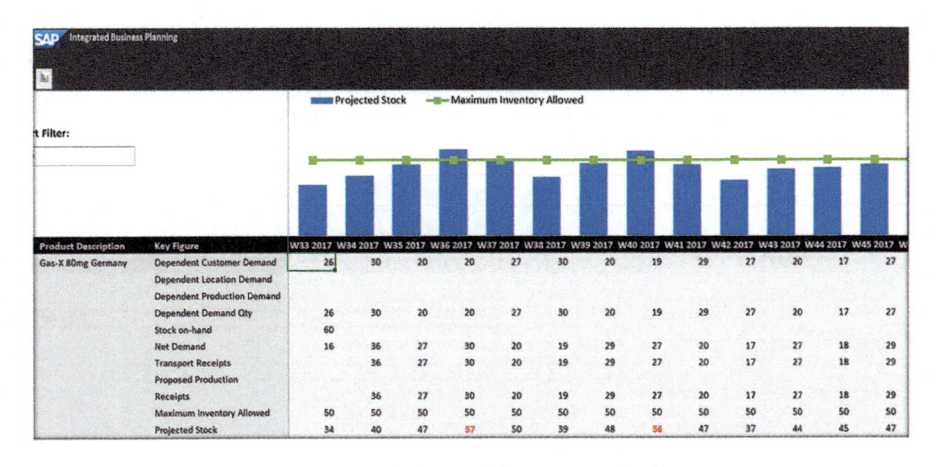

Product Description	Key Figure	W33 2017	W34 2017	W35 2017	W36 2017	W37 2017	W38 2017	W39 2017	W40 2017	W41 2017	W42 2017	W43 2017	W44 2017	W45 2017
Gas-X 80mg Germany	Dependent Customer Demand	26	30	20	20	27	30	20	19	29	27	20	17	27
	Dependent Location Demand													
	Dependent Production Demand													
	Dependent Demand Qty	26	30	20	20	27	30	20	19	29	27	20	17	27
	Stock on-hand	60												
	Net Demand	16	36	27	30	20	19	29	27	20	17	27	18	29
	Transport Receipts		36	27	30	20	19	29	27	20	17	27	18	29
	Proposed Production													
	Receipts		36	27	30	20	19	29	27	20	17	27	18	29
	Maximum Inventory Allowed	50	50	50	50	50	50	50	50	50	50	50	50	50
	Projected Stock	34	40	47	57	50	39	48	56	47	37	44	45	47

Fig. 4.39 SAP IBP—distribution center view with inventory projections

Once demand is propagated on distribution center level, planner could assess projected stock situation against maximum allowed target levels. This can be seen as soft constraint; actions supported with workflow could be triggered to address those if needed (Fig. 4.39).

As part of the planning process, demand planner receives many inputs, and one of them could be an additional demand. Sales and marketing went for a tender and wanted to simulate end-to-end view and impact. Once tender is being captured as scenario and demand propagated, it is obvious that we have supply asset utilization which needs to be addressed (Fig. 4.40).

Unconstrained planning run (heuristic) did expose overutilization of assets. In the example below, drug substance production plant was heavily overutilized because of tender.

Supply planner decided to run supply optimization to constrain supply and visualize impact on market level. Some production was pulled earlier; supply

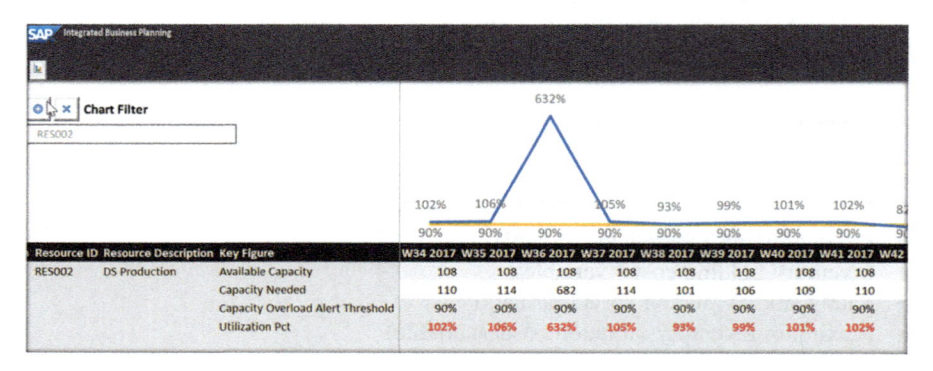

Fig. 4.40 SAP IBP—drug substance impact of the finished good tender

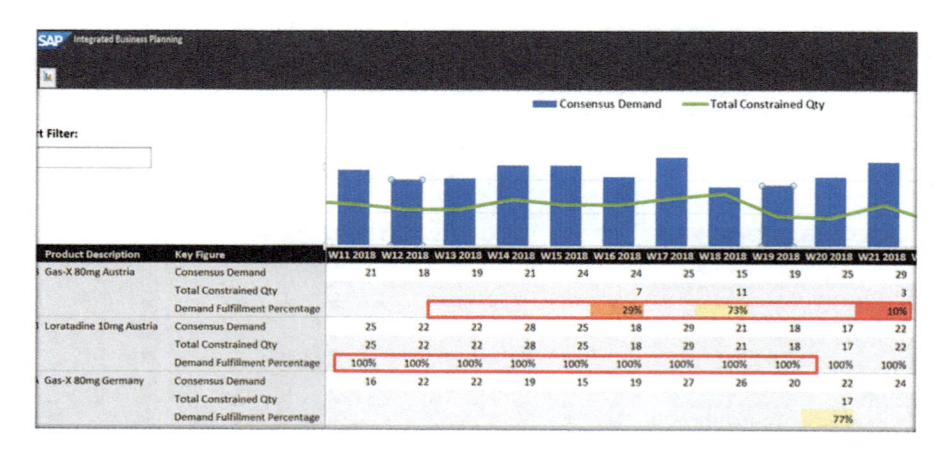

Fig. 4.41 SAP IBP—constrained plan impact on market level

4.2 Tactical S&OP

optimizer has propagated supply back to markets and exposed large gaps in demand fulfillment for two products which were produced with same production active pharma ingredient (drug substance) manufacturing assets. In this case optimizer did prioritize supply against lower costs (Fig. 4.41).

Sales and marketing were not happy with it; therefore, there was a request if simulation of end-to-end impact could be done with extensions of production line which was supposed to be operationalized shortly (Fig. 4.42).

New alternative resource was added into planning, and optimizer did consider it when generating new supply plan.

Finally planners had an opportunity to address various risk and opportunities like tenders, line extensions, and cost optimization and be able to compare impact of it in volume and value or just demand fulfillment ratio (Fig. 4.43).

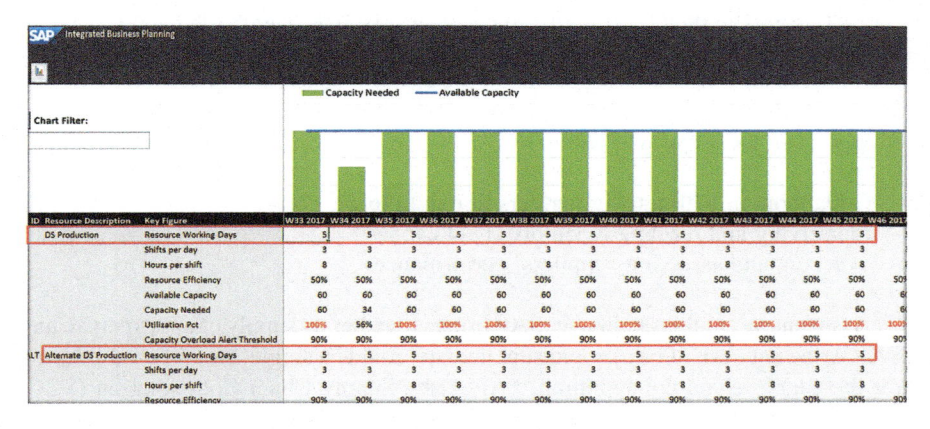

Fig. 4.42 SAP IBP—production line/plant extension simulation

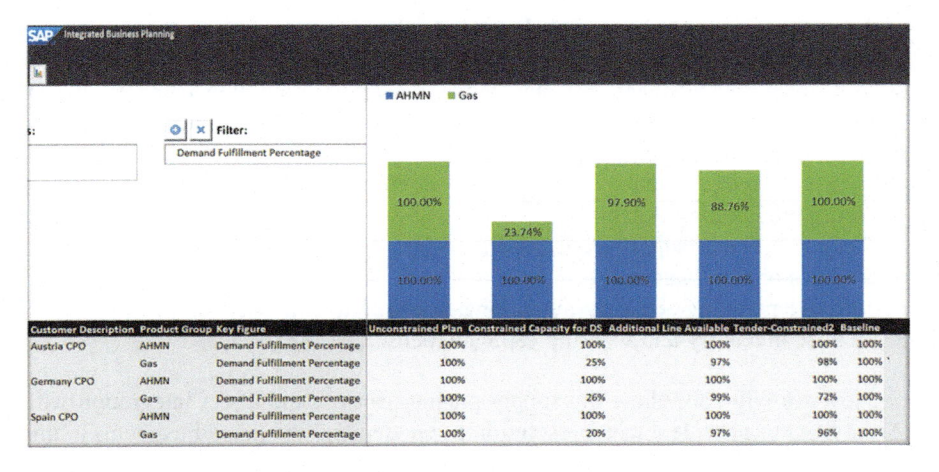

Fig. 4.43 SAP IBP—supply planning scenario comparison

Comparison of scenarios was summarized from market perspective. Management based on this information took a decision to accept tender and progress faster with production line extensions even with extra costs.

4.2.5 Improve IBP Supply Chain Planning with ARIBA Supplier Collaboration

With supply chains that are increasing in complexity, incorporating global outsourcing, and sometimes tracking up to the third tier suppliers, companies have to mitigate more diverse risks like supply disruptions caused by economic instability, foreign regulations, longer lead time, volatile exchange rate, etc. Preventing and minimizing such disruptions require visibility not only over their own operations but also across suppliers. It is difficult to make data-driven decisions when there is a high variation in data type and format, having a point-to-point collection of electronic data interchange (EDI) messages and spreadsheets sent via email. Achieving the necessary visibility is highly dependent on the adoption of the right technology/right supply chain tools that will allow:

– Collaboration with trading partners in real time
– Identifying and reacting to supply chain events
– Tracking and assessing suppliers' performance

As an answer to this challenge, SAP brings together its supply chain expertise and SAP Ariba network of buyers and suppliers to provide a single, cloud-based solution for the supply chain collaboration. SAP Ariba Supply Chain Collaboration (SCC) comes as an extension to the supply chain planning and execution processes simplifying and automating the collaboration with the trading partners like suppliers, service providers, or contract manufacturers across systems and geographies.

From operational to tactical and strategic planning, there are several use cases where a seamless integration between IBP and Ariba SCC will lead to an effective supply chain management, by managing complexity with transparency. It will enable companies to take informed decisions in dealing with frequent supply and demand variations leading to:

- Better predict the availability of supply.
- Reduce the total supply chain lead time by allowing faster reaction to demand changes or supply shortage.
- Improve planning accuracy by moving from silo to collaboration planning.
- Reduce inventory and working capital expense.

Now we will show how the supply planner can use the direct integration with Ariba SCC to provide a faster resolution to the demand volume adjustment. In this example, the adjustment implies an increase of the consensus demand with extra 25% in November and December. The only possible risk identified by the supply

4.2 Tactical S&OP

planner after propagating the new demand throughout the supply chain network is at the level of the component supply. So, before the supply planner is able to confirm the demand increase, he will quickly check whether the increase can be supported by the component delivery. There are currently two suppliers for which procurement contract exists, but one of these two suppliers, Supplier 101, gets a volume quota of 70% due to cost reasons (Fig. 4.44).

The unconstrained forecast is propagated across the bill of material levels and supply chain network, and it creates a component projection which is then integrated into Ariba SCC. Both suppliers were confirmation of their production capabilities in forecast commit. We can see below how the planning user interface looks for Supplier 101 highlighting also the quantity that changed since the last plan. However, due to some operational challenges, the supplier cannot confirm not even based on the previous plan. He is undercoming a longer time horizon. This could lead to a serious supply disruption if the second supplier, Supplier 102, is not able to cover the requested volumes (Fig. 4.45).

Integrating data back in IBP happens at the hit of one button from the supplier's side. Immediately the buyer's supply planner was notified about the component shortage and can drill down into the details (Fig. 4.46).

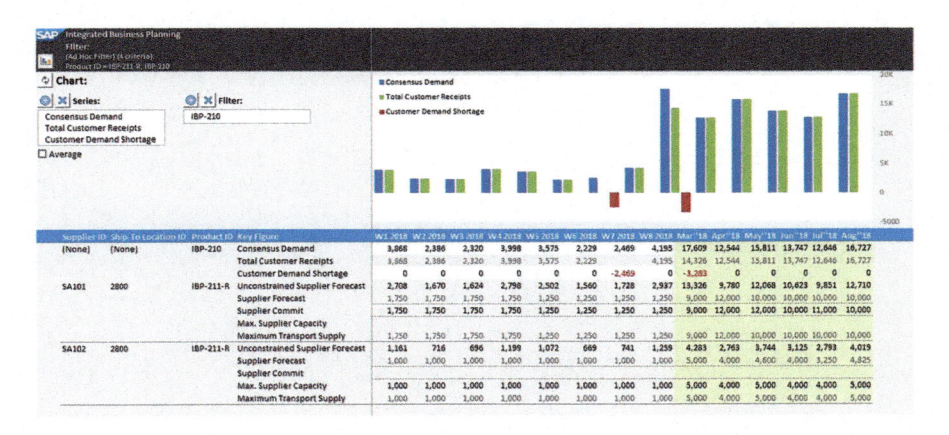

Fig. 4.44 SAP IBP—demand propagation for supplier components

Fig. 4.45 SAP Ariba supplier collaboration

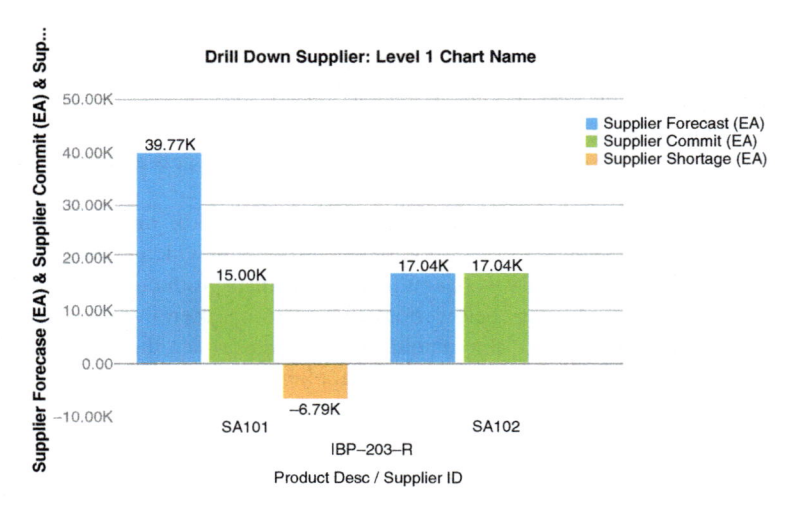

Fig. 4.46 SAP IBP—difference between supplier forecast and supplier commitments

Supplier ID	Ship-To Location ID	Product ID	Key Figure	W43 2017	W44 2017	W45 2017	W46 2017	W47 2017
SA101	2800	IBP-203-R	Supplier Forecast	1,500	1,500	1,500	1,500	1,500
			Supplier Commit	1,500	1,500	1,500	1,500	1,500
			Supplier Commit Upside					
			Maximum Transport Supply	1,500	1,500	1,500	1,500	1,500
SA102	2800	IBP-203-R	Supplier Forecast	2,500	2,500	2,500	2,500	2,500
			Supplier Commit	2,500	2,500	2,500	2,500	2,500
			Supplier Commit Upside	2,500	2,500	2,500	2,500	2,500
			Maximum Transport Supply	2,500	2,500	2,500	2,500	2,500

Fig. 4.47 SAP IBP—supplier integrated confirmation

Planner immediately saw that Supplier 101 under-commits but Supplier 102 positively responds to the volume changes and also has the availability to further increase.

Those confirmations which were send back automatically to IBP were developed as realistic integrated business plan and used in supply propagation across the network to demand customer locations.

We have seen large number of use cases for IBP-Ariba integration in business models where contract manufacturing/tolling was extensively used. Direct material procurement or production done outside of your own premises could be integrated via Ariba into IBP in a very effective way (Fig. 4.47).

4.2 Tactical S&OP

4.2.6 Improve Financial Outcomes with "What—If" Simulations

As part of Integrated Business Planning process, we have seen many times that there is a need to simulate price changes, combine it with cost-optimized supply plan, and see impact on revenue and profit. Below we will illustrate that need with two real use cases.

4.2.6.1 Revenue Projection Based on Country Price Tactics

Initial price tactics were defined on country level. Sales and marketing with finance were reviewing forecast price on regular basis.

Forecasted price did drive calculation of sales forecast revenue and profit. In this particular case, margin was loaded at aggregate country level (Fig. 4.48).

Demand manager and finance controller connected inputs provided by sales, marketing, and supply and proposed scenario where unit margin and unit price were adjusted at sales area level. The starting point to develop this scenario are price tactics which were introduced on sales area level (see Fig. 4.49). At demand review meeting, all functions have contributed to the development and agreement on

SKU	Country	Key Figure	2018	Jan'18	Feb'18	Mar'18	Apr'18	May'18	Jun'18
IBP-300	US	Std. Price	$30	$30	$30	$30	$30	$30	$30
		Forecasted Price	$30.25	$30.25	$30.25	$30.25	$30.25	$30.25	$30.25
		Sales Fcst Qty	167.7K	12.9K	13.0K	16.2K	12.9K	16.1K	13.1K
		Sales Fcst Rev.	5.07M	$390.2K	$391.8K	$491.1K	$389.9K	$486.2K	$395.1K
		Std. Margin	$5.8	$5.8	$5.8	$5.8	$5.8	$5.8	$5.8
		Std. Profit	$972.4K	$74.8K	$75.1K	$94.2K	$74.8K	$93.2K	$75.7K

Fig. 4.48 SAP IBP—price tactics on country level

SKU	Country	Sales Area	Key Figure	2018	Jan'18	Feb'18	Mar'18	Apr'18	May'18	Jun'18
IBP-300	US	(None)	Std. Margin	$5.8	$5.8	$5.8	$5.8	$5.8	$5.8	$5.8
IBP-300	US	North	Forecasted Price	$31	$31	$31	$31	$31	$31	$31
			Sales Fcst Qty	92.2K	7.1K	7.1K	8.9K	7.1K	8.8K	7.2K
			Sales Fcst Rev.	2.86M	$219.9K	$220.8K	$276.8K	$219.8K	$274.1K	$222.7K
			Forecasted Margin	$6.5	$6.5	$6.5	$6.5	$6.5	$6.5	$6.5
			Std. Profit	$534.8K	$41.1K	$41.3K	$51.8K	$41.1K	$51.3K	$41.7K
			Forecasted Profit	$599.4K	$46.1K	$46.3K	$58.0K	$46.1K	$57.5K	$46.7K
		South	Forecasted Price	$29.5	$29.5	$29.5	$29.5	$29.5	$29.5	$29.5
			Sales Fcst Qty	75.4K	5.8K	5.8K	7.3K	5.8K	7.2K	5.9K
			Sales Fcst Rev.	2.23M	$171.2K	$171.9K	$215.5K	$171.1K	$213.4K	$173.4K
			Forecasted Margin	$5.5	$5.5	$5.5	$5.5	$5.5	$5.5	$5.5
			Std. Profit	$437.6K	$33.7K	$33.8K	$42.4K	$33.6K	$42.0K	$34.1K
			Forecasted Profit	$414.9K	$31.9K	$32.1K	$40.2K	$31.9K	$39.8K	$32.3K

Fig. 4.49 SAP IBP—price and margin tactics on sales area level

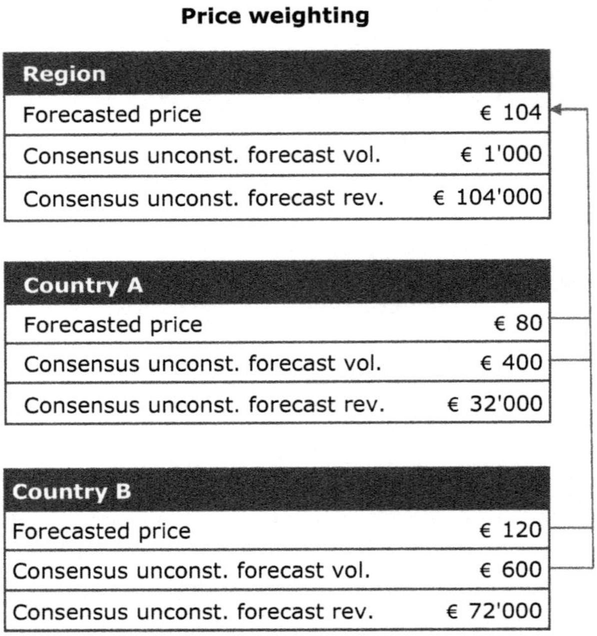

Fig. 4.50 Weighting of value key figures example

Price weighting

Region	
Forecasted price	€ 104
Consensus unconst. forecast vol.	€ 1'000
Consensus unconst. forecast rev.	€ 104'000

Country A	
Forecasted price	€ 80
Consensus unconst. forecast vol.	€ 400
Consensus unconst. forecast rev.	€ 32'000

Country B	
Forecasted price	€ 120
Consensus unconst. forecast vol.	€ 600
Consensus unconst. forecast rev.	€ 72'000

price elasticity and profit they want to have in specific sales area. They have considered competitor activity in those sales areas.

Once they have done that, they wanted to quickly have an overview of the forecast on country level again (Fig. 4.49). Special weighing with volumes was introduced, so figures make sense on low and aggregated level (Fig. 4.50).

4.2.6.2 Profit Projection Based on Cost Improvements

In the other company, there was a large Six Sigma improvement initiative in place which aims to reduce the waste from the production process in the manufacturing location that serves the sales area south region. We expected that it will lead to a reduction of the cost of goods sold. Before having the new COGS integrated from the leading system, we wanted to simulate how the projected reduction will impact the profitability.

For the simplicity of this example, the simulation was executed with a flat COGS reduction of 10% across 2018 and sales area south. The results were captured into an ad hoc scenario to allow an easy comparison with the baseline (Fig. 4.51).

It is easy to notice that the forecasted margin is immediately adjusted to reflect the new forecasted COGS which dropped from 4.5 in baseline to 4.05 in COGS variation scenario. Reviewing the profitability can be done.

Impact was visualized using analytics, where the forecasted profit was consolidated at country level (Fig. 4.52).

4.2 Tactical S&OP

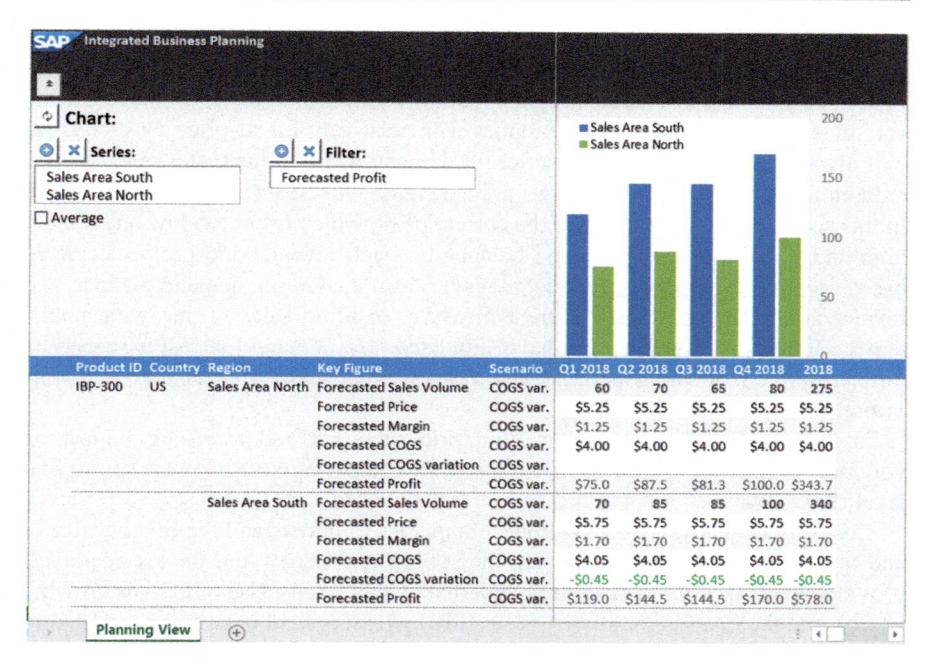

Fig. 4.51 SAP IBP—COGS reduction impact on profit

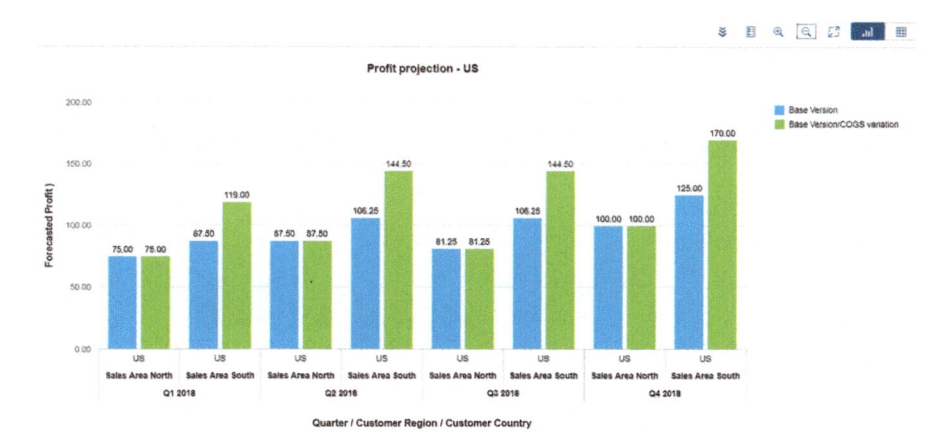

Fig. 4.52 SAP IBP—profit comparison

4.2.6.3 Revenue and Profit Projection in Cause and Effect Simulation

In one of the projects, we have seen that sales and marketing department wanted to simulate impact on volume based on price changes in a more scientific manner. We have used a more advanced statistical model called multilinear regression. In this model there is an assumed linear relationship between a target variable, usually referred to as dependent variable, and one or more variables which explain the target variable, usually referred to as independent variables or predictors.

In our business scenario, we talk about volume and price as two real-life variables. Assuming we have a product with relatively broad price elasticity, we will always expect to have a variation in demand as price fluctuates, e.g., a price reduction will boost demand, while a price increase will create a drop in the demand. In this scenario we wanted to find the correct price, which is not too low and not too high and be able to secure a good balance between revenue and profit calculated based on projected volume. Product manager from marketing, demand planner, and finance/pricing did evaluate different measures to bring sales in line with annual target. During this exercise, they have simulated how demand forecast is shaped by different price reductions/increase. Use cases were developed in separate scenarios in Fig. 4.53.

In the meeting we were simulating price changes and assessing impact on volume, revenue, and profit. Finally we were comparing scenarios on aggregated level (Fig. 4.54).

Cost service analysis (CSA) allows companies to understand the relative size of and the kind of relationship between the supply chain costs and the service levels provided to every kind of customers (internal and external). Use of CSA is growing in size, and the trend in familiarity is steadily increasing, and most firms use CSA to optimize inventory and pricing strategies. Mature (CSA) models enable useful "what-if" analysis and better understanding of SC trade-off impacts (Aronow & Barger, 2011).

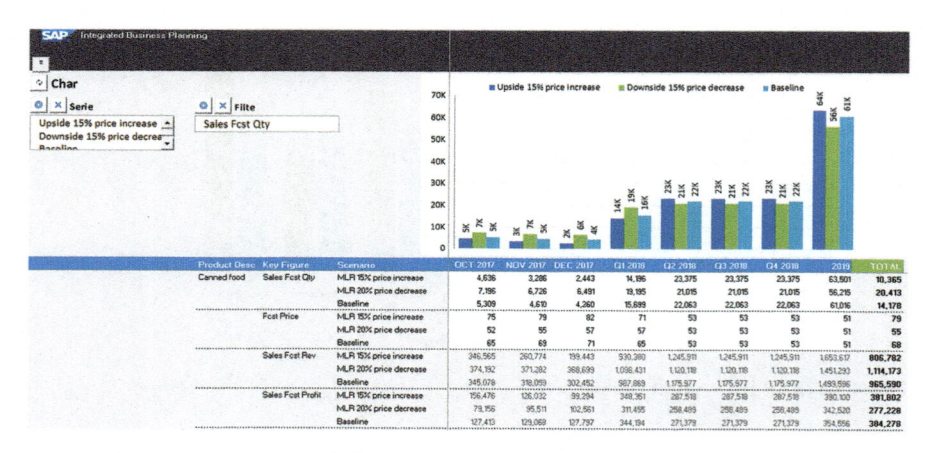

Fig. 4.53 SAP IBP—multilinear regression cause and effect scenarios

4.2 Tactical S&OP

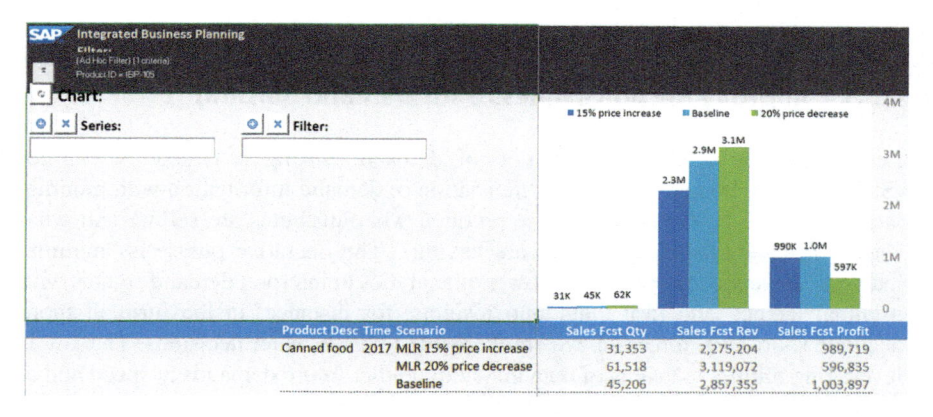

Fig. 4.54 SAP IBP—MLR scenario comparison

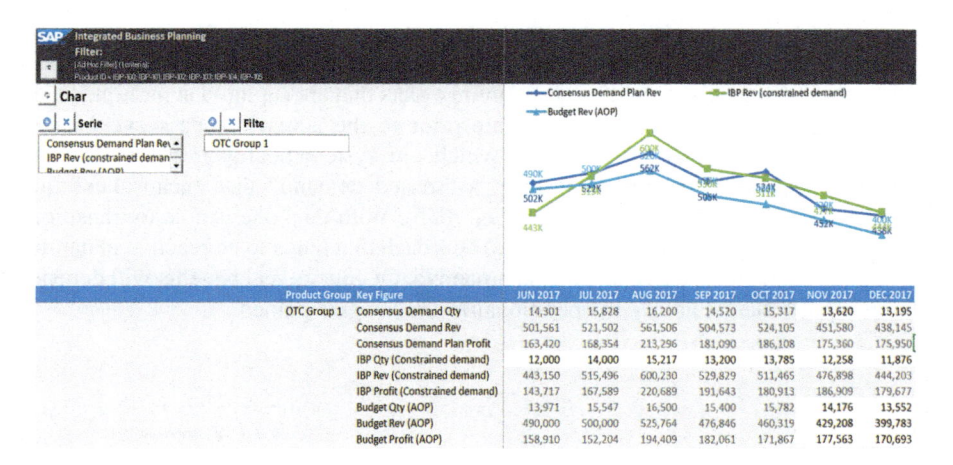

Fig. 4.55 SAP IBP—unconstrained forecast, optimized supply, and budget comparison

4.2.6.4 Comparisons of Demand Scenarios to Budget

We have seen many, many times that integration of financial data into Integrated Business Planning brings completely different quality of discussions. In most of the projects, we have developed solution which helps to assess differences between consensus unconstrained, constrained supply plan, and budget in volume and value. We have used scenario planning with different assumptions to expose gaps to budget and select leading scenario (Fig. 4.55).

With this approach we were able to define gaps to budget in a way it was actionable to create plan and allocate activities. We were able to expose gap on any level of material and customer hierarchy, define action plan to close it, and see progress in the next cycle.

4.3 Operational Planning

4.3.1 Improve Responsiveness with Demand Sensing

Let's start with a general definition of demand sensing provided by Gartner (Steutermann): It is defined as the "translation of demand information with minimal latency to detect who is buying the product, what attributes are selling and what impact demand shaping programs are having." The operative phrase is "minimal latency." If we are able to use the power of analytics to interpret demand signals with minimal latency and turn them into insights, for instance, in the form of more accurate short-term forecasts, we are then able to drive better decisions. The key is leveraging multiple streams of data that help predict future demands at speed and at scale. Clearly, the traditional principle of management by exception alone won't do. IBP's demand sensing algorithms provide the necessary tool support that allows interpretation of demand signals at speed and at scale. The illustration in Fig. 4.56 provides a conceptual illustration of the key principles at work. There are various inputs such as historical orders, historical consensus forecast (also known as consensus revisions—more on this later), future orders that are captured at multiple lags, and meaning at different points in time prior to the actual business event (say, customer order shipment) occurring, which are systematically processed by the demand sensing algorithm, to provide a "sensed demand" that encapsulates the insights of the various input streams (Fig. 4.56). With this, one is able to transition from a descriptive/diagnostic (a la alerts) approach that tends to be reactive in nature to a prescriptive/predictive one that is proactive. Of course, real benefits will depend on a supply chain's ability to operationalize the insights gained.

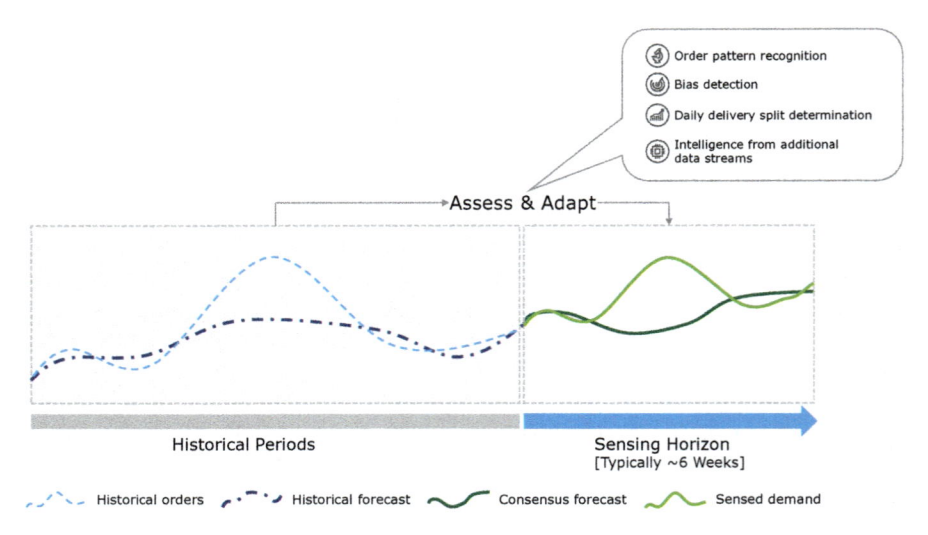

Fig. 4.56 SAP IBP—principles of demand sensing algorithm

4.3 Operational Planning

4.3.1.1 Variability Dampening

In the proliferation of SKUs, deep supply chain networks necessitated by customer proximity are key contributing factors to variability amplification as one gets closer to the customer: from a product structure standpoint, this could mean variability increase as one moves from raw materials to finished products. The increase is particularly pronounced in the case of divergent product flows (a lot more finished SKUs than input materials). From a distribution network perspective, this could mean a move from suppliers to retainers. From a time granularity perspective, this could be as one switches from months to days. This variability amplification is further exacerbated by the infamous bullwhip effect. This is illustrated in Fig. 4.57.

Demand sensing implies increasing the pulse, that is, systematically reacting to events influencing demand with minimal latency. This approach of using analytical support to process demand signals—both historical and forward looking—to make predictions in the near term leads to lowering of uncertainty "felt" by the supply chain. The dampening effect of increasing the number of demand observations on uncertainty (or variability) can be proved quantitatively.

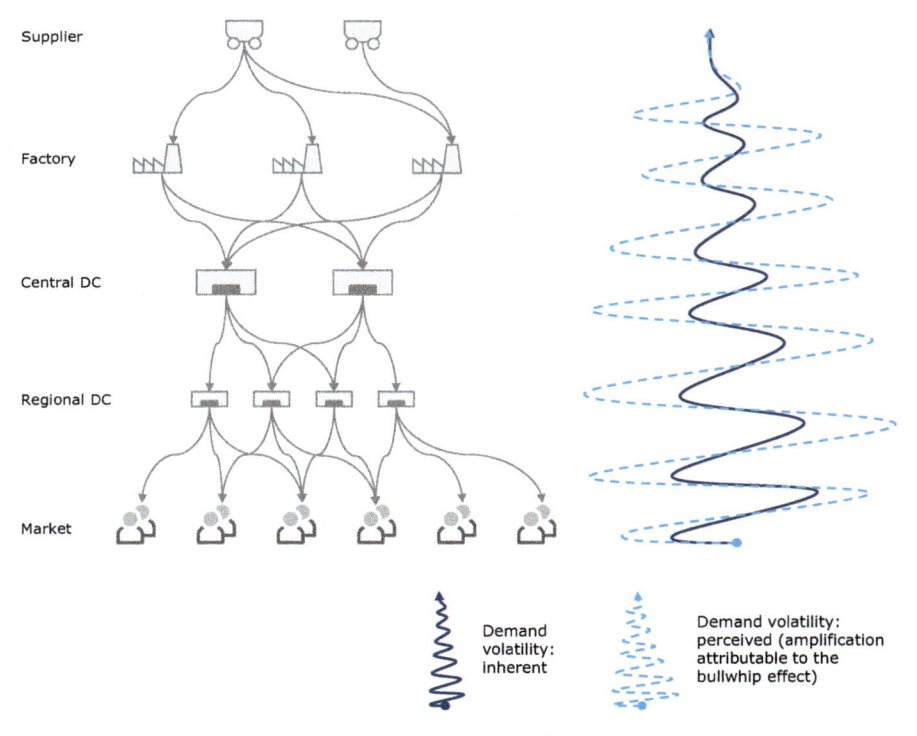

Fig. 4.57 Variability amplification as one moves closer to customer

Technical Note It can be proved that (Simchi, 1999):

$$\text{Variance of orders placed by the retailer at the manufacturer} \Big/ \text{Variance of demand as seen by the retailer}$$

$$\geq 1 + \frac{2L}{p} + \frac{2L^3}{p^3},$$

where $L =$ lead time and $p =$ number of demand observations.

4.3.1.2 Becoming Demand Driven

Demand-driven principles have been gaining traction with agility becoming more and more important to building "respond" capabilities. One of the core demand-driven principles is enshrined in the phrase "position and pull instead of push and promote" (Debra Smith, 2016). This means positioning the decoupling point further downstream, which could potentially lead to grabbing more market share by becoming more attractive (response time-wise) versus competition. The idea is illustrated in Fig. 4.58.

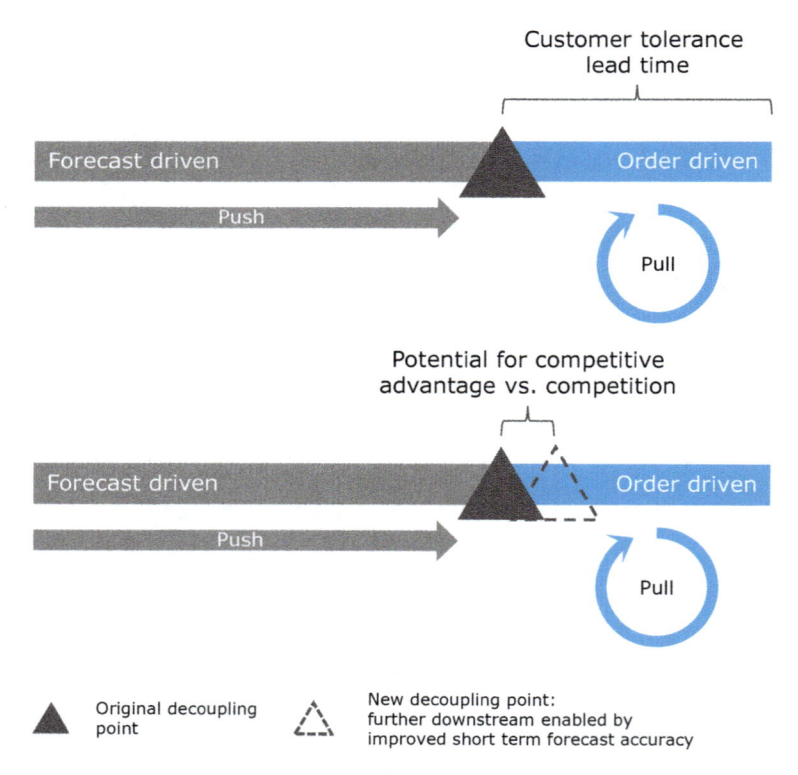

Fig. 4.58 Near-term forecast accuracy and decoupling point repositioning

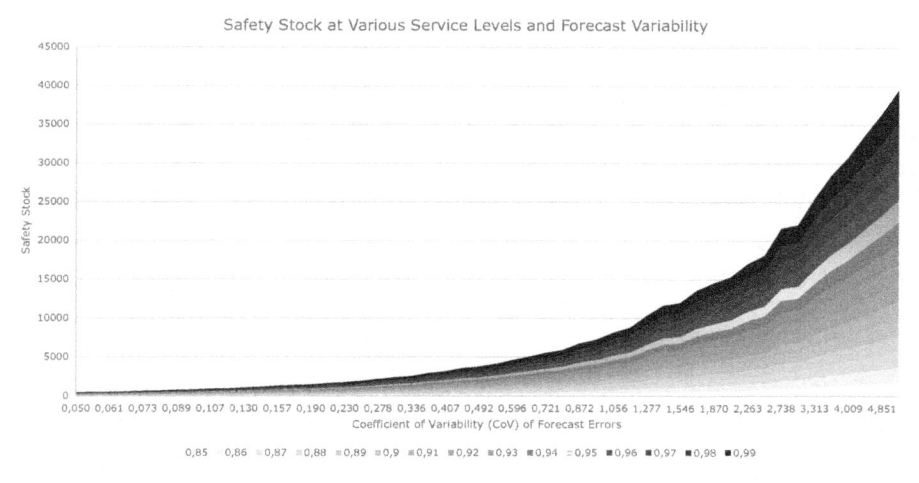

Fig. 4.59 Forecast variability, customer service level, and safety inventory relationship

4.3.1.3 Working Capital Rationalization

There is also a clear correlation between forecast variability and inventory. The greater the variability, the higher the required level of stocks to ensure a certain desired service level. As can be seen in Fig. 4.59, this relationship is nonlinear, and this represents a significant opportunity. Improvements in accuracy or reduction in variability can have a positive impact on working capital. One could either offer the same level of service at a reduced inventory or improve the service level keeping inventory investments the same.

4.3.1.4 Lead-Time Compression

Reduction of lead times is another area where demand sensing can bring in benefits. This is explained well using a numerical example: we have a bill of material (BOM) that consists of parts that are all made to order (say, because of high demand variability like in the case of a highly customizable product). Demands for these parts cannot be reliably predicted at higher lags (for instance, 30 days or more). However, let's say, by increasing the cadence and leveraging analytical support, forecast variability could be reduced for some of these parts to a level that makes a switch from make-to-order to make-to-stock viable. Let's analyze the impact of this. We'll do so by focusing on the critical path of the BOM, which is the longest path that represents the lead time experienced by the customer. The critical path changes as we progressively switch the strategy for parts where the variability decrease is significant enough to make this a viable option.

4.3.1.5 A Peek Under the Hood of SAP IBP's Demand Sensing Algorithm

Although the algorithm itself is proprietary and details of the inner workings are not in the public domain, the main steps can be deduced based on experimental results.

	Historical data for forecasting	Future order quantity	Sensed demand	Delivery quantity
Key figures	Consensus revisions / snapshots	Historical order quantity	Adjusted sensed demand	Adjusted delivery quantity

	1. Detect Bias	2. Recognize Order Patterns	3. Calculate Weekly Sensed Demand	4. Determine Daily Distribution Factors

	Bias horizons	Order quantity ratio calculation horizon	Min/max forecast adjustment bandwidth	Daily average calculation horizon
Settings	Lags		Minimum accuracy improvement threshold	Working days

Fig. 4.60 SAP IBP—demand sensing algorithm

The process described below is based on numerous runs of the algorithm for a number of deliberately created datasets to examine its behavior.

The algorithm can be said to consist of four key steps.[1] This is depicted in Fig. 4.60.

We have been running various tests with our customers and wanted to share briefly with you an example of how forecast bias can influence sensed demand quantity. Below figure illustrates that for Distribution Center 1, bias is very low; therefore, consensus demand plan and sensed demand are close to each other; then for Distribution Center 2, the gap between becomes bigger; and finally at Distribution Center 3, it is substantial due to growing forecast bias (Fig. 4.61).

A tool Du Jour

We are witnessing major shifts in the way supply chain planning is being done—it has a lot to do with the quantum of data supply chains that have to be processed. To make sense of all the data, tools that provide strong analytical support are of paramount importance. In the context of operational or short-term forecasting, demand sensing is a great example of one such instrument that helps predict demands more accurately by processing demand signals at speed and scale with the help of various algorithms. In fact, algorithmic supply chain planning is one trend that is bound to take hold as businesses start to embrace digital more and more. In the (Payne, 2016), the author argues that "competitive advantage will be determined by speed of understanding and adaptive response to environmental signals." The use of demand sensing for short-term forecasting is not just useful but essential for digital businesses to be able to adaptively respond to demand signals. We have talked about how traditional paradoxes are being overcome—particularly the one between cost-efficiency and responsiveness. Companies in their efforts to transcend

---

[1]This excludes any preprocessing steps. For example, cleansing the consensus demand of promotions is a typical preprocessing step. The assumption made is that the consensus key figure input is one without promotions.

4.3 Operational Planning

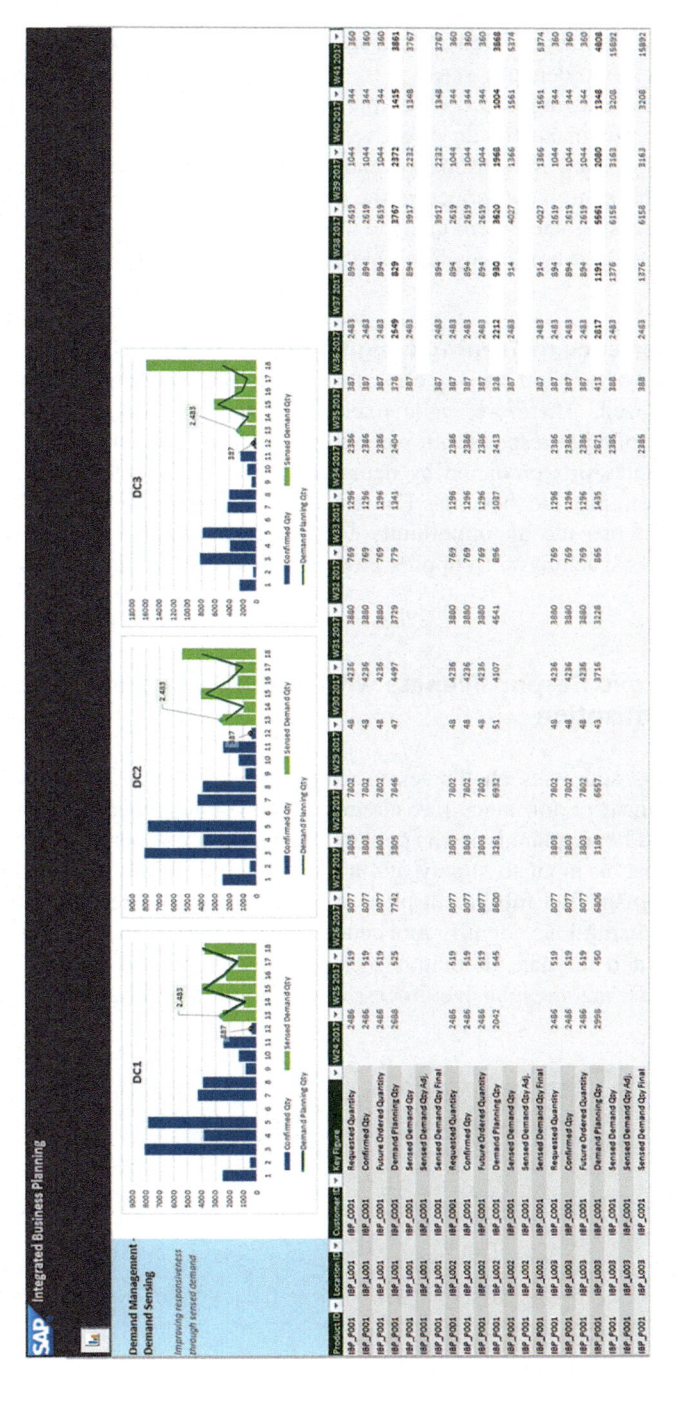

Fig. 4.61 SAP IBP—sensed demand impacted by DC forecast bias

trade-offs and move from "either-or" to "both-and" will need to use any and all means to minimize latency. Demand sensing is in many ways a tool for the times.

That being said, demand sensing in no way diminishes the importance of medium-term forecasting executed as part of tactical S&OP. A good consensus forecast is a prerequisite for an effective demand sensing process. For instance, demand patterns such as seasonality and trend are not detected by sensing. It assumes that these are incorporated in the consensus forecast and relies on insights gained by processing short-term demand signals and analysis of historical forecast performance to adjust consensus forecast (and derive sensed demand).

4.3.1.6 Importance of Turning Insights into Action

The true power of demand sensing cannot be realized unless insights gained cannot be operationalized. Therefore, agile execution processes are important to turn insights into profitable response. In some cases, even if lead times are too long to adapt to demand shifts predicted by demand sensing, early detection of potential issues can itself provide benefits. For example, being able to predict potential shortage might provide an opportunity to explore alternative scenarios, one of which could be switching to a supplier closer to home with a shorter lead time.

4.3.2 Improve Responsiveness with Short-Term Demand Prioritization

Responsiveness addresses challenges in short-term horizon. It is very often perceived as ultimate performance measurement of planning processes quality. Less firefighting and better planning. The demand plans that are generated in the mid- to long term go as an input to supply and allocation process and response planning where supply plans and fulfillment plans can be created to meet demand changes and/or supply disruptions, identify root causes and actionable corrections to demand infeasibilities, and simulate alternative corrective actions (Fig. 4.62).

There are two main responsive processes supported (Fig. 4.63):

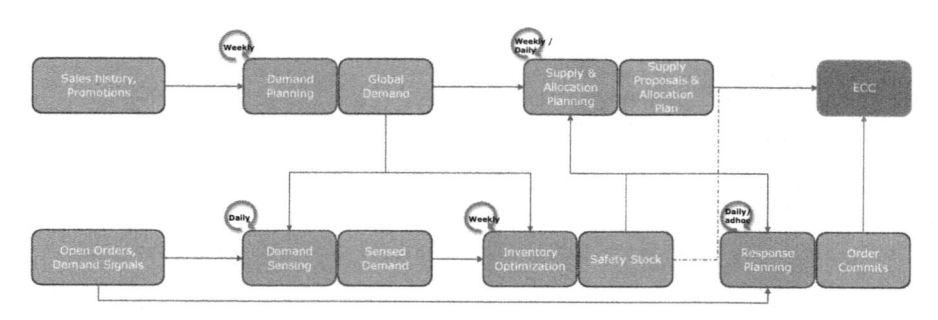

Fig. 4.62 Simplified IBP process

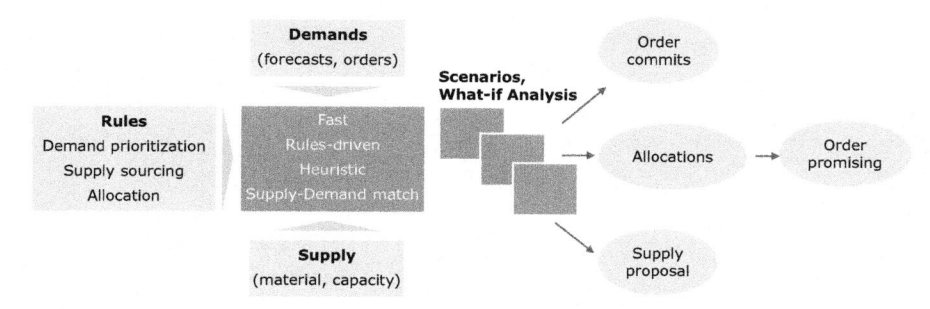

Fig. 4.63 SAP IBP—responsive process

- Supply and allocation planning: Create allocations and a supply plan based on prioritized forecast demands and supply chain constraints.
- Response planning: Create order confirmations and an adopted supply plan based on prioritized demands, allocations, and supply chain constraints.

Both processes work on tightly integrated information from ERP and allow for root-cause analysis and simulation of full and delta plans. The demand inputs for response processes include:

- Allocation run: Only considers forecast (single KF)
- Confirmation run: Considers forecast and sales orders

In future releases, customer can utilize several demand streams in the planning process (forecast, promotions, priority demand second priority demand, etc.)

4.3.2.1 Demand Prioritization

The demands in the system (forecast + sales orders) need to be prioritized for order fulfillment based on the business requirements.

- The rules are set up to prioritize the demands.
- Rules are used during planning run to prioritize the demands.
- Confirmation during planning run will be per prioritization.

A demand prioritization rule contains several segments and is ordered in a priority sequence for the segment as per Fig. 4.64.

Demand is being segmented, prioritized as per Fig. 4.65.

In SAP IBP, the account planner role provides access so several applications to maintain and view demand prioritizations, view product allocation profiles, and conformations and simulate sales orders (Fig. 4.66).

In demand prioritization, several rules can be defined, each with multiple segments. For example, the rule "Prioritize Sales Orders and Forecast by

Demand prioritization rule

- Rule contains segments

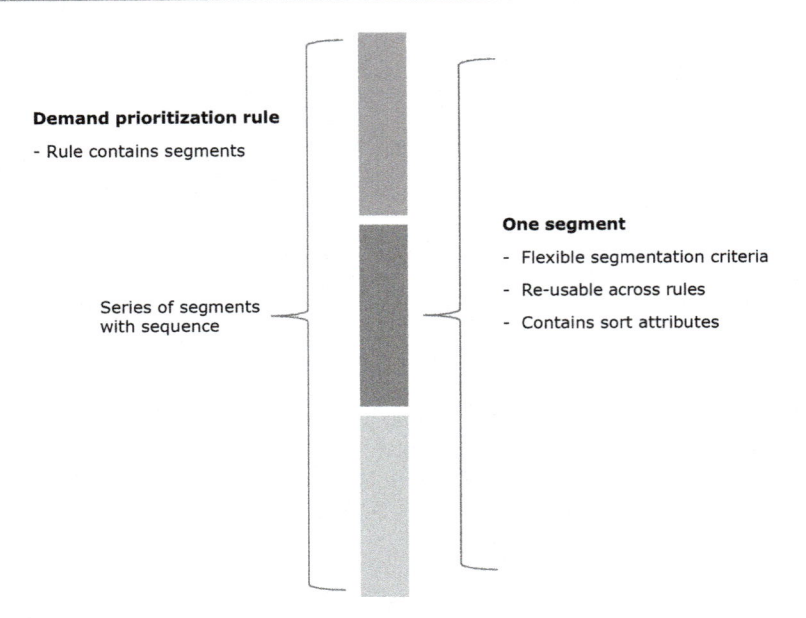

Series of segments with sequence

One segment

- Flexible segmentation criteria
- Re-usable across rules
- Contains sort attributes

Fig. 4.64 SAP IBP—demand prioritization concept

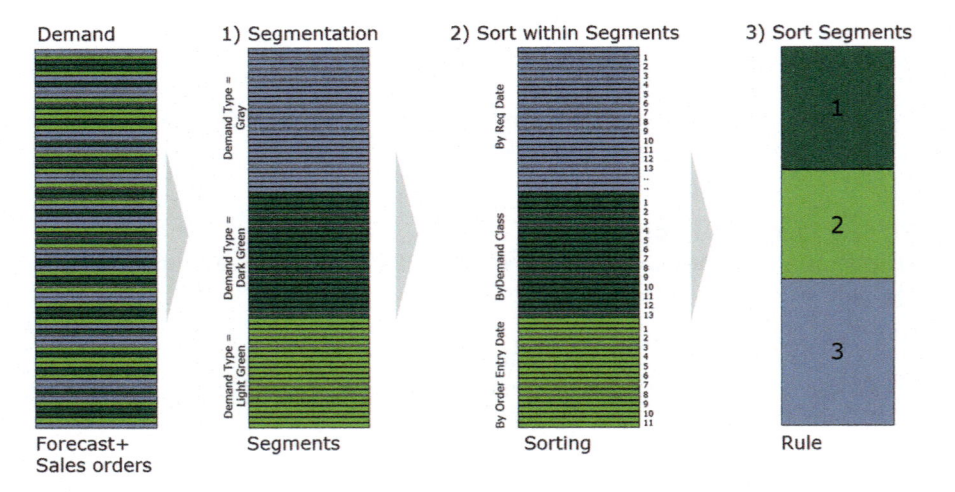

Fig. 4.65 SAP IBP—demand segmentation concept

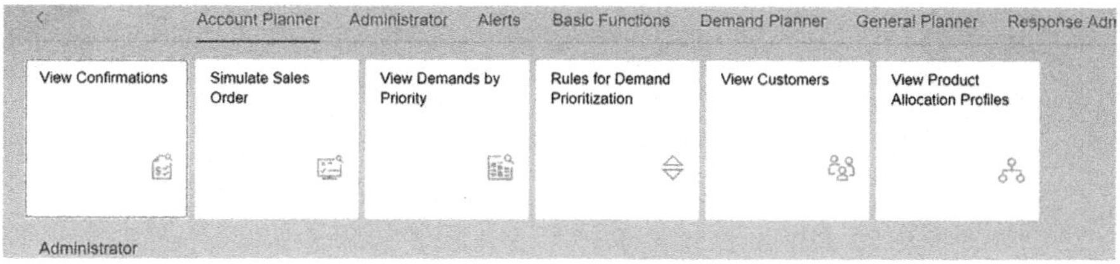

4.3 Operational Planning

| View Confirmations | Simulate Sales Order | View Demands by Priority | Rules for Demand Prioritization | View Customers | View Product Allocation Profiles |

Administrator

Fig. 4.66 SAP IBP—demand planner apps which help to increase responsiveness

Customer" can have several segments, each with segmentation criteria and sort attributes.

The supply and allocation run creates allocations and supply plan based on these prioritized demand forecasts and the supply chain constraints. Sales orders or forecasts are being prioritized, and some demand types may not be fulfilled (Fig. 4.67).

In the screen below, we see that some sales orders are exceeding allocation plan and forecast is not being fulfilled (covered). In this case for short-term planning, we identify demand which is at risk.

The response planning uses the prioritized demand along with forecasts and sales orders to perform a batch confirmation on sales order line level (Fig. 4.68).

Further **gating factor analysis** shows the reason the order was not fulfilled completely along with the other competing demands. A gating factor is anything that prevents you from fulfilling an order or forecast demand on time (Fig. 4.69).

With response management, you can analyze these gating factors and devise solutions to overcome them (Fig. 4.70). You can also make the necessary arrangements that might prevent these factors from arising in the future.

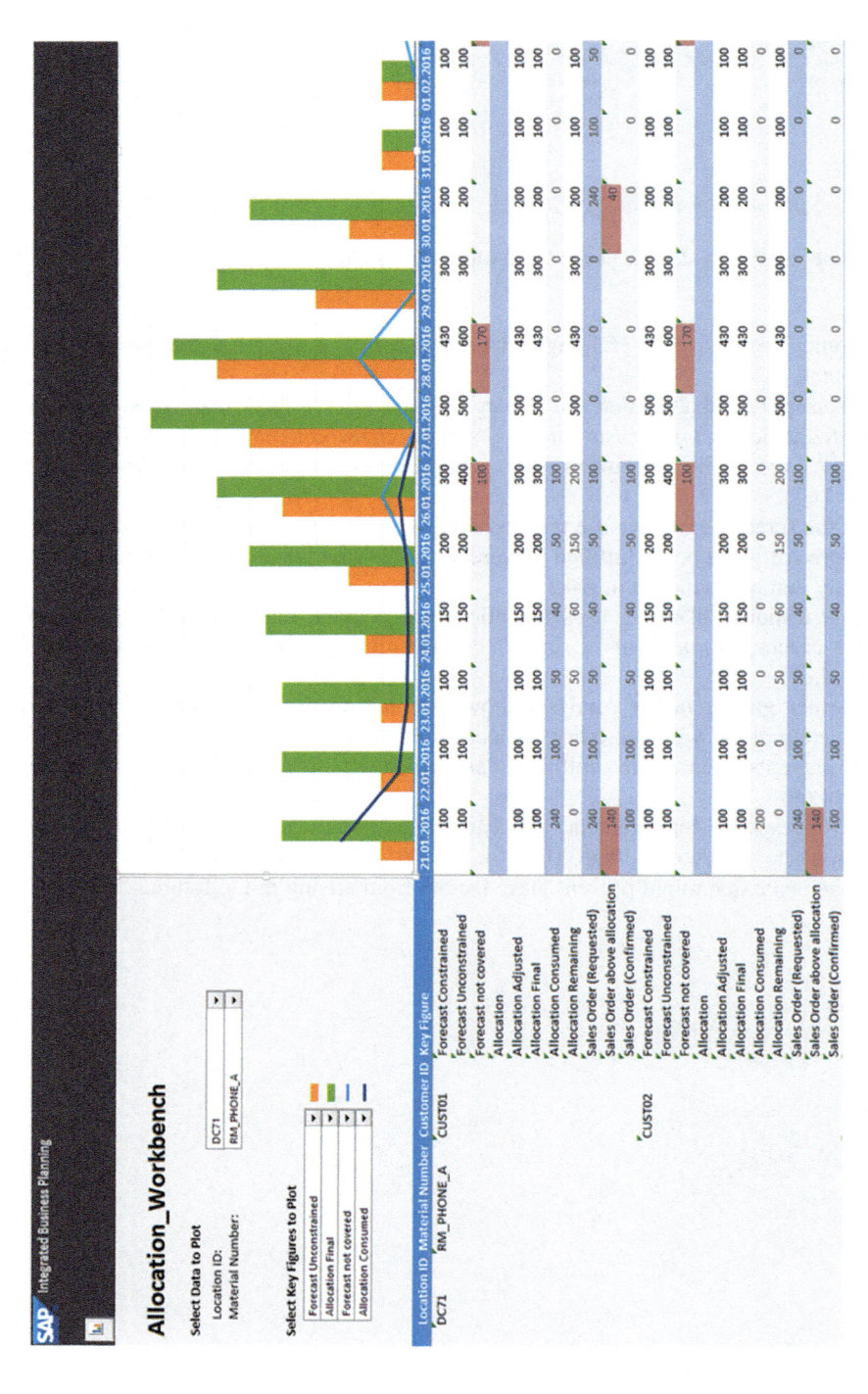

Fig. 4.67 SAP IBP—allocation to workbench planning view

4.3 Operational Planning

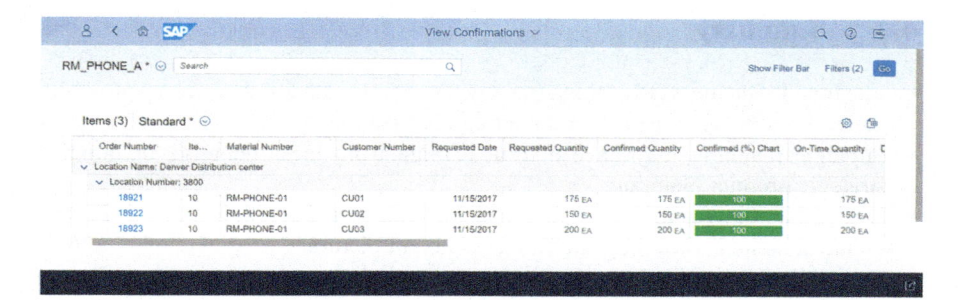

Fig. 4.68 SAP IBP—order confirmation app

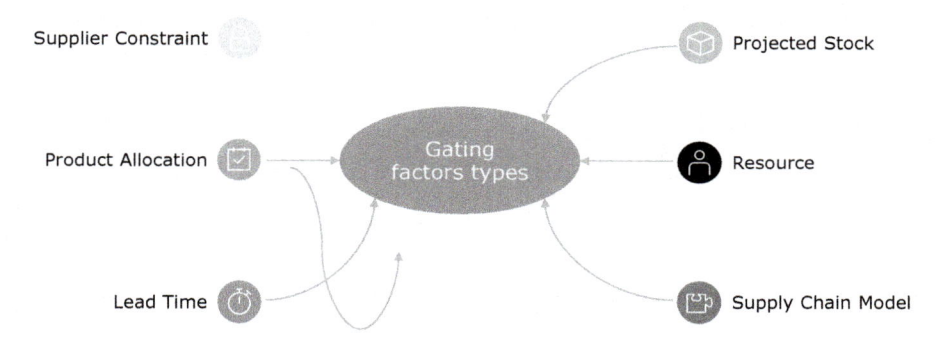

Fig. 4.69 Gating factor types

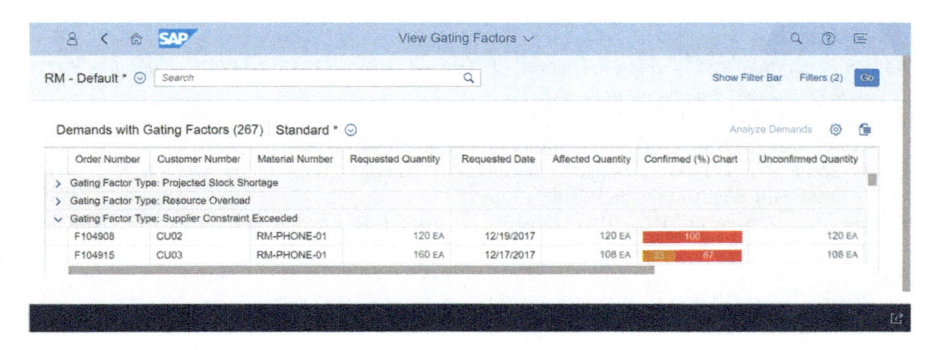

Fig. 4.70 SAP IBP—gating factors with pegged and affected orders

4.4 Summary

- Integrated Business Planning framework proves itself as a concept which integrates strategic, tactical, and operational planning.
- Strategic planning may have a form of annual business planning or monthly strategic product planning.
- Strategic initiatives of E2E assessment impacting product, demand, supply, and financial elements can be done in one coherent picture.
- Embedding financial elements (price, cost, margin, exchange rates) and finance controllers in the process brings management attention and realistic "what-if" scenario.
- Tactical S&OP can improve its focus with segmentation aligned to profitable growth and demand variability.
- Forecasting and demand planning can be done much more effectively and efficiently if you introduce differentiated forecasting, which cover different ways of working and different responsibilities and techniques for different product segments.
- Inventory availability and levels can be optimized with embedded in IBP inventory optimization algorithms.
- Supply plans can be constrained based on the availability of materials, machine, manpower, and cost optimized in same run.
- Supply plans can be more realistic if SAP Ariba supplier collaboration is connected to SAP IBP.
- In short-term horizon, pattern recognition embedded in demand sensing can improve your responsiveness to changes in demand.
- Prioritization of different types can help to improve your service levels and trade-off decision on order level.

References

APICS – module 3.D – Implementation of demand plans. (2015). *APICS – module 3.D – Implementation of demand plans.* APICS.

Aronow, S., & Barger, R., Jr. (2011). Understanding trade-offs: A practical supply chain cost-service analysis framework and maturity model. *Analysis*, (April).

Debra Smith, C. S. (2016). *Demand driven performance: Using smart metrics.* New York: McGraw-Hill Education. isbn:9780071796095.

Desmet, B., & Sterckx, P. (2012). Benefits of market-driven demand forecasting approach. *MÖBIUS*.

Mulllick Satinder, K. (1971). Tecnique, How to choose the right forecasting. *Harvard Business Review*.

Payne, T. (2016, September). Digital business requires algorithmic supply chain planning. *Gartner*.

Simchi, L. (1999). *Designing and managing the supply chain: Concepts, strategies, and case studies.* Boston: *McGraw-Hill*.

Steutermann, S., Salley, A., & Lord, P. (2012). Demand management elevates value network performance. *Gartner*.

Steutermann, S., Scott, F., & Tohamy, N. (2012). Building an effective demand-planning process. *Gartner*.

How to Manage Organization and Capability Change 5

5.1 Talent Acquisition

Why do we talk about talent acquisition? We have been asked many times in the projects what activities shall be planned to cope with the people impact coming from the Integrated Business Planning transformation program (Fig. 5.1). Transformation program may have a certain budget for finding new talents outside or inside the organization to cope with the change of capabilities required. It is essential to manage requirements for the adaption of capabilities with often limited budgets or possibilities in the organization. It is also essential to define how to align this with the overall company talent strategy by explaining how to build own talents. Let us explain what talent acquisition is and then discuss internal and external implications.

5.1.1 Talent Acquisition Is Not Synonymous with Recruitment

Talent acquisition can be defined as an approach that helps organizations to identify, attract, and bring on board top talents to fill the roles required to meet the company goals and effectively meet compelling business needs (Deloitte, 2016b). It is important to underline that the term talent acquisition should not be used synonymously with recruiting, as recruiting is a subgroup of talent acquisition and includes sourcing, screening, interviewing, assessing, selecting, hiring, as well as onboarding processes in some companies. Therefore, talent acquisition is not only recruiting: it embraces other crucial components necessary for effective recruitment and bringing highest values to the firm (Fig. 5.2).

In the workforce planning, staffing decision should be aligned with business strategy and enforced with understanding of the labor markets. Talent managers should not only know the company's labor pool but also understand their necessary skills and knowledge. Organizations should rationally plan all employer branding activities that enable them to build a company's image and reputation, help them

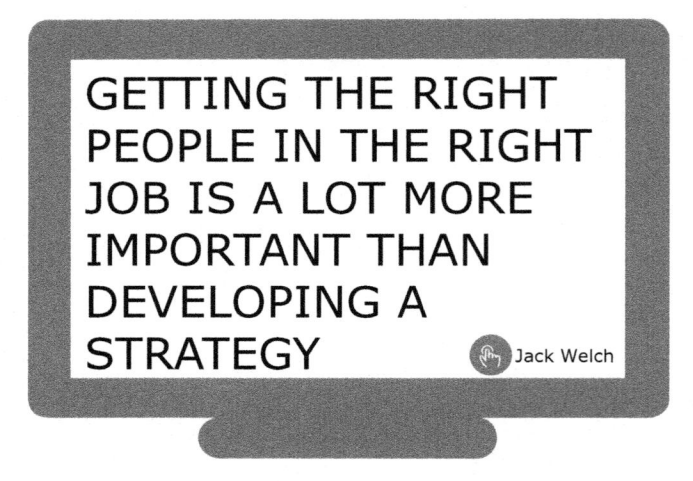

> GETTING THE RIGHT PEOPLE IN THE RIGHT JOB IS A LOT MORE IMPORTANT THAN DEVELOPING A STRATEGY
>
> Jack Welch

Fig. 5.1 Getting right people for the right job

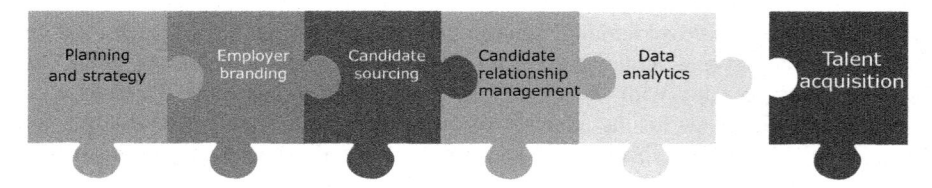

Planning and strategy — Employer branding — Candidate sourcing — Candidate relationship management — Data analytics — Talent acquisition

Fig. 5.2 Talent acquisition components

illustrate its culture as it improves their market position, and catch the interest of valuable candidates. It is important that an employer branding strategy conveys that organization culture, benefits, and growth opportunities are better than those of competitors. Especially nowadays that Millennials "judge the performance of a business on what it does and how it treats people" (Deloitte, 2016a).

As different sourcing strategies should be applied depending on the job and audiences, it is a crucial part in the talent acquisition process to define best talent/audiences whom to recruit for specific roles. In creating a positive candidate experience and candidate community, taking care of relationships with unselected candidates is an additional factor that should not be underestimated when talking about talent strategy. Remember that very often a pool of rejected candidates can be a good source of future recruitment participants. Additionally, they are the voice that can encourage or discourage other potential talents. To improve the talent acquisition process and to make better recruitment decisions, the talent management team should also ensure that all useful talent data is adequately tracked and analyzed. Within these mentioned elements, we find tasks, tools, selected technologies, and partners as key elements of a company's talent acquisition strategy (Erickson Robin, 2012).

Why is it so important to have an elaborated talent acquisition strategy? Even though the term "war for talent," referring to an increasingly competitive landscape for recruiting and retaining talented employees, was defined by Steven Hankin in 1997, its relevance is surprisingly up to date. Today's market is still a highly competitive talent environment where companies face challenges in attracting and retaining workers with specialized competences. Additionally, as jobs change rapidly and skills evolve so fast, it is very unlikely to have people who will be able to continue doing their job without learning and developing their skills. Many businesses fail due to hiring unskilled or wrong candidates; replacing them is indeed very expensive. A recent LinkedIn global recruiting trends report reveals that 83% of recruiters indicate talent acquisition as the #1 priority in their company in 2017. Meantime, 2017 Deloitte's Human Capital Trend report *Rewriting the rules for the digital age* (Deloitte, 2017b) shows that attracting skilled resources now stands as a top concern of business leaders, ranking third in 2017 survey. More than eight in ten (83%) executives say talent acquisition is important or very important. All the abovementioned factors, together with the cost related to acquire new talents, underline the undoubted importance of talent acquisition.

External or Internal Talent Acquisition
As a consequence of the talent problems, when looking for a perfect demand planner, demand manager, finance controller, or other key roles in the Integrated Business Planning area, you need to weight the pros and cons to decide the best talent acquisition strategy. As a first step, you can start by thinking if an external or internal talent acquisition would be the best way for your company to find a specific talent.

An external talent acquisition approach usually brings a larger pool of candidates among which you can find qualified applicants who already have experience in the area. It is also tempting to hire someone who can bring diversity and a different point of view because of his/her fresh look on the organization. On the other hand, external recruitment means less information about the candidate, higher costs related to the process, and longer onboarding time as external hires need to learn and adapt to the culture and the policies of the organization. Above all, it does not build employee engagement as employees do not receive a clear message about the opportunities to grow and develop their career within the organization. Even though it seems that there are more constraints for external talent searches, it is worth to underline that internal acquisition is not the best strategy for every company. In an organization experiencing corporate turnarounds or strategy shifts, the most obvious choice will be to search candidates externally. This is especially true if we are looking for very specific skills unlikely to be found within the company and we have all the processes or job trainings in place to support an external candidate during the integration period. Another important factor that will drive the selection of external candidates would be the lack of knowledge in terms of the internal talent pool because of absent or inconsistent information related to succession planning and performance.

While we were building a shared service organization in Poland, we needed to hire around 60 people at once with very specific skills—HR experience combined with a proficient level of different languages. As it was impossible to fulfill this talent need with the available internal candidates, we decided to go with a very intensive external talent acquisition which appeared to be the best way of finding so many talents with specific skills and experience during the time of massive organization changes.

Assuming you decide to search for external talents, you have a wide variety of recruiting strategies depending on market, candidate audience, and other factors typical for your organization. As it is impossible to describe every possible method, let's mention only a few of them that can facilitate the finding of the perfect demand planner and demand manager. Before beginning any search, it is important to develop a job description which clearly defines what outcomes you need from an employee performing this job.

Why are job descriptions and the way they are written so important? Among many things, a job description should consist of elements as per Fig. 5.3.

On the top of it, job description should definitely have an aim to attract candidates to response.

There are different methods of writing a job description depending on the organization's culture and the candidate audience this is addressed to. It is also obvious that the internal description will be much detailed than the one predicted for an external talent pool search. Additionally, as we want to capture the external audience attention and convince candidates that it is worth to apply for the position in our organization, an external job ad will have more marketing flavor than the internal description (Fig. 5.4).

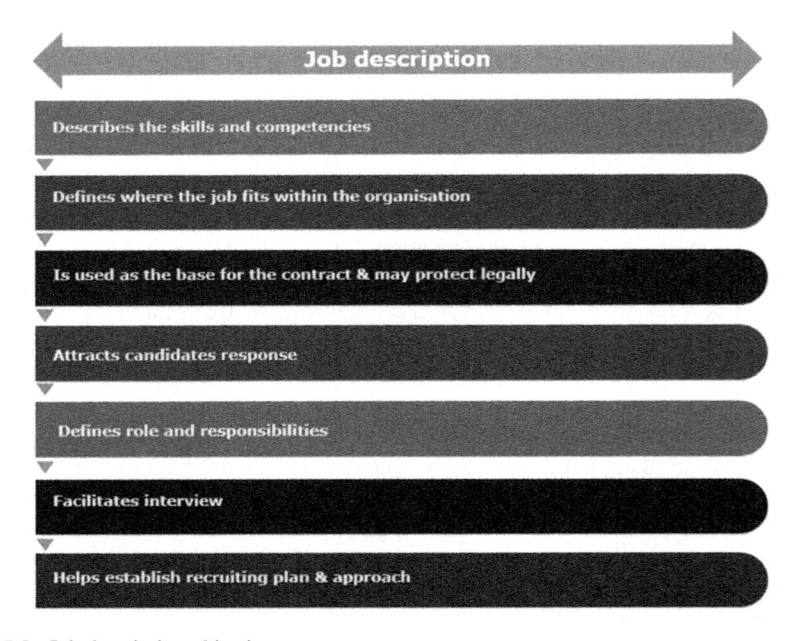

Fig. 5.3 Job description objectives

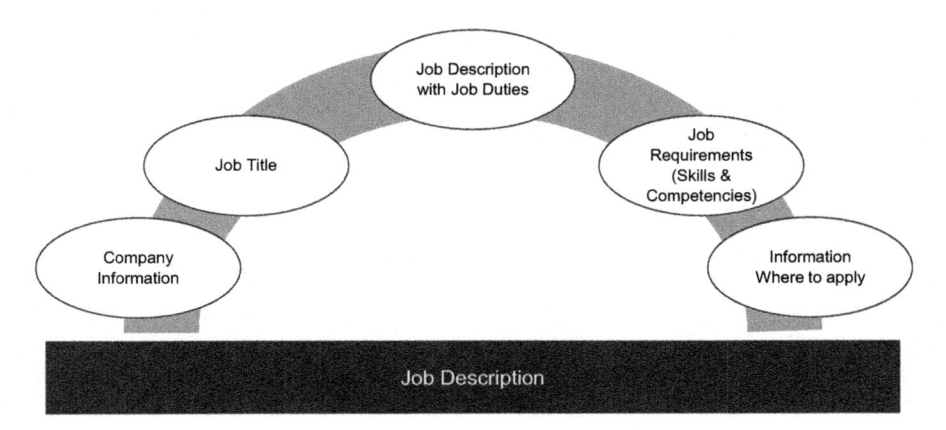

Fig. 5.4 Job description components

The crucial here is to understand with whom and how each of these critical IBP roles (demand planner, demand manager, finance controller) interact. Additionally, we should consider to have responsibilities, business impact, skills, and competences well defined for each of the roles. Required skills and competencies define the knowledge, skills, and attributes that the potential candidate should possess (e.g., analytical, data processing, and problem-solving skills). Based on the role definition, try to create a matrix that includes the competency, experience, and education that are required on each position. You can also identify the function which the competency supports and whether you think the competency is a minimum requirement or preferred requirement. When differentiating and describing roles, it is good to describe it taking into account responsibilities, business impact, skills, and competences related to focus areas.

Once we have a job description written, we can start choosing the best external talent source. All media (Internet, radio and TV, billboards, posters, and print publications) seem the most obvious ways of sourcing potential candidates and can be easily combined with all public relation activities related to employee branding. If you prefer to advertise your job opening to selected candidates, the best way is to use direct-to-candidate tactics among which are direct mail, tele-recruiting, or even workplace recruiting (reaching your candidate at his/her workplace). You can also use third-party recruiters and agencies if the position appears to be hard to fulfill but take into account that this is the most expensive way of recruiting. Government- and community-based programs assisting employers in finding and training candidate are also valuable sources of external talent pool of candidates. One of the most effective methods to attract best external talents is employee referral. Nowadays, many companies encourage their employees to participate in referral programs offering prizes or bonuses that underline the importance of this pool of sourcing.

How about finding internal candidates based on the knowledge you have and can easily obtain about your employees? What are the advantages of internal talent search? Is it only about cost-effectiveness? The answer of course is no. Finding internal candidate is not only cheaper. It is the way that enables an easier search because of the internal data that can help you assess the candidates and decide if he/she has the potential to do this job successfully. Contrary to external hires, internal candidates already know the organization, its culture, and environment so that their onboarding process will be much shorter than in the case of an external resource.

Additionally, it is proven that internals who change for a new role are less likely to leave the company, their loyalty, and engagement increase, and according to Deloitte's Human Capital Trends reports, companies' main effort is to drive higher engagement (Deloitte, 2017a).

Hiring internal candidate sends a positive message to all members of the organization as they see opportunities for career growth and development. As personal development, the ability to learn something new and get new skills is so important to Millennials; it is also a strong argument for winning this generation's loyalty. Another important factor that should not be ignored is cost as it is much more expensive to replace an employee than skilling him/her up.

Internal talent search is usually preferred by organizations who are growing with consistent and transparent succession planning and performance reviews. Skills required to perform the job that are not difficult to find in an organization is another important factor influencing that choice. Sometimes companies with no or few processes in place to support job training and integration decide to select internal talent acquisition as it is the easiest way to fulfill the role.

In one of the growing organizations we used to work for, we have decided to use available information related to succession plans and employees' performance to fill one position opening. As we wanted to hire someone highly motivated with good knowledge about the organization, we decided to seek for internal candidates with potential and interest in managing the human resource information system (HRIS) implementation as a project regional lead. We knew that the crucial factor wasn't experience in this area but the ability to perform successfully, motivation to grow, and skills easily to find within the organization. Based on knowledge we had, we managed to select internal talents that were able to perform this job. Additionally, with that internal selection, we sent a positive message to the company's employees whose motivation grows because of appearing possibilities for development.

In Fig. 5.5, you can find key differences between internal and external talent acquisition strategies.

Internal Talent Acquisition
Globalization, rapid changes, and demographics (aging society plus Millennials) create a huge demand for talents. How to find the right internal talent for IBP key stakeholders if they are already hired for another role? Internal talent acquisition usually embraces approaches that can be applied in combination or separately (Fig. 5.6).

Internal job posting is the easiest way to inform internal candidates about new open positions. Nowadays, most of the companies have their own recruitment platform where employees can apply directly whenever they find an interesting position. This is the fastest way to reach internal talents. Another way to find internal

5.1 Talent Acquisition

External TA
- Corporate turnarounds or strategy shifts
- No or inconsistent succession planning and performance information
- Skills not available within the organization
- Position integration support and training

Internal TA
- Growing organisation
- Consistent succession planning and performance information
- Skills available within the organization
- No position integration support and training

Fig. 5.5 External vs internal talent acquisition

- Job Posting
- Sponsorship
- HRIS Data

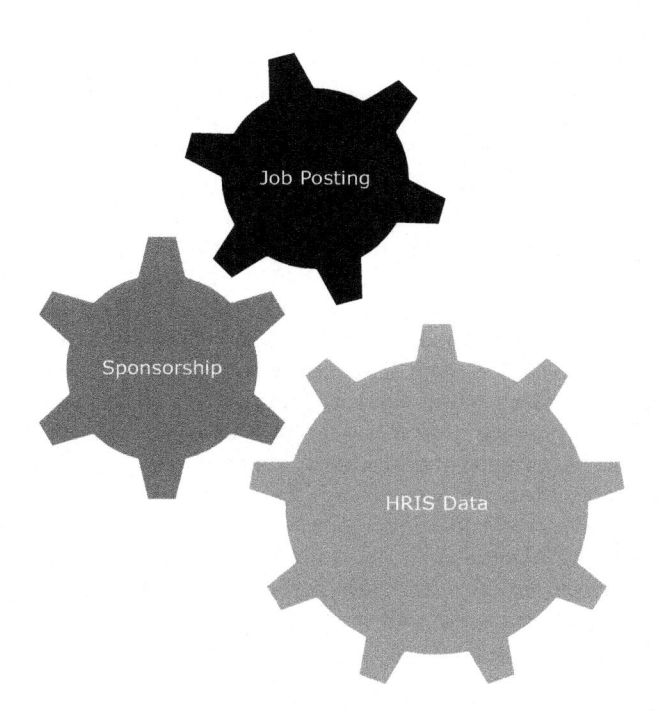

Fig. 5.6 Internal talent acquisition

candidates can be the manager nomination of high-performing employees. However, this may be perceived negatively as a symptom of favoritism. Last but not least, we can use data from the human resource information systems—data related to knowledge, skills, and abilities of candidates in combination with performance management, development plan, talent review, and succession planning information.

As part of your Integrated Business Planning transformation, you may consider to use two different talent acquisition approaches depending on the maturity of your organization and its talent processes and tools: use the data and talent applications already in place or elaborate the own tools to find the best candidate.

Assuming that your organization achieved talent management integration, your talent strategy (talent decisions supporting the business strategy) is aligned with the goals of the business and with the technology in place to support collaboration across processes. Integration means you have linked processes related to attract, manage, develop, and retain employees. Performance management, career management, succession management, leadership development, learning and capability development, total rewards, and talent acquisition are integrated through a common interface, data platform, workflow, and analytics (Buckingham & Goodall, 2015).

Taking into account the role definition of demand planner, demand manager, and finance manager, we know what responsibilities would be in the scope of these roles and what kind of skills and competencies are desired. Having an integrated process in place, we are able to use the necessary data to assess internal candidates. As a starting point, we can use HRIS data. In many companies, employees create their profiles in HRIS tools where they indicate their background, experience, skills, and knowledge. Sometimes we are even able to find on their information about their future goals and aspiration together with the data related to their performance review and development plan.

Performance management is the communication process between a manager and an employee that occurs throughout the year, in support of accomplishing the strategic objectives of the organization. During the interactions, the manager and employees have the chance to clarify expectations, set objectives, provide feedback, and review results. Using the performance management process and tools, we are able to seek for a candidate who is at or above their performance review. This means he/she is good at his/her job and will be good in their future role, an important factor to consider when looking for an internal candidate. The performance management discussions vary from year to year based on the changing objectives. The performance management process cycle includes planning, checking in, and reviewing. Everything begins when the manager and the employee review expectations and develop a performance plan that directs efforts toward achieving results aligned with the company's vision and support the employee's success. Throughout the year, goals and objectives are discussed during check-in meetings that provide a framework to ensure the employees achieve results through coaching and mutual feedback. At the end of the performance period, the manager reviews the employee's performance against expected objectives and discusses behaviors demonstrated in achieving those objectives.

It is worth to underline that today performance management is changing a lot: the focus is shifting away from annual reviews to a more ongoing form of accountability. Periodic meetings ensure more continual progresses, rather than a sudden push to meet goals at review time. Companies focus on ongoing processes that take place throughout the year and are very often more coaching oriented. To elevate the collaborative environment and strengthen the engagement, many companies decide to support a constant feedback environment. In some big consulting companies, employees receive regular peer-to-peer feedback and snapshots from their leader that are the basis for their performance and development discussion with their coaches (Buckingham & Goodall, 2015). This approach gives more data that can be used during the internal talent acquisition process. A constant feedback environment gives, namely, a more detailed look in a candidate's performance, his/her engagement, and his/her career aspirations.

The development plan is a group of activities and goals helping employees improve their performance and reach their career objectives. Usually, as a base of a development plan, organizations perform a development review to assess the competencies of the employee and the gap between the level that the employee represents and the level he/she should reach to improve their job or prepare for the next career step in the organization. Consequently, the manager together with the employees plans trainings or other development activities (e.g., mentoring, coaching, project) to improve employees' skills and competencies. As part of the development plan, the employee specifies his/her future career aspiration, interests, and mobility preferences that together with the knowledge about their competencies can be of great use for a talent search. Additionally, a development plan, if early planned, can be used to set objectives and define activities that can help the employee to develop the competencies and skills necessary to perform such a new role. To reach this, it is crucial to integrate the development plan into the employee's work and not underestimate its importance. In an organization where everyone understands the benefits of development plans and where everyone is supported by a strong learning culture, business results are better (Sherman, 2012).

When having processes and tools in place, the talent review and succession planning can be an additional source of knowledge for finding the perfect internal candidates. The talent review process is a series of talent review meetings to talk about business priorities, assess talents, and make decisions about the future. Meeting participants can go through activities similar to the ones highlighted in Fig. 5.7.

During the talent review, a nine-box chart can be created to represent any level of the organization and distinguish between high performers, those with high potential ready for new opportunities and those performing below expectations. In many talent review tools, comparison against different filters is possible. In addition, individual's data, including performance and potential ratings, experience, education, certifications, and mobility, can be easily stored in one place and successfully used to identify talents matching the demand planner, demand manager, and finance manager roles. Succession plans are one of the outcomes of the talent review process defining who will eventually replace people currently in key positions and naming activities to prepare successors for future roles via development plans. Succession plans specify a candidate's readiness to a job or position by using time frames or experience criteria. An HR/a talent manager when preparing succession plans defines the readiness level based on the knowledge about the candidate and whether the candidate has gaps between the current competencies and the skills required for the new role. Talent pools can be connected with succession plans to manage the development of a candidate, e.g., by creating goals for the candidates

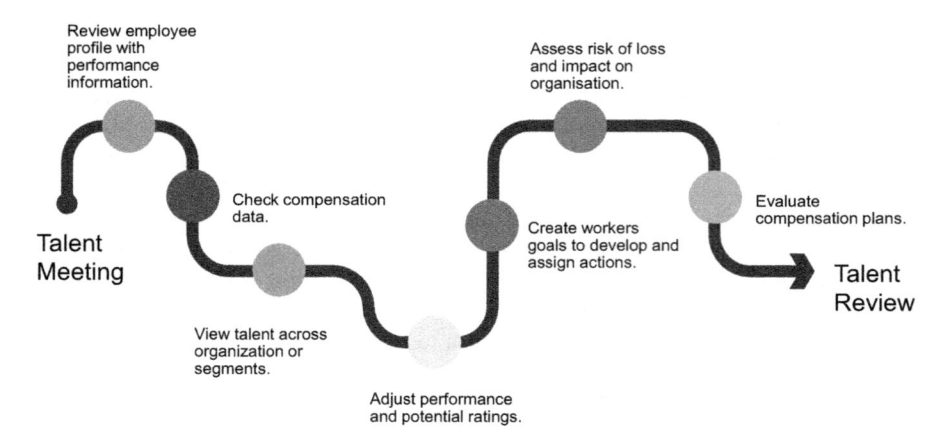

Fig. 5.7 Talent review meeting possibilities

that help prepare them for the job or position for which the plan has been created. All the above can be treated as useful for sourcing candidates for internal talent acquisitions.

If you do not have those processes and tools in place, it does not mean that you are unable to assess internal candidates. In this situation, it is good to create own "tools" for employee and manager assessment. To proceed, talent manager based on role definition can create forms (paper, excel, or online if tools in place) where all participants of the recruitment process can easily assess competencies and skills necessary for the successful performance in this position. Near each feature, assessors can evaluate if this is to be evaluated as excellent, good, fair, or poor and add comments if necessary. Additionally, a part related to experience and education can be placed. With this information in place, managers with the support from the talent manager side can decide if this candidate has enough potential to successfully perform required role (Fig. 5.8).

Another interesting way to find internal talent can be through internal mobility programs. To implement it or take advantage of it, you need to think about the candidate's potential to perform. To approach internal skill gaps, try to see what an internal candidate is capable of. Take a look at the candidates with cross-functional and crossover skills. Maybe you already have rotational programs for your employees that could be the perfect base to spot candidates with cross-functional skills and multidimensional points of view. Some companies use bungee or stretch program to keep their best people.

Google has developed "bungee program," which encourages employees to plunge into an entirely different department from 3 months to 1 year. It is proved that switching groups and roles not only gives the possibility to gain new skills but also fosters retention and a happy involvement in work. Bungee is a perfect opportunity to network and see new side of one another. When trying assignments in different areas, employees gain new skills and learn whether they like the new job and if they are good at it. Even if they return to their old role, they possess new knowledge and experiences that can be shared with their colleagues. New

Candidate Evaluation by Manager

Manager Name _____   Date _____

Employee Information

Candidate Name _____

Education _____

_____

Experience _____

_____

Skills Evaluation

Skills evaluation	Excellent	Good	Fair	Poor	Comments

Competencies Evaluation

Competencies evaluation	Excellent	Good	Fair	Poor	Comments

Manager Signature _____

Fig. 5.8 Internal talent assessment form

assignments can bring energy, fostering collaborations, creativity, and job satisfaction (Anderson, 2015).

5.2 Talent Retention

Retention management creates a working environment through the implementation of initiatives that focuses on forming, applying, and improving the workplace in which an employee is hired and thus encouraging employees to remain with their current employer.

In order to retain employees, human resources focus on areas within human resources. David J. Forrest (Forrest, 1999) defines five basic principles of retention management that lead to higher employee performance and satisfaction and therefore to their retention.

1. **People**:
   Employees need to feel they are being respected, appreciated, and valued and that their work benefits the overall company goal and direction.
2. **Personal development**:
   Employees need to have the possibility to grow both professionally and personally by recognizing and making the best use of their potential. The company should support personal growth by implementing development plans and investing in training and development programs in order to maximize on employee potential.
3. **Growth in responsibility**:
   Employees strive to grow and advance in their careers as part of their personal development. They need to feel they are gaining relevant experience, competencies, and opportunities to be more responsible in the work they do. Companies assist employees in managing them through their career by giving them more roles and responsibilities that are focused on performance and results. As part of their growth, the manager should map out what the employee is good at and possible areas for development, design a plan, and offer necessary tools and trainings in order to fill in the missing gaps. As the competency gap is met and they grow, employees should receive higher levels of responsibility and accountability in order to maximize their potential.
4. **Internal relationships**:
   Poor relationships with co-workers and the management can cause many employees to be disengaged and in turn cause lower effectiveness. Managers and employees alike have mass choices that can assist them in working together in order to improve their relationship and performance. Employees need to feel they are working for and around people they can respect, appreciate, and value. Primarily, it begins with the readiness from the side of senior executives and business owners to identify problems and find relevant solutions in order to improve interactions between managers and their employees.
5. **Success**:
   Employees need to feel valued and feel that they are successful in their deliverables. Their work needs to be meaningful and feed into the overall success of the business. A strong employee needs to be rewarded through different

domains within the major areas of human resources and also praised for assisting other employees to be successful.

5.2.1 Why Should Companies Invest in Retaining Employees?

1. **Financial effect**:
   Employee turnover is expensive, and companies with a high employee turnover rate typically incur higher costs. Replacing an employee heavily impacts the operational budget as additional costs of job advertising, training, development, and other organizational changes need to be incurred. While direct costs may be easy to measure, by their very nature indirect costs may be hidden and difficult to establish. New employees take significant time to go on board while they learn their job, which includes reduced quality, errors, and waste causing additional cost to the company.
   By retaining employees, the organization can keep overall costs and turnover to a minimum and keep morale and productivity on a high level.
2. **Productivity**:
   High turnover reflects on team morale and on the team's productivity which in turn affects the company as a whole. On boarding, new employees take time and energy from a significant amount of people (like HR and management) which should be focusing on the clients and the overall goal of the organization. It takes significant time and energy to help the new hire learn and adapt to the organization before the employee becomes fully productive.
3. **Competitors**:
   Companies that do not invest in retention risk their employees in leaving the organization and going to their direct competitors where they can apply the knowledge and skills they gained from the previous employment.
4. **Positive work culture**:
   Promoting a collaborative work environment in which employees work together rather than compete will help build stronger cooperation and understanding among them. The company should endorse and empower their employees to come together. Herewith they would feel to serve a common purpose while being in line with the company strategy. Employees that closely work with each other eventually adopt traits, complement strengths or weaknesses, and eventually adopt qualities from one another. Employees that collaborate for longer periods of time become in sync with one another and can develop shared processes for completing work in an efficient manner.
5. **Client satisfaction**:
   As the company's success is largely dependent on client satisfaction, an organization with a high employee turnover rate runs the risk of giving the organization a bad reputation. In addition to this, if clients work closely with an employee that is leaving, the company may risk losing the client to the new place of employment which more than often is the direct competitor. This results in a loss of revenue for the organization.

It is clear that having proper retention strategies is key in order to retain employees. Retention strategies are favorable to companies that want to retain employees within the organization, keeping costs of turnover down. More than often, employees that remain with the company for a longer period of time are respected, appreciated, given feedback, provided with growth opportunities, and given work-life balance options and have trust and confidence in their managers. In order to foster an environment that motivates and stimulates employees, managers need to incorporate motivation-building practices into their corporate culture which increases employee effectiveness.

By making employees feel comfortable in the workplace, retention rate will go up and so will the overall success of the organization.

To keep good employees in the company, Ryan Holmes, founder of Hootsuite, decided to adapt "google bungee program," claiming that great employees are great no matter what their roles are and also because of their attitude (Holmes, 2016). Based on that, he decided to give them a chance to try new positions within the company to prevent them from leaving. This is a very positive approach, especially taking into account Millennials that are willing to develop, learn, change a job every 2.5 years, and switch industries. In the summer of 2016, half a dozen participants joined the Hootsuite "stretch program." To be selected, they needed to perform at or above performance review levels and needed to have worked in the company for at least a year. Before joining, participants prepared learning plans approved by both the current and the rotational manager. During the program, they spent 90 days assigned to another department. Their current manager needed to agree on the reduction of their duties as they spent 1 day per week in the adoptive team. At the end of the 90-day program, if the new role was working for everyone, the employee could make the jump to full time, once his or her old role has been backfilled. If not, they were free to return full time to the previous role or try a new assignment.

No matter what was the final result of the stretch program, if they decided to transition to their new role or return to their old job, Hootsuite's CEO believes the program only brings positive effects as employees have the chance to try new positions without the risk of leaving the company. This unique program gives them the opportunity to network, get new skills, break silos, and take a look into other business areas. Keeping employees who want to grow and giving them the chance to evolve are really critical to attract and retain talent. This is also a great way to find a brand new career that can be used to find the perfect demand planner, demand manager, and finance controller as key IBP candidates. Additionally, it can support the different specialist and management career tracks for them.

5.3 Career Path Development

5.3.1 What Is a Career Path?

Employee path development provides information regarding the directions and career opportunities available within an organization. A career path displays the steps in a possible career and a plausible timeline for accomplishing them. Career paths must specify the qualifications needed to proceed to the next step and the minimum length of time employees must spend in each role to obtain and gain the necessary experience.

Employee career pathing is most effective when integrated into a company's overall talent management strategy. By aligning talent management processes and providing linkage between job roles, desired competencies, and key experiences, career paths direct employees toward the company's future competitiveness.

Integrated Business Planning is a very cross-functional process, and individuals who play a role in it may find various interest areas as part of the transformation program. Demand manager may understand more and get interested in marketing and product management, financial controllers may want to explore management roles, and demand planner may want to investigate roles in sales or even IT. IBP may open their eyes to any area of development they want to pursue.

5.3.2 What Are the Career Path Development Stages?

1. Create a career map:
   Career maps define common paths for moving within and across roles in ways that can facilitate growth and career development and display what a career looks like in terms of sequential positions, roles, and stages. Companies can use existing competency grades or job bands to define vertical and horizontal hierarchies if they have them implemented, and they can also compile organizational knowledge to create a general career mapping framework. Some organizations choose to provide additional information such as common transfers when changing careers, number of employees in a particular job role and the growth across those populations, and different job categories in particular business units. This information is particularly useful as employees become more versatile and move across job roles in different parts of the business to increase their expertise (Bopp, Bing, & Forte-Trammell, 2010; Carter, Cook, & Dorsey, 2009; Council. CEB Corporate Leadership, 2006).
2. Build position profiles:
   Position profiles create distinctions among job roles in career paths by outlining their core responsibilities, skills, and requirements. To do this, organizations consult subject matter experts, interview functional leaders, and conduct external industry benchmarking. It is also important to determine the qualifications and expertise associated with different career positions, roles, and stages. This might include the recommended or required education, skills,

technical training, licenses, and certifications for successful performance at each stage (Carter et al., 2009; Council. CEB Corporate Leadership, 2006).
3. Identify core competencies and expected behaviors:
    Competencies should outline behaviors that are displayed by outstanding performers and should serve as a performance basis that determine anticipated results in different roles. Competencies should enable performance and should be in line with the business strategy. Companies have introduced the concept of "vertically integrated" competencies in an effort to vertically align career path design with the strategic talent management process. These competencies tend to be the same from one career stage to the next; however, they differ between stages on what the expected scope is and the impact which the competencies should deliver (Bopp et al., 2010; White, 2012).
4. Incorporate training and development:
    Companies by prioritizing position profile characteristics and identifying key experiences that employees should acquire can link career paths to employee growth. Developmental opportunities can include leadership training courses, additional assignments, cross-functional team responsibilities, profit and loss ownership, and/or international exposure. All these examples should be interlinked in the company strategy and should provide the opportunity to develop competencies that are important for the next career stage (Bopp et al., 2010; Carter et al., 2009; Council. CEB Corporate Leadership, 2006; White, 2012).
5. Establish accountability:
    Companies should create tools to ensure effectiveness using the large amount of resources invested in the career pathing process. These tools should determine accountability for the job and define roles and responsibilities of individuals who support it, ensuring it can adapt to changing business conditions in order to meet the company's strategy (Council. CEB Corporate Leadership, 2006).

5.3.3 What Are the Key Factors for Successful Implementation of Career Pathing?

- Communication:
    Companies should communicate to their employees about the organization's career development approach. Important areas that should be addressed are: What is the role of the employee versus the role of the manager? Should employees drive their own career move, or is it the responsibility of the managers to assist them with their career moves? Moreover, what is the company's perspective on career success factors, international assignments, and level of mobility? All these important factors are needed to assist the employee in making the right career decisions (Carter et al., 2009; Filmer & Jeffay, 2010).

- Support:
  The necessary tools, guidelines, templates, and incentives must be provided to the employee and their manager to ensure that both sides understand the importance of and are committed to their role in the career development process. Potential career management resources may include physical or virtual career development centers of excellence, career advisors, training to help managers become better career coaches, employee self-assessments, and career discussion guides (CEB Corporate Leadership Council, 2002; Council. CEB Corporate Leadership, 2006).
- Networking:
  Encouraging networking within the company is also a great way for employees to explore career opportunities and gives the grounds for employees to better understand the working of the company and enhances learning and development. Some companies set internal professional groups, networking events, common interest groups, social media platforms, and mentoring programs (Bopp et al., 2010; Carter et al., 2009).
- Strategic Analytics:
  Functional competencies linked to career stages tell companies what capabilities are needed to reach the company strategy and what capabilities the company already has within the workforce. The gap between the two gives the company a picture of the capability transformation that the company will need to put in place in order to help meet their (White, 2012).

5.4 IBP Center of Expertise: Leadership!

Understanding how to sustain change in your organization should be on the top of your agenda. We are not saying how to reach a go-live but how to embed changes in the process and in people behaviors. It is a topic which addresses the importance of company culture (Fig. 5.9). The Integrated Business Planning Center of Expertise could make transformation adaptable to changing business environment and could take ownership to introduce and sustain change in processes, organizational structures, capabilities, and technology.

It has been proven by many studies that ca. 70% of the transformation programs did not deliver what was intended. Many problems with the realization of these programs come from the failure associated to the lack of a change sustainability framework and the lack of leadership or management support. There are many reasons for this: some important ones are the resistance to change and the lack of proper management buy-in. Transformation is often treated as an extra task for "line" organization senior management, tasks which are often not being measured. This makes it easy for the responsible person to agree to anything but apply "my" ways of working. When driving change, personal connection becomes critical, and the same goes for sustainability of change in organization. You should know what is in it for

> **CULTURE CANNOT BE COPIED, STRATEGY CAN**
>
> Gostick & Elton

Fig. 5.9 Culture cannot be copied

you, right? That is what business line experts and leaders expect to understand. We should understand some common pitfalls that transformation programs fall into:

– Make a change which is not lived.
– Implement change without influencing behaviors.
– Neglect relationship between "project" and "line" organization.
– Lack of focus on cross-functional process excellence.
– Lack of focus on knowledge sharing.
– Lack of focus on proper documentation.

This is exactly what IBP CoE should focus on. Sustainability of transformation is mainly focused on people; therefore, the IBP center of expertise should focus its efforts on:

– Process improvement or lead transformation
– Transparency regarding project information and objectives
– Coordinate learning and development of various stakeholder groups
– Building education framework and knowledge sharing platform
– Continuous improvements by design
– Process governance
– Talent management.

The IBP Center of Expertise should leverage cross-functional expertise from:

– Demand planning
– Finance
– Supply and operations
– Sales and marketing
– IT/system

5.4 IBP Center of Expertise: Leadership! 147

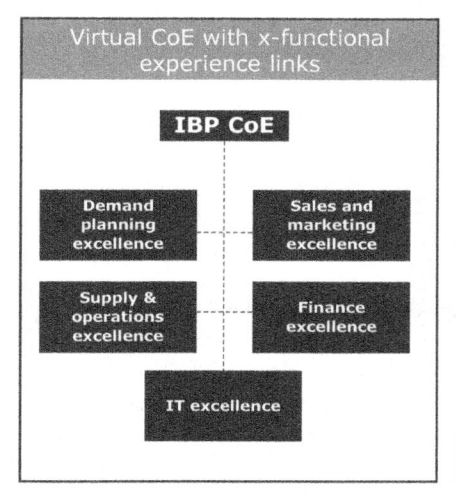

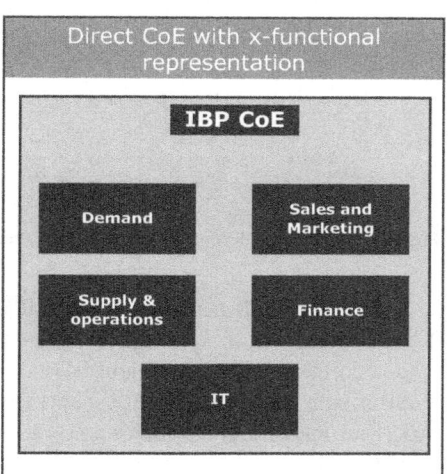

Fig. 5.10 IBP Center of Expertise (excellence) virtual vs direct model

Let us start from how to organize an Integrated Business Planning CoE. In most cases, there is a possibility to leverage existing excellence teams and form the IBP CoE as a "virtual" one but led and organized by an IBP champion.

The other approach could be to form the IBP CoE as an organizational unit which truly holds IBP transformation and improvements together on a global scale (Fig. 5.10).

Which one is the better approach? There is no single, universal answer. You need to decide what you want to achieve or what is really possible to be achieved with an IBP transformation program and then pick a model which matches those expectations. Running CoE as a soft virtual link between existing functionally focused expertise teams may work, but it all depends on the IBP champions and teams. In the other model, you are less dependent on the interactions between the experts managed by different functional managers and driven by different KPIs. In both models, the challenge of business operating model transformation stays the same.

You may think to adopt IBP CoE approach as (Fig. 5.11):

– Centralized, where IBP CoE will overarch business units
– Decentralized, where IBP Coe will be business unit specific

The centralized approach is good in homogeneous, relatively small, or less complex organizations. The decentralized model may be good in large, heterogeneous, and very distinctive business models operated under the same formal umbrella. If you go for decentralized model, you would invest time to find synergies between business units and take as much efforts as required to unify the IBP CoE.

Decentralized		Centralized	
Business unit A	Business unit B	Business unit A	Business unit B
IBP CoE	IBP CoE	IBP CoE	

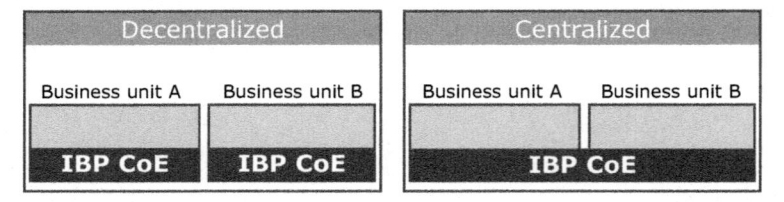

Fig. 5.11 IBP CoE decentralized vs centralized model

Let us scratch the surface of the challenges linked to deployment of CoE concept. You should define and agree with your senior management what kind of responsibilities IBP CoE should have. What do we mean by that? There should be a clear split of responsibilities between the organizational unit which run the processes and the one which takes care of transformation and improvements. We see CoE as responsible for the design, understood as in Fig. 3.2. Design is not how it looks but how it works in business, yet departments who run specific parts of IBP should be accountable for the results.

As we have highlighted above, demand and forecasting excellence may be integrated virtually into IBP CoE but still should be understood as:

- Mix of people with high statistical skills (demand analytics) and people who work closely to market businesses (demand planners)
- Demand analytics as useful and meaningful input and KPIs to the demand planners, so that they can make the right adjustments
- Not to rely on gut feelings but on the right amount of competences mix
- Position demand champions to drive the journey to become demand driven (Chase, 2016)

5.4.1 Let Us Talk About IBP COE Leadership!

Research within S&OP implementations has proven that adequate leadership is of high importance in particular when linked to the IBP champion role.

IBP champions should ensure that their employees feel "engaged, enabled, and energized." This approach is what makes employee performances increase and thus benefits the company. To ensure an effective "E + E + E" approach, the IBP champion should lead by example and:

1. **Define the burning platform**: managers need to instill employees' commitments by letting them understand the importance of their contribution to the cause.
2. **Create customer focus**: employees should develop and build a customer-focused relationship to enhance loyalty and satisfaction.
3. **Develop agility**: customers and employees need to be able to cope effectively and efficiently with change.

5.4 IBP Center of Expertise: Leadership!

4. **Create an open culture**: managers need to create an open and transparent platform for communication.
5. **Partner with your talents**: be inclusive, open for discussion with your team, and treat everybody as equal, allowing conversation around important topics.
6. **Encourage support and praise for each other**: higher level of goodwill and thanking each other for the results achieved.
7. **Establish clear accountability:** monitor performances by making employees accountable for their results and goals achieved (Gostick & Elton, 2012).

Having said the above, IBP champions should be a "people's person" rather than a "techy person." The IBP CoE team should provide all required expertise to the IBP champion, and they, as a result, should fully understand IBP. Champions should have operational experience in leading one of the functional pillars of IBP like process owner, organization change lead, capabilities transformation, or system manager. There should be a certain degree of functional knowledge needed by an IBP champion but focus should be mainly on "people."

The IBP champion may take into account the following approach:

- Establish clarity of intent and personal well-defined accountability.
- Introduce a scorecard method to evaluate, account, reward, or discipline (Howells, 2017).

And the IBP champion should ensure that the following areas are covered:

1. Building knowledge and skills for practical execution
2. Embedding leadership behaviors to build process sustainability
3. Developing cross-functional capability (James, 2015)

The business environment has changed over the recent years, and leadership should catch up with the new challenges that this entails. Leadership is essential to the success of a transformation, and many companies see leadership different than they did in the past.

Let us have a look on selected characteristics of the competency/leadership model introduced at Merck:

- A strong connection and awareness of the corporate strategy.
- Ethics oriented.
- Englobing technology and innovation.
- Result-oriented approach.
- Building trustworthy collaborations.
- Every single person around the globe has to embrace the new competency model. It needs to be lived (Berkmann, 2017).

In the above Merck model, leadership is understood holistically and distributed on all levels and not only associated to senior roles within the organization.

Good leadership is a transferable skill and is important in all areas of the business. Practitioners' view (Bradberry, 2017) explains what makes a great leader/IBP champion:

- An outstanding ability in communication that ensures connections and quick understanding.
- A brave heart that makes tough decisions in difficult times and that inspires and protects collaborators.
- With a leader, the so-called golden rule reaches a higher level: treat each person as he or she would like to be treated.
- A clear understanding and awareness of his week and strength points.
- Passion and enthusiasm.
- A leader needs to be humble, honest, and authentic and sometimes has to do the dirty work.
- Care about people not just for a team perspective but for human generosity.
- A strong vision that always transpires during conversations.
- A great understanding of people and a positive approach that spurs new ideas flow among colleagues.
- Taking responsibilities.
- Vision and purpose.

Many of us think that the soft skills that are required to lead are gained with time and experience, but actually this is not always the case. Emotional intelligence is defined as "the capacity to be aware of, control, and express one's emotions, and to handle interpersonal relationships judiciously and empathetically." Emotional intelligence is a skill that can be learned and is a mark of professional maturity; it can take years to develop and a lifetime to master.

We should be aware that the majority of people that want to lead are driven by feeding their egos, without considering if their lead could really bring an added value to the team (Feloni, 2016).

Let us think out of the box and bring examples of leadership from two Navy SEALs: Jocko Willink and Leif Babin. They summarize some key leadership characteristics, which may be very valid in defining IBP leadership model (Fig. 5.12):

- Take full responsibility—do not blame the others but act proactively to solve issues.
- Build a united team and help employees develop within them, minimize team conflicts, and manage team dynamics.
- Believe in your mission and do not forget there is always something to learn—admit your weaknesses.
- Do not go alone, but move in unison with your members.
- To proper execute a mission, you have to keep it simple!
- Prioritization, especially when everything cannot be handled in the same moment or simply because the right time has not come yet.

> **THERE ARE NO BAD TEAMS, ONLY BAD LEADERS**
>
> Jocko Willink and Leif Babin

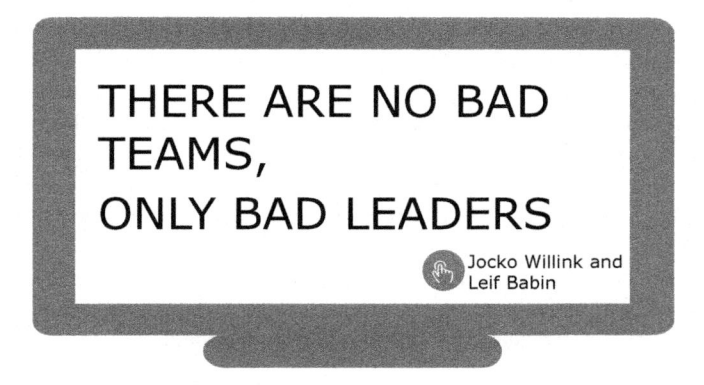

Fig. 5.12 There are no bad teams, only bad leaders

- Decentralizing decisions allowing others to take decisions when circumstances require it. Decision-making should be both top-down and bottom-up.
- Not complaining but acting savvy toward top management if task objectives are unrealistic or hide too much difficulties.
- Being firm but resolved, avoiding hostile circumstances getting you paralyzed (Hittelet, 2017).

5.5 Summary

- Integrated Business Planning opens opportunities for new skill sets and cross-functional organizational structure alignment to support vertical and horizontal integration.
- New business needs related to capabilities exposed with IBP can be addressed with the blend of internal and external talent acquisition.
- There is high cost associated to lack of talent acquisition and talent retention strategy. Cost appropriation should not be the only criteria in talent acquisition and retention strategy.
- Job description exemplifies if you know what you want.
- Internal talent acquisition is mostly done by organizations with consistent and transparent succession planning and performance reviews.
- Internals who change for a new role are less likely to leave the company.
- Very specialized roles or new competencies are often sourced externally.
- Trend is being observed that talents want to change their assignments, gain new skills, and learn whether they like specific aspect of the job and if they are good at it.
- Trend is being observed that companies walk away from annual performance review toward frequent check-in meetings and performance snapshots.
- Talent retention may impact company financials, productivity, outflow to competitors, work culture, and customer satisfaction.

- Talents tend to leave not their companies but their bosses.
- Career paths to success depends on communication (e.g., who drives it, manager or employee), support (e.g. tools, guidelines), networking (e.g., planner community), and analytics (e.g., as is capabilities versus needed capabilities).
- IBP Center of Expertise can be positioned as virtual or direct organizational unit which aims to sustain capability, process, and technology change.
- IBP Center of Expertise should be cross functional and should be led by IBP champion.
- Talent diversity may increase productivity and creativity; therefore, consider blending Millennials, boomers, male and female, cultures, and backgrounds.
- There is no effective change without well-rounded leaders.

References

Anderson, K. (2015). *Help others be happier and higher-performing together at work*. Retrieved from http://www.huffingtonpost.com/kare-anderson/help-others-be-happier-and-higher-performing-together-at-work_b_7081608.html

Berkmann, K. (2017). *A new leadership approach for the changing working environment*. Retrieved from https://www.linkedin.com/pulse/new-leadership-approach-changing-working-environment-kai-beckmann

Bopp, M. A., Bing, D. A., & Forte-Trammell, S. (2010). Agile career development: Lessons and approaches from IBM. *IBM Press*.

Bradberry, T. (2017). *The daily habits of exceptional leaders*. Retrieved from https://www.linkedin.com/pulse/daily-habits-exceptional-leaders-dr-travis-bradberry

Buckingham, M., & Goodall, A. (2015). Reinventing performance management. *Harvard Business*.

Carter, G. W., Cook, K. W., & Dorsey, D. W. (2009). *Charting courses to success for organizations and their employees*. New York: Wiley.

CEB Corporate Leadership Council. (2002). Career pathing strategies. *CEB Corporate Leadership Council*.

Chase, C. W. (2016). *Next generation demand management: People, process, analytics, and technology*. Hoboken, NJ: Wiley.

Council. CEB Corporate Leadership. (2006). *Career pathing processes and tools*. CEB Corporate Leadership Council.

Deloitte. (2016a). *2016 Deloitte Millenial Survey: Winning over the next generation of leaders*. Deloitte Touche Tomhmatsu Limited.

Deloitte. (2016b). *Talent acquisition*. Retrieved from http://blog.bersin.com/recruitment-is-not-talent-acquisition/

Deloitte. (2017a). *2017 Human capital trends: The new organization: Different by design*. Deloitte Touche Tomhmatsu Limited.

Deloitte. (2017b). *Rewriting the rules for the digital age*. Deloitte Touche Tomhmatsu Limited.

Erickson, R. (2012). Recruiting is NOT talent acquisition. *Bersin by Deloitte*.

Feloni, R. (2016). *Former Navy SEAL commanders explain why "there are no bad teams, only bad leaders"*. Retrieved from http://uk.businessinsider.com/former-navy-seals-no-bad-teams-only-bad-leaders-2016-9?r=US&IR=T

Filmer, S., & Jeffay, J. (2010). Rethinking career management in a changed business environment. *Human Capital Perspective*. Mercer LLC.

Forrest, D. J. (1999). *The foundation of employee retention*. Uniregistry Corporation. Retrieved from http://www.keepemployees.com/?f

Gostick, A., & Elton, C. (2012). Culture eats strategy for breakfast. *LinkedIn*.

References

Hittelet, P. -Y. (2017). *Leadership: 12 lessons from the Navy SEALs*. Retrieved from https://www.linkedin.com/pulse/leadership-12-lessons-from-navy-seals-pierre-yves-hittelet

Holmes, R. (2016). An unexpected way to stop people from quitting. *LinkedIn*. Retrieved from https://www.linkedin.com/pulse/unexpected-way-stop-people-from-quitting-ryan-holmes

Howells, R. (2017). *How to win with the right people in your digital supply chain*. Retrieved from https://www.forbes.com/sites/sap/2017/03/02/how-to-win-with-the-right-people-in-your-digital-supply-chain/#34658624618d

James, N. (2015, December). *3 Ways coaching & mentoring will improve your S&OP programme*.

Sherman, S. (2012). *High-impact performance management: Improving development planning*. Bersin by Deloitte.

White, D. G. (2012). Driving change through career models: An operating system for integrated talent management – rationale, approach, and the story at Microsoft and ITT. *Ontos Global LLC*.

How to Enable Change with SAP IBP Technology

6.1 SAP IBP Applications Overview

SAP Integrated Business Planning is a real-time supply chain planning solution purpose built to profitably meet future demand by optimizing the supply chain. Built natively on SAP HANA and deployed in cloud, SAP IBP provides the flexibility, agility, and performance to meet complex planning requirements of the next-generation supply chain. With integrated planning covering strategic, tactical, and operation level planning and a unified integrated model covering sales and operations planning, demand planning, inventory optimization, response and supply, and control tower, SAP IBP provides a single platform for all the planning needs. Together with robust planning algorithms, real-time simulations, what-if analysis, dashboards and analytics, alerts, embedded social collaboration, and data integration with external sources, SAP IBP is the state-of-the-art planning solution (Fig. 6.1).

6.1.1 Application Modules in SAP IBP

IBP for Sales and Operations Planning
Senior management business process to profitably align demand and supply to arrive at one business plan for the company. Typically executed as a monthly business planning process, IBP S&OP supports real-time what-if scenarios and simulations, collaborative planning, process management, and analytics to support a mid- to long-term aggregated tactical business plan.

IBP for Demand
With focus on attaining higher demand forecast accuracy, SAP IBP demand consists of:

– Mid- to long-term demand planning capabilities

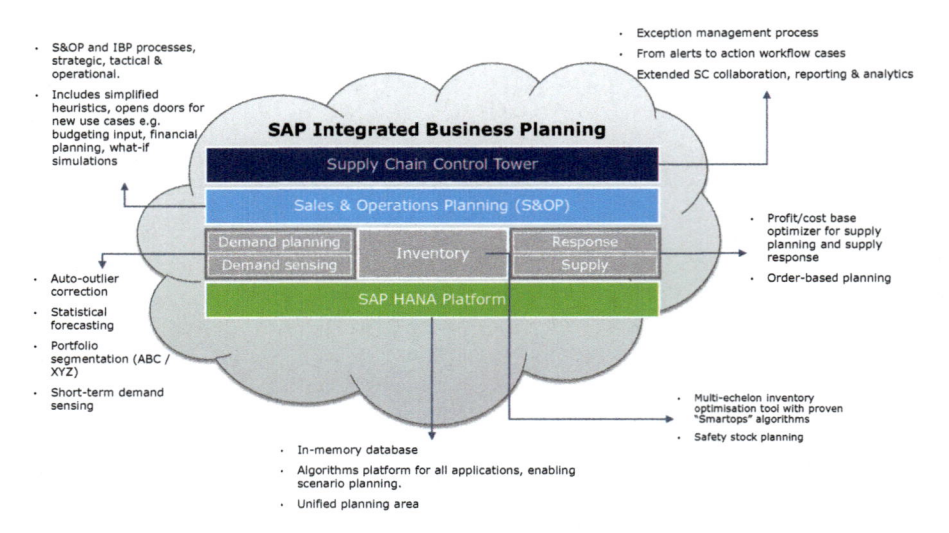

Fig. 6.1 SAP IBP applications overview

– Short-term demand sensing to provide a short-term sensed demand considering short-term demand signals analyzed using predictive pattern recognition algorithms

The demand planning capabilities include statistical forecasting, historical data analysis, product life cycle management, portfolio and customer segmentation, forecast error analysis, and demand classifications.

IBP for Inventory Optimization
Provides optimal stock recommendations together with inventory components at every stage of the supply network by performing multi-echelon inventory optimization balancing customer service and inventory levels. Provides the right mix of inventory considering forecast errors, demand variability, and supply uncertainties.

IBP for Response and Supply Planning
Supports tactical time series supply planning for S&OP process with unconstrained heuristics or constrained optimization, operational supply and response planning to generate constrained supply plan and allocation, and short-term order confirmations and deployment process. Generates supply proposals to execution systems.

Supply Chain Control Tower
Provides end-to-end supply chain visibility and insights to action for supply chain problems; exception management, analytics, and case management to uncover and resolve supply chain issues; performance measurements KPIs to monitor supply chain health; and support for business network collaboration with Ariba.

6.1 SAP IBP Applications Overview 157

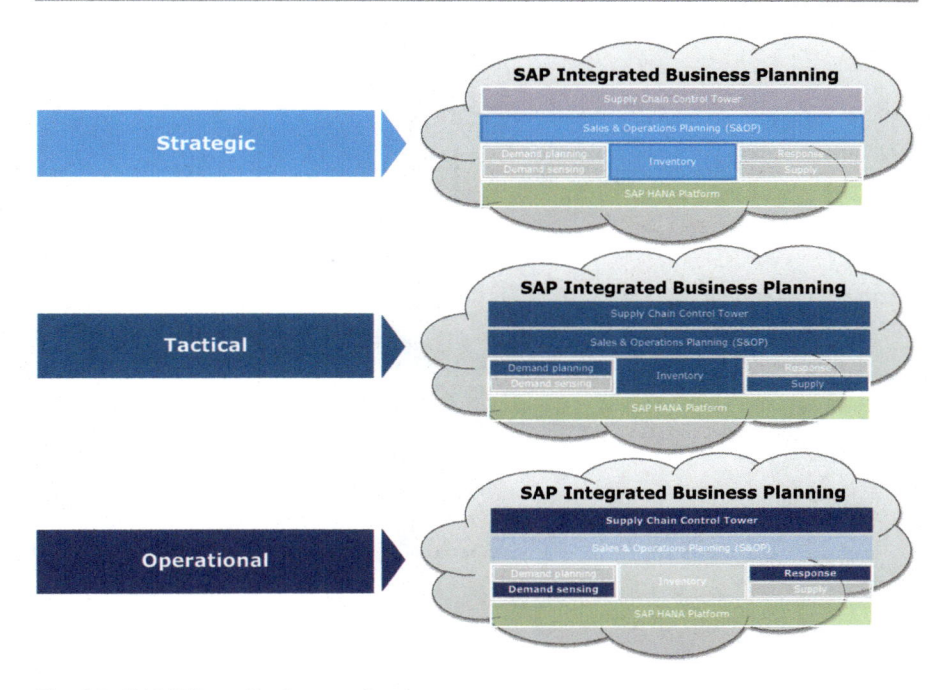

Fig. 6.2 SAP IBP applications vs planning type

SAP IBP covers business planning processes in a single application ranging from the strategic level long-term planning with focus on long-range demand plans, capacity, and financial projections to tactical level plans for mid- to long-term horizon to operation plan for short-term planning horizon with focus on reactiveness and agility in the frozen planning window. Figure 6.2 shows how each application module fits to the strategic, tactical, and operational planning. Supply chain control tower provides visibility across all the planning levels and horizons.

We now look at each of the applications of SAP IBP and their key capabilities in more detail.

6.1.2 IBP for Sales and Operations Planning

Sales and operations planning balances demand and supply plans aligned with the financial targets of a company. Typically run as a cross-functional, mid- to long-term tactical planning at a monthly or weekly level for 3–24 month horizon, S&OP is a bridge between strategic plans and the operations/execution. As shown in Fig. 6.3, S&OP takes inputs from strategic, operations, sales, and financial plans and arrives at one business plan that is agreed by the executive team.

SAP IBP for sales and operations provides the functionality to run an S&OP process for a company. The key enablers for:

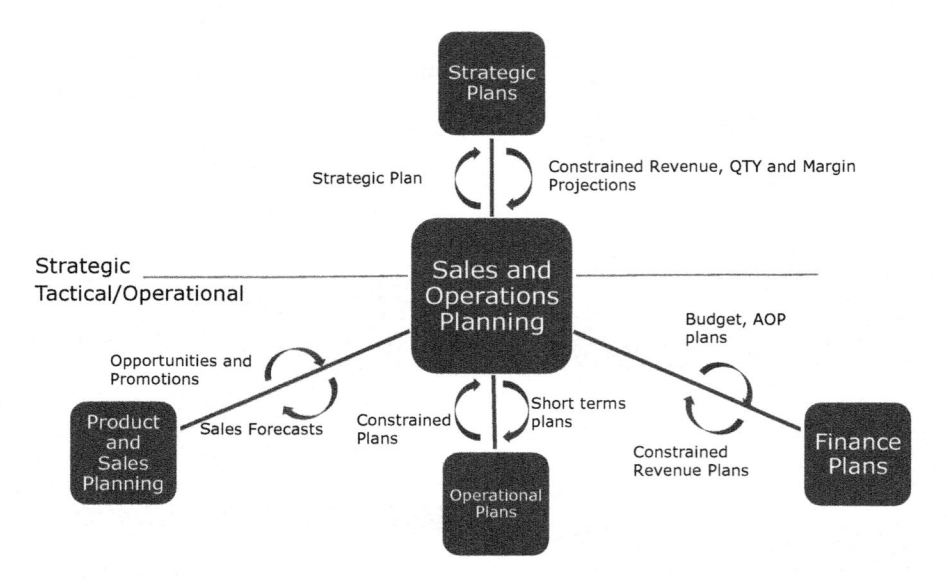

Fig. 6.3 Business operations overview

1. Unified data model and planning capabilities for demand, supply, and finance: A single unified data model that combines demand, supply, and finance integrated from a functional and process standpoint supporting critical planning functions like aggregations, disaggregations, planning at multiple levels of hierarchy without the need for data replication, or logging to multiple systems. The model is highly flexible and can be customized to the business process of each customer and adapted as the business model changes.
2. Real-time planning with scenarios, versions, and what-if simulations: An important aspect of S&OP is to perform what-if analysis by making changes to the base plan but without making them as "productive". Planner can focus on creating several scenarios and evaluating the best option, sharing results, and performing a collaborative business planning. Further versions help in analyzing mid- to long-term impact like adding onboarding strategic customers, product line launch, adding transportation lane, make vs buy decisions, changing sourcing, etc.
3. Process management: Provides the ability to orchestrate a business process across several geographies, business units, and hundreds of users working on an S&OP process. Task management, adherence to process deadlines, and automation of process activities increase process adherence and success of running an automated S&OP process.
4. Analytics and dashboards: At every stage of S&OP process, there are review meetings with cross-functional teams. Analytics and dashboards in IBP provide end users the ability to create and share relevant charts that provide end-to-end visibility and quick insights into important issues and help in decision-making.

6.1 SAP IBP Applications Overview

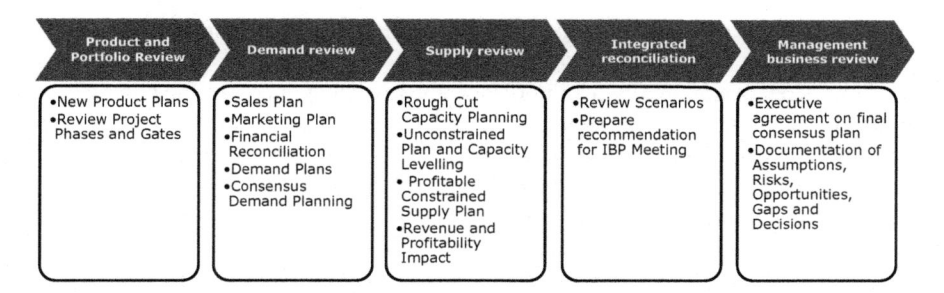

Product and Portfolio Review	Demand review	Supply review	Integrated reconciliation	Management business review
•New Product Plans •Review Project Phases and Gates	•Sales Plan •Marketing Plan •Financial Reconciliation •Demand Plans •Consensus Demand Planning	•Rough Cut Capacity Planning •Unconstrained Plan and Capacity Levelling • Profitable Constrained Supply Plan •Revenue and Profitability Impact	•Review Scenarios •Prepare recommendation for IBP Meeting	•Executive agreement on final consensus plan •Documentation of Assumptions, Risks, Opportunities, Gaps and Decisions

Fig. 6.4 SAP IBP supported business process overview

5. Social collaboration embedded in IBP: SAP IBP includes social collaboration platform SAP JAM which is embedded in Web UI and Excel to enable collaboration on planning activities and decisions across cross-functional teams. This increases transparency and drives toward a collaborative business planning.
6. Integration with external systems: SAP IBP provides integration with external systems like SAP ECC, SAP BPC, SAP C4C, Ariba, TPM, etc. to support connected planning with integration to several other systems where the detailed planning happens. In addition, data from external system outside SAP can be easily integrated to SAP IBP using SAP Cloud Platform for integration—data services.

The business processes supported in SAP IBP are shown in Fig. 6.4.

SAP IBP provides high flexibility to model customer's business model. Since most customers have different levels of planning structures, planning hierarchies, and planning horizons, the model can be set up to adhere to the business processes and planning structures. That is why SAP IBP S&OP has gained great traction in the market with flexibility to model business process across multiple industries like consumer products, chemicals, hi-tech, oil and gas, pharma, etc.

6.1.3 IBP for Response and Supply

SAP IBP for response and supply includes the supply chain planning processes with focus on supply planning for tactical S&OP, operations supply and allocation planning, short-term order confirmations, and deployment planning.

6.1.3.1 Tactical Supply Planning

Tactical S&OP supply planning using time series heuristic and optimizer models, arbitrary deep supply chain network with arbitrary bills of material, production steps, and multi-level sourcing. Supply planning in S&OP is used to plan and gain visibility on mid- to long-term supply plan to make important decision on how to profitably meet customer demand based on supply situations, e.g., make vs buy decisions, adding new shift, outsource to contract manufacturer, etc. The supply chain network is modeled as master data giving high flexibility to model any supply chain network.

Time series-based supply plan in IBP can be run using unconstrained heuristic or constrained optimizer. It generates time series-based distribution, production, and procurement plan. Key business processes covered are rough cut capacity, rough cut material planning, inventory projections, and coverages considering sourcing rules like customer source, location source, and production source of supply and constraints like resource capacity, material constraints, lead times, lot sizes, and adjustments to the plan. Several stages of production for finished goods from subassembly and components across different resources can also be modeled.

IBP S&OP heuristics show bottlenecks in supply chain and generate an unconstrained supply plan to meet the demand. It considers quotas to propagate the demand to downstream nodes.

Optimizer considers the supply chain costs and results in a feasible supply plan based on cost minimization or profit maximization. The output is a constrained demand plan or supply plan along with production, distribution, and procurement plan. Optimization in IBP is performed using a mathematical model using MILP and uses the following input.

- Min-max and incremental lot size
- Optimizer costs: nondelivery cost rate, production costs, transportation costs, external procurement costs, inventory holding costs, safety stock violations, max inventory violation

Hard constraints include resource capacities, max stock, lot sizes, stock, lead times, nonnegative projected stock, manual adjustments to plans for customer receipts, transport receipts, etc.

Optimizer supports several important capabilities for a tactical S&OP like aggregated constraint, late demand fulfillment, minimum resource utilization, fair share, build ahead scenarios, receipt balancing, etc.

Both heuristic and optimizer handle the following:

- Mixed sourcing: quotas, productions, external for make and buy decisions
- Production and handling resources
- Manual adjustments to the plan
- Sub-network planning
- Frozen horizon
- Simulations based on changes in sourcing, capacity supply, etc.
- Support for technical weeks
- Target periods of coverage/target inventory
- Projected inventory and projected coverage
- Co-products
- Scenario planning—supply recommendations for integrated reconciliation meetings
- Check mode for network consistency
- Manage master data: add new product, location, lane, etc.

6.1.3.2 Operational Planning: Order Based Supply and Allocation

Besides the times series supply planning, IBP for response and supply provides order-based operational supply planning and allocation plan capability based on tight integration with SAP ECC using open API ERP add-on. This integration allows for near real-time integration of master data and orders between ECC and IBP. The operational planning of SAP IBP uses external order-based data model.

Supply and allocation planning generates midterm supply and allocation plan based on fast, priority-based, rule-driven heuristics. The constrained forecast run takes forecasts as input along with prioritization and segmentation of demand streams together with supply constraints, and the supplier commits and outputs constrained forecast plan based on available supply allocated to customers based on prioritization. It generates order-based supply plans, i.e., planned orders, purchase requisitions, and stock transfer requisitions. It further generates allocations to feed live ATP process. IBP for response and supply allows for fast simulation and what-if scenarios to quickly evaluate various supply scenarios. Excel user interface provides the planners the well-known intuitive user interface to run response and supply planning scenarios.

SAP IBP response and supply also provide gating factor analysis to analyze the root cause of why certain demands are not fulfilled and what are the gating factors that need to be resolved.

Figure 6.5 shows the standard business catalogue of general response planner and supply planner with their set of supported Fiori applications (Fig. 6.5).

6.1.3.3 Operational Planning: Order Based Order Confirmation

The response/order confirmation creates order confirmations using allocation as constraints along with material and capacity constraints. It also considers prioritized demands like the constrained forecast run. The demand streams (forecast and sales orders) are prioritized based on the business rules. The demand prioritization rules

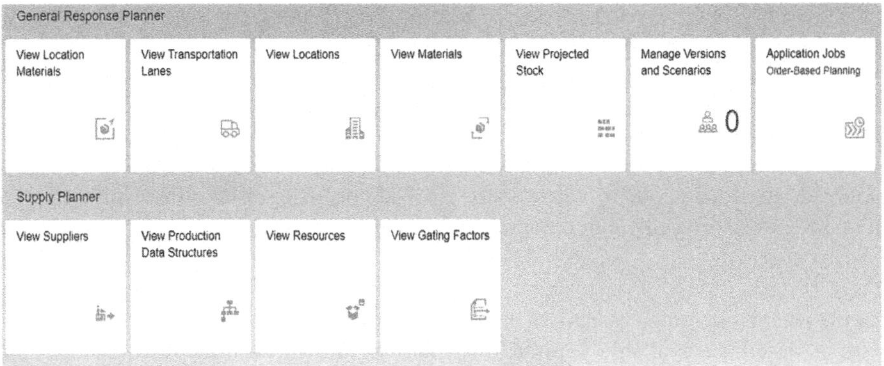

Fig. 6.5 SAP IBP—standard business catalogue of general response planner

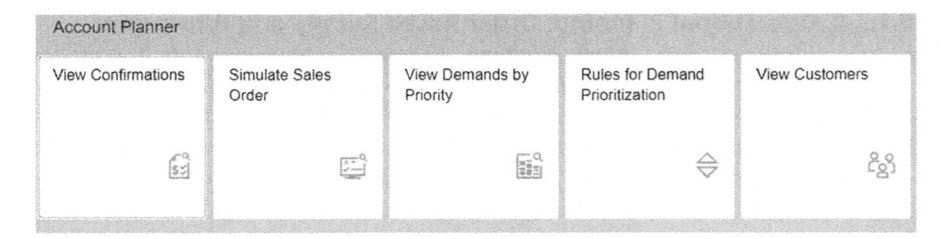

Fig. 6.6 SAP IBP—business catalogue for account planner

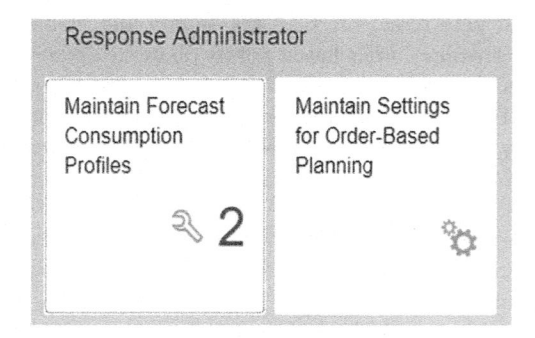

Fig. 6.7 SAP IBP—business catalogue for response administrators

contain several segments ordered in sequence. Each segment contains the criteria for segmenting the demand streams and sorting of attributes, e.g., by requested date of sales orders.

In addition to order reconfirmation proposals to ATP, response planning can also publish short-term supply proposals to ECC.

The figures show the business catalogue in IBP for account planner (Fig. 6.6) and response administrators (Fig. 6.7). The account planners can set up rules for demand prioritization, simulate sales orders, and view confirmations using the Fiori apps provided in IBP.

Gating Factor Analysis Peggings and root cause analysis for gating factors if certain sales orders cannot be confirmed fully can be done using the gating factor analysis application. It provides analysis of supply usage; identifies high-priority demand, unused supply, and competing demands; and displays pegging in graphical order network.

Deployment planning, as part of operational supply planning, re-plans the distribution based on available supply to demand in the short-term planning horizon. Deployment planning is a finite priority-based multistage planning with short planning horizon of about 6 weeks for use cases like shorter-term demand increase in one market over the other. The result of the deployment planning creates

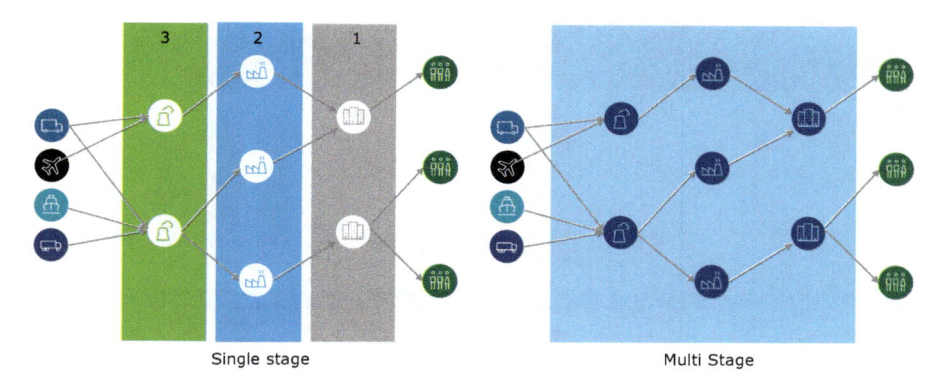

Fig. 6.8 SAP IBP—single stage vs multistage inventory planning overview

deployment stock transfer requisitions that can be sent to SAP ERP for execution of physical transportation of goods.

6.1.4 IBP for Inventory

SAP IBP for inventory provides inventory optimization capabilities to balance customer service levels and inventory levels and investments in the supply chain network. The goal is to find the right mix of inventory at every stocking node in the supply chain network.

By optimizing inventory at multiple stages of the network simultaneously instead of the traditional approach of isolated planning at every stage, SAP IBP for inventory provides optimal inventory targets that meet the customer service levels and reduce working capital. Figure 6.8 shows the difference between traditional approach of inventory planning and the multistage optimization in SAP IBP.

The business processes supported include:

- Review inventory drivers: demand forecasts, target service levels, lead-time variability, lot sizes, replenishment frequencies, etc.
- Calculate forecast errors as inputs to inventory optimization
- Multistage inventory optimization
- Safety stock recommendations and adjustments
- What-if scenarios
- Review inventory components

SAP IBP for inventory supports the following planning algorithms:

1. Single-stage inventory optimization: local calculation of recommended safety stock for each product location combination. Used to simulate the impact of local changes to the input key figures on the safety stock recommendations

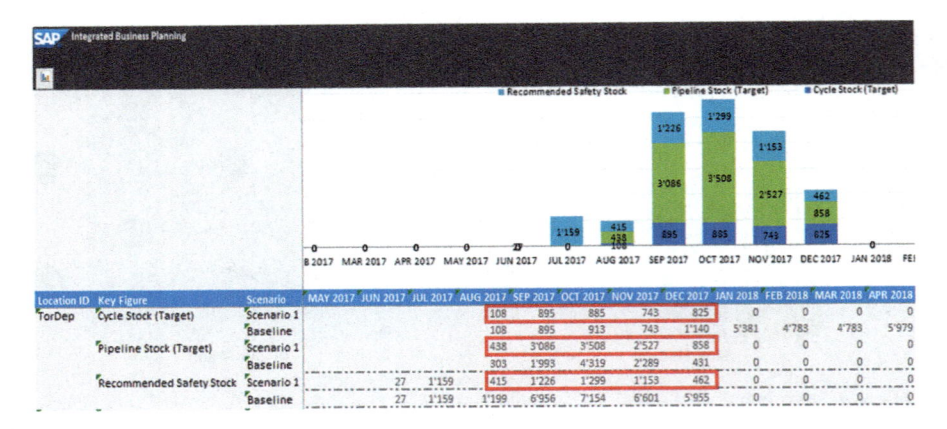

Fig. 6.9 SAP IBP—inventory optimization scenario planning by inventory types

2. Multistage inventory optimization: calculates recommended safety sock across all product/locations in the supply chain network simultaneously by minimizing inventory holding cost to meet the customer service levels
3. Expected demand loss: calculates the expected loss demand quantity for the demand distribution and inventory plan
4. Forecast error CV calculator: calculates forecast error coefficient of variation that is used to estimate the demand variability. This serves as inputs to the inventory optimization runs
5. Calculate inventory components: estimates the inventory components (inventory position, cycle stock, on-hand stock, pipeline stock, and merchandising stock) that make up the total inventory. Calculates reorder point

SAP IBP provides fast scenario planning and simulation of inventory by allowing the planners to work in Excel add-in for all inventory planning activities. These include viewing and changing drivers for inventory (demand, forecast error, replenishment frequency, min order qty, target service levels, lead times, and variability at every level in supply chain), running multistage inventory optimization, and viewing impact on inventory for the various scenarios (Fig. 6.9).

Further the analytics and network visualization provide end-to-end visibility of inventory in the supply chain network and quickly identify locations in the global supply chain where there is excess or shortage of inventory. Planners can visualize the network and drill down to any level to view the detailed inventory position.

Integration with other modules: Inventory optimization takes as input from IBP for demand the mid- to long-term demand planning qty, short-term sensed demand, and calculated forecast errors for IO to provide recommended safety stock targets. This goes as inputs to IBP for sales and operations supply planning and to IBP for response and supply planning for constrained forecast run and order confirmation. Further the weekly safety stock targets can be sent to ERP.

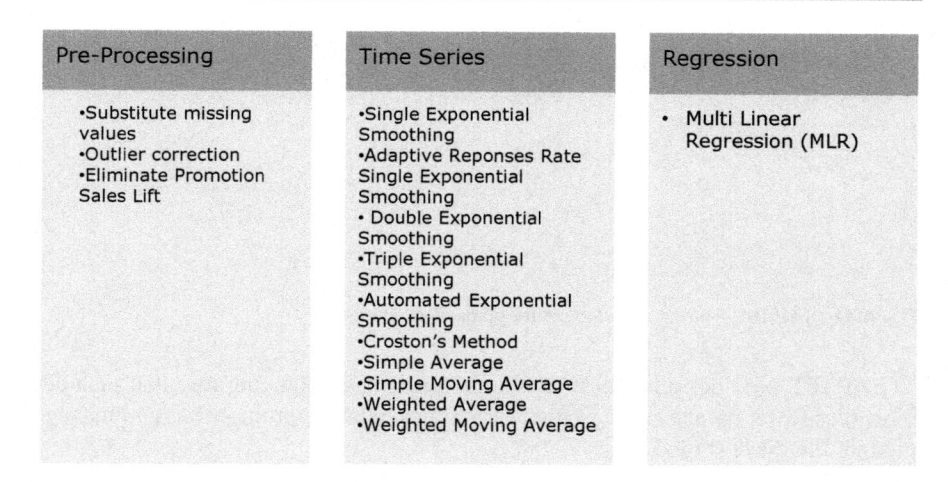

Pre-Processing	Time Series	Regression
•Substitute missing values •Outlier correction •Eliminate Promotion Sales Lift	•Single Exponential Smoothing •Adaptive Reponses Rate Single Exponential Smoothing • Double Exponential Smoothing •Triple Exponential Smoothing •Automated Exponential Smoothing •Croston's Method •Simple Average •Simple Moving Average •Weighted Average •Weighted Moving Average	• Multi Linear Regression (MLR)

Fig. 6.10 SAP IBP demand planning statistical models (status 2017)

6.1.5 IBP for Demand

IBP for demand includes the demand planning for mid- to long-term statistical forecasting and demand sensing for short-term forecasting. It combines specialized demand planning processes and tools to drive to an accurate demand plan, to identify opportunities to improve forecast and efficient exception management, and to identify and resolve deviations from forecast accuracy.

Demand Planning The mid- to long-term demand planning uses sales history as input to generate statistical forecasts. The powerful statistical methods in IBP are grouped under pre-processing, time series, and regression methods (Fig. 6.10).

Statistical forecasting can be executed interactively in Excel at any level of aggregation or can be set up as a batch forecasting run. Several forecast error measures can be set up to measure the accuracy of the forecast: these include MAPE, MPE, MSE, RMSE, MAD, WMAPE, MASE, etc.

The business processes supported by IBP for demand include the following:

- Mid- to long-term demand planning: add business insights and market intelligence on top of the generated statistical forecast.
- Advanced statistical forecasting: management and assignment of forecast profiles.
- Role-based local and global demand plans.
- Gather and cleanse historical data.
- Forecast errors and accuracy analysis.
- New product introductions and product life cycle management.
- Segmentation: ABC and XYZ classification.
- Integrating promotion data in forecasting and promotion analysis.

Demand Planner				
Manage Forecast Models	Assign Forecast Models	Analyze Promotions	Manage Product Lifecycle	Manage Forecast Error Calculations Demand Planning
				Error

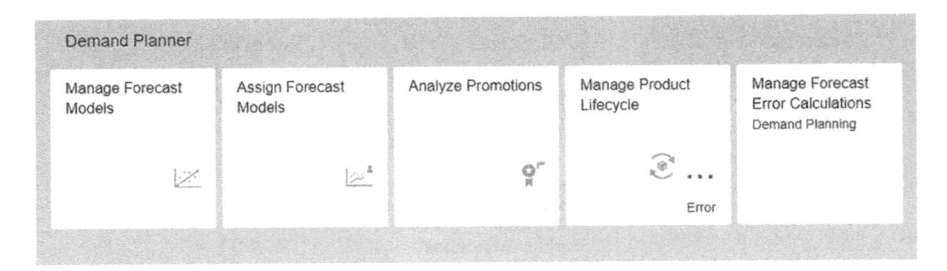

Fig. 6.11 SAP IBP—business catalogue for demand planning

SAP IBP provides a business catalogue for demand planning role that includes Fiori tiles to set up and manage forecast profiles, analyze promotions, and manage product life cycle (Fig. 6.11).

Demand Sensing SAP IBP for demand calculates the sensed demand plan for short-term horizon of 6–8 weeks in daily buckets by taking into account the demand drivers like open orders, history, and demand forecast. Demand sensing uses pattern recognition algorithms that consider seasonality and trends.

Demand sensing is typically applicable to companies with volatile markets and demand variability. It achieves better forecast accuracy in short-term horizon by considering order patterns and short-term demand trends. The results from the demand sensing algorithms can further be adjusted by planners considering the market intelligence and other influencing factors.

The short-term sensed demand when considered together with the mid- to long-term demand as input to inventory achieves better results for stock recommendations, higher customer service levels, and reduced stock outs.

Integration IBP for demand provides standard integration templates or best practices to integrate sales orders and deliveries from SAP ECC, point of sales data from SAP demand signal management, and trade promotions from SAP trade promotions management. Further sensed demand can be exported to SAP APO SNP as planned independent requirements.

6.2 Process Modeling

6.2.1 Global and Local Processes

To orchestrate a business process across multiple cross-functional units, a well-coordinated process management capability is required in an IBP application.

The process management capabilities synchronize and monitor several sequential and parallel processes with multiple processing steps along with collaboration

6.2 Process Modeling

U07 Sales and Operations Planning_October_2017: Supply Review

Fig. 6.12 SAP IBP—S&OP process chevrons

among the participants in a process. During the sales and operations planning process (Fig. 6.12), various steps occur to prepare the data for the process and to execute the various functions in the process and required actions as follow-up from discussions and analysis. The SAP sales and operations planning solution tracks these steps in a structured way and associates certain actions with these steps to improve the overall process and efficiency.

A well-coordinated IBP process should be able to achieve the following.

- Increase participation
- Adhere to process deadline
- Control information flow
- Improve automation and efficiency

Every customer has different ways in which they manage their business processes. There can be one global IBP process and several regional or country-specific IBP processes organized by product lines, brand, or category. Further each process may have multiple steps with different dates and participants. The implementation and structure of these process steps should be customized to each company's own business process.

To manage a global IBP process, there needs to be an overall process cadence and process discipline that need to be adhered and orchestrated across all local processes participating in a global process.

Per Oliver Wight, in general, product reviews and demand reviews are managed at a country level where the commercial organizations are working closely with the customers along with country-specific financial assumptions (Palmatier & Crum, 2003).

These country-specific product reviews and demand plans are then rolled up to a division or business unit level where the downstream processes like supply review, integrated reconciliation review, and management business review are conducted more at a global level for each business unit.

6.2.2 Process Cadence and Orchestration

When running a global IBP process, it is important to have a harmonized orchestration of the local processes to adhere to the process cadence of a global IBP process.

Therefore, there should be milestones and deadlines that need to be defined for the global IBP process and similar coordinated milestones for the local S&OP which is usually executed at country or country/business unit level.

The global process templates should be defined with the following characteristics:

- Well-defined and globally agreed IBP process steps.
- Milestones and durations for the process steps.
- Global process owners who monitor progress and adherence to milestones.
- Global agenda which can be modified locally/regionally in every cycle. Maybe even regional agenda should be developed.
- Global tasks which can be modified locally/regionally.
- Result of the meeting, e.g., documented assumptions need to be stored in collaboration platform and visible globally.

Local processes should have the flexibility to start process considering the size, complexity, and maturity of organization. Normally to run supply planning in global organization, you need to have all inputs from demand planning from all countries. Therefore, there should be flexibility on when to start the local product review and demand review step and adhere to global process milestones during the supply and management business reviews.

The local process steps should further have the flexibility on their planning processes (Fig. 6.13).

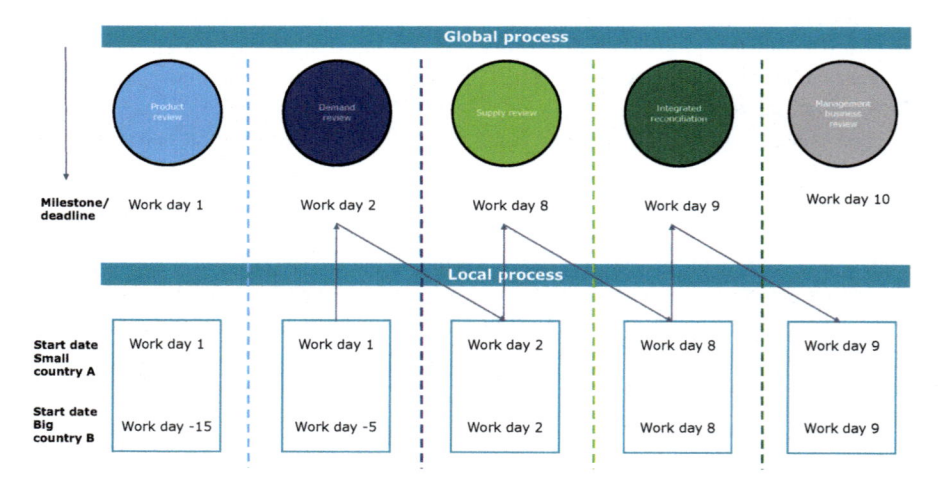

Fig. 6.13 Global process milestones local process flexibility

1. The dates on which the local processes can start can be defined based on the organization requirements. For example, the demand review step can start in month 1 (January) to cycle month (February).
2. Some process steps can be optional or not defined for a local process. Example Local Process 1 may not have a process review step and does not contribute to the overall global process for the product review step.
3. There can be flexibility in the definition of the process steps. For example, Country 1 has two separate steps, product review and demand review, whereas Country 2 has demand review process step that includes product review.
4. Some process steps can have different sub-steps representing differences in local demand planning processes. For example, County 1 could have sub-process steps, sales forecast → marketing review → consensus, whereas Country 2 may have statistical forecast → demand plan → consensus demand.
5. The local processes can have different collaboration groups for each of the process steps.
6. The local processes can have different meeting cadences for the IBP meetings and may include global process owners in each of the process review meetings.

As shown in Fig. 6.13, the local processes need to adhere to the deadline of the global process steps yet having the flexibility to run the process steps with localized duration. For example, the product review step of country A can start from Workday 1, whereas Country B can start from Workday 5. However, both need to complete by Workday 1 deadline of the global process. The steps within a local process can also be parallel. For example, in Country A, the product review and demand review steps both start on Workday 1, but may have different duration of the steps.

One of the biggest consumer companies has built a central standard framework for demand planning process, composed of baseline generation by demand management, cross-functional forecast enrichment, and consensus approach. They have recognized the need to introduce light process variance across markets. Unilever predicts that within 10 years, demand in emerging markets will exceed the one in developed ones, which exposes challenges in demand planning if not addressed early enough. They wanted to adapt to each country's particularities in terms of market and of local employees skills, measure impact of demand-shaping activities, and incorporate lessons learned to improve forecasting quality. Hybrid approach was introduced where some process framework elements did exist like high-level forecasting process flow based on statistical forecasting with cross-functional inputs and a consensual demand plan built after a "forecast alignment meeting" but still decentralized in a bit tailored way (Blosch & Uskert, 2011).

6.2.3 Hierarchy of Processes

The process steps in an IBP process can be hierarchical in nature (Fig. 6.14). At an aggregate level, the process owners usually need to see the overall IBP process steps'

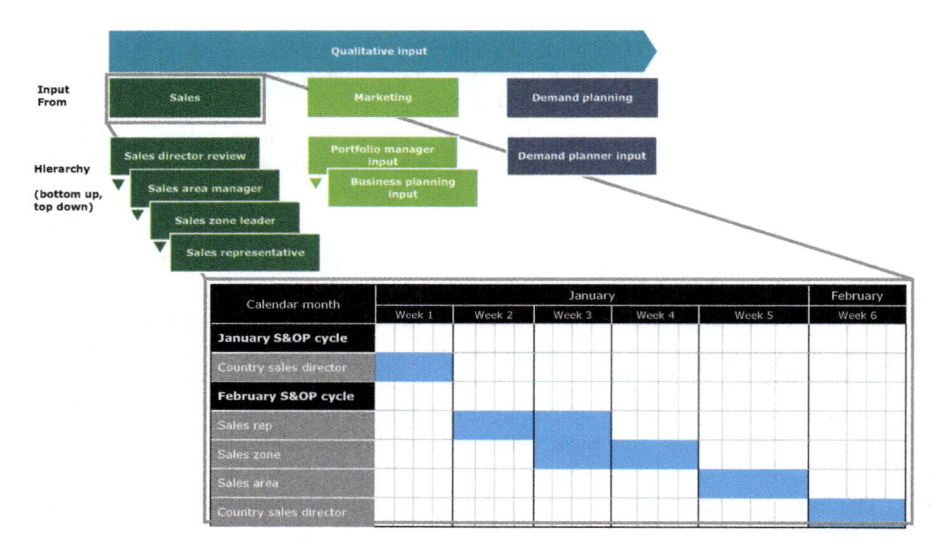

Fig. 6.14 Qualitative forecast input process hierarchy

milestones and the progress for each process step, whereas what happens within an individual process step is usually managed by the individual process step owners. The process steps can have sub-steps, and each of the sub-steps can have their sub-steps depending on the complexity of the overall process. However, for simplicity of managing the processes, the processes are usually maintained with one level of process steps, and the activities within a process step are managed with tasks.

S&OP process step: Demand review can have sub-process steps—qualitative input, quantitative input, demand review preparation, and demand review meeting. Each of the process step, for example, the qualitative input, can have multiple inputs coming from different planning organizations. Forecast inputs are collected from sales representatives rolling to the hierarchical organization levels of sales zone leader, sales area manager, and sales area director working with a bottom-up and top-down approach at different levels of planning hierarchies. This is where the process meets the planning aspects, where during each stage of the process there is a planning activity in terms of maintaining and managing plan across several users in the organization. A well-orchestrated process connects people, process, and planning activities in a collaborative planning process.

6.2.4 Process Management

Process management in IBP provides the capabilities to orchestrate an IBP process across a group of business teams involved in the collaborative planning activities. The coordination of planning activities across various groups with clear responsibilities, adherence to the process deadlines, handoffs between data and processes,

6.2 Process Modeling

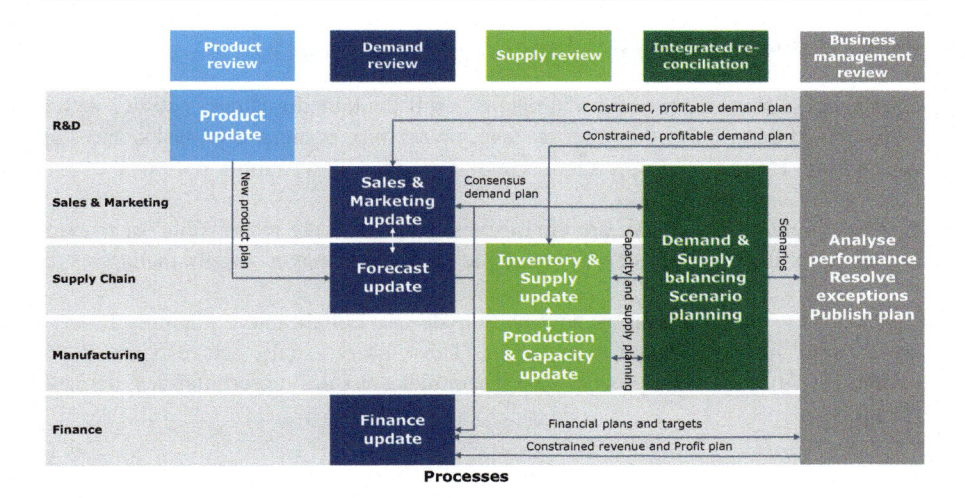

Fig. 6.15 Process and responsibility link

and transparency on the decisions and actions are important for the success of an IBP process (Fig. 6.15).

6.2.5 Process Template

A process template defines the blueprint of an IBP process for each organization. There can be multiple process templates created to represent the core activities in a business process. Each process has one or more process owners (e.g., S&OP coordinator) who are responsible for the execution of an IBP process in the organization. A template can have multiple process steps representing process stages. The building blocks of a process template include the following elements as per Fig. 6.16.

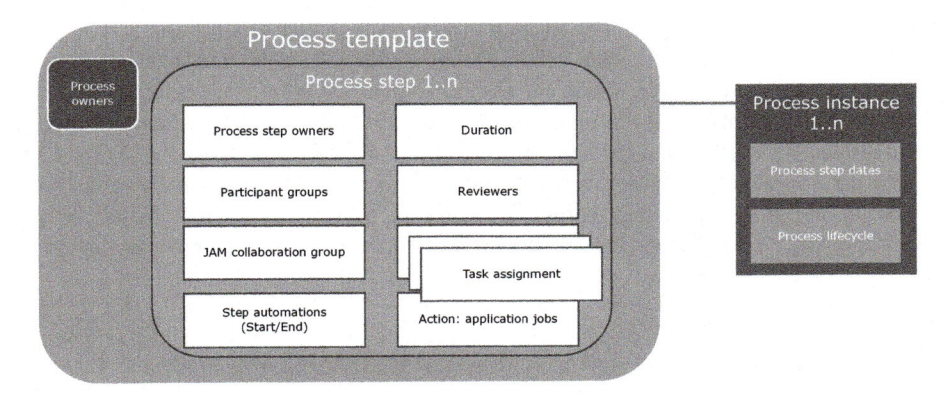

Fig. 6.16 SAP IBP—process template concept

6.2.6 Process Steps

Each process step in a process template is a self-contained business activity with a well-defined duration of the process stage, ownership, participation, tasks, and step automation. Examples are product review, demand review, supply review, etc.

Process Step Owners These are the business users who are responsible for managing the individual process step, for example, demand manager, supply manager, etc.

Participant Groups The users who participate in a collaborative planning process are grouped into participant user groups. These users usually are responsible for certain activities within a process step. Examples are sales representatives, demand planners, etc.

Reviewers These are the users who are involved in a process step to get a visibility into the overall progress of a process step; however, they may not be involved in individual activities associated with the step.

Duration This represents the number of workdays associated with a process step. For example, demand review step lasts for 7 working days in a planning cycle.

JAM Collaboration Group This is the collaboration group associated with a process step where participants can collaborate on activities, share information, maintain meeting cadences, and document decisions and actions. JAM group can also include other users beyond the participants in the process step.

Task Assignment For every step, there can be one or more predefined tasks that get executed in each planning cycle. These are the individual business activities in the process step that are assigned to one or more users of the participant groups. The completion progress of a process step depends on the task completion. For example, the demand review step can have the following tasks (Fig. 6.17).

Automation Settings The automation of starting and ending of a process step along with the dependencies between process steps is defined in the automation setting. For example, demand review step can start as soon as the prior product review step is completed. Supply review should start only when its start date has occurred. Integrated reconciliation step can end only when all the tasks associated with that step are completed. In addition, the application jobs can be triggered based on the start or end of a process step thereby orchestrating the application jobs based on the process stage completions. For example, run statistical forecast when the demand review process step starts.

6.2 Process Modeling 173

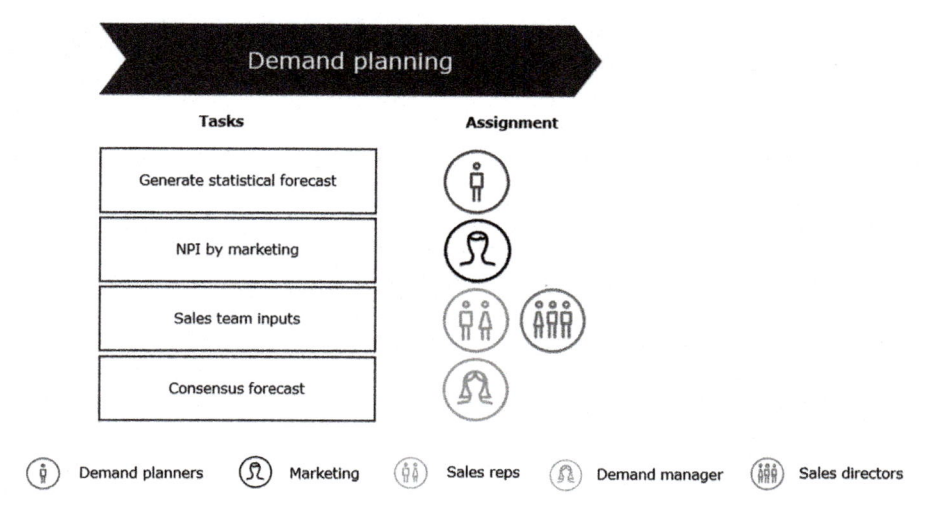

Fig. 6.17 Process step task, assignments

6.2.7 Process Instance

A process instance is a planning cycle for the defined business process in a process template. The process instance represents the planning calendar of a process template with defined process step dates (Fig. 6.18).

When a process template is instantiated, the workdays associated with a process template are converted to working dates for each step in the process. All the other settings of the process template are carried over to the instance. Process owner can create one or more process instances for a template. For example, a process template represents the S&OP process with duration for each step. There can be instances

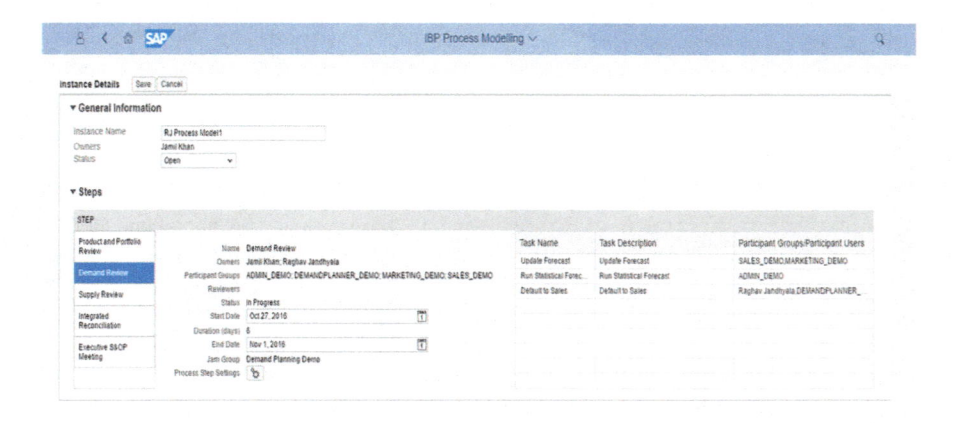

Fig. 6.18 SAP IBP—monthly S&OP process instances

created for the template representing the process for monthly S&OP cycles, i.e., January global IBP, February global IBP, etc.

6.2.8 Process Visualization and Monitoring

After the process instance has been instantiated for a process template, the monitoring and visualization of the process can be tracked in the IBP dashboard. Process charts can be created for each process instance and added to the IBP dashboard to view and track the progress of each process. The dashboard can show one or more active IBP processes at the same time to view at a global level all the regional or business unit-specific processes (Fig. 6.19).

Process instances can be supplemented with planning-related charts together in a dashboard (Fig. 6.20).

6.2.9 Task Management

Tasks in IBP are actionable business activities that are assigned to process step participants. These are required to be completed for the process to move forward. In S&OP process with several cross-functional business groups and hundreds of users in a business process, it is vital to make sure every user is participating in an orchestrated process by assigning tasks to users and monitoring their completions.

IBP process templates provide the default list of tasks that are carried out along with their assignment in every step of the process. These tasks get instantiated as JAM tasks when the process step is set in progress. There are different responsibilities related to tasks based on the roles of the users in a process. Task application in IBP provides an easy access for task owners to view and complete their open tasks and to create ad hoc tasks for a process cycle. A navigation is provided to the JAM task for

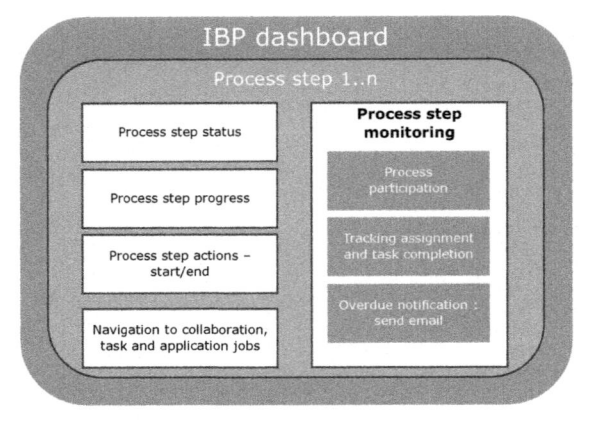

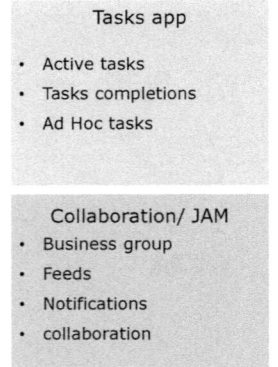

Fig. 6.19 SAP IBP—monitoring and visualization concept

6.2 Process Modeling

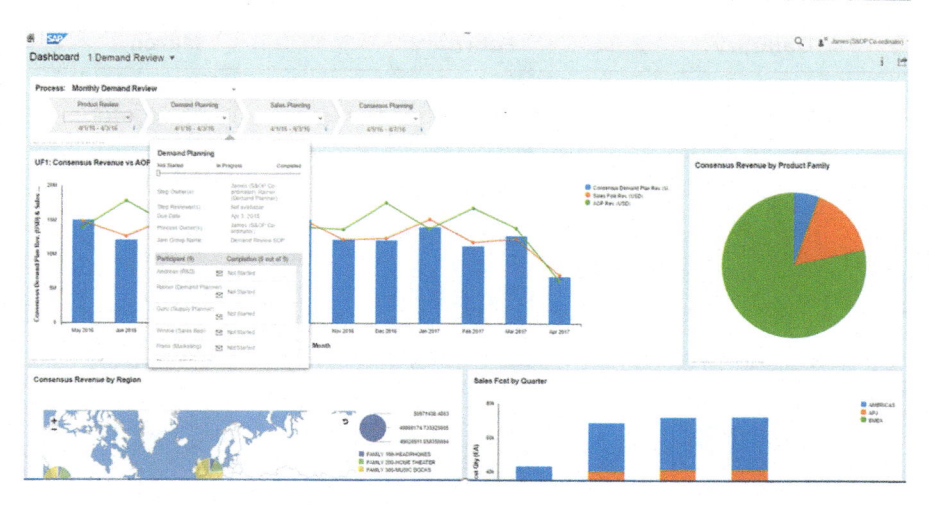

Fig. 6.20 SAP IBP—process chevrons and process status

the user to add further details to the tasks, start collaboration with others users, set up reminders, and adjust the tasks dates as required.

6.2.10 Process Automation

Most of the tactical/operational planning processes in an IBP process follow a monthly or weekly process cadence. For example, in IBP, you can define a monthly S&OP process template and instantiate a process instance for S&OP cycle each month. A process instance can have multiple process steps with different set of tasks and application jobs associated with each step. Therefore, it is important to have a harmonized automation of the process instances (Fig. 6.21), so that they can start and complete automatically based on the criteria defined by the process owners.

Process automation can be configured for each process step of a process template which defines how the step should start or end. Each process step has the following settings:

- Start and end dates
- Tasks [optional]
- Application job associated with start or end of the process step [optional]

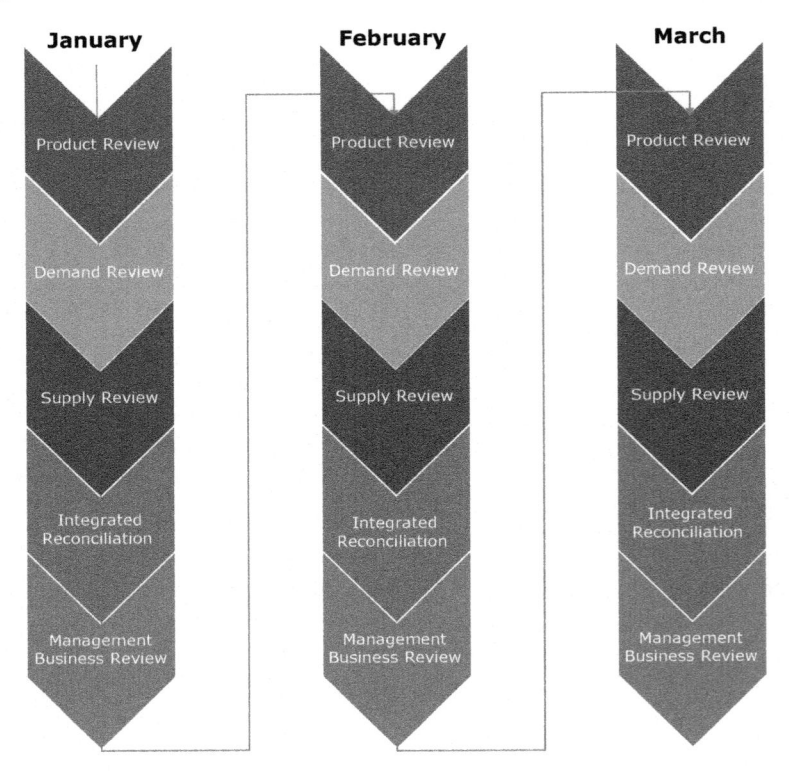

Fig. 6.21 Process automation for specific country IBP process

6.3 Organization Modeling

Why to model organization in your IBP? Modeling your IBP organization in IBP data model will ensure that your real-life processes are aligned to the ones executed in the system. It will help you to capture who executes, who is accountable, what is the performance against, inputs, decisions which are recorded and registered in the system by particular person. It may be very relevant for IBP since it has been proven that recorded decision when analyzed for specific individuals exposes some trends. Organizational design will facilitate creation of collaboration with the use of SAP IBP. We have run six sigma project once, which has exposed and proved that specific function and people were providing decisions and those decisions were having trends in bias. Removing of bias was addressed with specific individuals then.

Sales and Marketing
An important element on how to organize, monitor, and control qualitative forecast inputs is the knowledge about size, structure, and complexity of your sales

organization. This information should come out of your as-is assessment. You should be able to understand:

(a) Sales and marketing structure (e.g., sales representatives grouped by zone or customer type, marketing by portfolio or channels)
(b) Quantified complexity (e.g., number of forecasting combinations SKU/customer/sales representative)
(c) Past forecasting performance

Let's shortly highlight what to do with the data and information you have collected.

Ad (a) Information about organizational structures and marketing would need to be validated versus structures and available master data objects.

Some hints about what to look for:

- Are all the levels of sales team organization structure reflected in your master data objects?
- Which sales team levels are missing in the master data? What role might this level have in IBP process entry, review, and overall accountability?
- Do you have to face one customer in place? Does one sales representative visit a single customer and offer all products and services or multiple?
- How are your sales teams being organized by area? By portfolio? By type of selling? Combination of it? What master data objects describe that?
- Are all the levels of marketing organization structure reflected in your master data objects?
- Does your portfolio manager/brand manager have representation in the master data in transactional system? Which roles are missing in master data?
- How are your marketing teams being organized by portfolio/brands? By type of selling? By customer types/groups? Combination of it? What master data objects describe that?

Once you know the answers for those types of questions:

- Assess which missing objects are truly relevant for your data model.
- For existing objects fully understand the logic and configuration of your source systems.

Based on this mind map, you need to define which organizational elements will be needed in your IBP process framework. It would not be abnormal if some of the organizational dimensions in your IBP will be derived from transactional system and some additional ones would need to be maintained directly in SAP IBP.

It is highly probable that your sales organization reflected in the master data can be derived from transactional system. Most probably most of the levels would exist in some form in master data objects which drive order to cash process.

It is very common that marketing, finance, and part of supply organization are not mapped in transactional system. Some of the roles in those functions rarely play direct role in transactional/operational environment. An example is you may need to define how to map portfolio manager and finance controllers most probably in master data which is directly maintained in SAP IBP. Do not hesitate to do it. Organizational dimension are critical since they represent certain accountabilities for inputs which can be very important in process improvements and value-added analysis.

Ad (b) Information about complexity will help you to define the right level on which data should be stored or integrated; SAP calls it planning levels. It does not mean you would need to work on the level defined as SAP planning level since aggregation and disaggregation will help you to work on the level aligned to best insights.

Ad (c) Information about past forecast performance by function would help to define data flows within SAP IBP.

Examples:

- If you have sales input organized in structure like sales rep, sales zone, and country, then you may think of pre-filling the next level input by predecessor. It may help to clean up mistakes (errors) being done on the lowest level.
- Pre-fill marketing input done, for instance, on country level with latest aggregated to country sales input.
- Statistical forecasting might be pre-filled to defined level in sales team inputs.

We would strongly recommend to introduce a rule which helps to avoid inputs to be overwritten by multiple users. Do not create one input from sales overwritten by different roles, e.g., sales rep, sale zone lead, country manager, etc. Protect inputs—this may be gold. Forecast value-added analysis will tell you which creates value in the process and which does not, but at the beginning of your journey, capture all in separate key figures, and manage information flow with the use of copy operators.

Finance and Pricing
In Integrated Business Planning process, finance and pricing managers will play key role in the monetization of forecasts and plans.

In big organizations you may consider to map finance business partners, managers, controllers, as well as pricing managers in master data attributes to enable a controlled way to provide input and analysis. We would imagine that finance or pricing representative would not be derived as master data objects from the transactional system and therefore may need to be considered to be mapped directly in SAP IBP.

Demand Planners and Demand Managers
Demand planners and demand managers have to be mapped in your IBP master data. We do not expect those roles every implementation to be derived from transactional

system. Often we see that demand planners or demand managers are not mapped in ERP systems. Often they have market-oriented roles, and ERP system is not always good in that master data orientation. In this case it is highly probable to map those roles directly in IBP data model.

Supply and Logistic
Supply and operations roles usually are mapped in transactional system master data (e.g., supply planners, supply schedulers, customer service, distribution planners). Their accountability orientation can vary significantly; it can be product, plant, and market oriented. We recommend a detailed analysis to be performed if those roles will run some of the IBP process.

6.4 Data Modeling

A planning model in IBP provides the following capabilities to support different business processes:

1. Highly flexible configuration
2. Pre-configured standard leading practice content
3. Calculations and algorithms

A planning model in an integrated business planning covers planning processes with different periodicities, planning levels at which plans are run and different levels at which data is stored.

An IBP solution typically addresses process and data integration across various systems or applications. These processes can have different granularities of the planning hierarchies and time periods. Furthermore, the processes can have different frequencies of execution. The above example shows a planning process with short-, mid-, and long-term planning, with the focus varying from days to weeks, weeks to months, and months to years. There can be several different user roles accessing different aspects of an integrated process where demand planners focus on volume at detailed level of product/customer, whereas finance would have a view on value from detail to aggregated business units/category levels.

In SAP IBP, a unified planning model covers business process and data, across different application modules like demand, S&OP, control tower, inventory, supply, and response. The integrated planning process is a harmonized execution of multiple processes with the characteristics as listed in Fig. 6.22.

Integrated business processes do connect different sub-processes covering strategic, tactical, and operational planning in one coherent, transparent, and manageable process. These three process dimensions could be understood as:

Fig. 6.22 Integrated business process

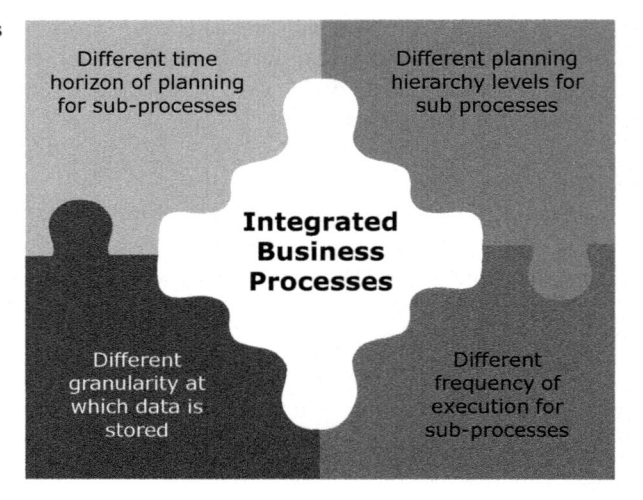

[Puzzle diagram: Integrated Business Processes at center, surrounded by four pieces: "Different time horizon of planning for sub-processes", "Different planning hierarchy levels for sub processes", "Different granularity at which data is stored", "Different frequency of execution for sub-processes"]

- Strategic view on long-term planning:
  - Strategic sales and operations planning
  - Long-range business planning
  - Network design and policy setting
- Tactical view on mid- to long-term planning:
  - Monthly sales and operations planning
  - Demand planning and demand management
  - Inventory optimization
  - Supply planning, allocations planning
- Operational view on short- to midterm planning:
  - Demand sensing
  - Demand shaping
  - Order confirmations and supply priorities

The above integrated process can have a huge time horizon span. It may start from the operational planning which covers up to 8 weeks, through the tactical planning which covers from 3 to 36 months, and finally to the strategic planning which often goes even beyond a 5-year horizon.

The above planning process operates on different planning hierarchy levels and time periods:

- S&OP process is usually viewed and run at an aggregated product family and country/region level.
- Demand planning at monthly or weekly—product, customer, and location level.
- Demand sensing at daily—product, customer, and location level.
- Exception management on daily product location level or KPIs like perfect order fulfillment executed on order level of sales orders and deliveries.

6.4 Data Modeling

Furthermore, these processes operate on a different granularity at which the data is stored. Processes can have different granularities at which the data is stored for the underlying data involved in the process:

- Statistical forecasting quantity: monthly product/location
- Marketing forecast stored at monthly product line level
- Finance plan at quarterly product family and regional level
- Sales force forecast at monthly product/customer level
- Supply plan key figures like capacities at resource location level

Finally those sub-processes operate at a different frequency, e.g.:

- Strategic sales and operations planning on a yearly frequency
- Tactical sales and operations planning at a monthly frequency
- Demand planning, inventory optimization from a weekly frequency
- Demand sensing and control tower from a daily frequency

The underlying supply chain model and the planning engine provide the needed flexibility to meet the planning and analytical needs of each exemplary user as shown in Fig. 6.23.

The artifacts of the underlying supply chain planning model that supports the business processes include the following:

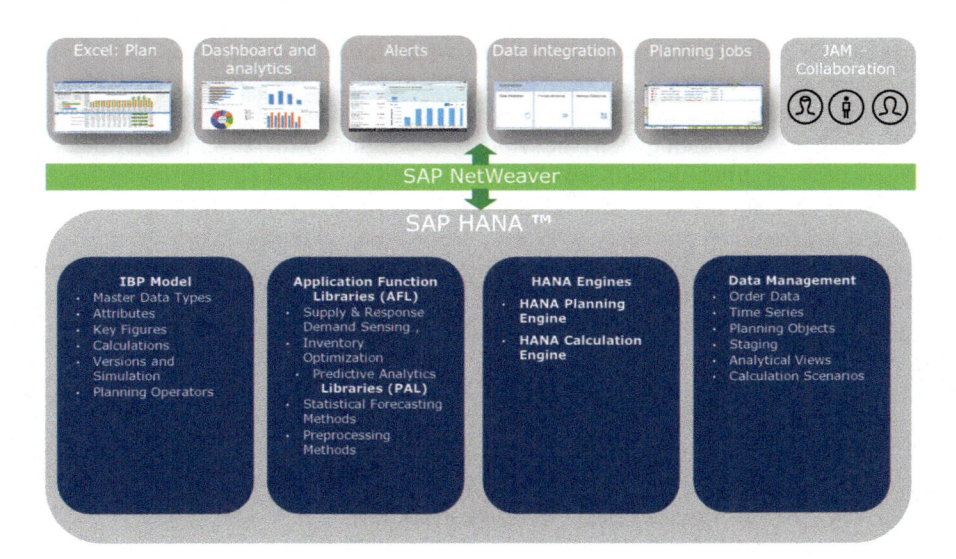

Fig. 6.23 SAP IBP on HANA

1. IBP configured model: a flexible configuration to define the supply chain planning model with key figures, planning hierarchies, versions, and planning operators
2. Algorithm libraries available in HANA:
   (a) Application function libraries (AFL): sophisticated planning algorithms, e.g., supply planning heuristics and optimization, multistage inventory optimization that run natively on HANA
   (b) Predictive analytics library (PAL): used by IBP for the statistical forecasting methods
3. HANA planning and calculation engine of the underlying SAP HANA platform
4. Data management: generated data model based on the pre-configured planning model that supports time series and order-based models

Let us define the fundamentals of SAP IBP data modeling.

Planning area in SAP IBP is a set of configuration elements that defines the data structure of a unified and Integrated Business Planning process. It brings together essential elements of planning processes like planning time periods and planning horizons, planning hierarchies, key figures, scenarios, and versions. Planning area may contain many plan datasets—one actual dataset and many version datasets. In IBP, the planning area artifacts like tables, views, calculation scenarios, and permissions are generated upon activation. These then form the basis for planning processes like data loads, calculations, planning views, planning operators, etc.; see Fig. 6.24.

A planning area is run natively in HANA within the planning and calculation engine. This allows for faster calculations where the data and calculations are run in-memory.

In SAP IBP, the key figures are stored and/or calculated. The calculated key figures have calculations on the stored key figure with several intermediate calculations at different levels of hierarchies. Only the stored key figures are stored in the HANA in-memory database, and the calculations behind the calculated key figures are executed on the fly whenever user queries such key figures from Excel, analytics, planning operators, etc. Aggregations on the fly are performed on the stored data and in-memory utilizing the power of SAP HANA, so there is no need to store aggregates or intermediate calculation results.

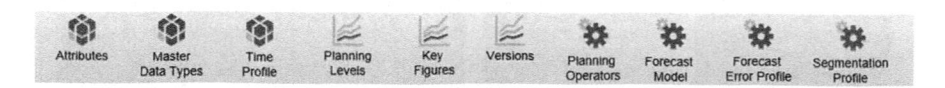

Fig. 6.24 SAP IBP—planning area configuration dimensions

6.4 Data Modeling

6.4.1 Elements of a Planning Area

The following illustration (Fig. 6.25) shows the primary entities of a planning area. A planning area is representative of multidimensional cube with several hierarchies of master data dimensions, time dimension, key figures, and versions. A planning area is composed of multiple key figures. Each key figure has a base planning level which represents the primary master data key structures. For example, sales forecast is stored at a planning level that has a product ID and customer ID as root characteristics along with time level as month. There can be several planning operators that can be associated with the planning area which operate on the data, e.g., statistical forecasting, supply planning heuristics, snapshots, etc. A master data type can be associated with one or more planning areas giving the flexibility to model a unified planning area or several planning areas sharing master data.

We will highlight in more detail only few critical elements of planning area.

6.4.2 Master Data Types

A master data type in IBP can be defined as simple, compound, reference, virtual, or external master data type. These types of master data types give flexibility to model different dimensions of data along with their referential integrity (Fig. 6.26).

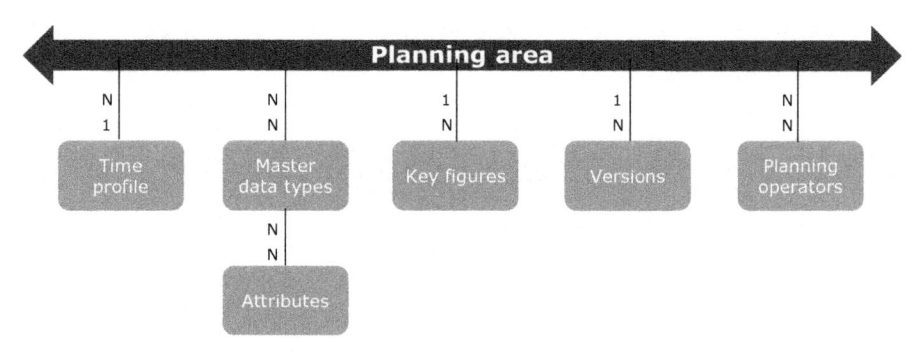

Fig. 6.25 SAP IBP—planning area

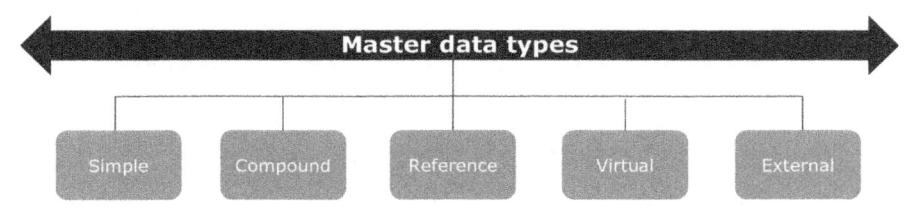

Fig. 6.26 SAP IBP—master data types

6.4.3 Key Figures

Key figures represent values of data in combination with time level and planning attributes. Key figures are sometimes also called measures and hold transactional data like price, quantity, value, ratio, etc. Key figures can be imported into the IBP system, calculated, and/or manually edited. Some examples of key figures include sales forecast, marketing forecast, consensus unconstrained forecast, projected inventory, or actual data such as sales orders and shipment history.

Each stored key figure has a base planning level which defines the keys at which the data is stored, e.g., sales forecast is by month, product ID, and customer ID.

Figure 6.27 shows the properties of a key figure. A planning area can contain multiple key figures which are the key elements of planning in a business process. The key figures have several properties like aggregation, disaggregation, calculation definitions, and display settings. These key figures are classified as per Fig. 6.27. Some key figures can be tracked for changes if needed.

User does not configure the data model. We want to highlight the key aspects of how user interacts with data with use of SAP IBP user interfaces. The main user interface of SAP IBP is Excel UI (Fig. 6.28).

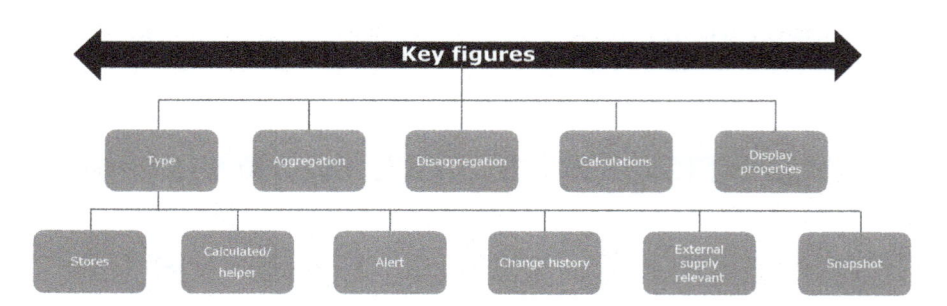

Fig. 6.27 SAP IBP—key figure types

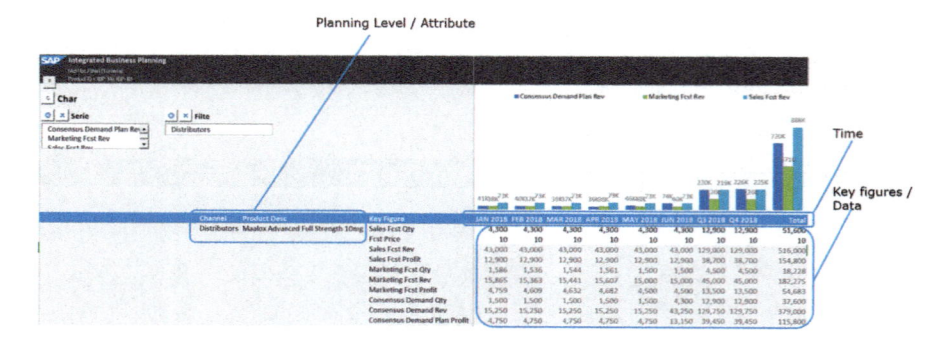

Fig. 6.28 SAP IBP – Excel UI planning screen overview

6.4 Data Modeling

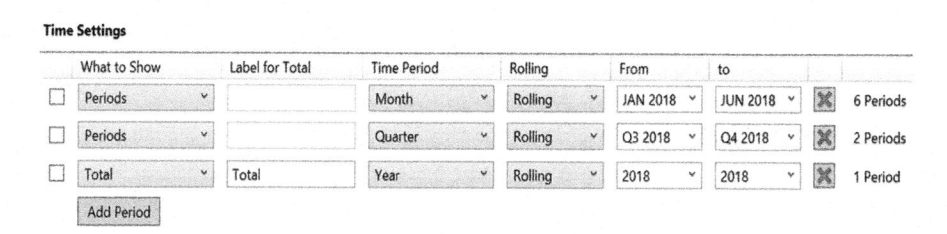

Time Settings								
☐	What to Show	Label for Total	Time Period	Rolling	From	to		
☐	Periods		Month	Rolling	JAN 2018	JUN 2018	✗	6 Periods
☐	Periods		Quarter	Rolling	Q3 2018	Q4 2018	✗	2 Periods
☐	Total	Total	Year	Rolling	2018	2018	✗	1 Period
Add Period								

Fig. 6.29 SAP IBP—time dimensions in Excel planning view

In the implementation process, either you start from predefined templates (example shown above) and you modify them or you start from scratch.

SAP IBP is oriented in large for "self-service." User can create their own ways of working aligned to their insights. They can create out of default project or SAP template their own favorite where they can change and adjust how they interact with the system and data.

Time Horizon and Periodicity User can select how they display data on time axis per their needs. This feature will help you to have details on shorter horizon and aggregation in long term (Fig. 6.29).

Key Figures Data shown in volume or values, totals and displayed in the view. Some key figures are stored like sales fcst qty, and some are calculated like sales fcst rev. Further key figures have properties of what can be edited and what can be viewed only.

Planning Levels The key figures are viewed and edited at any chosen level of data, e.g., product family and customer region. These are the planning levels at which the data is viewed and can be edited. However, each of these key figures could be defined at different base levels like sales qty is defined at product/customer and month level.

User interacts with data in similar way like in MS Excel pivot table (Fig. 6.30).

User can select *versions and scenarios* which represents alternate plans (Fig. 6.31).

We would like to bring user experience comparison brought by our colleague (Fig. 6.32).

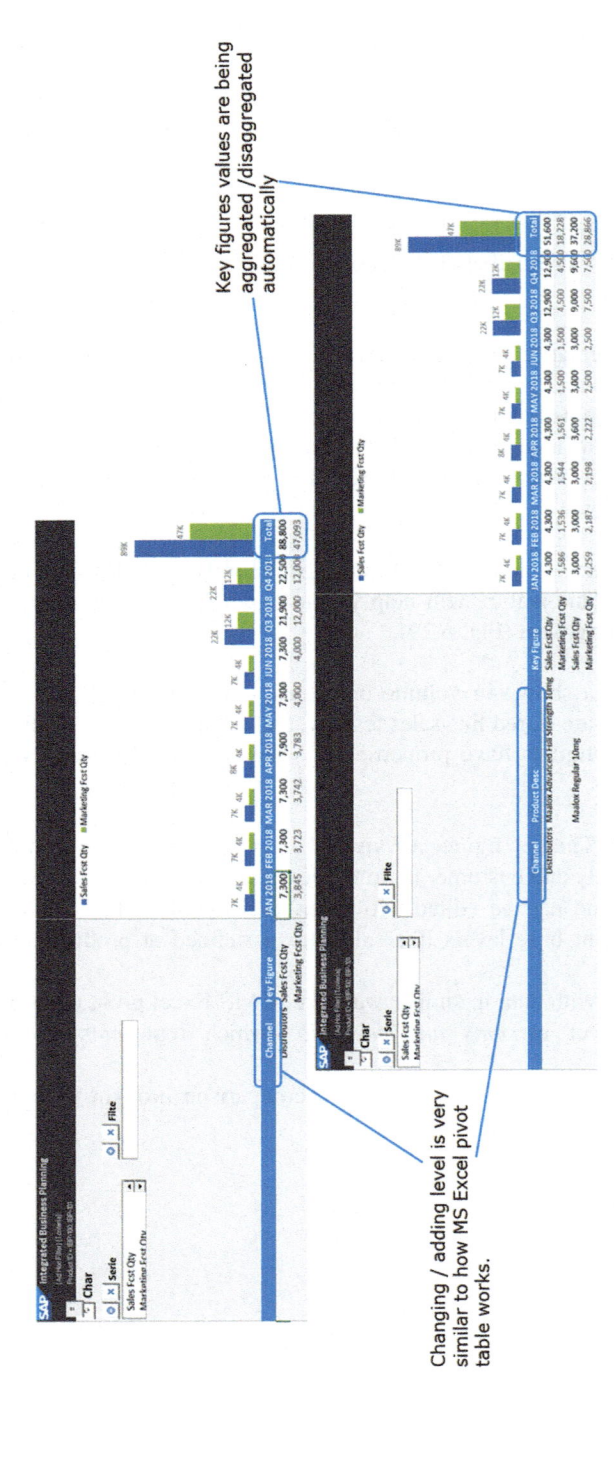

Fig. 6.30 SAP IBP and Microsoft Excel pivot table analogy

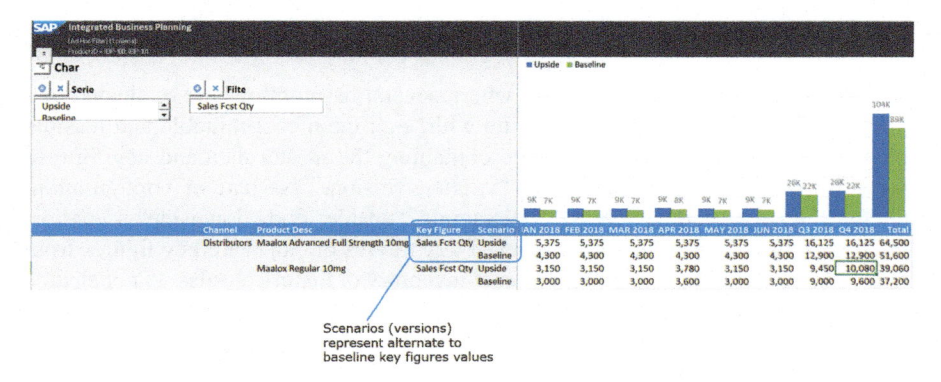

Fig. 6.31 SAP IBP—scenario display in Excel UI

Fig. 6.32 SAP IBP like Excel pivot table

6.5 Versions, Scenarios, and Assumptions

Performing "what-if" scenario planning and defining alternative plans to manage business risk and opportunities are important capabilities of SAP Integrated Business Planning system. Often in an IBP process, several alternate plans need to be evaluated based on the different assumptions. These alternative plans should coexist just like the baseline plans but provide flexibility to do ad hoc or streamlined analysis for decision-making without affecting planning data and sometimes even master data of the base version.

These alternative plans could have different business purposes where some are more focused on evaluating long-term strategic planning situations while some are more focused on evaluating options for any type of planning. SAP IBP provides two options for "what-if" scenario constructs, namely, "versions" and "user-defined scenarios." The section below explains the purpose of each and how versions and scenarios together can be used for evaluating alternate plans.

6.5.1 Versions

Versions are alternate plans of data where several assumptions are evaluated and uncertainties are factored in to come up with, e.g., the most profitable and feasible plan. When a planning area is created containing the master data and key figures, these by default become part of a "baseline version." As part of configuration, alternate versions can be defined, for example, "upside" and "downside" scenarios. Each version can have their unique set of key figures or can share key figures from the "base version." For example, on-hand inventory or historical sales do not change between versions, so these can be defined in a version to have data referring to a base version. By default, master data is shared across all versions in a planning area. However, based on the type of alternate plans to be evaluated per the business needs, version can be defined with version-dependent master data in which case the master data must be loaded to a specific version (see new sales channel mapped in the strategic planning use case).

Versions are configuration entries, and like a planning area base version, the artifacts like tables, views, etc. are generated during planning area activation. Therefore, it is required to know upfront and define the version that needs to be used in a planning process. Further a clear definition of what key figures should be included in a version must be predefined along with settings of version-dependent or version-independent master data making it less flexible for changes unless planning area is activated. A planning area can have one or more versions, and each of the version can be master data shared or version-specific master data. The data model or planning area provides all the necessary functionality and user access such that the alternate plans can coexist with the baseline plan without affecting data in the base version.

6.5.2 User-Defined Scenarios

Unlike versions that are pre-configured and available to all users, the user-defined scenarios can be created by end users as part of the planning process to evaluate multiple scenarios in parallel to the base plan. The results of a simulation can be stored by end users in its own scenario. Scenarios provide an own workspace for the planners to work on the plan. These scenarios are deltas on top of the baseline plan and can be managed without affecting the base plan.

Scenarios in IBP can be defined on a base version or configured versions or a combination of both. Scenarios are private to the user who defined them and can be shared with other users for collaborative decision-making. Typically, in a planning process, a planner works on several changes to the data based on planning assumptions and works on validating these multiple assumptions and collaborating with other users before making the change final. These final changes are then promoted to the baseline plan.

6.5.3 User-Defined Scenario Management

All user-defined scenarios can be created and managed in the Excel user interface of IBP where it is most relevant. These include sharing scenario with other users, promoting a scenario to baseline, resetting scenario to its original state, and deleting and duplicating a scenario (Fig. 6.33).

Scenarios can be selected in Excel and analytics to compare and analyze planning results between scenarios.

6.5.4 Version and Scenario Comparison

In Fig. 6.34, you will find the summary of differences between versions and scenarios.

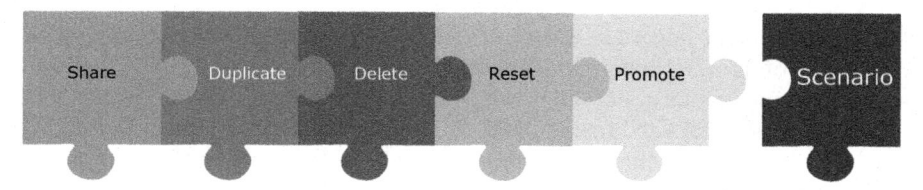

Fig. 6.33 SAP IBP—management of scenarios

	Versions	User defined scenarios
Purpose	Copies of planning dataset from base version	Saved simulation of planning data on top on versions(incl base)
Use case	Evaluate long term revenue and margin projection on adding a new product line	Evaluate impact on change in price or increase in demand for a customer.
Visibility	All users who have access to versions	Planning user who created the scenario and to whom the scenario is shared
Creation	Pre-defined as part of planning area configuration	Created on the fly in a planning process.
Who manages creation and changes	Planning area admin	Planning user who created
Data copy	Full copies of data	Deltas from baseline
Master data	Version dependent master data can be configured or share master data from base version	Shares same data as base version

Fig. 6.34 SAP IBP—versions vs scenarios

Versions and user-defined scenarios complement each other to providing high level of flexibility for real-time "what-if" analysis in IBP process. The benefits of such include the following:

1. What-if analysis can be run on all or selected dataset.
2. Real-time analysis and calculation of profitability and revenue projections of the alternate plans.
3. Faster what-if analysis of changing assumptions and evaluating impact on the plan in a separate workspace from the baseline plan.
4. Single data model that supports multiple versions, scenarios, and base version to coexist without affecting the base plan.
5. User permission is applied to the data they can view and manage.
6. Life cycle to copy, promote, and delete versions and scenarios.
7. High usability and efficiency in S&OP meetings by presenting the alternate plans in easy-to-use and visual analytical charts and Excel planning views.

Modeling of risks and opportunities is done in SAP IBP with use of versions and scenarios. It is an important aspect of every review step in IBP. Definition and evaluation of risks and opportunities and taking actions to overcome risks and choose the best opportunities are important for decision-making in IBP. There are characteristics of risks and opportunities that need to be captured and evaluated in a planning tool so that their effect is clear on the plan. Characteristics like probability, budget, drivers/notes, and actions of risks and opportunities are qualitative information that needs to be tracked as part of the planning process. In a planning process, the risks and opportunities can be managed as separate key figures that are considered in the overall business plan. The individual risk and opportunities can be modeled as an event, and different scenarios can be planned based on risks and opportunities. Or they can be grouped together into a single key figure for risks and opportunities. Often risks and opportunities are derived from the assumptions and changes to the assumptions. Both risks and opportunities can be defined at different planning levels of hierarchy. During each review cycle, assumptions, risks, and opportunities and the net effect of risks and opportunities are evaluated. As a result of the review meetings, the risks and opportunities can be adjusted, or new ones can be added based on the changes in assumptions. Further the following information like gaps identified, measures to close the gaps, and decisions/actions are captured in the review meetings. These can be recorded in the JAM Collaboration of IBP for documentation, traceability, and transparency.

6.5.5 Assumptions

Many companies that have succeeded in their planning processes have realized that the plans are only as good based on the qualitative information that drives the quantitative numbers. Therefore, the assumptions that drive the change are as important to be captured as the changes to the numbers.

The numbers alone are not sufficient to be captured. The qualitative input that drives the numbers should be captured, and plan and their changes should be based on assumptions.

Assumptions and the business drivers are unique to a company, and the different categories of assumptions vary by different industries. Common assumption categories include market conditions, growth assumptions, competitions assumptions, performance assumptions, etc.

These assumptions are then associated with a certain planning hierarchy, for example, at a brand level or category/region level where they are more relevant. Assumptions can keep changing for each planning period, and therefore the planning numbers are also changed and tracked together with the changing assumptions.

6.6 Collaboration

Why Is Collaboration Necessary in IBP?

IBP is a planning process across cross-functional business units and lines of business with tens to hundreds of users driving toward one plan that profitably meets demand and supply, aligning with the strategic objectives of a company. Therefore, it is very important that all stakeholders involved in this harmonized business process are engaged in making collaborative decisions based on provided transparency of information. Collaboration in an IBP process provides the following:

1. Collaboration across cross-functional teams
2. Record decisions and actions
3. Document storage and sharing
4. Collaborative decision-making
5. Better communication
6. Transparency of information
7. Easier user onboarding and higher user adoption

In this era where social collaboration is part of everyday life with user-friendly, easy to adopt collaborative platforms like Facebook, Twitter, messengers, etc., the need for collaboration quickly moves also to the enterprise platform where collaboration and social media engagement are necessary for the business community.

Companies are measured by how they engage their user community and customers. Internally it is important for the different cross-functional groups in a company to align on how the departmental plans achieve the strategic growth plans of the company. In a typical setup, the board and leadership team are responsible for defining the strategic direction of the company. These strategic goals are then translated to the tactical and operational goals of the company across several different business units, divisions, and functional units. For example, company sets a goal for top-line revenue increase of 20% over the next 3 years. This translates to R&D goals of accelerating new product launches, sales targets of reaching new markets and customers/upselling, technology team goals of driving toward new platforms and reducing infrastructure costs, etc.

Often how strategic objectives are achieved by the tactical, operations, and executions plans are not transparent, and departments work in silos thereby hindering the overall growth of the company. Therefore, a need for a well-established collaborative platform where people are engaged, objectives and information are transparent, and decisions are made in collaboration significantly increases achievement of the business goals.

6.6.1 Collaboration in SAP IBP

SAP integrated business process provides the necessary functionality and tools for a collaborative and integrated business planning in IBP. SAP JAM is the social collaboration platform that is embedded and seamlessly integrated in the SAP IBP application. Collaboration in IBP is achieved by the following:

1. Embedded JAM Collaboration
2. Process management integrated with JAM
3. Collaborative sharing of content: Excel views, analytics, scenarios
4. Case management for alerts in supply chain control tower

6.6.2 JAM Collaboration

SAP JAM is an enterprise social collaboration platform that is heavily used for collaboration across various groups, to exchange information, share document, etc. This is a well-proven platform that has been used by several customers to connect internal and external stakeholders, to exchange information, and to collaborate on important activities.

SAP JAM is a cloud-based enterprise collaboration with seamless connectivity on mobile devices providing structured collaborative tools like ranking, forums, tasks, etc. for collaborative decision-making.

SAP IBP uses SAP JAM providing JAM collaborative functionality directly embedded in IBP application. Single sign-on and direct navigation to JAM from IBP provide users the seamless collaboration across all areas of IBP application. In the IBP launchpad, the collaboration Fiori app provides a direct navigation to JAM Collaboration where the logged in user can see both the public and private collaboration groups that he/she is part of.

Though there are several scenarios for collaboration in IBP, we start with a collaboration scenario in an IBP process where during a demand review step in IBP, the demand planners identify a gap between the plan and the targets and works with various stakeholders across sales, marketing, and finance to close the gap to the target and present results for decision-making in the management business review meeting.

6.6 Collaboration

Scenario Demand planner collaborates with sales, supply, and finance team to close the gaps to meet AOP targets. A monthly IBP process for the USA is in progress for the May cycle of the year with a mid- to long-term horizon of 3 months to 2 years for the Cosmetics Business Unit of the Consumer Products Company ABC. To manage the collaboration across several stakeholders, a JAM group has been created, and the stakeholders have been invited to the group.

Demand planner John identifies that the demand projections for the May cycle of the S&OP process do not meet the AOP targets set by the company. He then collaborates with the stakeholders across marketing, sales, finance, and supply chain as to options to close the gap.

In the demand review step of IBP process, the current situation about gap between consensus demand plan revenue and annual operating plan/budget is identified and posted to the JAM feed providing visibility of the situation to other stakeholders involved in the planning process (Fig. 6.35).

The **JAM group** demand review is a private group with participants who are invited to join the group by the owner of the JAM group. A JAM group organizes all the required collaboration activities among the involved users by sharing and broadcasting information. Groups can be public or private depending on their usage. For example, the company has public groups providing information about the company goals and objectives, onboarding information, frequently asked questions, videos, documents, etc.

In our scenario demand planning group is a private group where important issues are discussed, documents are shared among stakeholders, and decisions are made.

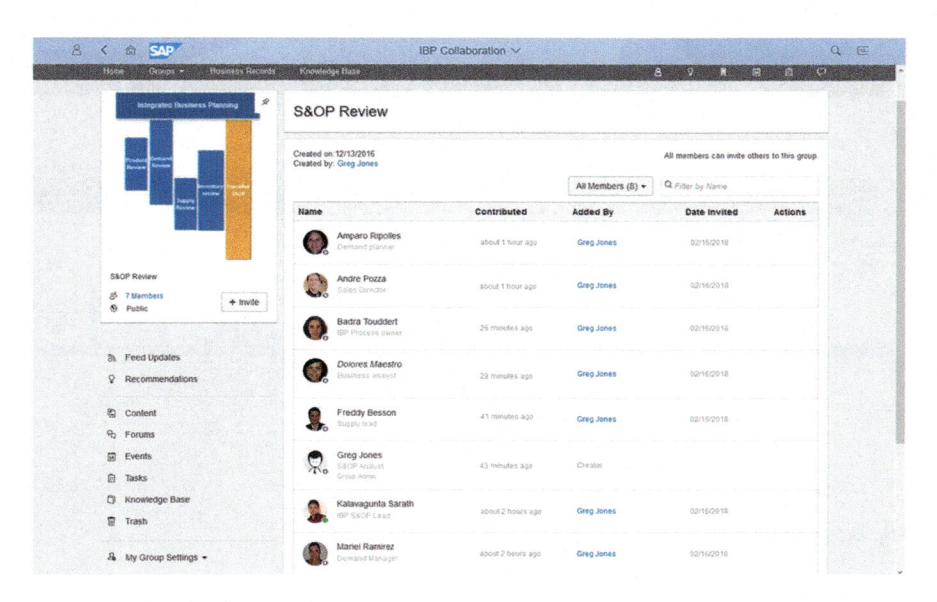

Fig. 6.35 SAP IBP JAM Collaboration

After the feed is posted to the JAM group with the chart showing the gaps, the users get notified immediately or based on their notification settings, and they can provide their feedback/comments on how to resolve the current issue. In this case Jeff from sales posted the note that there is an opportunity for a large deal happening with a new retailer in Q2 that can then be accounted for the demand plan. This looks like a good solution to solve the situation; however, the sales bias, risks, financial impact, and supply feasibility for the demand need to be accounted before a decision is made.

The sales planner makes the quantitative adjustments to the sales forecast quantity and provides qualitative notes and summary of the change in the reason code dialog that appears when changes to the plan are saved. In the reason code dialog, the user enters the reasons for the change along with a comment and chooses the JAM group to whom this information needs to be shared (Fig. 6.36).

Upon saving, the reason code and comments then get available instantly in the JAM feed for the JAM group to which the feed has been posted. Users in the JAM groups get instantly notified about changes to the plan. They can see in the **JAM feed** when the change was made, by whom, and the date/time for the change.

After the end of the sales input cycle, the demand planner can look at the list of all changes in the planning cycle for the demand review phase and finally arrives at a consensus demand plan that needs to be supplied. In the scenario for sales increase, the demand planner analyzes that historically the sales planner has had bias in his sales numbers. The demand planner therefore adjusts the consensus plan by taking into consideration the sales bias and other forecast intelligence measures to arrive at a consensus forecast. This is also then posted to the JAM feed, and all the stakeholders are informed.

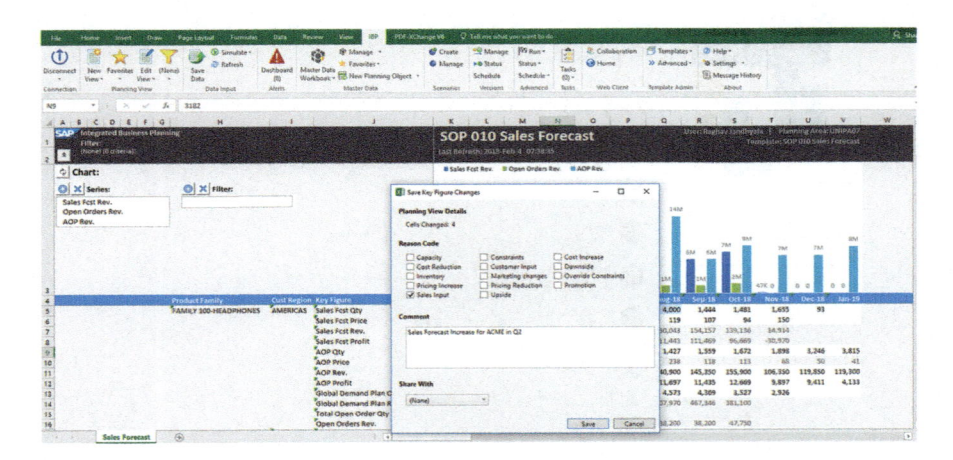

Fig. 6.36 SAP IBP JAM reason codes

6.6 Collaboration

Fig. 6.37 SAP IBP JAM decision matrix entries

6.6.3 Validating Options

After the demand review and supply review step are completed, the next process step is the integrated reconciliation where the demand and supply match happens together with financials to determine the scenario that needs to be recommended for the IBP meeting. Here JAM plays an important role in allowing for structured collaboration across the stakeholders by providing several decision-making tools like polls, decisions, pro/con table, ranking, and comparison table (Fig. 6.37).

As a preparation for the integrated reconciliation meeting, the supply options to meet the gap between AOP target and demand plan are evaluated, and each participant can add to the pros/cons for the list of options. Finally, a ranking tool would allow for participants to rank their option. Other collaborative tools in JAM can also be used to enhance the collaborative decision-making process. These activities are then instantly available in the JAM feed and allow all stakeholders to get a clear understanding of how a decision was made, what factors were taken into consideration, and who were involved in the decision make thereby providing a transparency on the decision-making process (Fig. 6.38).

6.6.4 Meetings and Decisions

The next step in the process is the IBP meeting. Using the JAM Collaboration tool, the S&OP process coordinator sets up the meeting with an agenda and list of documents that need to be reviewed during the IBP meeting (Fig. 6.39). In our scenario, the leadership team across all departments attend this meeting to decide on the final plan taking into consideration the risks, opportunities, and assumption. The decision from this meeting drives the operation and execution aspect of the plan.

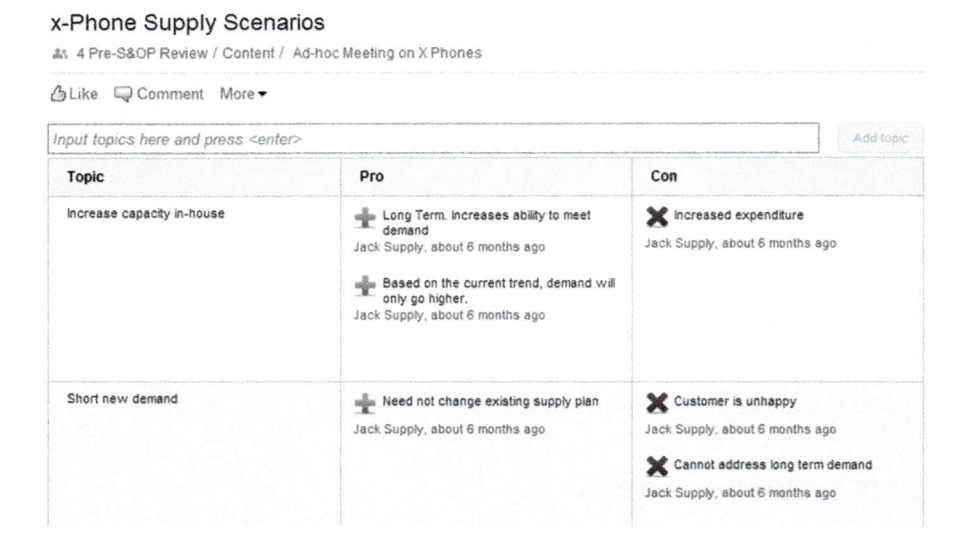

Fig. 6.38 SAP IBP JAM Collaboration decision matrix—pros/cons

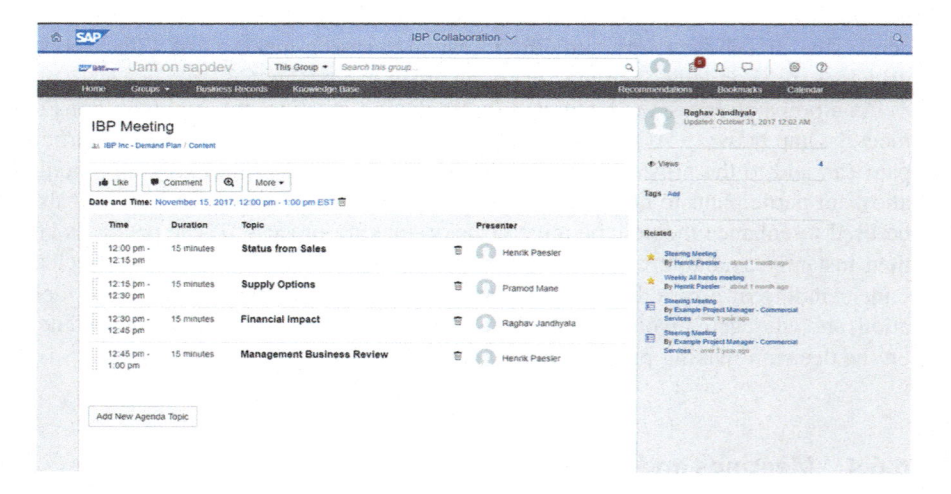

Fig. 6.39 SAP IBP JAM Collaboration groups

The meeting has been set up with the agenda of:

- Input from sales
- Review supply options
- Financial impact
- Decision and approval of plans

6.6 Collaboration

SAP IBP with embedded JAM Collaboration captures all the required structure collaborative steps unlike several undocumented and unstructured collaboration that happens in several organizations through emails, offline conversations, and phone calls.

6.6.5 Store and Share Documentation

The final step in the process after the management business review is to capture all the decisions, actions, meeting notes, and documents (Fig. 6.40). The decisions and documents from the IBP meetings for each of the planning cycles can be stored in the flexible folder structure that can be defined for the user to easily find and access information.

The content section of the JAM page is the access to all the documents and structured content. All the decisions that were taken and the planning processes can be easily accessed from this section thereby increasing transparency and information communication.

In summary JAM provides a good collaboration platform for IBP. The multiple work groups which can be dynamically created allow for context-driven communication and conversation between members, share ideas, provide comments, respond to questions, and interact with other members right from the planning tool. With so much information that is tracked, it is also very important to find the information quickly. The content search feature in JAM provides a free form search to instantly access any content. JAM augments the planning process with its rich set of tools to provide a qualitative input to otherwise quantitative-driven plans.

With any collaborative tools, the success of its adoption depends on the ease to use the tool, self-service with no trainings, seamless connectivity, and embedded collaboration as part of the planning tools. SAP IBP meets both the planning and collaboration done right from one place thereby increasing the user adoption and increasing collaboration across the team and company.

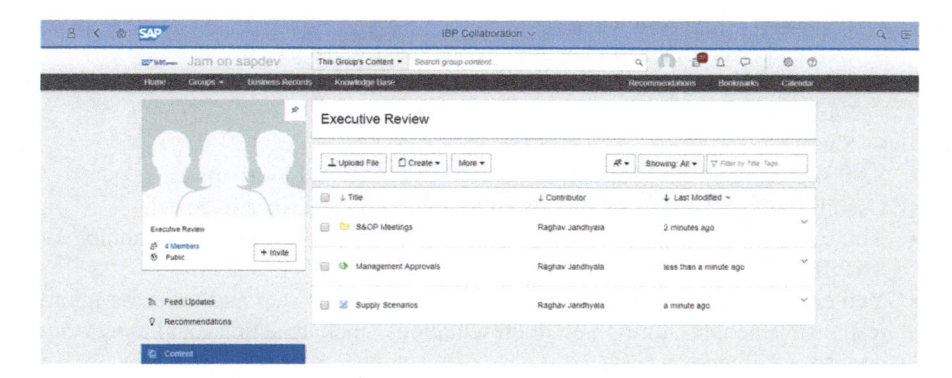

Fig. 6.40 SAP IBP JAM Collaboration tasks and S&OP document storage

Fig. 6.41 SAP IBP—case management

6.6.6 Case Management

Case management which is part of supply chain control tower allows collaboration and resolution of supply chain issues that have been identified from the custom alerts. Case management app in SAP IBP encapsulates all the information relevant to solve the issue and maintains a log of all actions that were taken to resolve an issue (Fig. 6.41).

Users can track one or more alerts in a case, take snapshots of the data, add comments, and track changes to the case in case history. Cases have a life cycle and status for users to focus on the most important ones. These cases can also be assigned to several users or user groups to collaborate and resolve the case.

6.7 Summary

- SAP IBP is a cloud system which has the following functional application running in the cloud on single HANA database without any internal interface:
  - Inventory optimization
  - Demand (with demand planning and demand sensing)
  - Response and supply
  - Supply chain control tower
  - S&OP
- SAP IBP comes with Web UI, Excel user interface and Fiori apps.
- Usability of SAP IBP is strengthened by main user interface in Excel.
- You can run strategic planning, tactical S&OP, and operational planning on SAP IBP.
- You can orchestrate planning process by modeling its step and tasks, assigning responsible people, storing S&OP presentations, tracking actions, and monitoring process adherence.

- You can introduce global process framework and local variation, all working according to same milestones, supported by process automation, e.g., releasing S&OP process instances on regular basis.
- You can model organization as part of data model, e.g., for the purpose of process improvement, analytics, KPI linked to organizational units, and roles.
- SAP IBP comes with pre-configured process and data model. You can configure nonstandard processes with standard instruments allowing you to configure key figures, master data, routines, flows, and KPIs.
- You can leverage flexibility of configuration done in HANA and combine it on user interface with feature of Microsoft Excel.
- SAP IBP supports creation of alternate plans with the use of user-defined scenarios where you can modify data (e.g., change price) but share same master data and more extensive versions where you can change data and model new master data objects (e.g., add new sales channel, production plant extensions)
- SAP IBP supports with JAM tool collaboration between IBP stakeholders. JAM supports:
    - Chat and data collaboration across cross-functional teams
    - Record decisions (pros and cons) and actions
    - Store and share documents
    - Collaborative decision-making with case management
    - Ad hoc communication
    - Transparency of information in one repository
    - Easier user onboarding and higher user adoption
    - S&OP page

References

Blosch, M., & Uskert, M. (2011). Unilever develops demand planning capability in developing and emerging markets. *Gartner*.

Palmatier, G. E., & Crum, C. (2003). *Enterprise sales and operations planning: Synchronizing demand, supply and resources for peak performance*. Boca Raton: J Ross.

How to Measure Transformation Success 7

7.1 Why Measure, Relevance in Performance Measures

Management guru Eliyahu Goldratt, best known for his book "The Goal" (Goldratt, 1984), said "...tell me how you'll measure me and I'll tell you how I'll behave." This vividly illustrates the need for performance measurement, particularly in the context of Integrated Business Planning[1] where influencing the right behaviors is at the heart of achieving superior outcomes (Fig. 7.1).

Great outcomes are borne out of great decisions, and great decisions get made based on relevant facts (and corresponding measures).

However, facts do not appear out of thin air. More often than not, they start out as opinions. A good decision-maker seeks out facts and measures to either validate or invalidate her/his opinion. It is important to note, though, that what is a fact in one field of study may not be one in another—they are highly context sensitive. Peter Drucker in his book "The Effective Executive" (Drucker, 2007) illustrates this with the example of taste. He points out that taste is not relevant and therefore not a fact in physics, but is of utmost relevance when it comes to cooking. Now let's take an example closer to IBP. To estimate demand for a new product, the relevance of competition or competitors depends on how unique the new product is. If the product is unlike anything out there in the market, one can reasonably spare efforts to seek out facts regarding competition to test opinions about market demand. This goes to show that criterion of relevance is an important criterion to identify facts or measures significant to the decision at hand.

> Whenever one analyzes the way a truly effective, a truly right, decision has been reached, one finds that a great deal of work and thought went into finding the appropriate measurement (Drucker, 2007).

---

[1] In this chapter, terms planning and Integrated Business Planning will be used interchangeably.

© Springer International Publishing AG, part of Springer Nature 2018
R. Kepczynski et al., *Integrated Business Planning*, Management for Professionals, https://doi.org/10.1007/978-3-319-75665-3_7

Why measure?
Concept of relevance in choosing measures

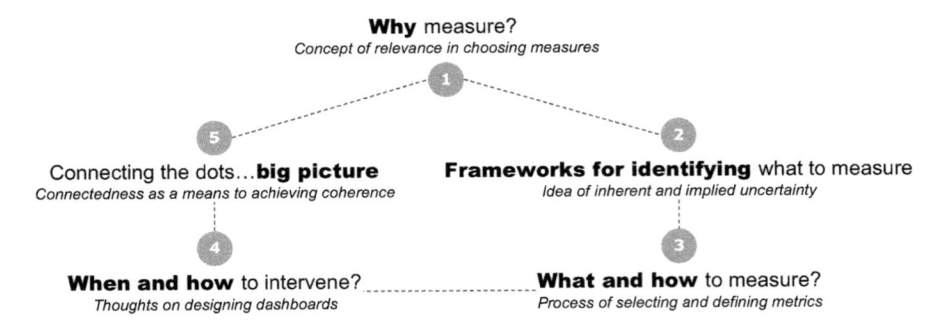

Connecting the dots...big picture
Connectedness as a means to achieving coherence

Frameworks for identifying what to measure
Idea of inherent and implied uncertainty

When and how to intervene?
Thoughts on designing dashboards

What and how to measure?
Process of selecting and defining metrics

Fig. 7.1 Structure of the "How to measure performance" chapter

Finding the appropriate measurement for a given situation also depends on how one approaches decision-making. As a decision-maker, it is tempting to want to reduce the burden on oneself by restricting opinions on the matter. This would be the wrong approach. Being transfixed on one opinion could easily lead to confirmation bias. Statisticians will tell you that if you are persistent, you will find the facts to support your opinion. It is important therefore to encourage diverse and often dissenting views. This would lead to diversity also in the form of measures, each one providing a different perspective to the same problem and letting the decision-maker choose the measure that's most relevant to the decision in question.

The anecdote below highlights how a new opinion or a new way of thinking sparks the need for new measurements that eventually leads to better decisions:

> The story of how McNamara, who was a defense secretary under President Kennedy, instituted measures to improve inventory performance of the military, should help underscore the importance of measurement and choosing the right measures. It was in the aftermath of the Korean War when McNamara was brought in. The procurement and inventory policies were in a state of disarray. The measurements were based on total dollars or numbers in procurement and inventory. McNamara challenged existing notions and instituted new measurements that acknowledged a key fact: only around 5 to 6 percent of items in inventory were responsible for 90% of procurement dollars and/or were needed for combat readiness. So, the new policy was designed around managing these items in minute detail and the rest using the principle of management by exception. This change immediately led to a significant decrease in effort and improvements in decision quality. This anecdote shows how selection of the right measures helps focus on leverage points in the process—that is, those aspects that wield a disproportionate impact on performance. It also highlights the importance of challenging traditional metrics as they may have become out of touch with the new reality.

Using the above anecdote as the basis, the following illustration shows how a different (in this case, a better) opinion can lead to fresh insights (Fig. 7.2).

Opinion 1 is based on a traditional and dated way of thinking that all items are created equal and therefore connects to a measure that is reflective of an undifferentiated way of looking at procurement spend (total $ in procurement and inventory).

However, opinion 2 is a recognition of the Pareto principle at work—in this context, related to procurement spend and inventory management. Consequently, the

7.2 What to Measure

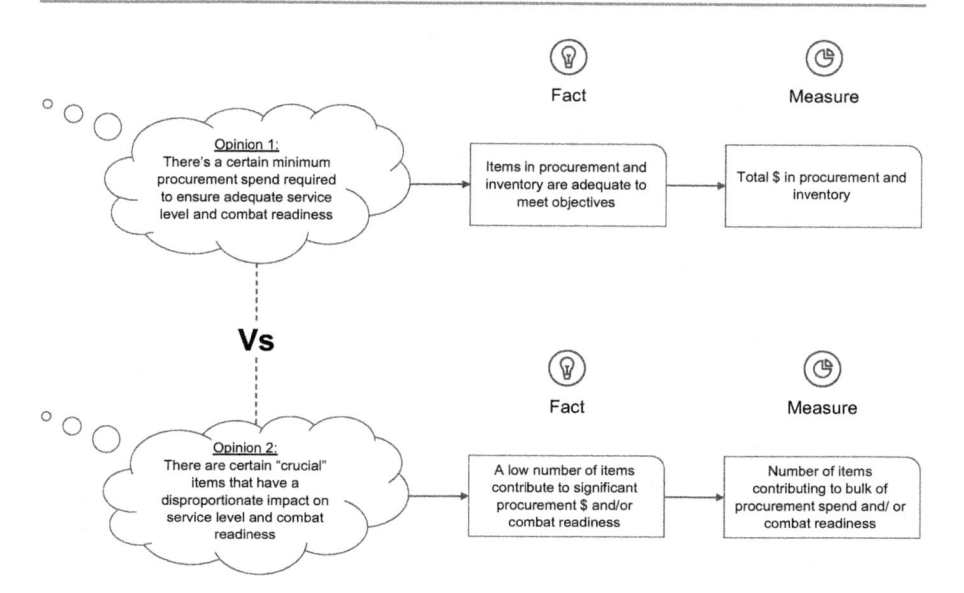

Fig. 7.2 From opinion to facts and measures

measure chosen looks at the % of items that contribute to the bulk of procurement spend. This leads to the insight that these "crucial" items need special treatment. An example of a different (and in this case a superior) outcome is brought about by choosing a better measure to support procurement and inventory decisions.

7.2 What to Measure

In the previous section, we talked about the idea of relevance in choosing measures. Let's dwell on this topic a little more as it plays a pivotal role in the selection of the right measures.

For driving effective decisions in an integrated planning context, one needs to select the most relevant set of metrics to measure the level of alignment between (integrated planning) capabilities and overall firm strategy.

For example, for a firm that lays a strong emphasis on product variety (a broad variety of product offerings), its planning capabilities vis-à-vis ensuring high level of SKU-level accuracy such as product life cycle management, demand forecasting, demand shaping, and sensing should be on par with its ambitions for such a strategy. By extension, its metrics portfolio should consist of measures that monitor performance of these capabilities that are essential to delivering on the promise of broad variety.

In general terms, right metrics are a function of capabilities that are essential to deliver on a firm's chosen strategy.

Market Needs ≡ "True" Uncertainty

↓↓↓↓
━━━━━━━━━━━━━━━━━━━━━━━ Deliberate strategic choices
↓↓↓↓

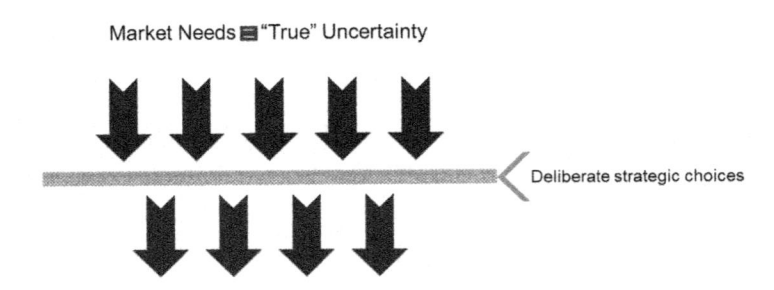

Needs a firm chooses to address ≡ "Implied" Uncertainty

Fig. 7.3 True uncertainty and implied uncertainty

There is an emphasis on "chosen" as a firm deliberately chooses what it will and it won't do that in turn informs its strategy. In order to measure alignment between capabilities and strategy, the concept of true and implied uncertainty (Chopra & Meindl, 2014) is quite useful. This concept is illustrated in very simple terms in Fig. 7.3.

The market needs along several attributes such as variety, volume, response time, etc. translate to a certain uncertainty profile—demand as well as supply—that represents the true or inherent uncertainty. However, a firm through what it chooses or chooses not to do is exposed to a level of uncertainty, which can be termed as "implied" uncertainty.

Let's elaborate on this a little further with an example.

Customers can be segmented based on how they prioritize product-oriented attributes such as quantity, variety, service level, response times, price, level of innovation, etc. (Chopra & Meindl, 2014), into homogeneous segments or segments consisting of customers with similar needs. A company then has to make conscious choices regarding segments it will cater to, since these choices will determine what is relevant for the company. These conscious choices inform a company's *competitive strategy*.

Competitive strategy provides a filter of relevance that helps narrow down needs that a firm seeks to satisfy. The example illustrated (Fig. 7.4) shows two customer segments—gray and blue—that differ along various attributes that are an expression of needs. Clearly, blue is a more demanding segment in that these customers demand greater range of quantities, variety, higher service level, lower response times, and higher level of innovation. If a firm needs to cater to both these segments, the implied uncertainty will be a lot higher than when it chooses to cater to one or the other only. In the example, the firm has chosen to address the needs of the gray segment only,

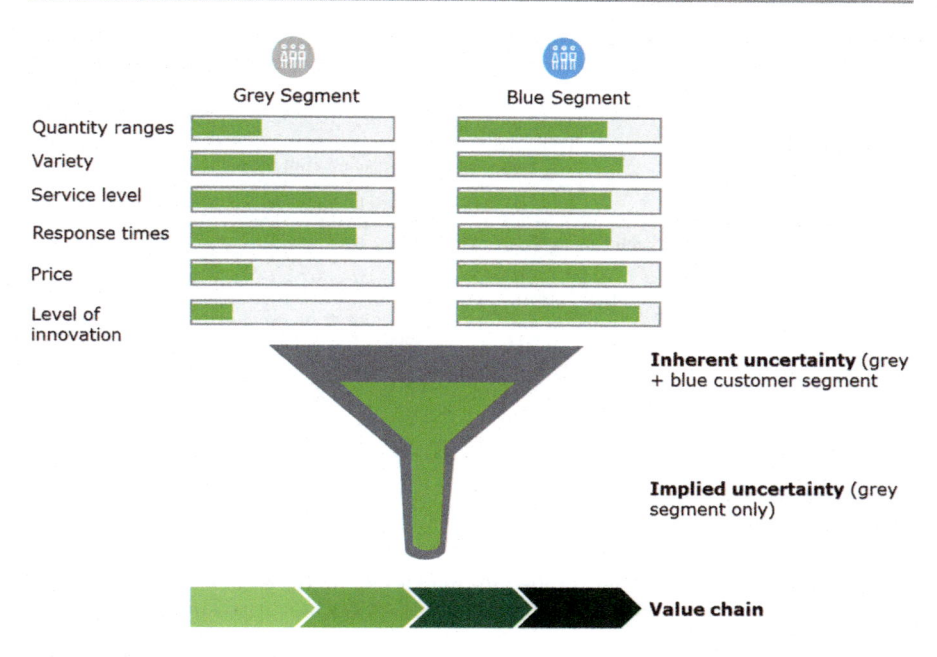

Fig. 7.4 Inherent vs implied uncertainty

thereby making implied uncertainty significantly lower than true uncertainty (if it were to cater to both segments.)[2]

From a planning perspective, the key question therefore is, what capabilities require special attention in order to be optimized for the level of implied uncertainty they are expected to handle? With this question in mind, let's turn our attention to two interesting conceptual constructs that can help us establish a framework for choosing the right metrics.

Functional and Innovative Supply Chain Characteristics
Seminal article "What Is the Right Supply Chain for Your Product?" (Fisher, 1997) points out that there are essentially two categories of supply chain costs—physical costs and market mediation costs.

Physical costs are incurred in transforming raw materials to finished goods, whereas market mediation costs are a result of communication of demand information across the supply chain and activities undertaken to ensure adequate supply. He further argues that the relative significance of these two categories of costs is owed to the nature of products being dealt with—functional or innovative (Fig. 7.5).

---

[2] Please note that a firm can also choose to only partially satisfy the needs of a certain segment and through that limit the uncertainty it is exposed to. So, it doesn't have to be an all or nothing equation when it comes to staisfying needs of a certain segment.

Functional SC characteristics	Innovative SC characteristics
• Standard products • Lower lead times • Lower demand variability • Higher numbers of stages • Flexible contracts • Cheaper modes of transport (between stages) • Lower product costs/prices • Typically, a make to stock manufacturing environment is to be found • Higher levels of inventory	• Higher level of innovation and customized products • High lead times • Very high demand variability • Lower number of stages (agile) • Relative stable supplier contracts • Higher transportation costs (between stages) – sometimes to compensate for high lead times • High products costs/prices • Typically, a make to stock manufacturing environment is to be found • Lower levels of inventory (especially finished goods inventory)

Fig. 7.5 Functional vs innovative characteristics

This distinction is a very important one in identifying the right set of metrics. A functional supply chain dealing with standard products requires different set of planning capabilities, and related metrics, compared to one dealing with innovative products. For example, an innovative supply chain calls for a much more sophisticated NPI capability, and metrics thereof, than a functional supply chain as the pace of introduction of new products is much higher in an innovative supply chain.

Responsiveness and Efficiency

The second framework, which talks about the efficiency-responsiveness continuum, is closely related to the functional-innovative distinction. For instance, a firm dealing with functional products ought to be a lot more focused on cost efficiency given thinner margins compared to an innovative supply chain. On the other hand, an innovative supply chain that faces short product life cycles, high rate of product obsolescence, and quick response times needs to be more focused on building responsiveness capabilities. This idea is illustrated in Fig. 7.6.

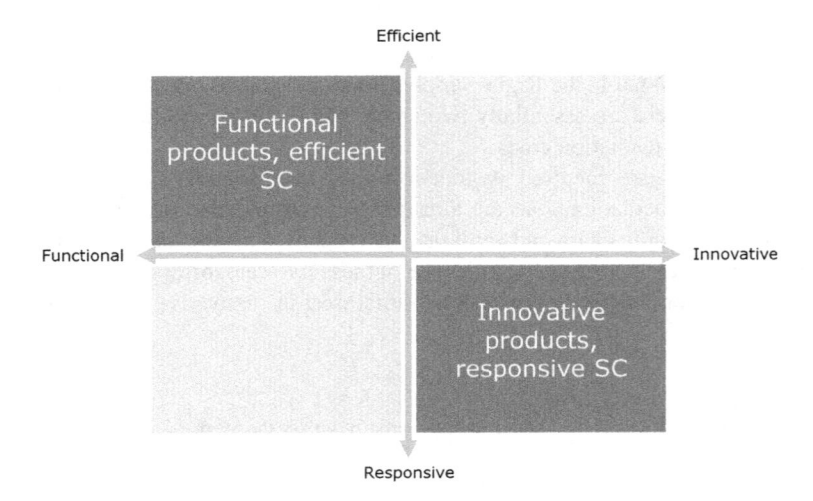

Fig. 7.6 Functional-innovative and efficiency-responsiveness concepts

7.2 What to Measure

The top right and bottom left areas show a misalignment—that is, an innovative product not supported by responsive processes or a functional product not supported by efficient processes (Fig. 7.6). If metrics were to be designed keeping in mind capabilities needed for a strong alignment with the type of products a firm is dealing with, potential misalignments will be brought into sharp focus.

An alignment or fit is achieved when the responsiveness is right for a given level of uncertainty. We can call it "strategic fit" (Chopra & Meindl, 2014). It is of paramount importance to carefully design metrics to help with measurement and monitoring of alignment and, if required, perform course correction.

Examples of Fit/Misfit

A supply chain like Walmart faces a low level of uncertainty as its products fall squarely on the functional side of the functional-innovative continuum. It does not mean, though, that Walmart does not innovate—it does, but its innovation is centered on process innovation rather than product innovation. Cross-docking, which is a logistics concept pioneered by Walmart, helps minimize or even completely eliminate the need for intermediate storage by coordinating inbound shipments to its DCs that allows for quick consolidation and reconfiguration into outbound shipments. This is an example of process innovation that improves efficiency and is one among several of Walmart's strategies to achieve fit.

Barilla's (Hammond, 1994) use of just-in-time distribution (JITD) is another case in point. Despite the functional nature of pasta, Barilla was faced with high variability in its supply chain due to the dreaded whipsaw or bullwhip effect. This was caused by the ordering patterns of its distributors. The JITD program was introduced to reveal hidden information, which in this instance is true demand as seen by distributors, resulting in reduction of uncertainty exposure (see technical note Fig. 7.7) that ultimately led to efficiency gains.

Technical note. The following equation quantifies the variance of demand (D) as seen by a supply chain node to orders (Q) placed by it to its upstream node. L stands for lead time between the nodes and p for the number of demand observations the order is calculated based on.

$$\frac{Var(Q)}{Var(D)} \geq 1 + \frac{2L}{p} + \frac{2L^2}{p^2}$$

As can be seen, the variability of ordering increases with increasing lead times and decreases as the number of observations that inform ordering decisions are increased. For example, if we assume the lead time to be one period and the number of observations to be four, we get:

$$\frac{Var(Q)}{Var(D)} \geq 1.63$$

That is, the variance of orders placed (Q) will be 60% higher than the true variance of demand (D). It is to be noted that variability increases as one moves upstream and is more severe (increases multiplicatively) if ordering is based on decentralized versus centralized information.

Fig. 7.7 Orders versus demand metric

In the above two examples, the focus is on efficiency given the functional nature of the products. From a metrics perspective, this would require a strong emphasis on cost-centric metrics.

To illustrate this point, let us take the example of a manufacturing company dealing in highly engineered products. The planning department at this company was used to ordering materials by analyzing requirements project by project without any regard for cost implications such an approach might have on ordering costs of materials used across multiple projects. To mitigate the situation, an analysis of historical data was done to identify such "standard" materials, and an inventory policy that uses economic order quantity based on an estimation of annual demand was instituted. To measure the impact of this change in policy, a simple cost-focused process metric was used: number of POs created for materials identified as standard over a reporting week. A trend chart that plots this metric was included in the supply chain manager's dashboard, which helped assess the effectiveness of the policy change and also provide an early indication in case things start to regress. This metric was linked to higher-level metrics like supervisor productivity and purchase planner productivity and then all the way up to operating margin. Poor performance of any one of these metrics could be analyzed, and the linkages offer a way to explore causality and assess impact.

For functional supply chains, the risk of misaligned incentives leading to inefficiencies is particularly high. The classic example of Campbell Soup is a case in point (Narayanan & Raman, 2004). Campbell's distributors were indulging in forward-buy to avail of promotional discounts for its chicken soup. This was placing a heavy strain on Campbell's supply chain. Campbell's hope was that the distributors' savings were being passed on to retailers. As Campbell was only collecting data regarding distributor purchases, this assumption couldn't be validated. Campbell was able to disconfirm this assumption once it started collecting sales data from its distributors. This led to Campbell modifying their incentives to only offer discounts for sales and not purchases. More generally, promotions are a good example of a policy that artificially inflate uncertainty faced by a supply chain leading to higher supply chain costs being incurred than could be justified by the implied uncertainty faced.

On the other hand, for supply chains dealing in innovative products, metrics definition requires a different approach. Excessive focus on cost-centric metrics here could lead to actions that are wrongheaded.

7.3 How to Measure

The previous section dealt with a conceptual framework for choosing metrics in a way that helps achieve tight alignment between strategy and capabilities required to execute on that strategy. In this section we turn our attention to the actual process of identifying a portfolio of such metrics.

The focus of the selection process should be the fostering of capabilities that reinforce the fit between a company's strategy and capabilities that help deliver on the chosen strategy. What does this mean in reality? What does a firm have to do to identify such capabilities and define metrics that are congruent with its overall business goals?

Process metrics measure performance of processes that are logical groupings of activities in support of primary activities along the value chain, performed to achieve stated business objectives.

But how does one ensure designs of processes are aligned strategically? That is, how does one design processes that are tailor-made to achieve favorable outcomes and to meet performance targets of lagging metrics, which are mostly financial in nature (return on assets, profit margin, markdowns as a % of sales, etc.). There are some constructs that offer guidance.

Chopra and Meindl (2014) have talked about the concept of drivers of supply chain performance. They have proposed three logistical (L) and three cross-functional (CF) drivers, namely, facilities (L), inventory (L), transportation (L), information (CF), sourcing (CF), and pricing (CF). The supply chain drivers can be viewed as components of the supply chain strategy, which in turn is one component of a company's functional strategies (others being new product development and marketing and sales strategies).

The supply chain strategy needs to be defined so as to strike the right balance between efficiency and responsiveness given the level of implied uncertainty. This is accomplished by designing processes that lend themselves well to decision-making and resolution of trade-offs along the drivers that results in their optimal performance vis-à-vis the overall strategy.

The idea is visualized in below figure. Supply chain strategy (part of functional strategies) is built on a foundation of competitive or business strategy. The processes are visualized as pillars, and these provide the framework for making the right trade-offs (along the supply chain drivers of performance) resulting in desired outcomes and generation of anticipated value (Fig. 7.8).

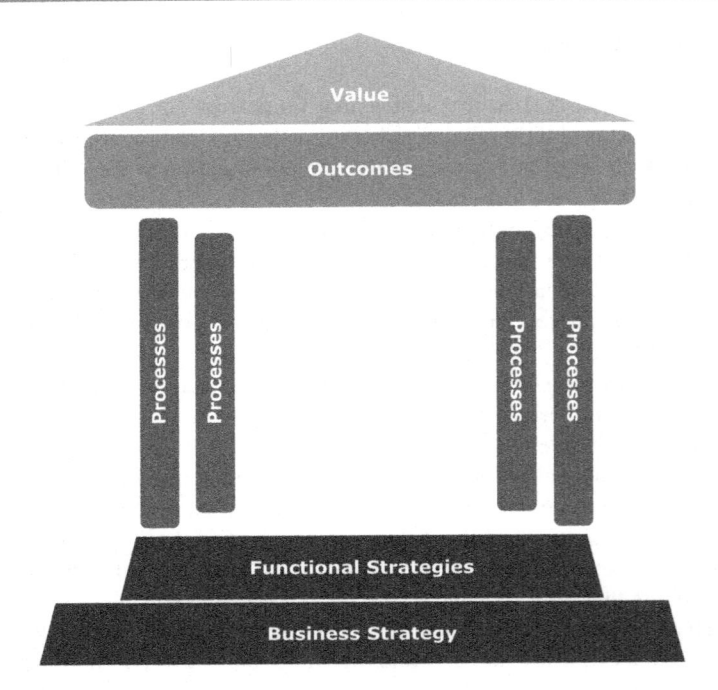

Fig. 7.8 House of value

To describe the concept of trade-offs with regard to supply chain drivers, a comparison is made between a typical functional supply chain and an innovative supply chain, and some examples of process design focus and metrics are provided for each of the drivers (Fig. 7.9).

One can see from the objectives and metrics provided in the example in Fig. 7.9 that drivers of performance for a functional supply chain are cost focused, whereas for an innovative supply chain they are velocity focused.

In summary, selecting the right metrics is a function of capabilities that need to be cultivated in order to achieve strategic objectives. We have seen that selecting the right capabilities requires an understanding of the "implied" uncertainty facing the supply chain, which is in turn a result of deliberate choices a firm makes vis-à-vis its strategy. We have also seen how the nature of the product influences selection of capabilities – a functional product requires efficiency-focused capabilities, whereas an innovative product requires responsiveness capabilities. Performance metrics, therefore, should be chosen in a way that helps assess, diagnose, and correct (using terminology from Gartner (Hofman, 2015)) alignment between strategic imperatives and capabilities designed in response to these imperatives. A graphical version of this summary is presented in Fig. 7.10.

7.3 How to Measure

Supply chain driver	Functional / efficient supply chain		Innovative / responsive supply chain	
Location	⊚	Economies of scale/scope	⊚	Proximity to customers
	⊘	Utilization	⊘	Flow efficiency
Transportation	⊚	Cost efficient	⊚	Rapid transportation
	⊘	Inbound/outbound shipment costs	⊘	Fraction transported by mode
Inventory	⊚	Availability	⊚	Strategic positioning to reduce cycle time, increase throughput
	⊘	Fill rate	⊘	Obsolescence costs
Information	⊚	Use of information for optimal utilization of assets	⊚	Reduction of latency in communication
	⊘	Forecast horizon	⊘	Forecast error
Sourcing	⊚	Flexible contracts	⊚	Strategic contracts, supplier collaboration
	⊘	Purchase price	⊘	Quality, reliability
Pricing	⊚	Stability to reduce bullwhip (e.g. Every Day Low Price)	⊚	Differentiated pricing to shape demand
	⊘	Days Sales Outstanding	⊘	Profit margin

⊚ Objective   ⊘ Measure

Fig. 7.9 Examples of process design focus and metrics for functional SCs

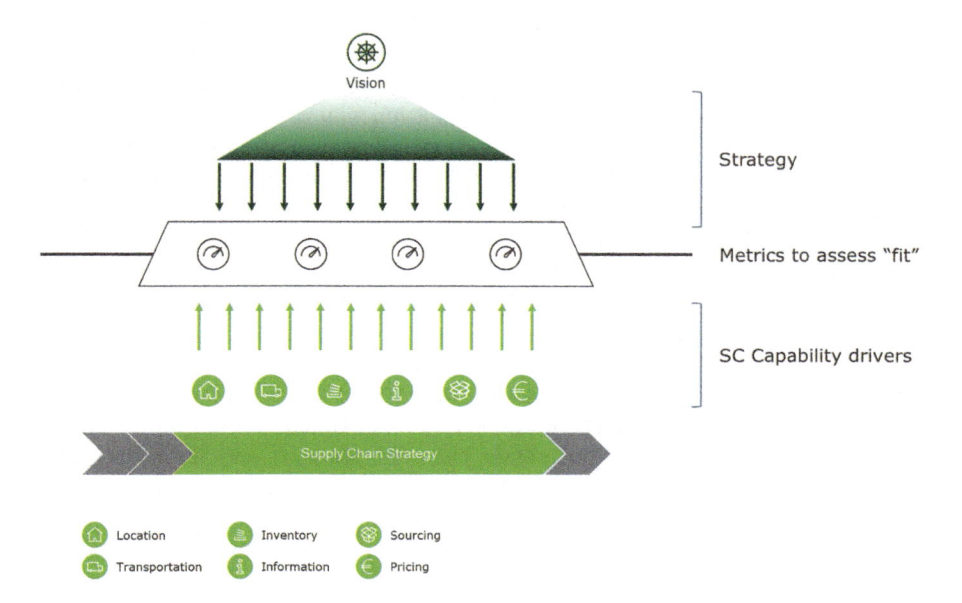

Fig. 7.10 Design metrics to assess the level of fit between strategy and capabilities

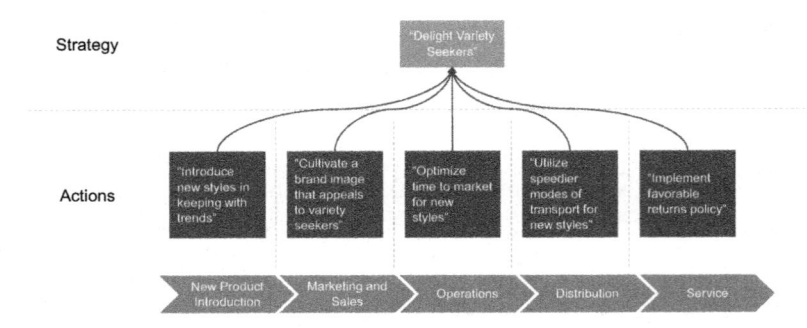

Fig. 7.11 Acme capabilities to foster the strategy of delighting variety seekers

In the illustration above (Fig. 7.10), the assessment of "fit" restricted to supply chain capabilities put in place in response to overall strategy. This is because, as noted earlier, the six drivers of performance we have discussed relate to the supply chain function. Similar capability drivers can be thought of for the other functions, namely, new product development, and marketing and sales to then make a more holistic assessment of fit. The following example adopts such a view.

Let's take the example of a fictitious company called Acme Corporation, a manufacturer of fashion garments with a strong online presence. It caters to a targeted segment of customers that place a premium on variety. Let's call this group "variety seekers" following the typology proposed by Rohm and Swaminathan (2004) in their research on online shoppers.[3] Using this terminology, Acme Corporation can be said to place particular emphasis on wooing variety seekers. From the discussion earlier on framework for selecting metrics, we know Acme's exposure to uncertainty (implied) is a function of varieties it promises to offer and, given that it has chosen a strategy of attracting variety seekers, this uncertainty is higher than it would have been if it had chosen to focus on, for example, fewer varieties. Accordingly, its capabilities need to be geared toward performing well under this level of uncertainty.

If we go along the value chain (see Fig. 7.11), Acme's chosen competitive strategy should be reinforced by its functional strategies. This could translate, for example, to capabilities that are conducive to introduction of new styles in keeping with trends (new product development), creation of a brand image that's attractive to variety seekers (marketing), activities that are geared toward being responsive in order to reduce time to market for new styles (operations), placing a premium on speed rather than ensuring full container loads (distribution), and favorable returns policy to make online shopping a viable alternative for variety seekers (service).

Supply chain excellence in general, and integrated planning excellence in particular, is about being able to resolve trade-offs in a way that leads to favorable business outcomes. Metrics should help determine if this is indeed happening. For the above

---

[3] According to the typology, online shoppers can be clustered into four segments based on shopping motivations: convenience shopper, variety seeker, balanced buyer, and store-oriented buyer.

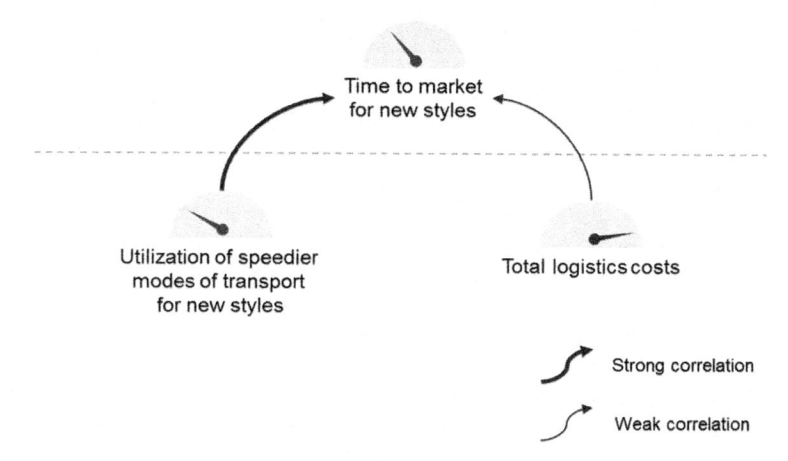

Fig. 7.12 Comparison of responsiveness metric compared to a cost-centric metric

Acme case, assuming time to market for new styles is performing below target, the fact that slower modes of transport are being overused might indicate that the trade-off between transportation cost and responsiveness is not being handled in congruence with the overall strategy. In other words, a metric that measures agility such as "utilization of speedier modes of transport" has a better predictive quality when it comes to explaining the poor performance of time to market compared to a cost-centric metric such as "total logistics costs" (Fig. 7.12).

Taking this analogy further, if the selection of metrics had not been careful enough and there is a predominance of cost-centric metrics, it might lead to a false sense of self-satisfaction. Joel Shapiro (Shapiro, 2017) calls this the importance trap whereby metrics are designed without evaluating their importance in light of the firm's business priorities.

You may be wondering: if right metrics drive right behaviors, how should these be used to shape actions taken on a day-to-day basis?

To answer this, one has to invoke the notion of process hierarchy (Fig. 7.13). We have talked about some metrics tied to activities along the value chain. They'd have to be decomposed to metrics for processes and sub-processes to meaningfully discuss things like how actions performed on a daily basis contribute to higher level business objectives.

Going back to the Acme example, one of the key metrics on a value chain level could be markdowns as a percentage of sales. Given Acme's focus on variety, this metric is quite relevant as it encapsulates the firm's ability to deliver the variety demanded by the market at the right time and in the right quantities. This is a typical example of an outcome metric or a lagging metric. That is, it allows one to get a measure of an outcome and respond to it, but it is not really useful when one wants to proactively shape it. An appropriate process metric in this case would be forecast

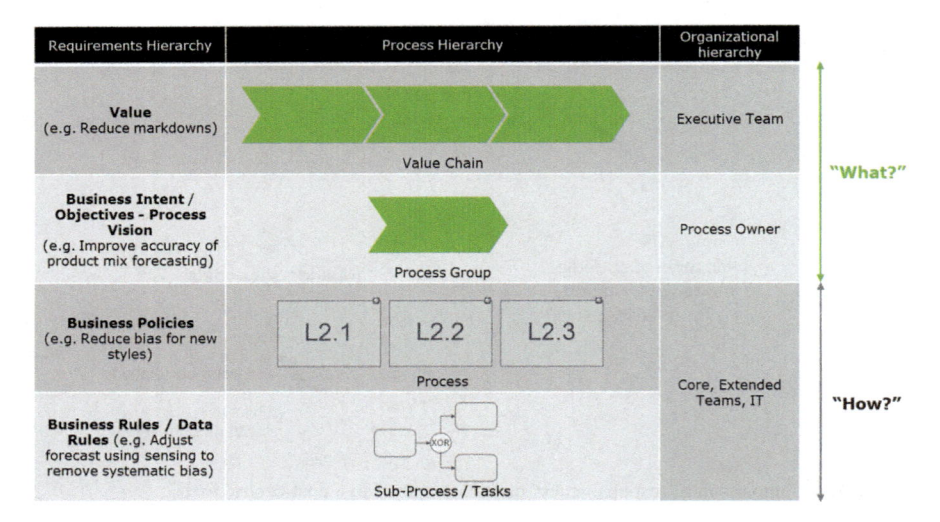

Fig. 7.13 Process hierarchy for process measurement

bias for new styles. This metric has a predictive quality to it and therefore can be termed a leading metric.

There is also an organizational link to the process hierarchy and the hierarchy of metrics. Value chain level metrics are apt for the executive and senior leadership teams. Process owners (be it functionally oriented or cross-functional processes) are the primary audience for process group level metrics. Process teams are the target demographic for process and task level metrics.

Note that focusing on responsive process capabilities does not mean completely ignoring efficiency considerations (or vice versa). Here, the idea of qualifiers and differentiators might help provide clarity. Qualifying level performance is the price of admission. Differentiating performance is what sets your company apart from the competition. So, an innovative supply chain needs to do exceptionally well on metrics centered on responsiveness but needs to turn in at least qualifying level performance on efficiency metrics. How can this insight be applied during process design? We turn to the next construct that comes in handy—one of process segmentation. This idea is depicted in Fig. 7.14. Processes are segmented on the basis of their uniqueness in relation to competition. Differentiating and innovative ideas are where the firm needs to perform exceptionally—this is what sets it apart and makes it tick. On the other hand, common ideas represent commodity processes, and here the focus is just to perform well enough to clear the barrier for entry, pay the price of admission.

In the following paragraphs, we'll explore the process metric in greater detail. We'll start by exploring the anatomy or the building blocks of a process metric. We'll then turn our attention to different aspects of measurement and the topic of formal definition of metrics. Finally, we'll explore the topic of connectedness between metrics and how to avoid suboptimal lagging metrics (value chain and

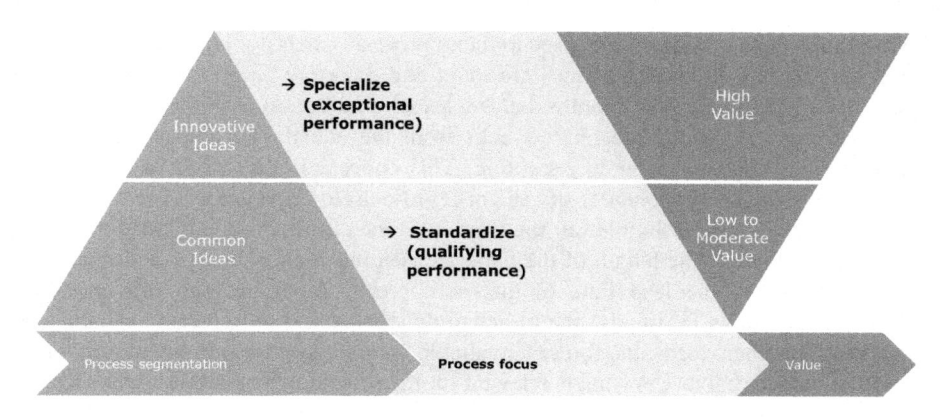

Fig. 7.14 Concept of process segmentation

firm level) caused by optimizing functional metrics without due consideration for interdependencies in the last section titled "Big Picture."

7.3.1 Components of a Process Metric

These are essentially three—purpose, timeliness, and level.

Purpose Purpose brings in a cross-functional orientation to measurement. It brings the context in which the measurement is being made into sharp relief.

Continuing with the Acme case, the process neighbors for the forecasting process are procurement and replenishment that rely on the quality of the forecast for making decisions in their respective functional domains (Fig. 7.15). Therefore, the forecasting process needs to be acutely aware of upstream and downstream processes that are influenced by the quality of its outputs, in other words, cognizant of its purpose.

Although both procurement and replenishment processes need forecast as an input, they differ in terms of *when* they need this information and how *detailed* this information has to be. This brings us to the next component—timeliness.

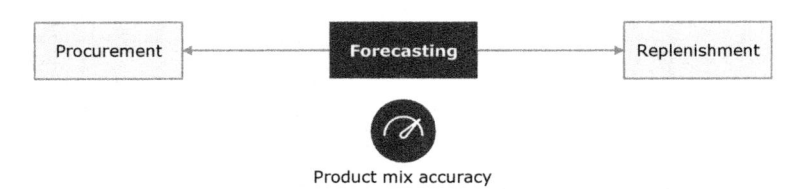

Fig. 7.15 Process neighbors of forecasting

Timeliness Let's assume the procurement process needs to order fabrics from overseas suppliers. The lead times are long, and therefore an accurate forecast of fabrics is needed several months before actual production. On the other hand, replenishment decisions are made weeks from the actual sale and can therefore benefit from updates closer to execution. This concept is illustrated in Fig. 7.16. Imagine typical components of an order-to-deliver lead time: procurement, manufacturing, replenishment (all the way up to the customer facing location), and customer delivery. The length of the bars representing each of these components is representative of the lead time of that component. As is evident, procurement decisions are made far in advance of actual delivery based on forecast available at that time. In other words, the forecast available "procurement commitment horizon" ahead of actual delivery is what is relevant for the procurement process. Any update made after "procurement commit" is irrelevant as the supplier is, more often than not, unable to react to that. However, replenishment can benefit from updates made closer to delivery. The "deployment commitment horizon" is the key consideration here. One of the rules of forecasting is that the further out the event that is being forecasted, the worse the quality. In our Acme case, this'd mean procurement that has to deal with the longest commitment horizon is far worse off than other functions. This would be true if it were finished goods that are externally procured. In Acme's case though, what is being procured are fabrics (raw materials) that will be processed into finished goods. Given that Acme focuses on variety, we have a case of a divergent bill of material (few raw materials, but very many finished goods). Therefore, the answer to the question "is procurement much worse off?" is more nuanced. We'll have to bring in another component of measurement—level.

Level The question of level of detail of forecast can be resolved by using the criterion of relevance. In Acme's case, procurement is interested in the demand for

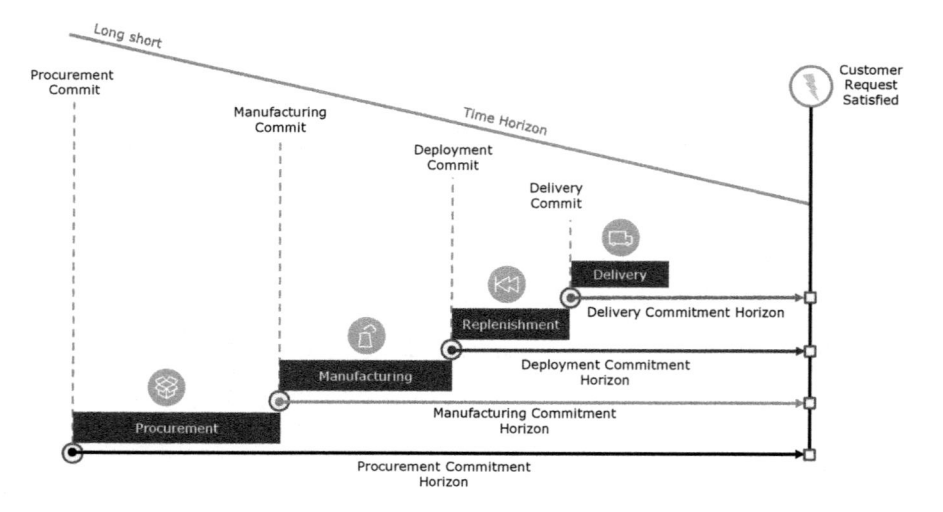

Fig. 7.16 Timeliness in measurement—concept of forecast commitment horizon

fabrics at the time it has to place orders to the supplier ("procurement commit" in Fig. 7.16). Therefore, from a procurement perspective, it really does not matter if the product mix that gets eventually sold is different from what was assumed at the time of ordering at the supplier as long as the demand for fabrics the product mix translates to is accurate. Therefore, the level that is relevant for procurement is raw material. As one gets closer to execution, the level of detail increases. Replenishment relies on accurate forecast of demand on SKU customer facing location (location from where customer orders will be delivered) level. There are other aspects as well, besides product structure, which contribute to the increase in level of detail as one gets closer to the event that is being forecasted, for instance, location. It may not be important for the supplier to know the manufacturing location(s) to which the fabrics need to be supplied to at the time of ordering. This can be resolved close to the shipment being organized. Similarly, the DCs to which stock that is being manufactured needs to be deployed is not relevant for production planning and scheduling and will only have to be resolved latest at "deployment commit" (see Fig. 7.16). As the examples illustrate, level of detail needs to be seen in conjunction with the time dimension—the longer the horizon, the lower the level of detail and vice versa. This idea is presented in Fig. 7.17.

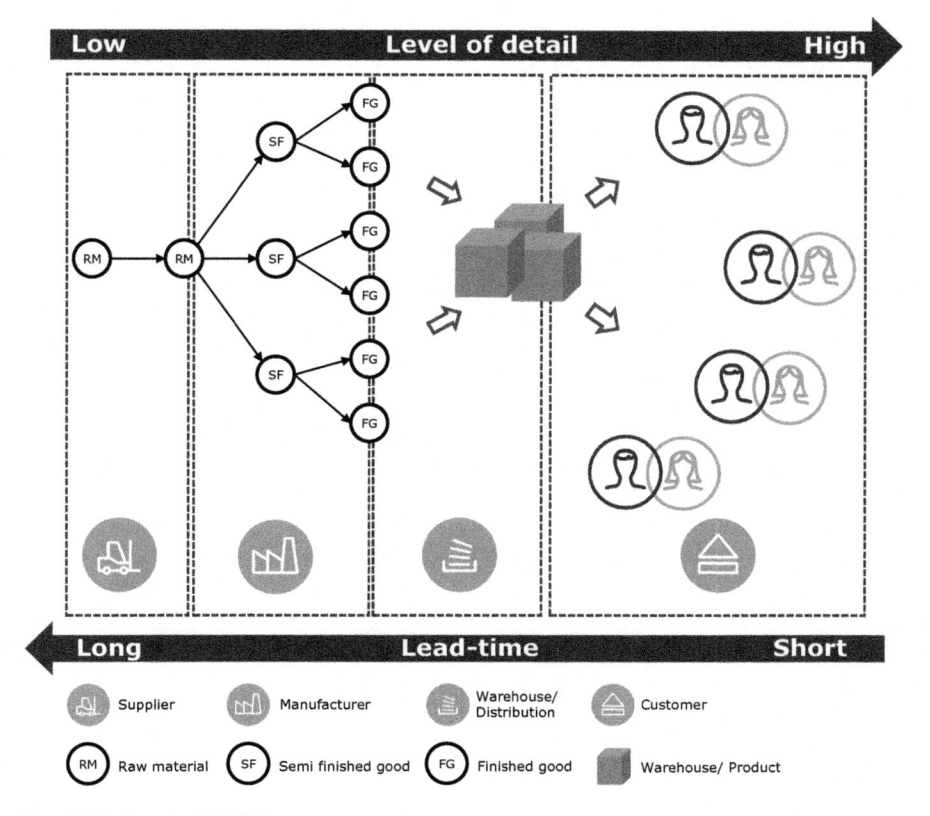

Fig. 7.17 Level of detail in measurement

It is therefore important, when designing process metrics, to consider the components of measurement described above. In the case of procurement at Acme, for example, forecast accuracy on fabric level that is available at the time of "procurement commit" is what possesses explanatory value to quality of decisions that follow and, therefore, should be the metric that is tracked and included in a functionally oriented dashboard.

7.4 Process Measurement

Once the performance that ought to be measured is clear, the definition of metrics needs to account for the mechanics of the process itself. We'll talk about mechanics in general terms before dwelling on the specific example of demand management. The mechanics are simple enough: a process receives inputs, performs certain activities, and generates outputs. The primary focus when it comes to performance measurement, and consequently, the definition of process metrics, is of course output effectiveness (and associated metrics). However, sole focus on output-centered metrics disregards factors (inputs and activities) that contribute to the observed output (effectiveness); see Fig. 7.18.

A more comprehensive approach gives confidence to this holistic view of looking at performance and focuses on three aspects: effectiveness, efficiency, and adherence (Fig. 7.19).

What do you gain from these three aspects?

- Effectiveness measurement, which is a measure of process output, will explain how good you are performing.
- Efficiency measurement, based on process activities and process inputs, will explain how time-consuming or complex your processes are.
- Adherence/quality measurement, which is all about measuring process activities, will help you to understand if forecasting inputs are provided on time and if sales and marketing leaders are available on review.

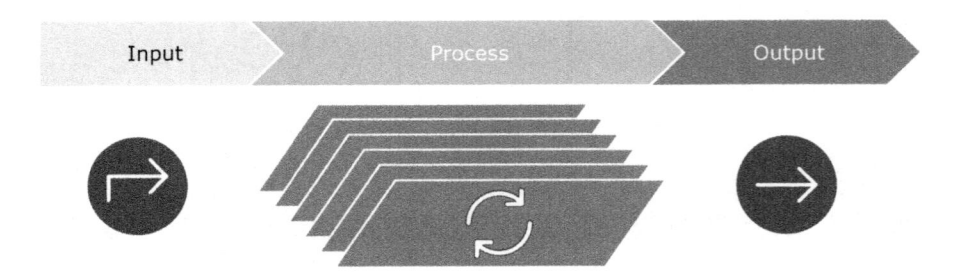

Fig. 7.18 Process mechanics

7.5 How to Measure Effectiveness, Efficiency, and Adherence

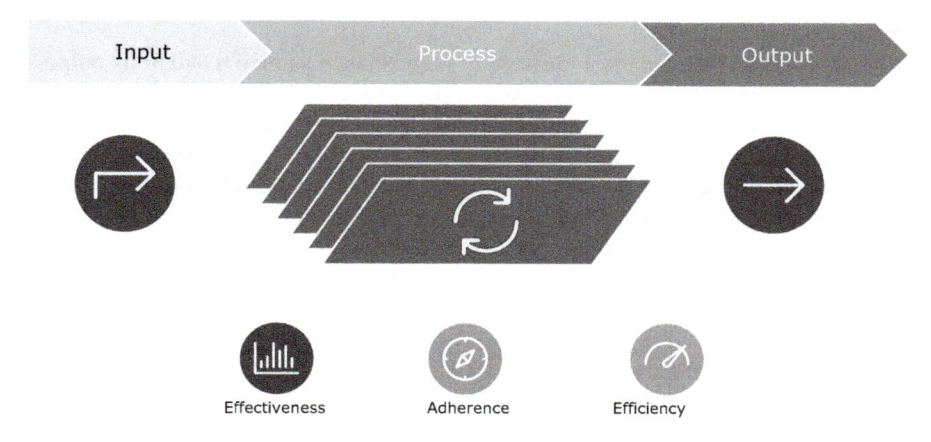

Fig. 7.19 Three aspects of measurement

7.5 How to Measure Effectiveness, Efficiency, and Adherence

There were a lot of publications about what is the most suitable way to measure forecasting process. We would like to group them into three categories (Fig. 7.20).

We'll discuss these aspects in turn as they relate to the demand management process.

Before we go into how to measure maybe a thought from Charles W. Chase (Chase, 2009) where he states that "People do not want to be measured, because they are scared of their performances instead of seeing it as an improvement process".

Process adherence
Set of measures which help you to check if process steps are executed according to agreements e.g. if stakeholders are present and provide input

Process measurement:
- Measure process output
- Focus on essentials
- Introduce measurement aligned to your process maturity

Process efficiency
Measures which help you to monitor how your process improvement affect time being spend on e.g. forecasting

Process effectiveness
Measures which help you to understand your process output performance and help to initiate corrective actions. The best practice is to use multiple measures in conjunction

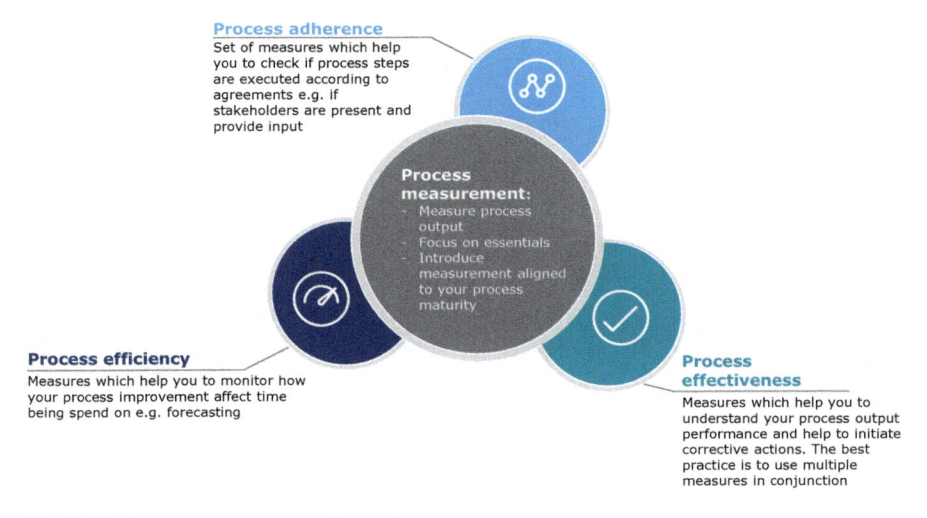

Fig. 7.20 Process measurement dimensions

Effectiveness

Effectiveness of a process is a measure of performance as they relate to its outputs. Process metrics that measure this aspect of performance wield the most influence on the performance of downstream processes. There are several ways to measure effectiveness and therefore several choices for metrics. When carefully done, a multitude of metrics can actually reveal details about different attributes of performance and together paint a wholesome picture. The analogy of an airplane cockpit, which is often invoked, is entirely apt. Each control in isolation provides a useful but limiting view. However, the cockpit as a whole, provides great insights regarding the health of the airplane—a prime example of the whole being greater than the sum of its parts.

In Fig. 7.21 the three most important effectiveness metrics are depicted, namely, forecast accuracy, bias, and stability. As can be seen within the triangle, the cogs represent decision variables (can be seen as inputs, activities) that contribute to the overall performance as reflected in the effectiveness metrics.

Forecast Error To be able to measure accuracy, one has to quantify errors. Forecast errors are a function of forecast variability and are a key decision variable in the calculation of time, capacity, and inventory buffers to ensure adequate levels of service.

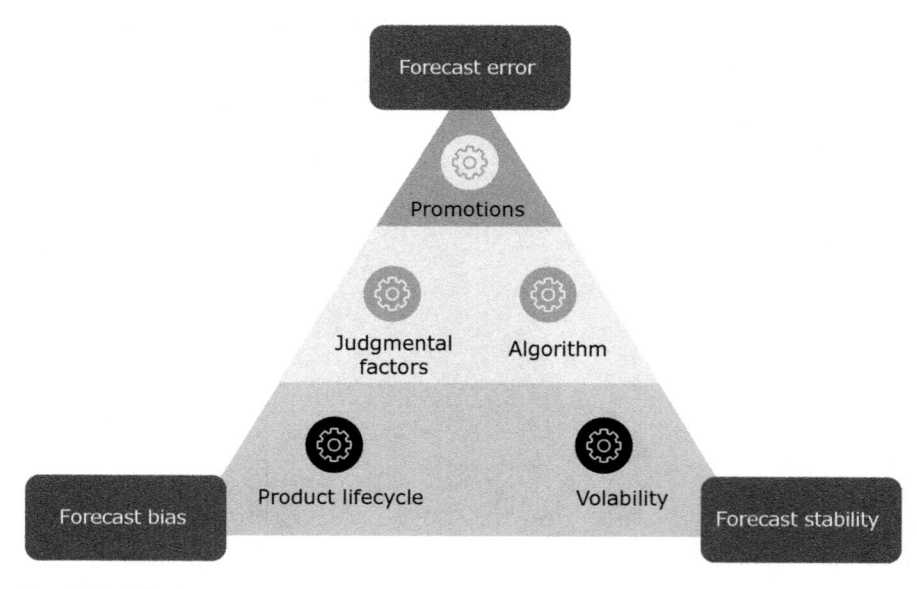

Fig. 7.21 Effectiveness measures

7.5 How to Measure Effectiveness, Efficiency, and Adherence

Forecast error metrics	Formula	Guidelines for use
Mean square error (MSE)	$\frac{1}{n}\sum_{t=1}^{n}(F_t - D_t)^2$	+ Good for penalizing large errors - Not so intuitive to interpret / visualize
Mean absolute deviation (MAD)	$\frac{1}{n}\sum_{t=1}^{n}|F_t - D_t|$	+ Intuitive and easy to visualize (same units as demand) + Good for small numbers
Mean absolute percentage error (MAPE)	$\left[\frac{1}{n}\sum_{t=1}^{n}\left|\frac{F_t - D_t}{D_t}\right|\right] * 100$	- Not affected by magnitude of demand quantities + Expressed in % - lends itself easily to comparisons + Good for seasonal patterns + Good as a leading summary metric
Weighted Mean absolute percentage error (MAPE)	$\left(\frac{\sum |Forecast - Sales|}{\sum Sales}\right) * 100$	+ Affected by magnitude of demand quantities + Expressed in % and easy to understand, used to visualize process error on aggregated level - "Promotes" over forecasting - Not good in handling zero demand or zero forecast

Fig. 7.22 Comparison of forecast error measures

In Fig. 7.22, the three measures are compared with some guidelines for use.

Forecast Bias Forecast bias is used to uncover systematic biases in the underlying forecasting process leading to consistent over- or under-forecasting. There are several formulas that can be used. A selection of typical formulas and guidelines for their use is presented in Fig. 7.23.

Forecast Stability Forecast stability measures the stability of the forecast for the same time bucket produced in different time horizons. This is visualized in Fig. 7.24. The changes to the forecast from a certain reference point (say, the highest lag; lag 5 in the example visualized) are measured at multiple lags. The height of the red diamonds in the graphic depicts the magnitude of change from the reference point.

Numerically, the following formula can be used to calculate this metric:

$$\text{Forecast Stability} = \left(1 - \frac{\text{Mean Absolute Deviation}}{\text{Mean}}\right) \times 100$$

For example, if lag [1–3] forecasts are 500 PC, 30 PC, and 115 PC, respectively, mean is 215 PC, and the mean absolute deviation is 190 PC (abs (500 − 215) + abs (500 − 30) + abs (500 − 115)/3 = 190 PC). Therefore forecast stability would be (1 − (190/215)) 10%, which is a very low number as is intuitive, given that the forecasts at different lags vary significantly from each other.

Forecast Bias Formula	Guidelines for use
$$\dfrac{F-A}{F+A}$$ F = Forecast A = Actual Sales	+ Forecast bias is a % value constrained between -100% and 100% + Useful metric for item level bias measurement (results in division by zero only if both forecast and actual are zero) - Not easy to interpret bias in terms of sales
$$\dfrac{|F-A|}{F+A}$$	+ Forecast bias is either +/- 1 + Can be used to identify systematic bias – for example, if for a given number of historical periods, bias exceeds a certain threshold model is said to exhibit systematic bias - Extent of bias is not given representation – both small and large biases are treated the same
$$\dfrac{F-A}{A}$$	+ Bias as a % of sales + Lends itself to intuitive interpretation - Not very suitable as an item level formula for bias, particularly for sporadic demand items (prevalence of zero actual sales)
$$\dfrac{\sum F - A}{MAD}$$ MAD = Mean Absolute Deviation	+ Numerator is the error total and the denominator the mean absolute deviation. Useful summary metric, which is also called as tracking signal + Relationship between MAD and standard deviation (1 sigma ≈ 1.25 * MAD) allows for interpretation of bias in terms of standard deviation and to establish threshold limits, which when exceeded can be used to trigger exceptions - Better used in conjunction with another bias measure as the results are not easy to interpret intuitively

Fig. 7.23 Comparison of forecast bias measures

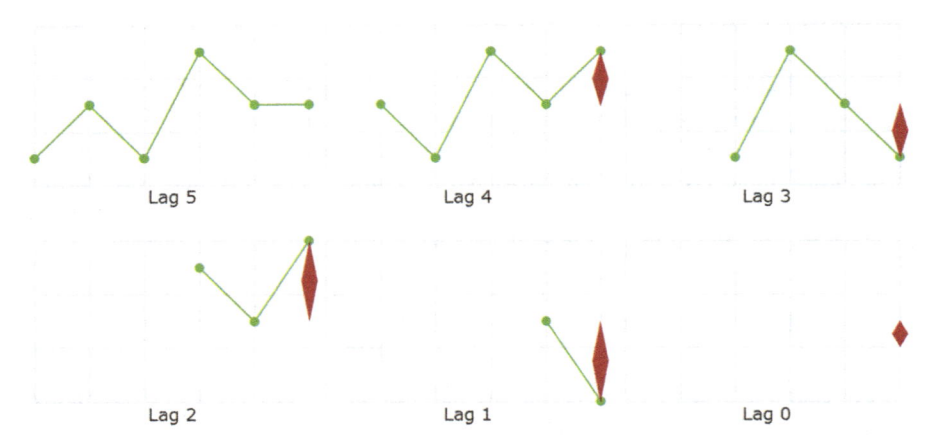

Fig. 7.24 Forecast stability metric

7.5 How to Measure Effectiveness, Efficiency, and Adherence

7.5.1 Correlation of Metrics

As we discussed before, correlation of measures gives much better insights about forecast error than a single one. Let us illustrate that on selected forecast effectiveness metrics (Fig. 7.25).

We see magnitude of the error is substantial, and we understand that we under forecast therefore are exposed to stock-outs and finally that we have made an error which may be perceived as big as 1400 tons which in chemical industry may be relatively big. Effectiveness metrics should be analyzed, visualized in year-to-date and time series manner. Figure 7.26 illustrates selected key metrics which you may select as valid to measure your process effectiveness. You see as well their purpose. One measure will not tell you if performance is good or wrong, what corrective actions to introduce. It is always about correlation of few measures which brings

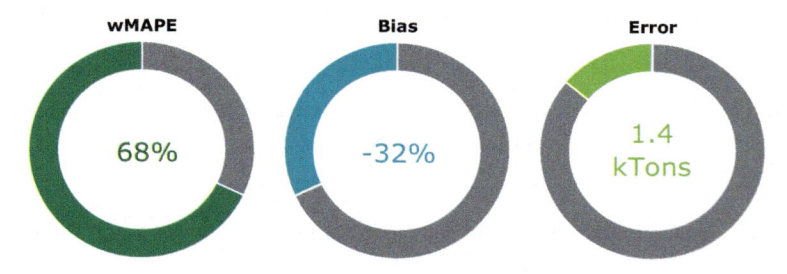

wMAPE 68%   **Bias** -32%   **Error** 1.4 kTons

Fig. 7.25 Correlation of effectiveness measures

Forecast effectiveness
- Forecast percent. error wMAPE (%)
- Forecast bias (+/- %)
- Forecast error (+/- volume)
- Forecast stability

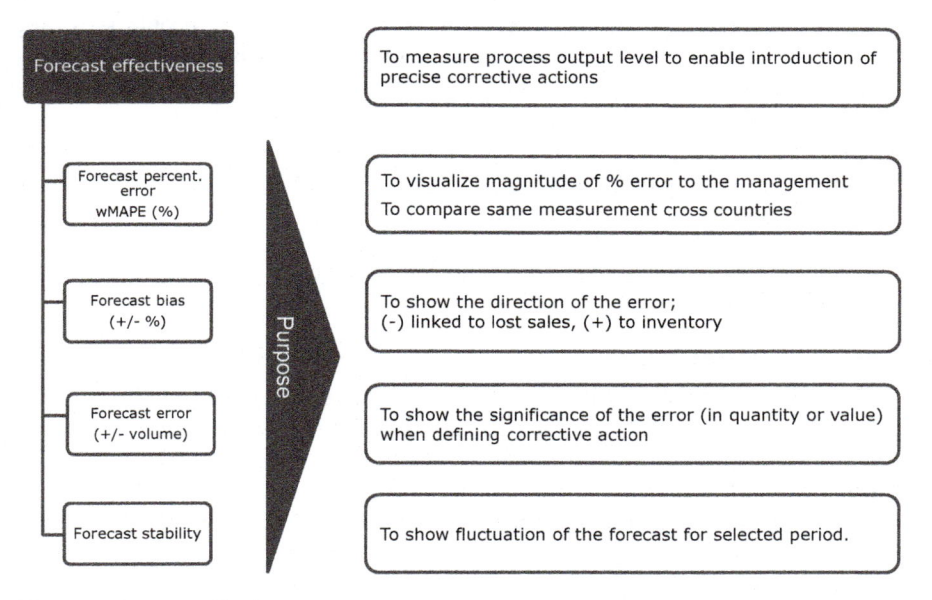

Purpose:
- To measure process output level to enable introduction of precise corrective actions
- To visualize magnitude of % error to the management. To compare same measurement cross countries
- To show the direction of the error; (-) linked to lost sales, (+) to inventory
- To show the significance of the error (in quantity or value) when defining corrective action
- To show fluctuation of the forecast for selected period.

Fig. 7.26 Forecast effectiveness measures

understanding of error nature. When you know the cause, it is easier to trigger and deploy corrective action.

Efficiency
Measurement of process efficiency can be understood through:

- Value add—metric which should describe what value is generated by specific process steps versus statistical forecasting, naïve. We often use MASE (mean absolute scaled error) developed by professor Rob J. Hyndman which can measure selected input in reference to naïve forecast.
- Forecasting combinations over time—metric which should help you to describe how many forecasting combination for specific process you have.
- No. of phase-in vs phase-outs—metric which will help you to understand if product review coordinated by demand planner does produce more and more materials or as well helps to manage long tail of SKUs and removes some SKUs from range.

Measuring efficiency is not easy; you would need to make decision which metric will describe the best your way of measuring how efficient your process is.
Some examples:

1. No. of forecasting combinations—to monitor potential no. of touch points available in forecast inputs (sales, marketing, demand planning).
2. No. of people providing forecast inputs—to monitor if the no. of people providing input does change over time. You may be surprised with degree of correlation between specific forecast input error and no. of people providing forecast input. Very often the more people touching forecast, the worse it gets.
3. How long does it take to forecast—to monitor how long in average does it take to provide forecast input.
4. Phase-in vs phase-outs—to monitor if you only add new SKUs in IBP portfolio and do or do not manage long tail of SKU. Some should be removed from the range.

Why should you measure forecasting process efficiency?

- To identify areas of improvement
- To visualize improvements
- To understand how efforts in collecting inputs are correlated to forecast performance

Adherence
Measurement of process quality/process adherence could be understood through:

- Presence on the meeting—it may sound weird to some of you, but especially at the beginning of your journey or improvement, it is quite important to check if

stakeholders who either are responsible to provide input or the ones who review it are present on scheduled activities.
- Input provided on time—in large organizations where many inputs are qualitative, you would need to set up time slots by when particular input has to be finalized. You should set up calendar of activities but as well you should go further and start to measure if inputs are provided against agreed calendar of activities.
- Qualitative inputs up to date—many times you may ask yourself as demand planner if input provided is up to date or not. Visualization of last change time stamp might help to assess it. We are not recommending to update forecast for the sake of updating it, but you may look on forecast input provided by sales rep which is 6 months old differently than on the one which was updated just yesterday, don't you think?

Measuring process adherence/quality is important. Adherence to process rules may be differently organized in large or small organizations but make very sense. Strength of your process will be described by degree of adherence to the rules you defined with your management.

Some examples:

1. Frequency of forecasting combination updates—you may have defined rules how frequently to update forecast for different product segments. It does not stop you to capture changes as needed (new deal, new customer, etc.) but to set up rule how frequently in average it should happen.
2. Last forecast update for qualitative inputs—to monitor how up to date the forecast input is. In some cases it may help you to understand the reason of forecast input error.
3. Process step completeness as per schedule—to monitor individual person routine and compliance with rules.

7.6 Big Picture: How to Link Measurement to Shareholder Value

The fact that process metrics provide a performance profile of individual processes raises the risk of one falling into the trap of a myopic view. Excessive focus on single metrics oftentimes leads to suboptimal performance on a firm level. Lora Cecere in her book *Metrics that Matter* (Cecere, 2014) writes "best operating strategies and metrics portfolios are built when companies translate business strategy into tactical plans." This connectedness has been the cornerstone of the field of systems dynamics. In this context, a soccer analogy courtesy of Fred Kofman (Kofman, 2006) is quite pertinent. When he coaches companies and teams, he often brings up the example of soccer and asks what the objective of a defensive/offensive player is. He points out that even seasoned executives get tripped up and answer "to save goals" or "to score goals," whereas the true objective of everyone on the team should be for the team to win. In the field of systems dynamics, it is a well-known fact that to optimize a system, you will often have to sub-optimize subsystems. The same is true for supply chain processes in general and IBP in particular. This speaks to the irrationality of focusing purely on functional metrics hoping to achieve favorable outcomes on a firm level. Performance of a certain process and accompanying metrics needs to be seen in the context of the overall network of processes and its role in the interplay of metrics (i.e., correlation between metrics).

For example, a company that is focused on efficiency wants to be the best in class in terms of cash-to-cash cycle (C2C). It embarks on an initiative to cut inventory without thinking holistically and addressing underlying variability that is resulting in poor forecast accuracy. The result will most likely be that customer service suffers leading to lost sales and poor financial results. The problem lies in a certain lack of recognition of the fact that a company is a complex system and that understanding and optimizing parts of it is not the same as optimizing the whole. An example of the perils of such silo thinking is an old one but very illuminating (Hau, 2004). HP's integrated circuit division in order to optimize on its metric of low inventory held very low inventories of ICs. However, this resulted in long lead times for printers, which the company could ill afford. This resulted in HP carrying inventory of assembled printers (a classic case of tail wagging the dog)! Such situations can be avoided by connecting metrics, which allows for viewing performance not in isolation but through the lens of a firm's overall strategy.

There have been several frameworks proposed that give due consideration to the importance of this connectedness we talk about. We'll briefly review a few of them.

DuPont This is one of the earliest examples of a framework aimed at breaking down financial performance to its constituent parts. The model consisted solely of financial metrics (Fig. 7.27). Nevertheless, it helped break down the enigmatic idea of shareholder value to more manageable parts.

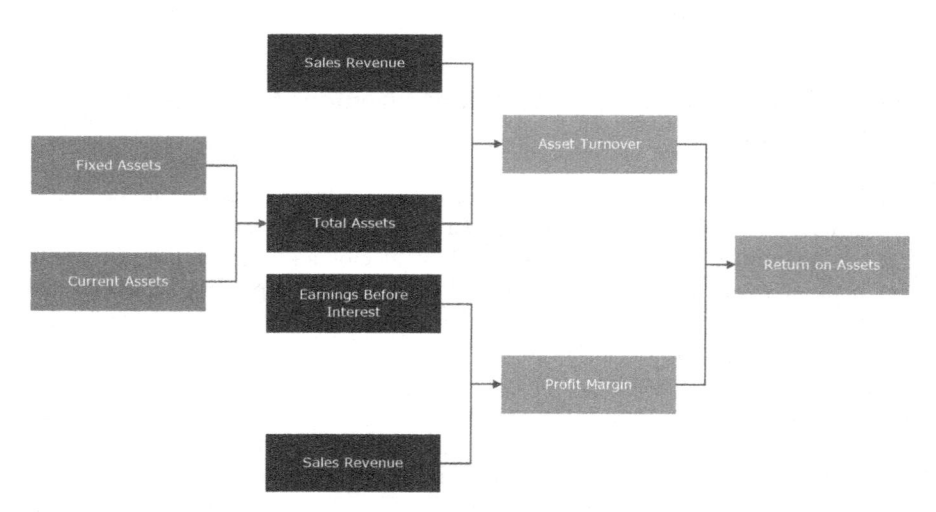

Fig. 7.27 Simplified version of DuPont financial measurement model

7.6 Big Picture: How to Link Measurement to Shareholder Value

Financial — To succeed, how should we appear to our shareholders?

Customer — To achieve our vision, how should we appear to our customers?

Vision and Strategy

Internal Business Process — To satisfy our shareholders and customers, what business processes must we excel at?

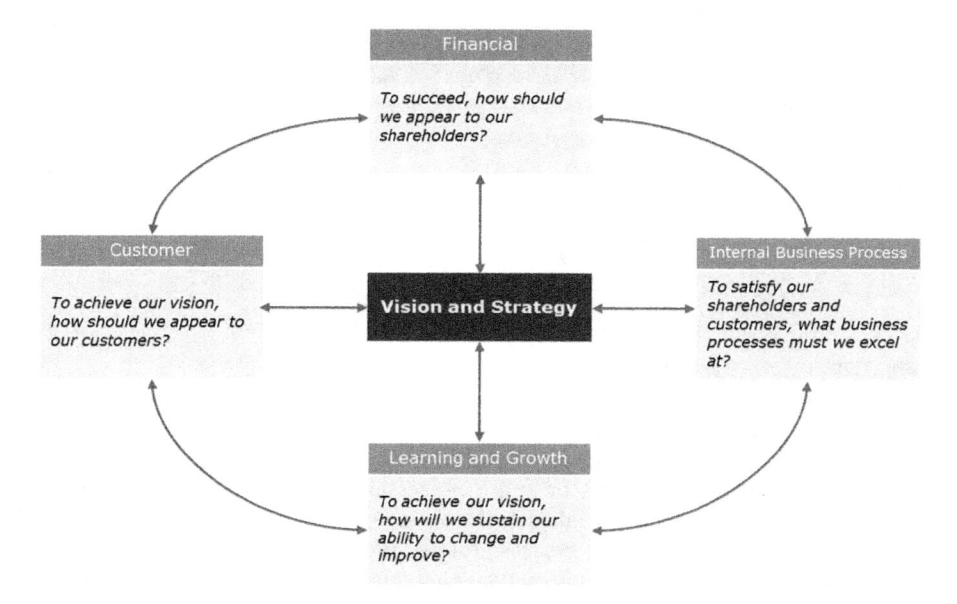

Learning and Growth — To achieve our vision, how will we sustain our ability to change and improve?

Fig. 7.28 Balanced scorecard framework

Balanced Scorecard The balanced scorecard developed by Robert S. Kaplan and David P. Norton addresses the dangers of excessive focus on financially oriented metrics. They propose four perspectives that provide a more comprehensive treatment of performance metrics: financial, customer, internal business process, and learning and growth (Fig. 7.28). There are goals and measures defined along each of these perspectives that together are intended to create a virtuous cycle of high performance.

Deloitte's Enterprise Value Map (EVM) Deloitte's enterprise value map aims to address the drawback in DuPont model in that it is solely financially oriented. EVM is a framework that connects financial performance to levers of performance that runs the whole gamut of activities—be it strategic, tactical, or operational. The framework can be used either to analyze reasons for poor performance by using a top-down approach—following financial/lagging metrics to actions that influence those—or a bottom-up approach, identifying actions that are appropriate given performance goals a firm wants to achieve (Fig. 7.29).

There is a common thread that connects the frameworks discussed—it is that there is a hierarchy (actions connected to business objectives and processes connected across multiple levels), which can be translated to a metrics hierarchy. Let's take, for instance, process hierarchy as it relates to metrics. Process hierarchy typically consists of (from lower to higher) tasks, sub-processes, processes, process groups, and finally value chain functions (see Fig. 7.13). One can design metrics

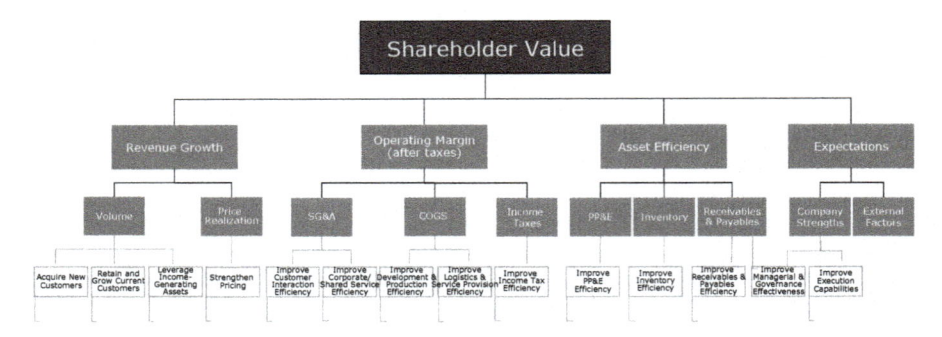

Fig. 7.29 Deloitte's enterprise value map framework

along these levels, and the metrics so designed will exhibit a certain latency between what is being measured (tasks or entire processes) and their impact on metrics. Latency is lower for metrics linked to lower levels (say, tasks or sub-processes) compared to higher levels (say, process groups). Based on latency, metrics could be classified into leading (low latency) and lagging (high latency) metrics. Managing by lagging metrics alone can be likened to driving by looking through a rearview mirror. There needs to be a healthy mix of both. Leading metrics give an opportunity to not just observe, but shape performance. Frameworks like EVM allow for creating of a coherent hierarchy of metrics, with leading metrics on lower levels and lagging metrics, typically consisting of financially oriented metrics, on higher levels. An implementation of such an idea is presented in Fig. 7.30. It shows a set of improvement actions that are tied to leading indicators that are linked to lagging indicators and, all the way up to, value levers and eventually shareholder value that sits atop the value hierarchy.

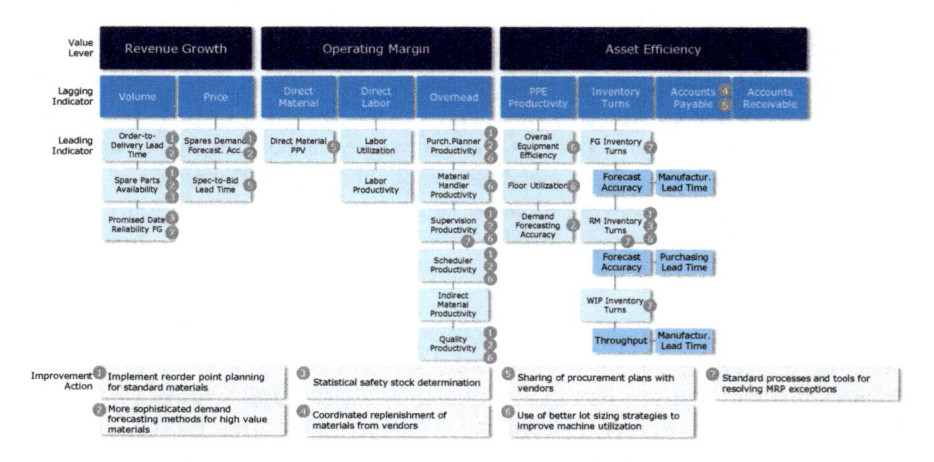

Fig. 7.30 A connected and coherent portfolio of leading and lagging metrics

7.6 Big Picture: How to Link Measurement to Shareholder Value

Although the abovementioned frameworks help see interdependencies between metrics, one needs to be careful not to fall into what Joel Shapiro calls the "causality trap"—seeing causal links where in fact none exist. The analogy he uses is that of carrying lighters/matches and cancer—one wouldn't assume a causal link between the two, but, unfortunately, in business contexts people are only too eager to attribute causality (Daniel Kahneman uses the term coherence—a wish for coherence favors overconfidence). In order not to fall prey to this, Rhian Silvestro (Silvestro, 2016) argues that "assumptions about what drives financial performance have become so widely accepted that they are often viewed as facts." Therefore, there is a need for relationships to be investigated and the correlations validated. Otherwise, it could lead to incorrect incentives and behaviors. The author further recommends use of a tool such as topology mapping to introduce rigor.

In this method, statistical significance of relationships is tested and visualized. The example effectively highlights the importance of testing hypotheses regarding correlations between metrics. The prevailing assumption when it comes to service industries is that there is a mirroring effect between employee satisfaction and loyalty and customer satisfaction and loyalty and that these correlate positively with financial performance. However, as the topology map in the example, that of a superstore retail chain, shows, this is not supported by evidence in this particular instance. You can see that there is actually a negative correlation between employee satisfaction/loyalty and profit. This was because the key determining factor for profit in the case studied was store size—the larger the store, the greater the product offering and the higher the profits. However, store size had a dampening effect on employee satisfaction and morale, and since larger stores were typically located in competitive labor markets, retention rates were low.

Having said that, there are a number of examples of metrics where the relationships are clearly documented and understood—for example, between inventory, throughput, and cycle time or forecast variability and inventory turns. To be precise, these are metrics that ideally ought to be correlated, and if seen not to be the case, it should be a cause for concern and analysis. Orbit charts can be a great tool in visualizing such correlations where Walmart has not really been able to translate gains it has made in inventory turns to commensurate operating margin gains. The best scenario is progression toward the top-right corner where improvements in inventory are matched by operating margin improvements. On the other hand, Target has seen improvements in operating margin, but hasn't really been able to move the needle on inventory turns. As a side note, one can see that by adding a time dimension, which orbit charts make possible, one can move beyond averages and track year-on-year performance, which as this example suggests can be highly illuminating.

A discussion on big picture cannot be complete without talking about the rapid pace of change in supply chains, accelerated by trends such as digitalization, big data, IoT, AI, etc. This is resulting in supply chains moving away from being "strategically decoupled and price driven" to "strategically coupled and value driven" (Melnyk, Davis, Spekman, & Sandor, 2010). The authors in "Outcome Driven Supply Chains" talk about supply chains designed to deliver specific outcomes such as cost, responsiveness, resiliency, security, sustainability, and innovation. Garner talks about the need for bimodal supply chains that combine core capabilities with "disruptive, innovative and aspirational" capabilities (Johnson, Jacobson, Barrett, Stiffler, & Tohamy, 2017). At any rate, this represents additional complexity when it comes to performance measurement and particularly in being able to connect the dots. Being able to successfully combine outcomes that may be at odds with each other means superior capabilities in analyzing and resolving trade-offs and incenting right behaviors through metrics. This can only be achieved through a connected portfolio of coherent metrics that reflect the causal relationships between actions and their consequences and in the context of overall firm objectives.

7.7 When Things Go Wrong

In this section we will discuss some design principles for analytics and dashboards that can accelerate the process of gleaning insights from data.

We talked about process mechanics visualized in Fig. 7.18.

The anatomy of a process (i.e., inputs → process → output) can serve as a template for analyzing the roots of performance.

A carefully chosen set of metrics can help peel off layers that contribute to performance and analyze each one in turn.

Wrong Outputs
Let's start with outputs. Metrics that relate to outputs are effectiveness measures or outcome measures. A useful principle here is to go for a smart selection of effectiveness measures, each one complementing the others in providing a certain perspective and together resulting in a better appreciation of performance that is being observed.

Some examples:

- Consensus forecast accuracy and statistical forecast accuracy. Comparisons can yield insights as to the added value of enriching statistical forecast or the value of statistical forecasting.
- Consensus baseline accuracy and consensus total (baseline plus promotions) accuracy can provide insights about the accuracy and value of promotional forecast enrichment.
- Statistical bias and demand planner bias: if the statistical bias is greater, for example, it can be an indication that model and/or parameters are a poor fit for the product in question.

In visualizing performance measures, the concept of small multiples can be used quite effectively as a storytelling device. Edward Tufte (Tufte & Edward, 1983) who is a strong proponent of this idea describes it as "(small multiples are a) series of graphics showing the same combination of variables indexed by changes in another variable," e.g., support for school vouchers across states in the USA. The indexing in this case is along two dimensions: on the x-axis it is by income, and on the y-axis it is by race. This type of visualization is very effective in studying correlations and identifying leverage points (variables that have a disproportionate impact on what is being studied).

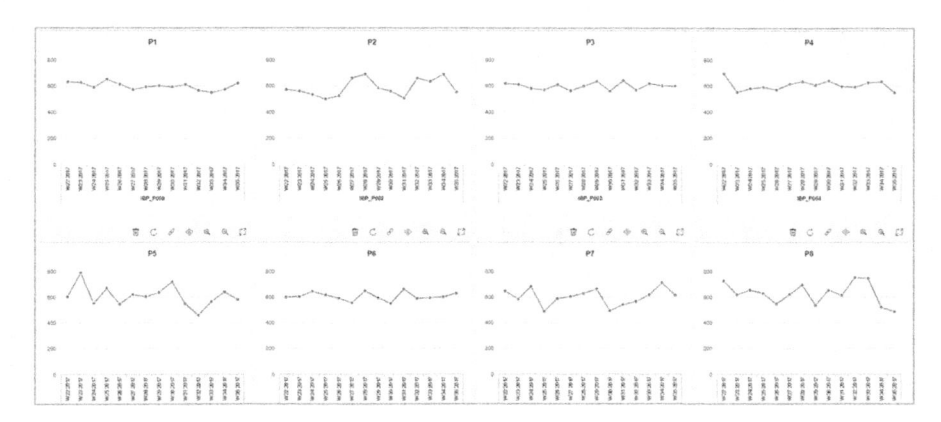

Fig. 7.31 SAP IBP—example of small multiples in a dashboard

Such visualizations can be developed in IBP by creating multiple charts and including them in a dashboard. An example is shown in Fig. 7.31.

Wrong Inputs

Turning to inputs, metrics that measure the accuracy of inputs can help with root cause analysis—to answer questions such as "can poor performance be attributed to wrong assumptions? Incorrect information coming from upstream sources?" Inputs can also be analyzed from the perspective of level of detail. If inputs are gathered on multiple levels of detail—on a more detailed or the same level of granularity as required to be delivered to downstream process, an analysis of accuracy of inputs can reveal if effort expended in gathering more detailed inputs are bearing fruit. For example, let's say sales representatives are delivering plans for key accounts, which are then aggregated to a customer facing location level, whereas the demand planner is already planning on the customer facing location level. If it turns out that, systematically, the aggregated sales representatives' forecast is worse than demand planner forecast, one can reasonably question the effort expended in collating sales representatives' forecast.

On the flipside, it can also be analyzed to see if there are inputs that are being provided on a high level of accuracy but not really utilized in the process. Taking the same example from above, it might be that a significant portion of demand for a certain product is coming from a handful for key accounts and forecast for key accounts made by account representatives are very accurate. However, they are not sufficiently considered in the final consensus forecast leading to poor overall accuracy. An analysis of input accuracy can lead to uncovering of improvement potential such as this.

Wrong Process

This crucial step is responsible for transforming inputs into outputs. From an analytics perspective, the key question to answer is if the level of effort is justified by the quality of outputs. The graphic in Fig. 7.32 illustrates this idea. One is said to operate on the efficiency frontier if the cost of planning (or effort spent) is commensurate with the accuracy of the results. The cost of planning can be estimated by

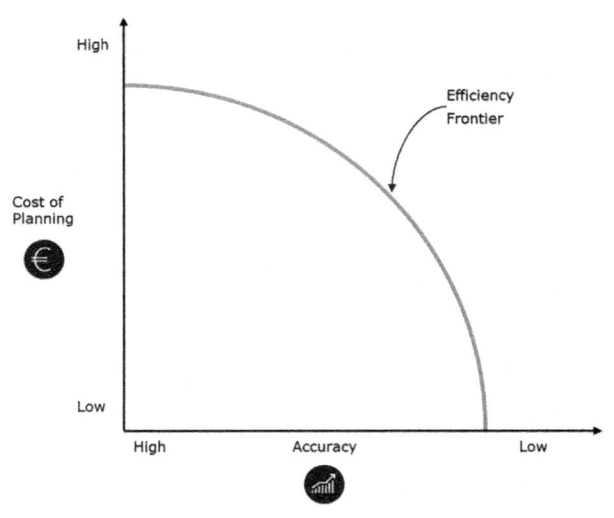

Fig. 7.32 Processing effort and accuracy: operating on the efficiency frontier

analyzing factors like implementation complexity and the complexity of maintaining and operating the planning solution, effort spent in collecting and processing inputs. This can be a qualitative analysis. If it turns out that the effort is disproportionately higher compared to the accuracy of results, actions in terms of reducing solution complexity and/or effort investment in planning are required.

In a demand side of IBP, the MASE (mean absolute scaled error) metric is quite useful in determining whether one is operating efficiently. MASE is the ratio of forecast error (using the present model) to forecast error if one were to use naïve forecast (NF1) where the forecast for the subsequent period equals the observed demand for the current period. The formula is presented below:

$$\text{MASE} = \frac{\frac{\sum_{t=1}^{n} |F_t - Y_t|}{n}}{\frac{\sum_{t=2}^{n} |Y_t - Y_{t-1}|}{n-1}}.$$

This means that, with MASE, the accuracy of the model in use is expressed in terms of the improvement it offers over NF1. Concretely:

If MASE = 1: the model is only as good as NF1. You could just as well spare additional costs potentially incurred by using anything more advanced.
If MASE > 1: model in use is worse. This definitely calls for deeper investigation. It can also be that the planning cluster (owing to its importance) demands an advanced model, but it has not been set up properly and is grossly underperforming.
If MASE < 1: model is better than NF1. How close it is to 0 than to 1 is a measure of how good the model in use is.

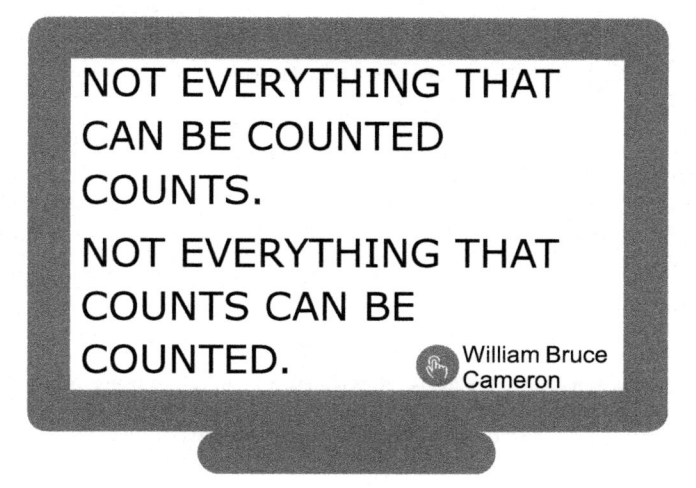

> NOT EVERYTHING THAT CAN BE COUNTED COUNTS.
>
> NOT EVERYTHING THAT COUNTS CAN BE COUNTED.
>
> — William Bruce Cameron

Fig. 7.33 Count what matters

Finally let us close this chapter with the following quote shown in Fig. 7.33.

7.8 Summary

- Identify what needs to be measured by applying the lens of relevance.
- Adopt a conceptual frame of reference (e.g., innovative/functional or responsiveness/efficiency) to identify capabilities required to deliver on strategic imperatives.
- Define metrics to measure the level of alignment between (integrated business) planning capabilities and overall firm strategy.
- Use a diversity of measures to measure different aspects of performance, which delivers better insights into root cause for poor or good performance.
- Achieve holistic view by connecting metrics in a way that is in alignment with business strategy.
- Use a healthy mix of leading and lagging metrics. Leverage leading metrics to shape performance and use lagging metrics to observe performance and determine need for intervention.
- Use a portfolio of coherent metrics to understand trade-offs in order to resolve them with a view to creating specific outcomes and generating anticipated value.
- Leverage visualizations to peel off layers of performance and analyze each one in turn to understand roots of good or bad performance.

References

Cecere, L. (2014). *Supply chain metrics that matter*. Hoboken, NJ: Wiley.
Chase, C. W. (2009). *Demand-driven forecasting: A structured approach to forecasting*. Hoboken, NJ: Wiley. Retrieved from https://books.google.com/books?hl=en&lr=&id=iVIbAAAAQBAJ&pgis=1

Chopra, S., & Meindl, P. (2014). *Supply chain management: Strategy, planning and operation.* Boston: Pearson.
Drucker, P. (2007). The effective executive. *Harvard Business Review.*
Fisher. (1997). What is the right supply chain for your product? *Harvard Business Review.*
Goldratt, E. (1984). *The goal.* New York: North River Press.
Hammond, J. H. (1994). Barilla SpA (A) case study. *Harvard Business Review.*
Hau, L. (2004). The triple-A supply chain. *Harvard Business Review.*
Hofman, D. (2015). How to use interdependencies to turn metrics data into action. *Gartner.*
Johnson, J., Jacobson, S. F., Barrett, J., Stiffler, D., Johnson, J., Jacobson, S. F., Barrett, J., Stiffler, D., & Tohamy, N. (2017). *For supply chain executives: The bimodal challenge.* Gartner.
Kofman, F. (2006). Conscious business: How to build value through values. *MIT Sloan Management Review.*
Narayanan, V. G., & Raman, A. (2004). Aligning incentives in supply chains. *Harvard Business Review.*
Rohm, A., & Swaminathan, V. (2004). A typology of online shoppers based on shopping motivations. *ScienceDirect.*
Shapiro, J. (2017). 3 ways data dashboards can mislead you. *Harvard Business.*
Silvestro, R. (2016). Do you know what really drives your business's performance? *MIT Sloan Management Review.*

How to Build Transformation Path 8

A transformation project should always start from the knowledge of the as-is situation. This is obvious, yet it is essential to make a step back and do it right. You need to assess your as-is maturity and the state of IBP from an organizational, capability, process, and system perspective. Framework explained here (is used by leading consulting company) helps you go through the steps leading to the development of road map and business case (Fig. 8.1).

The assessment can be done on both qualitative and quantitative inputs. Combining both normally leads to the most valuable insights. The assessment should be done against following "dimensions": objective (business priorities), process, organization, performance management, and technology. These dimensions may have a different maturity and therefore very often a differentiated approach should be followed. As we describe the methodology, we try to illustrate it with demand planning and demand management use cases.

8.1 Qualitative Assessment

Questionnaire
The following questionnaire is a list of questions which will help you to understand the current state of a particular process/subprocess within the Integrated Business Planning framework. You may need to differentiate questionnaire per different group of stakeholders leading operational planning, tactical S&OP, and strategic planning. Questionnaires are typically used to:

- Conduct interviews
- Facilitate workshops
- Assess business processes (along with maturity models)

The insights and key questions listed for each level should help you to understand the as-is state of the process, organization, capabilities, and technology.

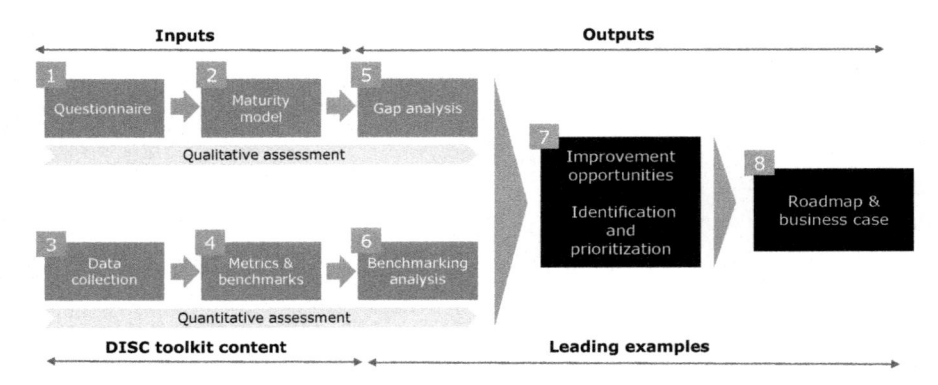

Fig. 8.1 Key elements of Deloitte integrated supply chain assessment framework

Example (Fig. 8.2) on forecasting process, organization, and system.

The depth of the questionnaire should depend on your business drivers and requirements for the transformation program. The more comprehensive the assessment is, the better the sets of insights on your as-is process will be. These can be used to define a way to organize the transformation program.

Finding an answers to the above questions will also help you to map your processes against maturity model, desired to-be state.

There are many ways to organize the information collecting process. In a big and complex organization, the questionnaire could be organized with a simple web page. On the contrary, in rather lean organizations series of meetings with key stakeholders on various levels could be good enough.

Try to collect input from experts and the management and do not be surprised if there are major discrepancies on how management and experts see their processes.

Maturity Model

You may look at maturity models as an instrument which provides descriptions of typical practices at varying levels of maturity—lagging, developing, performing, and leading:

- Lagging: The process does not exist or is rudimentary.
- Developing: Functional process exists with scope for major improvements.
- Performing: The process meets all basic functional needs, but leading practices are not adopted across the process.
- Leading: Leading practices are adopted across the process.

Maturity models are typically used to:

8.1 Qualitative Assessment

Level	Insights / Key Questions
Forecasting process	Evaluate if process is repeatable and systematic. Does it fit to the global calendar of activities? What are the main process steps which define forecasting? How are inputs from various functions provided? On which granularity, timing and frequency? Does the process deliver consensus driven unconstrained demand forecast in volume? Does the organization understand what it means to become demand drive? How is the monetization of the forecasts done? What nonstandard revenue drivers are included in the forecasts? Which form phase in and phase out forecasting is being integrated into the process? How are marketing events being considered? What level of collaboration with external partners is introduced? Does the process have global milestones and local variations? How are these addressed? How are functions captured? What are typical internal and external risk and opportunities? Is there a common definition and understanding of how the process is measured? What are the measures and parameters to evaluate performance? ...
Forecasting organization	Evaluate who provides inputs. Which functions review and approve the forecasts? Which roles from specific functions have insights to provide input and do they provide input on the level that speaks to them? Who is a consumer of the forecasts? Are these being used end to end? Do we have appointed stakeholders who are authorized to make decisions in case of lack of consensus? Who does ensure that the process is executed timely and deliverables are realized and understood? How statistical forecasting is organized? Who performs data cleansing and what inputs are being used? How are organizationally changes between cycles controlled? Is there an organizational bias embed in process design? ...
Forecasting technology	Evaluate how current solution supports data integration. From how many systems is what data being integrated? What does the integrated data really means? Is there a business definition of data? Who owns the master data? How is aggregated and detailed forecasting being managed? Does the system support scenario planning and multiple inputs to be reconciled in various unit of measures? What are the functionalities to support data visualization? Does the functionality support exception management? How is this linked to introduction of corrective actions? How does the organization use the system for collaboration? What are current system constrains and inefficiencies? ...

Fig. 8.2 Evaluation of levels

- Describe general leading practices or industry leading practices.
- Compare the current state of practices with the average performance of "peer group and industry leading practices."

Example (Fig. 8.3) on forecasting data input.

Maturity models should be developed for the key areas that drive your process, organization structure and placement, required capabilities, available data, functionality, and scalability of the system.

It does not mean that in every transformation program you need to address all at once, but please consider that the output of the transformation programs depends on

Level	Stage1 (Lagging)	Stage2 (Developing)	Stage3 (Performing)	Stage4 (Leading)
Forecasting — what primary data input is being used to predict the future	Total invoiced volume netted with returns

No separation of base line from quantified risk and opportunities

Granularity of process is dictated by granularity of the financial data

Data input is driven by internal financial flow | Total invoiced or total shipped quantity

Debit and credit invoices separated from each other

Shipments expose typical lack of synchronization to invoice quantity

No separation between input for standard/direct sales and consignment sales

No separation of base line from quantified risk and opportunities

Process granularity is compromised by internal material flow data granularity

Data input is driven by internal material and financial flows | Total historical sales orders, classified by deviation from customer requirements (cancelled, inventory not available)

Standard/direct business and consignment business model separated

Valuation of forecasts follows volumetric figures

Input from direct customers is being considered

Base volumetric input separated from risk and opportunities

Process granularity is aligned to best "internal" insights

Data input is driven by internal material flow | Demand signal, Points sales data

Repositories and PoS data management platform

Total classified historical orders are combined with PoS data

Process granularity is differentiated and opened for outside view

Data input is combining inside with outside view, data signal is demand market driven |

Fig. 8.3 Maturity stages per level

the required maturity of processes, organization structure, capabilities, data, and system. Do not underestimate the importance of sustainability of change and how to make sure to identify your capability to embed the change.

Thought leader Charles Chase assesses in his publication (Chase, 2016) that even though complexity and market volatility increase, cost pressures are still present, product life cycles are shortened, and new products/SKUs are launched more frequently, many companies still:

- Do not think about how to leverage "big data."
- Struggle with forecast accuracy, synchronization, and lack of cross-functional collaboration.
- Go more and more global which cannot mitigate volatility with inventories.
- Use customer orders and shipments instead of POS data to shape and predict demand.
- Lack specific human-related competencies and experience misalignment in terms of cross-functional KPIs.

Gap Analysis

Once you understand your perception of the as is and maturity of the process, organization, capabilities, data, and system, you should think about how to expose the gaps to the required maturity level.

Gap analysis:

8.1 Qualitative Assessment

- Uses questionnaires and maturity models to identify qualitative gaps in capability. This information is used to validate/disprove a hypothesis for the transformation program focus.
- Often helps to answer the question "Why" and helps to determine the root cause of suboptimal performance.
- Helps to run rigorous and competent analysis which is the foundation for opportunity identification and the subsequent business case.

It is important to identify gaps per area, but it is even more critical to define what the expected or acceptable maturity is that you want to achieve. You do not need to be on a leading stage in every area but definitely on the ones critical for your business.

Let us give you an example for that: Point of sales data might not be at all available or may form a very small part of the input in your business models. In this case, being on a performing or even developing level is absolutely good and acceptable. You do not have to aim high if this will not give you the right improvement impact.

In the gap analysis phase (Fig. 8.4), discussions with stakeholders about the desired maturity stage become essential and extremely important. Plan to do that in an informed manner and be clear about what you want to achieve.

Criteria	Current state	Gap between current state and target state				Target state
		Lagging	Developing	Performing	Leading	
Forecasting Primary data input	Currently invoice data netted with return is being used.	●		●		Total historical orders classified by deviation from customer expectation will be used as primary data input. Data for base line will be separated for risk & opportunities
Forecasting Organization	Demand planning roles & responsibilities are mixed supply planning, lack of demand planning excellence, lack of demand planning champion	●			●	Organizational structures, positioning, roles and responsibilities will be aligned globally. Demand planning excellence led by experienced forecasting champion will be embedded in Integrated Business Planning center of expertise.
Forecasting Capabilities	Lack of statistical forecasting capabilities and data processing & management for PoS signal	●		●		Build statistical forecasting in house capabilities supported in interim stage with external service. Not required to build PoS data processing skills.

● Current State   ● Target State

Fig. 8.4 Gap analysis—current vs. target state examples

8.2 Quantitative Assessment

Data Collection

Combining data analysis with a qualitative view, as highlighted above, brings the best results. In this case, with term "results," it is meant to have understanding of where you factually are and where you should be (what maturity level you want to achieve). As we want to stay with demand planning and demand management example, you would need to define data requirements, data collection plans, data sources and granularity, and the business definition of the data.

Data collection should be understood as:

- Data collection plan, which lists data items that are needed to quantitatively assess the current state of demand planning and demand management (like forecasts and actuals) used in the process. We would not advice to collect results of measurement (wMAPE, Bias) but rather data inputs for measurement (actuals, forecasts, and data attributes) and then calculate a performance measurement in the benchmarking step. The data collection plan should identify the purpose/objective of data collection on the item level.
- Data collection execution. As the data collection very often might need to be executed by many people, you might need to define very specific data request templates.

To perform data collection, you need to define all data sources and systems required in the assessment.

In data collection and data validation, you may want to leverage techniques which are part of the six sigma data-driven improvement methodology.

Metrics, Benchmark

Once we have collected the data, we need to define metrics and parameters of the metrics. Metrics relevant for this function can be grouped into the following categories:

- Process effectiveness
- Process efficiency
- Process quality and adherence

In one of the last chapters of this book, you will find a detailed definition of performance measurement.

Metrics should be defined very clearly by their parameters, and these parameters should be aligned to the output you measure. An example of a forecasting measure is, e.g., wMAPE (weighted mean absolute percentage error) which has parameters like time lag, aggregation window, level, and data input. These parameters have to be applied properly to describe the process. If not applied properly, parameters of the metrics can seriously change the way you should look on your initiative. We have

8.2 Quantitative Assessment

seen that misuse of parameters is often happening in business environment. You should assess quality of parameters as well.

Last but not least, you need to approve the calculation of the metrics. Normally, this step should not be a problem since the standard formulas expressed in the leading literature should be used.

Metrics are typically used to:

- Compare current performance with external industry benchmarks, internal benchmarks, or targeted goals.
- Track the progress of an improvement initiative or program to the targeted goal state.

Example (Fig. 8.5) of forecasting metrics definition.

Benchmarking Analysis
The use of right metrics with clearly defined parameters will help you to position your as-is versus industry or general process leading practices.

Benchmarking analysis can be understood as:

Level		Metrics / Description
		Calculation formula: $$weighted\_MAPE = \left(\frac{\sum |Forecast - Sales|}{\sum Sales}\right)$$
Forecast effectiveness	wMAPE (weighted Absolute Performance Error)	Time lag: 3 (representing average lead time of this S&OP / supply chain)
		Aggregation window: data to be aggregated on single month. Process is executed monthly and has monthly implications on cost and revenue therefore aggregation window should be 1 month.
		Data input: Sales may equal Shipment, Forecast may equal Consensus Unconstrained Forecast both in volume. Use ABC/XYZ to align to profitability and predictability but do not mix volume and value dimensions.
		Level: should be aligned to process output linked to measured consensus unconstrained forecast e.g. Country / SKU / month.

Fig. 8.5 Evaluated metrics

Example: Benchmarking Analysis

Metric calculation — Average & leading benchmarks — Comments from gap analysis

Metric	Calculation	Benchmark			Performance indicator	Comments
		Actual	Lead*	Source		
Forecasting process effectiveness	wMAPE	57%	26%	*IBF research report 2003	R	Benchmark for applicable parameters
Forecasting process quality & adherence	On time country unconstrained forecast submission	11 out of 12 months		Internal study	G	Process is executed in very systematic controlled manner
Forecasting process efficiency	No of Phase Ins vs Phase outs	2:1		Internal study	Y	There are products not deleted from the portfolio even though no sales no forecast in last 3 years

Fig. 8.6 Benchmark analysis example

- Instrument which compares performance quantitatively against relevant benchmarks (e.g., peer group companies or internal targets) to identify potential improvement opportunities
- Elements which often help to determine the degree/severity of the business problem

Choosing the right set of metrics is the key to a correct diagnosis of the business forecasting or Integrated Business Planning problem.

The above table (Fig. 8.6) is an example of benchmark where performance indicators are visualized graphically and show how good or bad as is looks like.

8.3 Improvement Opportunities and Prioritization

Shall you consider to jump into this process step of analysis right away? We strongly recommend not to do so. Start with the identification of problem areas, define them, and combine gap analyses (qualitative) and benchmarking analyses (quantitative) to determine which improvement opportunities are worth pursuing. We were asking ourselves if we shall run this assessment even though the project has been initiated/started, if it makes sense to proceed with project without knowing scale change, impact.

In essence, this step is about the evaluation of the problem area and prioritization vs impact and ability to implement.

8.3 Improvement Opportunities and Prioritization

This step requires considerable judgment to determine the most logical grouping of gaps/solutions, the magnitude of the opportunity, and level of detail needed to quantify benefits. It is important to group qualitative and quantitative gaps into the initiatives. Each initiative should have a distinctive set of performance measurement.

As per example functional area of forecasting, assessment can address gaps identified in your organizational structure, missing or wrong capabilities, process design which follows the one size fit all method and systems that constrain your ability to reflect your business models. Once you have done your identification of improvement initiatives, you would need to assess their impact. Often, you would like to understand where to focus since maturity and gaps identify major transformation requirements.

You may consider to prioritize your initiatives based on the following activities:

- Identify and agree a list of opportunities, sorted by time horizon: short, medium, and long term.
- Confirm that each opportunity has quantitative benefits (e.g., savings ranges) identified.
- Determine the most important qualitative scoring criteria (e.g., ease of implementation, timeline for realization of benefit).
- Select the appropriate initiatives for the scoring survey.
- Combine scoring with quantitative prioritization ranking.
- Plot a prioritization chart based on qualitative and quantitative scores of the improvement opportunities.
- Discuss with stakeholders prioritization and investments (spend required).
- Develop the final agreed prioritization of improvement opportunities.

The prioritization matrix may highlight the type of the processes with colors like strategic planning, tactical S&OP, and operational planning. Below you see visualization (Fig. 8.7) of demand planning and demand management process prioritization.

Soft and hard factors may be used in prioritization. The completeness of the maturity assessment is vital. You should assess if your organization structure fits the purpose, if capabilities are allocated in the right places, if the processes are robust, and if the technology enables adaptation and is well positioned for the future.

Traditional S&OP becomes more demand driven these days and is seen more as a process to manage business, transforms into IBP. The transformation to such a state requires technology, business process improvement, organizational, and cultural resilience.

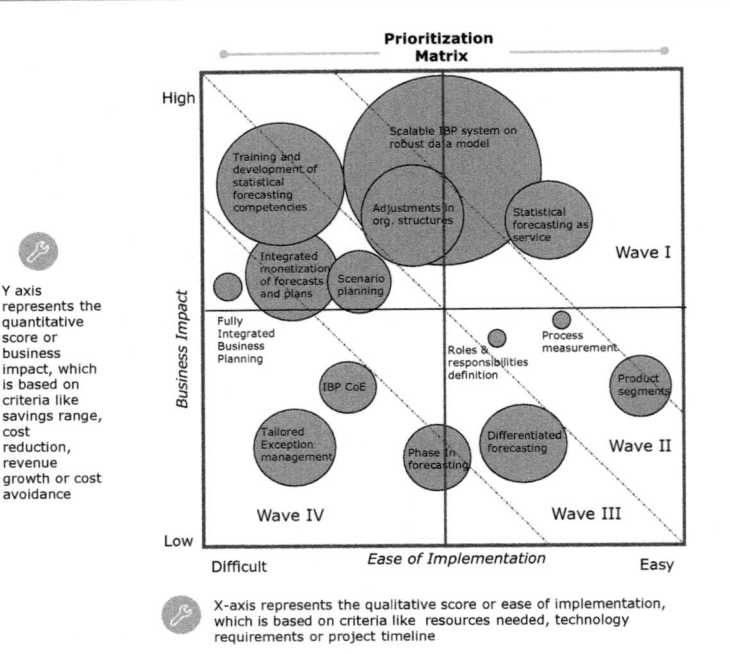

Fig. 8.7 Prioritization matrix

8.4 Road Map and Business Case

In a large or complex organization you may be required to take a very methodical approach to build your business case. A business case analyzes a proposed project, or a series of projects under the program, to determine if the project(s) should be undertaken. The business case helps to answer two questions:

- How much value will this project/program create?
- How long will the project take to implement?

You can take those five major steps to build your business case (Fig. 8.8):
When running those steps following activities may be considered:

- Define relevant and measurable financial and operational metrics.
- Establish baselines and achievable targets for the financial and operational metrics.
- Quantify project benefits and costs. Understand the risks involved with implementation of the project.
- Prepare incremental financial statements.
- Conduct financial analysis.
- Run sensitivity analyses to determine the results of various scenarios.

8.4 Road Map and Business Case

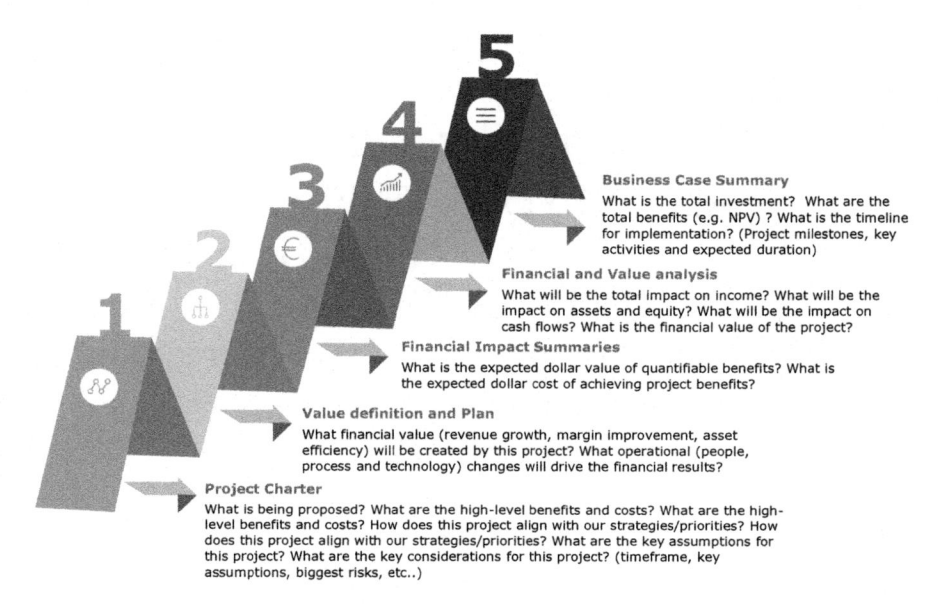

5. Business Case Summary
What is the total investment? What are the total benefits (e.g. NPV) ? What is the timeline for implementation? (Project milestones, key activities and expected duration)

4. Financial and Value analysis
What will be the total impact on income? What will be the impact on assets and equity? What will be the impact on cash flows? What is the financial value of the project?

3. Financial Impact Summaries
What is the expected dollar value of quantifiable benefits? What is the expected dollar cost of achieving project benefits?

2. Value definition and Plan
What financial value (revenue growth, margin improvement, asset efficiency) will be created by this project? What operational (people, process and technology) changes will drive the financial results?

1. Project Charter
What is being proposed? What are the high-level benefits and costs? What are the high-level benefits and costs? How does this project align with our strategies/priorities? How does this project align with our strategies/priorities? What are the key assumptions for this project? What are the key considerations for this project? (timeframe, key assumptions, biggest risks, etc..)

Fig. 8.8 Steps to develop complex business case

- If necessary, develop a scoring worksheet to communicate the results of the sensitivity or scenario analyses and weigh/force rank investment alternatives.
- Present a high-level summary of financial benefits and costs/financial impact.
- Summarize the results of the financial and value analysis.
- Based on the results of the financial and value analysis, fine-tune prioritization.

Many times you may be asked to build a transformation road map, which typically outlines:

- Project timelines
- Sequence of projects to be undertaken
- Key milestones
- Activities
- Resources and requirements
- Dependencies with other projects

When building complex transformation road map, which is based on many projects and initiatives, you may consider to:

1. Prioritize the series of projects based on financial benefits and costs.
2. Understand interdependencies between proposed projects and other ongoing projects.

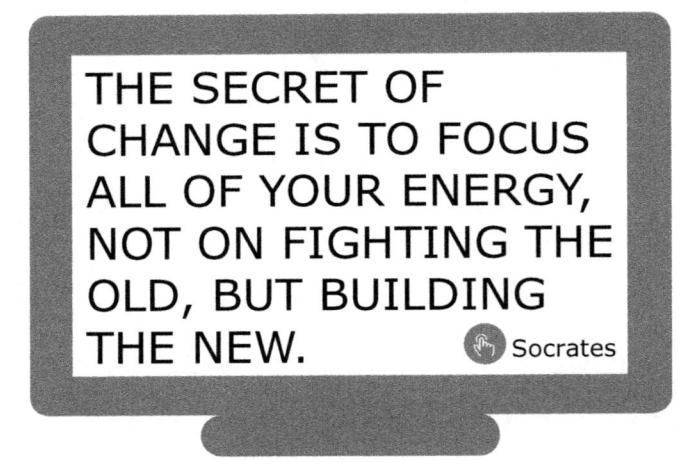

> **THE SECRET OF CHANGE IS TO FOCUS ALL OF YOUR ENERGY, NOT ON FIGHTING THE OLD, BUT BUILDING THE NEW.** — Socrates

Fig. 8.9 Approach to change by Socrates

3. Determine constraints for implementation of the projects.
4. Develop a sequence of projects for implementation with tentative timelines based on priority, interdependencies, and resource constraints.
5. Discuss and agree the project sequence with the stakeholders and adjust it, if required. Finalize the order of implementation of the projects.
6. Develop a detailed implementation plan for the projects. For each project, the implementation plan should include:
   – Project timelines
   – Project activities
   – Key milestones
   – Key stakeholders
   – Resources required/allocated
   – Other project requirements

Once you know you can afford a "change," get the right focus shown on Fig. 8.9.

8.5 Summary

- Lack of objective knowledge of "as is" in capabilities, org. structures, roles harmonization, processes, and technology maturity can heavily impact cost of implementation aiming to achieve unrealistic goals of "to be."
- Combine qualitative and quantitative methods to get the most reliable assessment.
- Your business most probably does not require that you are on "leading" maturity in all aspects of processes, organizational and capabilities, or technology.

- Transformation gaps should be defined versus desired state and not "cross industries best in class." Best in class performance should be used for benchmarking purposes.
- Quantitative assessment of raw data followed by performance calculation may expose that you are measuring wrong things or run measurement in wrong way.
- Business priorities are not the only one you should consider when prioritizing initiatives under IBP transformation. Prioritization of initiatives should be done with consideration of ability to implement change.
- Consider integrated design approach when planning IBP road map and business case.
- As-is assessment should not be positioned as performance check but as basis for transformation opportunity.

Reference

Chase, C. W. (2016). *Next generation demand management: People, process, analytics, and technology*. Hoboken, NJ: Wiley.

"Quo Vadis" Integrated Business Planning

9.1 Observations of Disruptive Technology Trends

Digitalization of supply chains and overall business and social environment is having a disruptive influence. Digitalization is definitely a challenge but creates game-changing opportunities. It concerns as well, where Integrated Business Planning is heading.

The third wave of IT-driven revolution is upon us (PC, Internet, and now digital), and it promises to be the biggest yet (Porter & Heppelmann, 2014) resulting in fundamental shifts in how value is created and captured. The imprint of this new revolution is digital omnipresence, and it is being orchestrated by an explosion of connected devices and accompanied by an explosion of data.

The reality for many companies wanting to partake in this digital revolution is that they are faced with more data than they know what to do with. But then, there are also companies that have managed to attain digital mastery (excelling along dimensions of digital capability and leadership capability) (Westerman, Bonnet, & McAfee, 2014). A key differentiator that separates digital masters from the rest could lie with their unyielding focus on business value: the realizations that investing in IoT (Internet of things) platforms and collecting humongous data from social media, etc. aren't goals in and of itself but are just a means to creating a superior value proposition for their customers. With revolutionary technologies, there tends to be an initial phase where technology is adopted for technology's sake. However, soon enough (perhaps once the novelty wears off), focus should shift to justifying investments.

This means organizations right now are asking themselves questions such as:

- How will IBP leverage huge amount of data about customer preferences, about our competitors, and about our products? How will IBP leverage "big data"?
- How will IBP leverage data and information available in extended supply chain, reality? How will IBP leverage Internet of things ("IoT")?

- How will IBP address a need to further personalize products, customized products and services, and how it will help us to make tradeoffs? How will IBP leverage machine learning?
- How will IBP address a need to differentiate the way we do planning for customized products and commodity products? How will IBP leverage machine learning?
- How will IBP address a need to have more data vs less data and more real data vs historical data per different categories of products and markets? How will IBP leverage big data and machine learning?
- When and how can we collect more data to make planning decisions? How will IBP leverage IoT?
- What capabilities will you need to have in-house vs outsource or buy to leverage big data, machine learning, and IoT in your business and in your planning?
- What capabilities are needed in the future of IBP? Is IBP really heading toward as some call it "self-driving" planning solution? Will people be able to execute all this complexity coming from personalization of targeting of products and services, or will we focus only on essentials? How will IBP leverage artificial intelligence? Will it steer at least the "self-driving" part of your products and services?

We see that:

- Business problem, e.g., competition pressure and innovation technology needed adoption
- Growth need, e.g., new market development, new services, and product offering

Drive business models to stronger digitalization (Fig. 9.1).

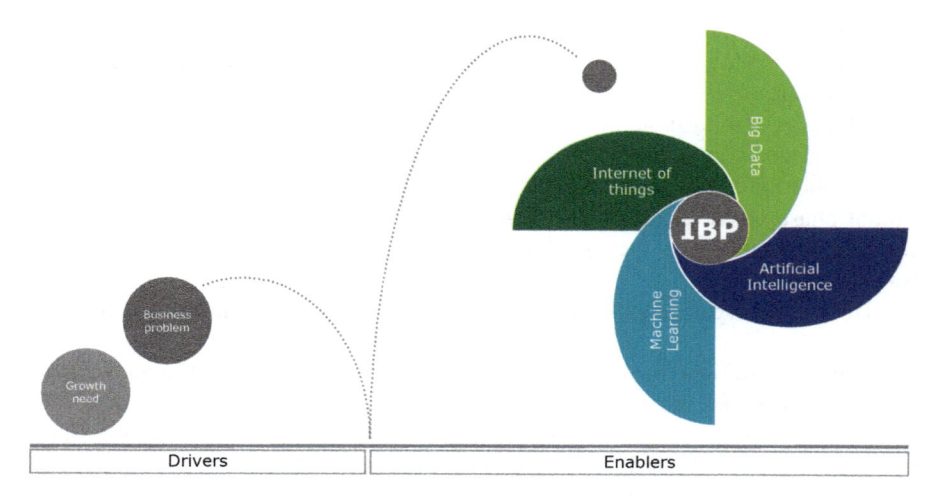

Fig. 9.1 Digital disruption drivers impact IBP

9.1 Observations of Disruptive Technology Trends

Digitalization becomes more and more integrated, and in many industries we observe stronger and stronger need to accelerate prototyping or building productive solutions leveraging IoT, big data, machine learning, or even artificial intelligence in connection to Integrated Business Planning.

In the above context of disruptive new technologies, we had many discussions with customers and colleagues, within professional communities, and came to three common conclusions:

First conclusion: Process differentiation and optimization were not perceived as a threat from the implementation standpoint. Many professionals said that process differentiation linked to diversified business model where product and services offering vary from commodity to highly personalized is an imperative. Process was perceived as the component of operating model, which is associated with lowest risk compared to people and technology.

Second conclusion: Ability to adopt, create, and continuously improve required skill sets, people capabilities, and organizational structures in own or from external sources was associated with high risk and high resistance out of other operating model dimensions.

Third conclusion: Ability to leverage and continuously adopt new technologies which help to become more effective and efficient, robust, and diversified was associated with high risk but great opportunity.

Furthermore, we have observed certain correlations which we want to bring to your consideration when building your IBP transformation road maps.

On the below chart (Fig. 9.2), you see correlation between the need for customization which grows with the need to access more data and in real time.

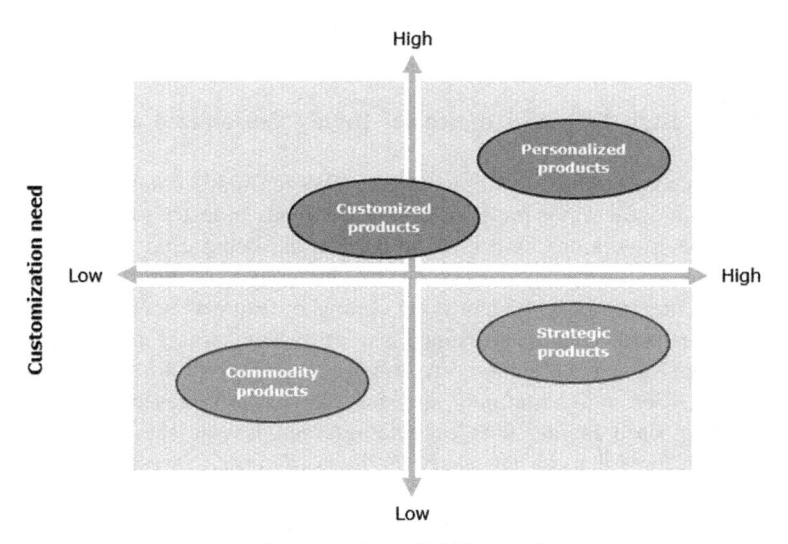

Fig. 9.2 Data size and real-time data availability vs product customization need

This correlation is quite common in consumer industry but as well in industrial companies. It does not mean that companies move completely toward more customizable products, but it means that in their product and services portfolio, those products tend to appear more and more often, and it is associated with higher flexibility, more data including consumer or customer buying preferences, and product feedback. The above correlation looks a bit different in consumer products industry marked in blue but as well in industrial companies marked in green.

9.2 Process Trends

Let's briefly discuss some of the trends and illustrate them with conceptual use cases (1, 2, 3, 4) which leverage new technologies IoT, big data, machine learning, and artificial intelligence in broadly understood planning processes.

Use Case 1: Life Science and Health-Care
LoT, big data, and machine learning linked to IBP for health-care industry—specific medicines have to be administered based on tests that are performed by patients themselves at home. Results of tests could be sent over the Internet to a central data repository, and, based on sophisticated machine learning algorithms, various workflows such as a consultation with a doctor or adjustments to existing dosage or replenishment of existing medication or orders for new medication, etc. can be triggered. The data that is generated becomes an input for pattern determination, which over large number of patients can be used to optimize the solution (e.g., better demand forecasting) and improve customer experience. Data which is gathered can be used in planning but as well in execution processes. This use case is imagined in Fig. 9.3.

Use Case 2: High-Tech and Industrial Highly Customized and Personalized Products
LoT, big data, and machine learning linked to IBP for highly configured products—in industrial, mobile applications or consumer goods industry sensors may detect how often specific options built into the product are being used. Data so collected could serve as input for analytics and machine learning algorithms that help uncover opportunities in terms of both identifying options or features underused or those that are in high demand. Insights so gained can help shape strategic activities such as product design, resource planning, investments, etc. (Fig. 9.5).

See Fig. 9.4 for an illustration of this idea. Green dots represent product features that are being used in line with expectations and investments made. However, crosses are features that do not justify the level of current investments (be it high or low). Such insights made possible through sensors and analytics can help mitigate risk of developing functionalities customers are unwilling to pay for or, on the flip side, help discover untapped or underutilized functionalities.

9.2 Process Trends

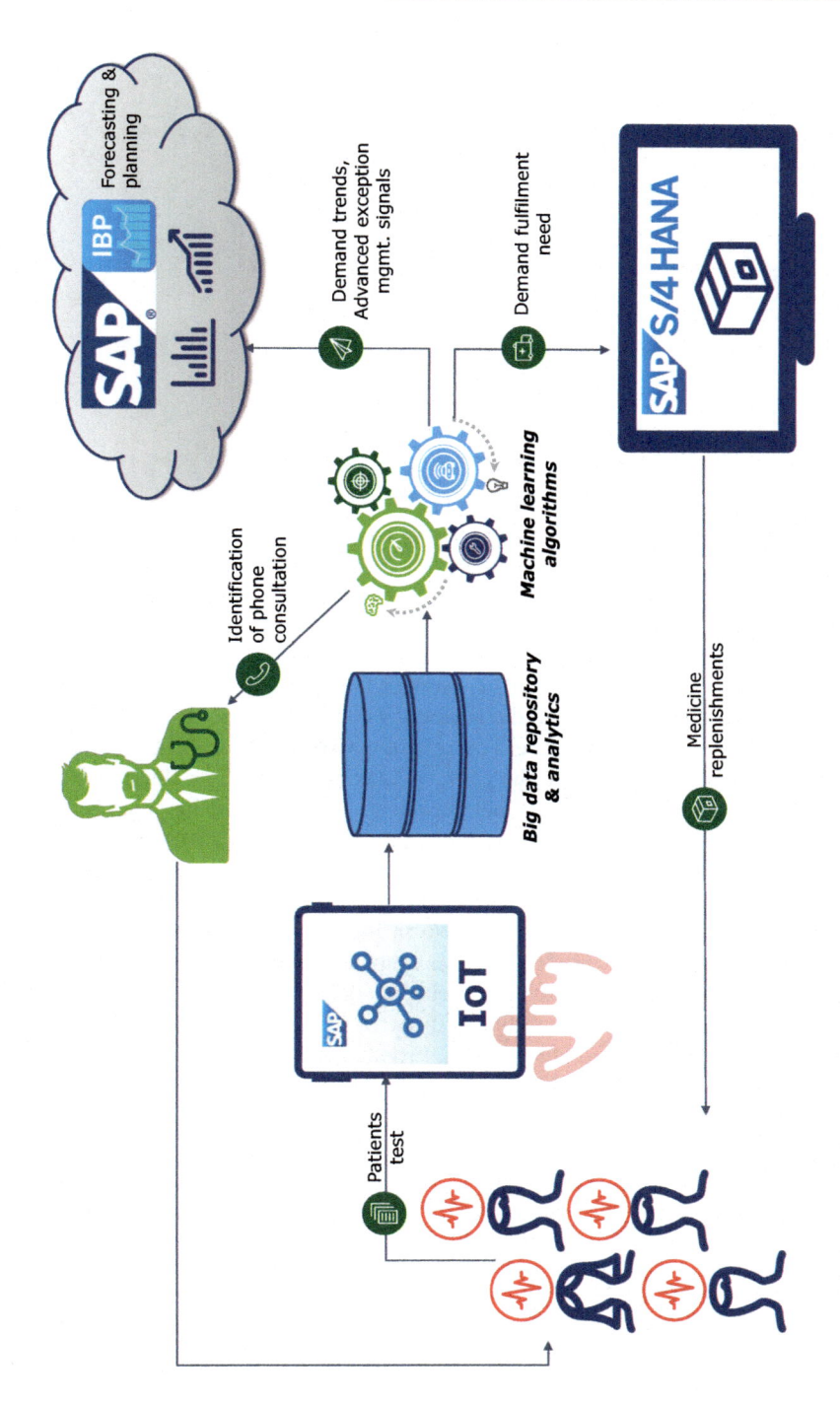

Fig. 9.3 Concept of IBP framework for life science and health-care industry

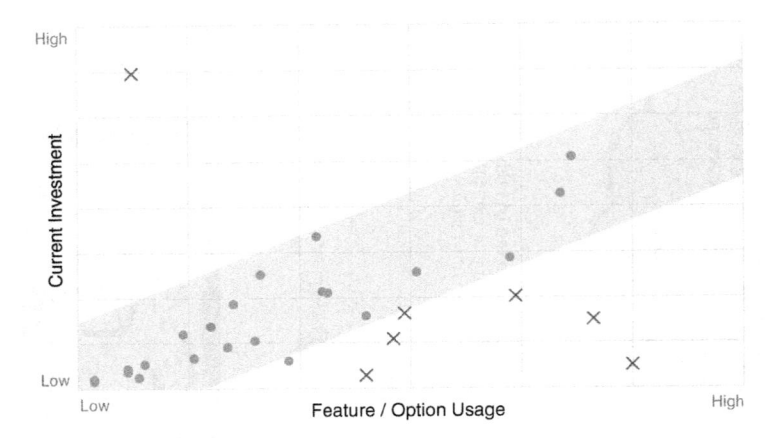

Fig. 9.4 Using usage statistics of features/options collected from embedded sensors

In both use cases (visualized in Figs. 9.3 and 9.5), there is a technology platform involved that facilitates delivery of certain services via mobile apps. This technology platform can also be called the technology stack that includes product data in the cloud, the physical product (hardware), and the software that is embedded in the product itself and a suite of services in the cloud that help monitor, control, and optimize (Porter & Heppelmann, 2014) product functions. The presence of a technology platform that allows users to connect and consume services can lead to what is called network effects. Network effects refer to a virtuous cycle caused by increase in number of users connecting to the platform making the platform that much more valuable. There are multiple factors that make it so: more users on the platform leads to more data generated, and the algorithms that deliver services have more data to work with (to train on) making them more useful. Then there is the fact that users can connect to other users via the platform thereby enhancing their experience. This virtuous cycle in the case of Uber is shown in Fig. 9.6. This virtuous cycle in the digital era has resulted in what is termed as demand economies of scale. "Demand economies of scale are driven by efficiencies in social networks, demand aggregation, app development that make bigger networks more valuable to their users" (Parker, Van Alstyne, & Choudary, 2016). From an IBP perspective, this speaks to the need for a holistic and extended integrated planning framework that makes the ecosystem more attractive to users and can feed off of positive network effects. We'll address this in the section "Planning applications observations."

9.2 Process Trends

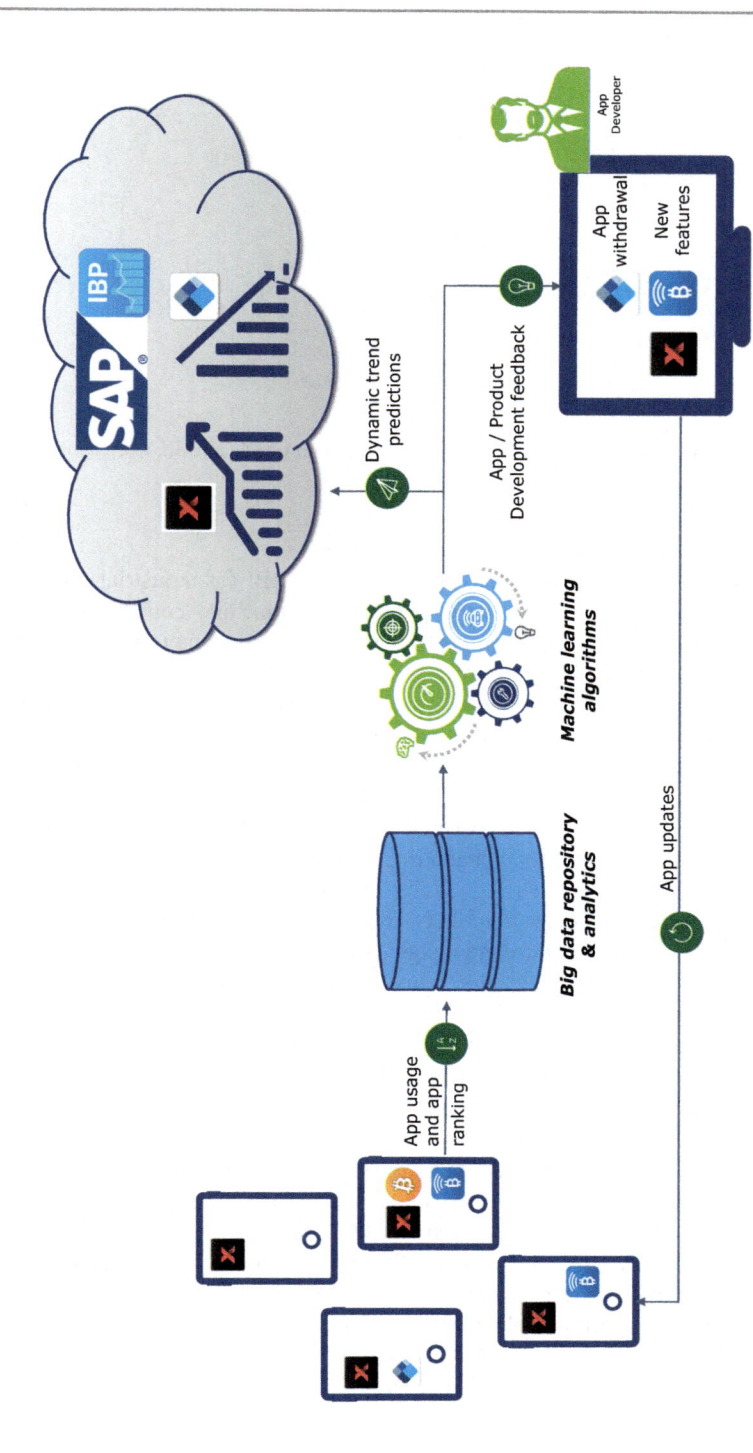

Fig. 9.5 Concept of IBP framework for configurable products in high-tech industry

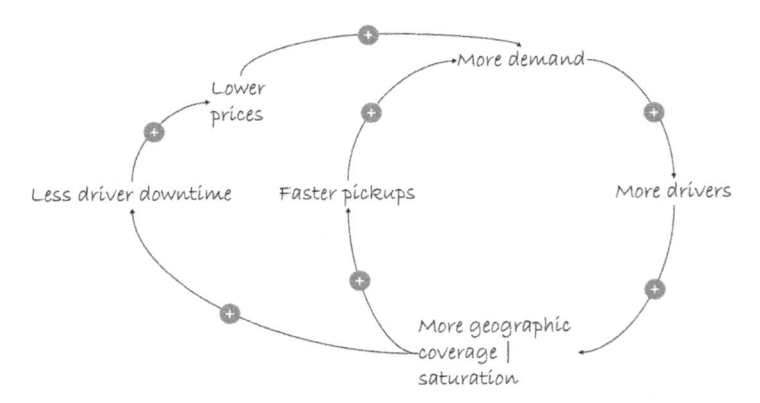

Fig. 9.6 Napkin sketch of how network effects have propelled Uber's growth. Recreation of David Sacks' napkin sketch/twitter post

Use Case 3: Industrial and Machinery Industry

LoT and machine learning linked to IBP and S/4 (ERP) for industrial, machinery products—Sensors placed in strategic parts of the machine collect information, which is analyzed on the fly and compared with historical data patterns and tolerance limits. Machine learning algorithms crunch through collected data and alerts experts and client that detect preventive maintenance is needed as vibrations detected lie outside tolerance limits ("learnt" from historical patterns). Information is integrated into ERP to block resource for maintenance. Simultaneously, information is sent to IBP to reduce available capacity for planning purposes. Additionally, data which is collected can be used in OEE (overall equipment efficiency) to recommend standards in routings used for scheduling and IBP planning. This use case is imagined in Fig. 9.7.

The key to successful integration of sensors and machine learning is in being able to deliver up-to-date information and insights to support decision-making. Ecolab is a shining example of a company that is using IoT successfully to deliver superior value to its customers (Bock, Iansiti, & Lakhani, 2017). It has deployed IoT assets in its water treatment operations to collect data from equipment that allows it to monitor performance. The company is then able to detect "potential problems, suggest and dispatch the best available technician, and minimize downtime or process disruptions" (Bock et al., 2017).

This can also lead to higher order benefits, say in the context of planning. Taking the example of Ecolab a step further, let's say certain spare parts and treatment materials are required to be carried by field service personnel when they are dispatched to perform a service. It is not difficult to imagine how data captured by IoT assets can be used as complementary inputs to generate sensed forecast in IBP that results in more accurate planning in the context of field service operations

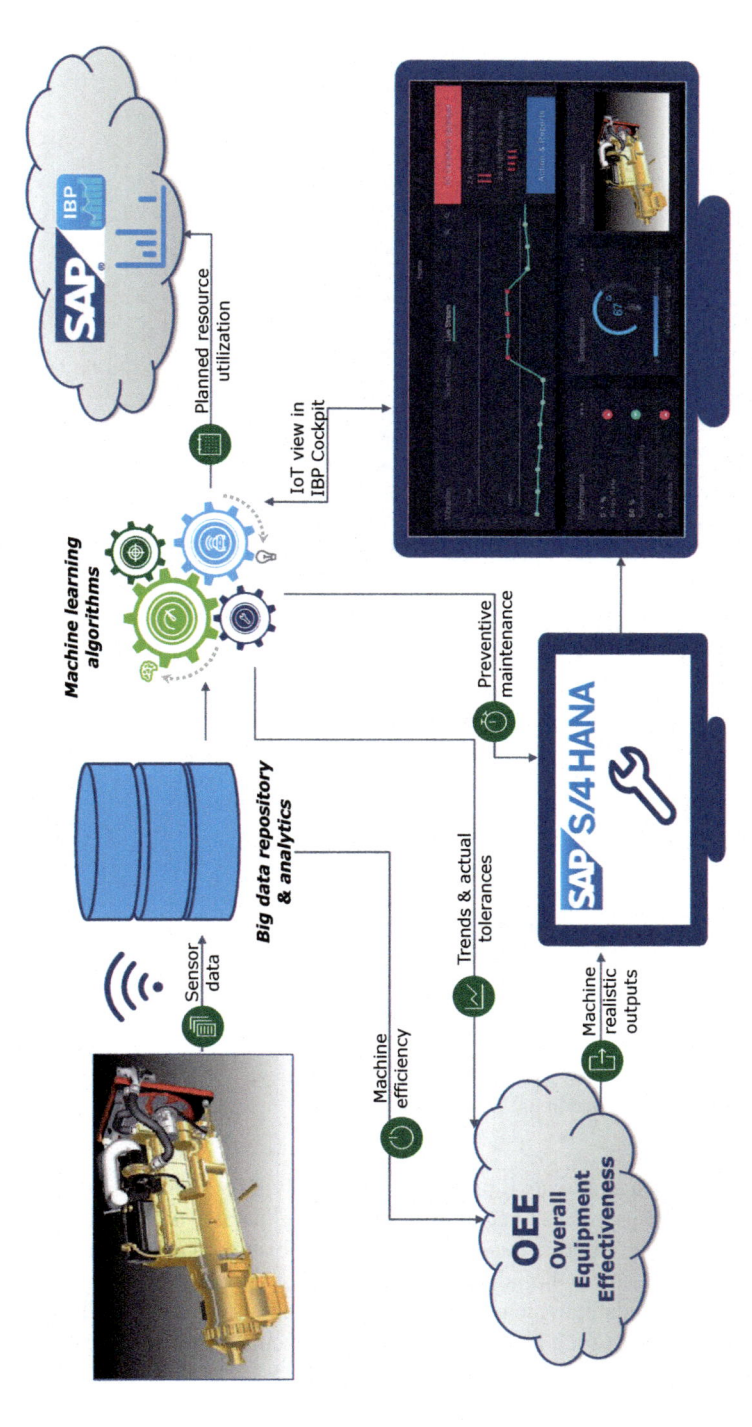

Fig. 9.7 Concept of extended IBP framework for industrial, machinery industry

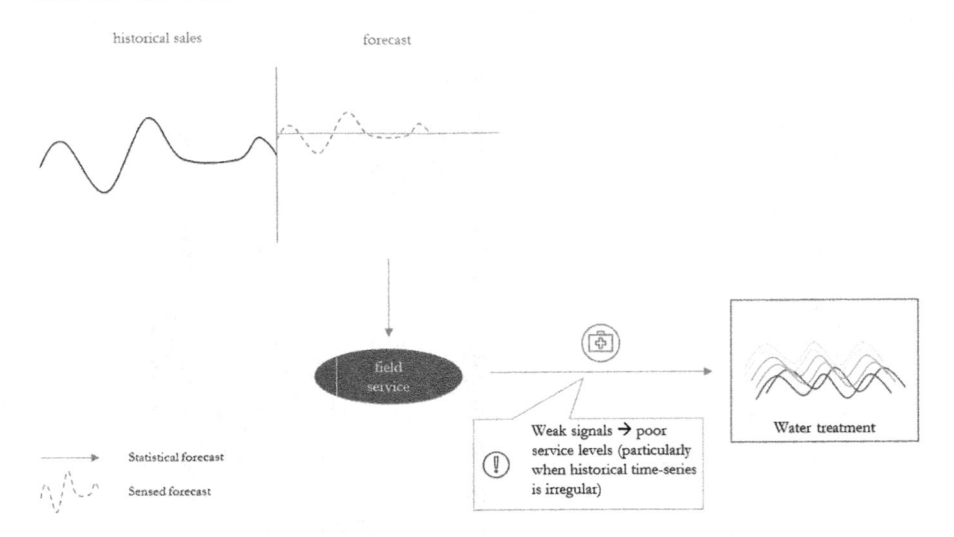

Fig. 9.8 Field service lack of IoT usage in recent past

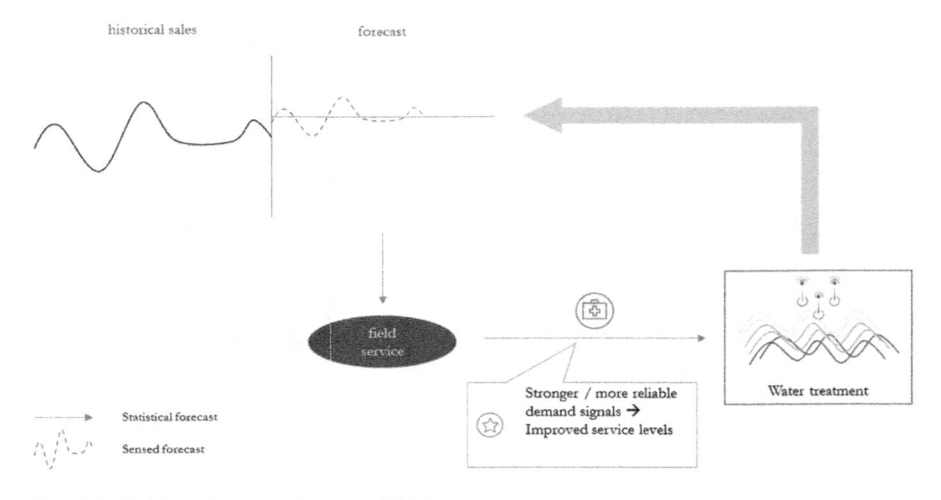

Fig. 9.9 Field service operation use of IoT present use case

(a before and after scenario are illustrated, respectively, Figs. 9.8 and 9.9). In a sense, telemetric data helps reduce uncertainty by turning what was essentially a fully stochastic process (predictive maintenance based on historical analysis of mean time to failure) into a somewhat deterministic process (impending failure detected through telemetric data, which in turn triggers actions). This can have several positive consequences such as improved planning accuracy, reduction in inventory, and better customer service.

Use Case 4: Consumer Products Industry

Big data, machine learning, and artificial intelligence linked to IBP for trading company which sells hundreds of thousands of products over e-commerce platforms—it was critical to optimize cost of operations and differentiate the way they operate by the type of product/market. Structured (big) data is collected in a common repository from various e-commerce platforms, analyzed by machine learning algorithms to then propose demand patterns in sales and in buying behaviors, which is then used by an AI assistant embedded in IBP to run planning processes autonomously for commodity products. For strategic or highly customized products as well, the AI assistant helps planners in making them faster and more efficient. This use case is imagined in Fig. 9.10.

In the previous use case, we have talked about use of AI to carry out planning tasks. It might at first seem farfetched that something as specialized as supply chain planning can be handled, albeit in a limited sense, by AI.

Let's ponder on this for a bit.

Serious researchers on the topic talk about narrow AI and strong AI. Narrow AI are software "that are capable of sophisticated analysis, decision making and reasoning within a relatively narrow field of application" (Ford, 2009). Strong AI on the other hand is true intelligence that, for now, lies in the realm of science fiction. When we talk about AI in the context of IBP, we refer to narrow AI. Narrow is more about brute force rather than demonstrating true intelligence. It is only as good as the datasets it is fed and trained on. It is less about true reasoning and more about responding to familiar or near familiar situations in a way that maximizes the chance of a favorable outcome—favorable in light of historical evidence. Martin Ford (2009) cites the example of Garry Kasparov's playing chess against IBM's Deep Blue in 1997. He argues that the advantage of the computer comes not from creativity (which by the way is needed by a human player in hordes) but in its ability to compute millions of possible moves and choose the best one (based on its rich memory of hundreds of thousands of matches). For an uninformed observer, this might seem like a feat of creativity until the details of what is really at play spoil the mystique. The same is true for an AI planning assistant. If we strip away the usual humanoid visualizations that accompany such discussions, an AI assistant is simply a software program that is capable of learning from experience (think datasets) and apply that experience to either autonomously make decisions or assist (like in the described use case) humans in doing so. In the context of planning, if we think about predictions as establishing correlations between present and the future, the idea of a machine doing a good job of it should not seem farfetched after all.

Above use cases illustrate requirements trend for tighter integration of new technologies into planning to be more:

- Holistic in the way we plan, due to system integration capabilities, IoT
- Aligned to consumer and customer preferences with big data
- Automatize with the use of machine learning
- Focused with the use of artificial intelligence assistants

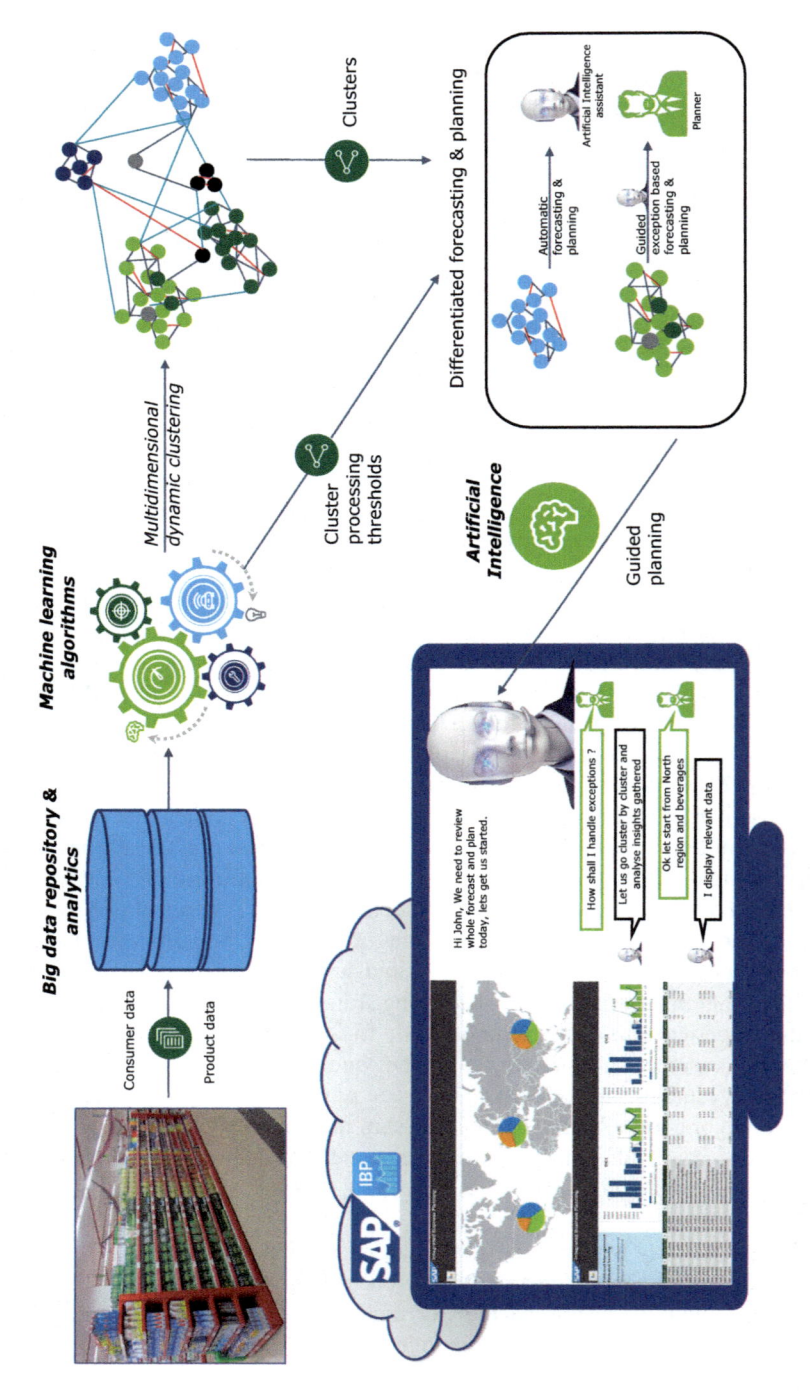

Fig. 9.10 Concept of extended IBP framework for consumer products industry

We see that for many cases complexity embedded in remote algorithms shifts toward machines, sensors, consumer, and customers. Algorithms shifts toward where complexity is being generated or captured.

9.3 Planning Applications Observations

From core planning application perspective, we see requirement to connect dedicated application or integrate specialized solutions under one holistic and extended integrated planning framework.

Extended planning application framework should enable acceleration of usage of new technology trends. On the other hand, framework would need to be open to be successful. If framework will be open for creation of new apps, it will unleash technology flexibility and innovation adoptions needed to support market needs.

We observe higher and higher demand to use IoT, big data, machine learning, and artificial intelligence in planning, which does accelerate the need to create better integration between specialized solutions.

We also see analytics being enabled across whole cloud applications in extended planning framework. Huge amount of data exposes stronger and stronger need for appealing visualization, data discovery, sophisticated segmentation, self-learning prediction, and self-learning prescription capabilities. You will not be able to work with big data which we talk about here; if there are analytical solution, machine learning algorithms and artificial intelligence solutions will not adopt its maturity with required fast pace.

In analytics we always struggle with the amount of data being replicated. We were wondering when it would be possible to read data from various non-harmonized sources instead of replicating them. What if we read and harmonize it on the fly? Will machine learning help to do that harmonization of master data objects on the fly, will accelerators help to connect and not replicate data, and will ability to create apps unlock flexibility and innovation?

Integration of applications and dedicated solutions under one framework accelerates digitalization of supply chain and whole company business environment (Fig. 9.11).

It could happen that integrated approach to big data, machine learning, IoT, and artificial intelligence connected dedicated applications will transform Integrated Business Planning solution from "planning system of records" into "system of innovation" or rather "solution of innovation."

Fig. 9.11 Is this where cloud integration of the whole SAP planning and analytics applications is heading?

9.4 Organizational and Capabilities Trend

We have observed correlation between the need for new digitalization technologies like big data, machine learning, IoT, and knowledge, experience, capabilities in markets/product and services/technology field (Fig. 9.12).

We see that companies take different routes on how to build or source new capabilities. There are some who build them in-house but many outsource.

We have seen that market and product knowledge capabilities are mostly kept inside the company, but we noticed some examples where big data, machine

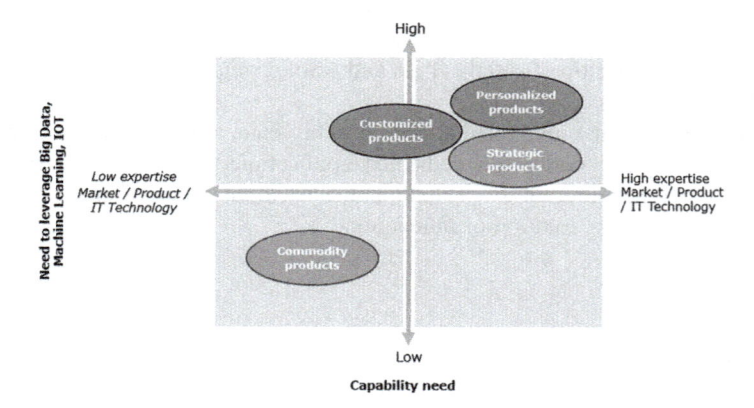

Fig. 9.12 Disruptive technology trends vs. capabilities

9.4 Organizational and Capabilities Trend

learning, or IoT is addressed through partnerships or outsourcing. Trend to keep technology disruptive capabilities outside company is common, but there are many companies which take a challenge and address it in-house if this is perceived as strategic advantage. Example of decision made in alignment of strategic advantage could be company Monsanto which acquired large "big data analytics" companies.

It means that new technologies generate the need for new capabilities and open doors for adjustments of business models. We see that people side of digital disruption evolves somehow toward "networks" operating with its own pace of transformation but connected between each other. We need to learn how to make organizational structures, capabilities, and talents to be more agile and "network" oriented. This way of management becomes a hard time for "control freaks" and those who define structures to manage full time of the team but has a great opportunity to facilitate innovation and improve adoptability. Organizational structures may lose their power to "networks." Operating in cross-functional network do increase degree of ambiguity and expose need for talents who cope with innovation, can explore and learn fast, and most importantly turn learning into action. People side of IBP may evolve into direction that organizational structures and capabilities are not fixed for years anymore.

Process and technology trends generate huge disruption; we need to define new ways on how we should operate them and ways on how we need to change. That's why we would like to bring few examples which expose concerns and opportunities:

1. We have seen a company offering their products on the market for years. They had enough of good data to improve their forecasting process with statistical forecasting. They have tried with simple time series algorithms and have not investigated any further with more advanced algorithms. Quality of simple algorithms was good enough for certain group of demand patterns but not for majority. Screening of data, detail analysis including forecast value added analysis, and ex-post forecasting have shown significant opportunities to improve forecasting if more advanced methods would be used. The management did not recognize this as an opportunity even though it was professionally presented to them. This change would require building new capabilities in company but no new head counts. It was an area which could not be proven without making proof of concepts and pilots. Step like that was not made. Forecasting still continues to be labor intensive.
2. Country IBP pilot project brought enormous exposure of value of cross-functional integration. IBP pilot has proven that embedding finance function and financial data into decision-making process, defined as part of IBP process and tool, was bringing a lot of value to local organization. Decisions became more profitable. Global finance management has understood during program rollout that in reality of countries, financial elements like costs, price, and margin were used to make decisions. To our big surprise, global function has strictly forbidden to use this data in IBP and gave strict instruction that local finance should focus on doing what they used to do before. It was a step back to maturity when finance

generated second "IBP" plan but after S&OP meeting. This second plan had different assumptions and different values.
3. Country organization has experienced fast and tremendous, year-over-year growth. There was a strong drive from management to adjust their organization, capabilities, and behaviors. Supply chain directors have convinced management to use supply chain planning technology implementation as "excuse" to introduce more integrated ways of working between departments. Team was formed from internal and external employees; team was extremely motivated and was supported by management on regular meetings. Regional operations director and regional finance director found time to understand and support change. S&OP type of process was enriched with financial information, previously not connected functions started to work together in integrated process on verified sources of data.
4. Regional demand and supply planning functions have recognized major differences in business models for their business lines. One of the business lines had large flexibility in manufacturing but was "cast in stone" on commercial side. They have understood that monthly S&OP process was not enough to manage demand, supply, and finance reconciliation. They have designed and introduced bi-weekly process which was connected to tactical S&OP. In new operational planning process marketing, sales and supply chain were involved and made very operational but impactful decisions. This process brought integration between regional planning function, sales and marketing, and site planning to the next level. The value of transparency exceeded their expectations.

Examples above illustrate that relatively simple solution requires transformation in people's behavior and this can be successful or not. The major difference between examples 1–2 and 3–4 came down to the ability to change behavior and strive to drive change, leadership, and dedication.

We think that IBP future depends on:

– Ability to change our behaviors and capabilities
– Ability to continuously manage technology adoption

George Westerman et al. (2014) have proposed a framework for looking at digital maturity along two important dimensions—digital capability and leadership capability. Digital capability is a technology dimension, whereas leadership capability is a people dimension. For truly leveraging benefits of IoT, big data, and AI, companies need to develop themselves along both these dimensions. Digital capability without strong leadership can lead to islands of digital excellence without an overarching vision and commitment to follow through. On the other hand, leadership capability without adequate digital capability can lead to poorly thought through and executed initiatives from a technology perspective that do not measure up to the vision put forth. The authors of the aforementioned framework studied 391 companies in 30 countries (restricting themselves to companies with revenues of $500 million or higher) and based on financials of 184 companies in this group that are publicly traded have seen that those that have strong digital and leadership capabilities (also called digital masters) are on average 26% more profitable than peers, generate 9% higher revenues from physical assets, and generally demonstrate better financial performance than companies whose capabilities place them in the other quadrants (fashionistas, beginners, conservatives).

Somehow, we have found it interesting that:

- People's ability to change behavior depends on **"people networks."**
- Technology adoption depends on **"technology networks."**

Those two abilities seem like primary focus areas in making the future of IBP happen.

Disclaimer In this chapter you will find Robert Kepczynski and Ganesh Sankaran observations of technology, business concepts, and trends, and it is not intended to be binding, aligned with SAP strategy.

References

Bock, R., Iansiti, M., & Lakhani, K. R. (2017). What the companies on the right side of the digital business divide have in common. *Harvard Business Review*.

Ford, M. (2009). *The lights in the tunnel: Automation, accelerating technology and the economy of the future*. Acculant.

Parker, G., Van Alstyne, M., & Choudary, S. P. (2016). *Platform revolution: How networked markets are transforming the economy*. New York: W. W. Norton.

Porter, M. E., & Heppelmann, J. E. (2014). How smart, connected products are transforming competition. *Harvard Business Review*.

Westerman, G., Bonnet, D., & McAfee, A. (2014). What is digital mastery? In Leading digital: turning technology into business transformation. *Harvard Business Review*.

Printed by Printforce, the Netherlands